DEFAMILIARIZING THE ABORIGINAL:
CULTURAL PRACTICES AND DECOLONIZATION IN CANADA

From the Canadian Indian Act to Freud's *Totem and Taboo* to films such as *Nanook of the North,* all manner of cultural artefacts have been used to create a distinction between savagery and civilization. In *Defamiliarizing the Aboriginal,* Julia V. Emberley examines the historical production of aboriginality in colonial cultural practices and its impact on the everyday lives of indigenous women, youth, and children.

Adopting a materalist-semiotic approach, Emberley explores the ways in which representational technologies – film, photography, and print culture, including legal documents and literature – were crucial to British colonial practices. Many indigenous scholars, writers, and artists, however, have confounded these practices by deploying aboriginality as a complex and enabling sign of social, cultural, and political transformation. Emberley gives due attention to this important work, studying a wide range of topics such as race, place, and motherhood, primitivism and violence, and sexuality and global political kinships. Her multidisciplinary approach ensures that *Defamiliarizing the Aboriginal* will be of interest to scholars and students of cultural studies, indigenious studies, women's studies, postcolonial and colonial studies, literature, and film.

JULIA V. EMBERLEY is an associate professor in the Department of English at the University of Western Ontario.

Cover illustration: *Transparent Parents Singing Hearts,* Jane Ash Poitras, 1998. Mixed media on canvas (36" X 48"). Image courtesy of the artist and Spirit Wrestler Gallery, Vancouver, British Columbia.

JULIA V. EMBERLEY

Defamiliarizing the Aboriginal

Cultural Practices and Decolonization in Canada

UNIVERSITY OF TORONTO PRESS
Toronto Buffalo London

© University of Toronto Press Incorporated 2007
www.utppublishing.com
Toronto Buffalo London
Printed in Canada

Reprinted in paperback 2009

ISBN 978-0-8020-9151-2 (cloth)
ISBN 978-1-4426-1025-5 (paper)

Printed on acid-free paper

Library and Archives Canada Cataloguing in Publication

Emberley, Julia, 1958–
　　Defamiliarizing the aboriginal : cultural practices and decolonization in
　　Canada / Julia V. Emberley.

　　Includes bibliographical references (p.[285]-302) and index.
　　ISBN 978-0-8020-9151-2 (bound). – ISBN 978-1-4426-1025-5 (pbk.)

　　1. Native women – Canada – Social conditions – 20th century.　2. Native
　　peoples – Canada – Social conditions – 20th century.　3. Native peoples –
　　Kinship – Social aspects – Canada.　4. Native peoples – Canada – Govern-
　　ment relations.　5. Family – Canada – History – 20th century.　6. Feminist
　　theory – Canada.　7. Indigenous peoples in literature.　8. Decolonization
　　– Canada.　I. Title.

NX652.I53E42 2007　　306.85089′97071　　C2007-902335-5　　NX652*

University of Toronto Press acknowledges the finanical assistance to its
publishing program of the Canada Council for the Arts and the Ontario
Arts Council.

This book has been published with the help of a grant from the Canadian
Federation for the Humanities and Social Sciences, through the Aid to
Scholarly Publications Programme, using funds provided by the Social Sci-
ences and Humanities Research Council of Canada.

University of Toronto Press acknowledges the financial support for its publishing activities of the Government of Canada through the Book Publishing Industry Development Program (BPIDP).

To Sophie

The family, as Foucault warns us, should not be seen as a haven from the sexualities of a dangerous outside world, but as the site of their production.

Ann Laura Stoler, *Race and the Education of Desire*

Contents

Illustrations

Preface

In 2004 the Native Women's Association of Canada in conjunction with Amnesty International launched a campaign, 'Sisters in Spirit,' to expose violence directed towards indigenous women in Canada. The release of their report, 'Stolen Sisters: Discrimination and Violence against Indigenous Women in Canada,' drew international attention to the stark realities of neocolonial violence in the lives of indigenous peoples.

This book contributes to a large body of anti-imperialist and anti-racist materialist feminist scholarship that is working towards clarifying the theoretical and practical dimensions of women and children's oppression in such diverse places as India, the Middle East, Latin America, China, and Eastern Europe. This particular project addresses the specificity of indigenous women's struggles in the modern Canadian state, but its vision, its theoretical trajectories and methodological issues, are, I believe, entirely relevant to a global context, if for no other reason than the fact that the 'globalization' of economic and political powers since the Second World War has *de facto* made it virtually impossible to think and act without knowledge of the larger picture. Furthermore, it is no longer possible to ignore the hidden complicities that exist between transnational capitalism and everyday life. Some may argue that uncovering those invisible connections will come about when women are no longer excluded from political leadership. The reality of women as political leaders, however, is no guarantee that a transnational feminist vision in support of indigenous women will be present. It is more important, I think, to consider the relative absence of indigenous women's struggles, inside and outside the home and in relation to domestic, sexual, and gendered violence, from the overall political agenda for social change. This book seeks to have violence towards women, and children, gay and lesbian youth recognized as advanced and technically efficient forms that are used today, as they have been in the past and in the more recent case of 'ethnic cleansing' in Eastern Europe, to maintain the oppression and impoverishment of indigenous peoples globally. It is with some urgency, then, that transnational feminists must take up the challenge of examining how the seemingly abstract global processes of dispossession are embedded in daily life. This is a large project and this book an initial attempt to grapple with the question of intimate violence as, perhaps, the most urgent problem facing transnational feminisms today.

Canada occupies a unique place in indigenous global histories because it is both a so-called First World country and a former colony of the British Empire. Thus, its historical formation has been crafted out of a national agenda that is also a neocolonial one. To a large extent, Canadian history is learned and taught from the perspective of competing national longings and belongings, based on the narratives of settler cultures, French, English, and otherwise, to the exclusion, dismissal, and even denial of Canada as a colonial and neocolonial state. While the discourse of postcolonialism in Canadian literary studies has tended to keep Euro-Canadian or 'settler' literature at the centre of its critical inquiry – as if the contradictions of the colonial encounter inhere primarily between English or French Canada and Britain, France, or other European nations – it must be continually pointed out that colonization and imperialism had its greatest and most detrimental impact on indigenous societies. Not surprisingly, for indigenous nations, the relationships among the Canadian state, immigration, and themselves constitute a complex web of power, and any attempt to isolate the history of colonization and postcoloniality from its effects on indigenous people is nothing more than the perpetuation of colonial violence and the sanctioned ignorance that reinforces its continuity. The tensions between settler cultures and indigenous nations must also be written; otherwise, the notion of a 'postcolonial' nation state that has exceeded its colonial history becomes nothing more than an extraordinary fiction. For how can a nation be postcolonial when it has yet to acknowledge or even address its colonial history? How is it possible to understand the importance of contemporary decolonization if the colonial past remains hidden from examination and discussion? From the perspective of cultural politics, it becomes important to study the historical mechanisms of colonial representation, especially, I would argue, by tracing how the figure of the Aboriginal was mobilized simultaneously and in conjunction with colonial state practices that ranged from genocide to assimilation.

This study brings the so-called new and old worlds of colonial contact into relation with each other through two notable figures: Aboriginal Man and Bourgeois Woman. It is a sort of critical cultural studies version of Tarzan and Jane, the wild man in the forest, the savage of colonial invention, finding his soulmate, the British petty-bourgeois woman, in the heart of the uncivilized jungle. Aboriginal Man and Bourgeois Woman: an odd couple, you might say. Most of us are familiar with the figure of the wild man, a solitary, nomadic, primitive, and savage creature epitomized by Rousseau's Noble Savage. The ideology of individualism perpetuated by the rise of the bourgeois family in the nineteenth century and its authoritative father figure created this singular focus on his significant Other. This text, however, places the figure of primitive man in relation to the bourgeois woman, and takes the position that both these figures were integral to an imperialist configuration in which racial and sexual difference, and colonization, were irreducible and entirely interrelated forms of power and domination.

Michel Foucault anticipated the historical situatedness of sexuality, but failed to notice some crucial aspects of its discursive and institutional emplacement, especially in relation to racial discourses and colonization. Postcolonial critics sought to demonstrate how sexuality, 'race,' class, and gender were deployed to invent, maintain, or destroy relations of political and ideological power to the benefit of the hegemony of European imperialist nations (Fanon 1967, Gilman 1985, McClintock 1993, Spivak 1988, Stoler 1989, and Young 1995). Such relations constantly shifted to recreate or sustain the equilibrium of an imperialist political economy. Thus, sexuality, along with race, gender, and class, intersected within such highly codified sites and institutional locations as 'the family,' schooling, government, and education to do the work of suturing closed the social ruptures that threatened to loosen the grip of bourgeois imperial governance and its industrial-capitalist economy. Sexuality *and* aboriginality were significant domains of power in the nineteenth century, discontinuous yet mutually reinforcing sites of institutional incorporation that were put to use in the violent and regulatory governance of 'the body.' For bourgeois

governance, sexuality, race, and aboriginality became important corporealities for the disenfranchisement of the labouring classes and indigenous peoples in the colonies. Labour was an immensely important site
of incorporation, especially for the economic institutionalization of
working life that was central to nineteenth-century industrial capitalism. Labour was the form of embodiment for the working class in the
factory and at home, in which working-class women's bodies established the continuity between the two in stark contrast to the bourgeoisie's governing strategies of separate spheres produced upon
ideologies of sexual and racial difference.

Bourgeois woman and aboriginal man represent two key figures to
emerge in the nineteenth century as central to the English bourgeois
family's conception of itself as having the rightful disposition to rule
domestic and foreign relations of economic and political power. The
domain in which these figures flourished was that of the domestic
sphere and the bourgeois family. By the end of the nineteenth century,
the distinction between family and empire would completely implode
– familial ideology would become civilizational ideology, and visa
versa, the one the microcosm of the other, universal and Other, primitive, domestic, and civilized – all signifying a world that was radically
shifting and slipping from a diversity of competing societies to a
homogenizing culture of commodification.

Whether as ideology, discourse, or signifying system, 'the family' figured as an Enlightenment metaphor for power. It replaced the dominant European and Euro-American Christian trilogy – Father, Son, and
Holy Ghost – challenging this autochthonous myth of human origins
and, instead, leaving a fantasy of familial love in a breeding ground of
competitiveness (as mere exhibition of sibling rivalry or simply the
age-old Oedipal struggle between father and son) and individuality
(the uniqueness and beauty of the bourgeois mother or daughter; the
successful oedipalization of the father/son). Sexual desire would be
strictly regulated by domestic violence and control of children's play-
mates. Mothers would act as equally dangerous instruments of control
over their daughters, ensuring that their ambitions would be thwarted
with financial decisions not in their favour. Any attempt to undermine
female children through the mother or older siblings would be considered normal familial tensions. The psychiatric profession would base
its entire existence on helping or further damaging the victims and
scapegoats of familial power relations; and all of this as a necessary precondition to accepting state power, the rule of a few men and their

mother-proxies, through violence, repression, and regulatory and normalization procedures.

It is by focusing on the bourgeois woman and aboriginal man, on prevailing ideologies of primitivism and Orientalism, and the imbricated histories of patriarchy, racism, and imperialism that a counter-hegemonic understanding of bourgeois alienation (that is, how the bourgeois family came to differ from itself) is possible. Through an examination of various visual and textual materials, including fiction, film, psychoanalytical discourses, and legislative policies, this book sets out to understand the underlying assumptions about gender, sexuality, and race these figures came to embody. Moreover, it seeks to situate their importance to the making of the Aboriginal Family through the interwoven practices, spectacles, histories, and knowledges of colonization.

This book is also concerned with understanding how representational technologies produce powers that cannot be subsumed under economic, physical, and epistemic forms of violence; images, too, exert their own power, sacrificing human subjects to a field of subjugation to advance colonial oppression and exploitation. Such semiotic apparatuses of subjugation must be examined on their own terms if the dual process of their reclamation and erasure on the part of indigenous artists and writers today is to be fully appreciated and understood as the dynamic and vital force for social change that it is. Thus, it is equally important to recognize the vital place of cultural practices as sites of social and political change.

Acknowledgments

I am grateful to the Humanities and Social Sciences Research Council of Canada for funding that made research for this project possible and the University of Western Ontario for a small research grant during the summer of 2004. Research for this project was conducted at the British Library, the Royal Museum of British Columbia, and the Whyte Museum in Banff, Alberta. I am grateful for the support provided by the people who work in these institutions.

I began this project during a sabbatical leave at the Center for Gender and Feminist Research at the University of British Columbia in 1999, and I am grateful to this institution for a memorable opportunity for intellectual exchange, and especially the opportunity to dialogue about my project with such wonderful colleagues as Lynne Bell and Rosanne

Kennedy. Cathy Denby, a front-line worker, indigenous scholar, and cultural activist in the struggle against violence toward indigenous women, transformed my comprehension of the language and meaning of justice and healing in decolonization, and for this I am very grateful. Many thanks to former colleagues at the University of Northern British Columbia, Tonia Mills and Perry Shawana, for the benefit of their intellectual acuity and commentary on previously published papers reproduced, in part, here. I am also grateful to the graduate students in both the Gender Studies Program at the University of Northern British Columbia and the English Department at the University of Western Ontario for their lively discussions and insights on the materials included in this book.

Many thanks to Siobhan McMenemy at University of Toronto Press for her wonderful editorial guidance throughout the publishing process. I would also like to thank the two anonymous readers for the University of Toronto who provided insightful commentaries and recommendations. I have tried to address all their concerns. The shortcomings that remain are entirely my own.

The following articles have been reproduced either in part or in their entirety in this volume: 'The "Bourgeois Family," Aboriginal Women, and Colonial Governance in Canada: A Study in Feminist Historical and Cultural Materialisms,' *Signs: Journal of Women in Culture and Society* 27.1 (Autumn 2001): 59–85; 'The Power in Written Bodies: Gender, Decolonization and the Archive,' *Genders* 23 (1996): 184–211, reprinted as 'The Logics of Discovery: Border/Body Disputes,' *Canadian Review of Comparative Literature* 22.3/4 (Sept./Dec. 1995): 603–21; 'Colonial Phantasms: Aboriginality in the Photographic Archive,' in *Recalling Early Canada*, ed. Jennifer Blair et al. (Edmonton: University of Alberta Press, 2005), 301–34; 'Colonial Governance and the Making and Unmaking of the Bourgeois "Eskimo Family" in Robert Flaherty's *Nanook of the North*,' in *Indigeneity: Constructions and (Re)Presentations*, ed. James Brown and Patricia Sant (Comock, NY: Nova Science Press, 1999), 96–117.

Finally, it remains for me to thank my partner, Elie Korkmaz, and my daughter, Sophie Emberley-Korkmaz, for their enduring and sustaining love during the writing and research for this book.

DEFAMILIARIZING THE ABORIGINAL:
CULTURAL PRACTICES AND DECOLONIZATION IN CANADA

Introduction: Of Soft and Savage Bodies in the Colonial Domestic Archive

This book examines the cultural representation of 'the family' as an institution of colonial power in early-twentieth-century Canada. My argument is that technologies of representation, including film, photography, and print culture, disseminated images that contributed, whether knowingly or not, to the imposition of the bourgeois European and patriarchal family on indigenous societies. However, the sexual codes and racial inscriptions of the nineteenth-century European and bourgeois family structure were not simply exported to colonial space and imposed on indigenous kinship structures. Rather, the very determining power of this familial structure was constituted both through and against indigenous kinship relations. This dual process of imposition and exploitation was accomplished, in part, through cultural practices and representations which collectively became a coercive form of power working in relation to political and economic forms of colonial domination. The purpose of this book is to historicize this mode of representational violence, and to study how its attendant formation of a network of images came to serve the interests of a colonial settler culture and form such a significant part of Canada's national imaginary.

For the most part, the argument developed in this book lies in the way I assemble materials so as to make connections that are not readily apparent and unmake or disassemble apparently fixed and immutable truths. This performative method of analysis can, perhaps, be usefully characterized as a analytics of dis/memberment, defined by this double movement of assemblage and disassemblage; hence the 'slash,' which signals this dual process of making and unmaking. The slash also has the additional force of calling attention to the body as a material site of dis-membering and re-membering, violence and healing. A materialist approach to the body and corporeal power is central to my understanding of how European imperialist nations oppressed and exploited their colonized subjects. I also want to suggest that this analytics of dismemberment offers up a strategic way of putting into play forms of knowledge that are subjugated or forgotten. For example, works of fiction, photographs, and advertisements are rarely if ever thought of or valued as knowledge. Moreover, and in keeping with its double movement to critically examine subjugated and sanctioned knowledges, this analytical approach seeks to demonstrate how the multiple realities of First Nations women and children, especially, have been displaced under colonization.

In an effort to gain a better understanding of the role of cultural practices in determining – and perhaps even liberating – social forms of existence, such as the family under colonization, a few historical references are needed.

In Canada during the late nineteenth century, and throughout the twentieth, colonial politics were engaged in developing and deploying techniques to dismantle indigenous kinship relations by imposing European forms of political governance. Specifically, a hierarchical division between public and domestic spheres was imposed upon gatherer/hunter societies. The European division of public and private spheres instituted and maintained colonial-patriarchal power through hierarchical formations both between and within these domains. In the public domain, bourgeois men occupied positions of power in juridical, government, financial, medical, military, and knowledge institutions. In the domestic sphere, power was maintained through the patriarchal figure of 'the father' and the economically, legally, and state sanctioned control of patrilineal descent. Although the gender division of labour that existed in many gatherer/hunter societies may have provided the basis for facilitating this process, there was, nevertheless, a significant difference between the two forms of political governance in the distribution of power. For gatherer/hunters, a gender division of labour did not automatically translate into a hierarchical division of power, as Eleanor Leacock demonstrated in her groundbreaking study of the Montagnais-Naskapi (Leacock 1980). In Canada, the hierarchical model was imposed on indigenous people largely through the regulatory agency of late-nineteenth-century government legislation leading up to and including the Indian Act (1876) and subsequent amendments. Constitutive of this legislative practice of colonial power was the making of the 'domestic sphere' into a significant site for the colonization of First

Nations women and children. Thus the equitable distributive powers of kinship relations among gatherer/hunters were destroyed and replaced.

One of the effects of the colonial state's control over this newly transformed 'aboriginal domestic sphere' was its self-appointed power over kinship relations and the pedagogical practices that took place there. As a result, the colonial state authorized the implementation of compulsory education in residential schools for First Nations children. Taken by legal force from their families, First Nations children and young teenagers were placed in Christian boarding schools. These schools were the site of an extraordinary 'policing operation' (qua Foucault) inasmuch as they set out to regulate aboriginal children's bodies to the assimilatory objectives of colonial dispossession, transforming those bodies into agricultural and domestic labourers. Such an operation eventuated in the loss of Native languages, the destruction of spiritual and cultural practices, and, with the dissolution of kinship relations, the collapse of a network of emotional, intellectual, spiritual, and physical support. In addition to these regulatory colonial practices of assimilation there was the now well-documented use of the coercive and violent practices of sexual and physical abuse (see Chrisjohn et al. 1997, Milloy 1999, Scott and Austin 2005, and Scott 2005). Such a history demands a response. Social scientists and historians have responded to this history and its violence. It is time for cultural critics to examine the multiple and conflictual ways in which cultural representations and practices colluded in colonial violence.

The following sections elaborate upon some theoretical and methodological problems that need to be addressed in pursuing a critical enterprise such as this one. Firstly, I address the emergence of 'the family' in the colonial context, what characters make up its socially imagined formation, and to what end the production of the aboriginal family served the interests of colonization. 'The family' in question here is an imaginary formation, but no less powerful in its real-world effects. Just how we characterize 'real-world effects,' however, must be situated, I argue, within the context of everyday life. Secondly, I examine how a 'worlding' of everyday life provided the basis for establishing interdependencies between women's and children's lives and the histories and present-day realities of colonial and neocolonial practices. The importance of familial everyday life to colonial and decolonial practices lies in how it materially inscribes the body with forces of subjugation and resistance. Such material inscriptions of body powers are themselves mediated by cultural as well as political representations. Thirdly, I emphasize the degree to which the figures of aboriginality created under colonization were gendered and racially inscribed. Moreover, they speak to the often uneven relations that exist in colonization between indigenous men and women, and how colonial practices sought to initiate certain forms of homosociality between indigenous and white men in order to implement the European bourgeois patriarchal and heteronormative model of the family.

In 'loco parentis': The Birth of the Family in Colonial Space

One is not simply born into a family. One becomes a family through juridical, educational, medical, ideological, and other institutional apparatuses and discursive practices. One also comes to identify one's familial location through various narrative techniques and representational strategies that construct the figures of the family. For example, there is the ideal family that emerged in the nineteenth century with the rise of industrial capitalism and bourgeois power in England. This bourgeois family was composed, imaginatively, of civilized man (the father as patriarch), bourgeois woman (the mother as commodity consumer), Oedipal son, and dutiful daughter. These figures existed, however, in opposition to a sort of shadow family, a phantom-like image of the Other Family composed of aboriginal man, hysterical mother, anti-Oedipal schizoid sons, and wayward daughters. In Sam Mendes's brilliant film of the late 1990s, *American Beauty* (U.S. 1999), an apparently dysfunctional family (the Burnhams), with its thin veneer of normality and respectability, only pales in comparison to the much more frightening image of the retired Colonel Fitts and his familial regime of domestic and homophobic violence. The spectacle of a domestic suburban dystopia that the film creates is only undone by an equally aggressive voyeurism on the part of the Colonel's son, who uses a camcorder (hand-held video camera) to record images of intense beauty and objects of love. Competing technologies of representation (the film itself and the hand-held video camera) construct different images of 'the family': on the one hand, it is a site of heterosexual and homosexual love, passion, and eroticism; and, on the other, it is full of terror, violence, homophobia, and pornographic violence. The family is a contested zone, a space of competing signs about familial relations and what constitutes them.

The tension between sexuality and violence in this particular filmic spectacle of the (sub)urban middle-class heterosexual family and its 'others' has a history of precursors that can be traced to a turn-of-the-twentieth-century configuration of Aboriginal Man and Bourgeois Woman. This is, of course, the story of Tarzan, the savage of colonial invention and yet of aristocratic origins, who finds his soulmate, Jane, an English petty-bourgeois woman, in the heart of the jungle. Together they nurture a child of undisclosed parental and cultural origins – 'the boy.' This seemingly odd couple has a whole other range of literary and dramatic antecedents as well as contemporary figures, ranging from Jean-Jacques Rousseau's eighteenth-century figure of the noble savage and the aristocratic women he disparages as a corrupting influence over his primitive man, to J.M. Barrie's early twentieth-century English classic *Peter and Wendy*, a children's version of Tarzan and Jane. In such narratives, Aboriginal Man is the hero, and the moral is a simple one: once his childlike ignorance of the ways of civilization is corrected and his primitive aggression tamed, Aboriginal Man is fit to enter the bourgeois household and take up his rightful disposition to rule family and state as the rational and civilized man of the Enlightenment. He is either idealized for his adventurousness and freedom from Victorian repression and domesticity, or demonized and feared as a symbol of repressed desire and violence waiting to be unleashed, as in Robert Louis Stevenson's brilliant short story *The Strange Case of Dr. Jekyll and Mr. Hyde*.

Essentially, then, aboriginal man stood for the bourgeois man's 'other,' the man he supposedly was in the linear evolution of civilization. In the late nineteenth century and well into the twentieth, European bourgeois masculinity was defined in relation to both romanticized and demonized figures of the ignoble (uncontrollably violent) and noble savage.[1] The bourgeois woman was the instrument of civilization who would produce and reproduce the culture of the proper body; from hygiene to sexuality, from the governance of children in the domestic sphere to the management of servitude and labour in the household, from the control of reproduction, racialized lines of descent, and their social and political economies of inheritance, the Mother was the agent of imperialism and capitalism in the interrelated spaces of empire and colony. The figures of bourgeois woman and aboriginal man disclose the interwoven histories of patriarchy, racism, and imperialism and open up questions concerning how such ideologies contributed to bourgeois alienation – that is, how the bourgeois family came to differ from itself, how it fractured along the fault-lines of its economic realities and ideological imaginings.

Figures of aboriginality and femininity were constitutive of the rhetoric of sexual and racial difference and provided the bourgeois family with a wealth of material against which to try to secure its economic and political hegemony, both 'at home' and in the colonies. During the late nineteenth and early twentieth centuries, European imperial powers enlisted various disciplines of knowledge in order to justify and assert their right to govern 'colonized peoples.' The duality of savagery and civilization shaped English ideas about indigenous cultures as essentially ones that existed in a savage infantile state in need of the governing rationality of a more advanced and enlightened bourgeois society. In contradictory fashion, science and aesthetics created representations of colonized Others that served as the basis for a progressive narrative of nature's terror and beauty, *her* unruliness and innocence. Like an overly aggressive child, *she* must be physically tamed, taught proper social values of work and family, theistic values of love, compassion, and forgiveness, and the meaning of applied intellectual and technological European superiority. Passive and childlike, and yet violent and threatening, contradictory figures of aboriginality became central to the making of European consciousness and shaped the meaning of the lives of the bourgeoisie not only in relation to colonized subjects but to itself as well as to European working classes. In resistance to the negative valance that bourgeois society attached to aboriginality, Karl Marx and Friedrich Engels took up Lewis Henry Morgan's anthropological study of the Iroquois confederacy and the 'communistic household' to launch a counter-discourse of European state-run communism; nevertheless, they both viewed indigenous peoples as belonging to a lower stage of human development, to the 'childhood of the human race' (Engels 1972: 87). Various European scientific discourses and aesthetic representations attempted to negotiate and stabilize the meaning of Europe's sense of its own progress and the value of the Aboriginal to the competing discourses of civilization.

By making the figure of the Aboriginal its founding subject, dominant as well as counter European discourses of primitivism would have an enormous impact on the actual lives of First Nations. Colonial space would be shaped and molded to European social, economic, and political architectonics. Colonial government policies, scientific and anthropological discourses on the 'racial origins' of Man, evolutionary and psychoanalytical theories, as well as photographic, filmic, and popular representations of 'primitive cultures,' contributed in various ways to subjecting the Aboriginal to a range of techniques and representational strategies designed to dismantle indigenous kinship relations. They also set out to recreate those complex social relations in the two-dimensional image of colonial bourgeois society with its hierarchical division between private and public spheres.

Through government policies and practices, the bourgeois family became established within colonial space. Its relations of power and politics of the flesh – the way aboriginal bodies were treated as objects of scientific and social experimentation in the name of a nurturing, caring, and benevolent state – came to determine and structure the meaning of the family for contemporary aboriginal cultures. On the one hand, the European model of domesticity was transplanted to the colonial environment and mapped onto indigenous kinship relations; on the other, the nineteenth-century European patriarchal bourgeois family came to depend on the colonies as the space within which to test as well as secure a representation of itself as socially accepted and, therefore, 'natural.' Thus the colonial encounter functioned as an oppositional site for Europeans to produce knowledge about themselves as members of civilized and enlightened nations. Such knowledge of the family competed with indigenous kinship relations. From the European perspective, conformity to the ideal of the 'Universal Family' was essential to a European self-definition; the family that did not conform was regarded as degenerate and uncivilized.

The so-called aboriginal family became a complex signifying practice, the site of contested images and discourses. Central to this historical contest was the attempt to obliterate existing kinship affiliations because such political kinships formed the basis of economic and social governance among gatherer/hunter societies. In the photographic image of figure I.1, its textual framing demonstrates how the bodies of indigenous people in Canada were inscribed within the oppositional ethnocentric logic of civilization (the bourgeois Christian family – 'Mr. and Mrs. Morley Beaver and Child') and savagery ('Western Indian, Squaw and Papoose').

The violent clash of signs contained in this photographic representation of the Aboriginal Family occurred during a period when anthropology, writes Rosalind Morris, 'assumed the inevitable extinction of Native cultures and drew much of its legitimacy from its claim to be salvaging what little remained of doomed peoples' (Morris 1994: 45).

I.1 'Mr. and Mrs. Morley Beaver and Child.' Stoney, c. 1910 (archival inscription). 'Western Indian, Squaw, & Papoose' (textual overlay).

Ethnographic writings and visual representations in film and photography served as such salvaging operations.[2] To paraphrase James Clifford, 'the other is lost, in disintegrating time and space, but saved in the text,' or, as the case may be, in film and photography as well (as quoted in Morris 1994: 45). The salvage mentality in ethnographic practices certainly underscored the ideological fear of lost origins. Such salvaging operations were, however, mythic to the extent that indigenous people and societies were not in actual fact 'vanishing.' Rather, their way of life was being re-signified through various technologies and techniques of representation. Various colonial legislative practices, scientific knowledges, and representational media contributed to making this semiotic apparatus of aboriginality. An economical and seemingly less violent process of ideological containment, this semiotic field of legislative, epistemic, and aesthetic practices did not require the actual 'extinction' of First Peoples, but the re-signifying of their kinship relations in the terms of the bourgeois family. Colonization had to invest in a new semiotic order, a new code of familial relations in everyday life, if it was to successfully contest indigenous relations of economic exchange and kinship governance. Doing so required not simply the destruction of the latter but its replacement by something else.

The early twentieth century was a time of self-consciousness in modernity, a time of coming to terms with the radical changes wrought by capitalism and imperialism throughout the nineteenth century, including the rise of counter-hegemonic and competing ideologies, practices, and theories of suffragism and socialism, as well as the emergence of the new science of psychoanalysis. This historical moment also witnessed a dramatic change in British imperialist politics and policies from imperial state-sanctioned violence to 'self-governance,' from direct political and military intervention to neocolonial economic and political practices, such as 'indirect rule' in the colonies. Importantly, the invention of the new mechanical technologies of representation such as photography and film, along with print culture, gave rise to a visual representation of colonization. Crucial to this transatlantic study of the making and unmaking of the Aboriginal Family in the British Empire, English Canada, and indigenous territories is the understanding that its invention was the result of the iterative capabilities of the technologies that reproduced images of the Aboriginal Family. This iterative capability constitutes a specific mode of colonial violence, a sort of spectral violence named as such not only because of its ability to create the spectacle of the family but because such images would come to haunt the desires of a civilizing colonial consciousness. Spectral violence constitutes a specific form of cultural hegemony that may intersect and work with the organized militaristic violence of the state, but is neither supplemental nor tangential to it. In other words, it cannot be reduced to its merely symbolic component either as a reflection of 'real' violence or as textual instances of colonial ideology formalizing the actual violence that served to consolidate the state's social, economic, or political interests. During the hegemony of British imperialism in the late nineteenth and early twentieth centuries technologies of representation were strategically deployed as part of a complex web of colonial power which, in addition to political and economic violence, set out to constitute the colonial subject as *Aboriginal*, while simultaneously obliterating any trace of this 'originary' subject. In so doing, this mode of representational violence fixed meanings and values, and bound and reduced the complexity of indigenous lived experiences to a fixed set of images, a panoramic phantasmania of *aboriginality* whose ghostly presence would haunt the apparent immortalizing technologies of re-production. Thus, aboriginality signifies both a semiotics of subjugation and a mode of colonial representational violence in which the subject is made to vanish from historical veracity and reappear as a simulacrum. What images propose as the truth of 'aboriginal peoples' is, ironically, a substitute for something that may never have existed to begin with. The figure of 'aboriginality' – *ab origine* (from the beginning) – belies the rupture that exists between the lived experiences of indigenous peoples and the impoverished spectacle of colonial representation, the Aboriginal. This is to say that colonial knowledge did not discover the lives of Aboriginals (*qua* ethnography); rather, it constructed figures of aboriginality through various signifying apparatuses, systems, and technologies of representation. It emerged at a certain distance and separate from indigenous peoples' existence and worked to circumscribe a provisional domain of the real and its representative proxies, attempting to render place and people finite as partial objects of knowledge. At once both remarkably familiar, and yet *not* known, the uncanny figure of the Aboriginal would constitute a powerful figure that would transform daily life among indigenous people.

There are three key features of representational violence operating spatially in the semiotics of subjugation. They include:

1 spatial practices of violence: locations

2 spatial representations of violence: discursive, textual, epistemic, corporeal, and visual
3 spaces of representational violence: the family portrait

On one level, we can say that violence often takes place in particular locations, circumscribed by real material boundaries, such as the house, the schoolyard, the urban street, or the war zone. The spatial practice of violence in these particular locations is rendered visible or invisible depending on covert or overt strategies of legitimization. The spectacle of war and street violence is a visible practice designed to be a 'show of force.' The violence of sexism and racism in the schoolyard or the home is generally covert and surreptitious; its dangers to the perpetrator as well as the victim often result in focusing the public's attention on the agent of violence. The known dangers of military, domestic, and pedagogical violence are perceived through the concrete and empirical spaces they occupy. Thus, the physicality of violence is itself localized and located within an experiential and perceived dimension, a known place.

Articulated to the spatial practices of violence are spatial representations of violence conceived in discourses of resistance and oppression that work to delimit the very meaning of violence as well as the places in which violence occurs. This is the realm of an epistemology of violence and the study of knowledges, signs, codes, representations, and practices about violence. For example, the study of *violence against women* is encoded by multiple terms used to decipher the specificity of gendered violence: domestic violence, sexual abuse, wife battering, youth violence, the violent school girl, rural violence, pornography, family violence, intimate violence in families, abused children, and lesbian battering. Media studies in representations of violence in comic books, television programs, and films, for example, interrogate the border between real and imagined violence from the assumption that however complex such a relationship is, fundamentally, these forms of violence are interrelated in deterministic and causal ways.

The organization of knowledge can itself be a mode of representational violence, such as the way the Royal British Columbia Museum, discussed in detail in chapter 5, arranges certain images under the heading 'Family Groups' and others under the heading 'Indian Family Portrait.' There is no category entitled 'Colonial Family Portrait' or

'Non-Indian Family Portrait.' How subjects are categorized and orga-nized and what forms of regularity emerge from the types of classifica-tions used, constitute spatial modes of epistemic violence.

The third configuration combines the knowledges gained from real spatial practices of violence and the various spatial representations of violence. What characterizes these spaces are actual examples, such as the Family Portrait. My intent here is to read the spaces of representa-tional violence in order to rupture the image from its seemingly normal and naturalized context, thus allowing for the possibility of intervening in the space between reception and meaning. The latter constitutes a strategy in de-signification in which the Aboriginal Family is rendered *unfamiliar.*

As a site of social regulation in colonial space, the colonial bourgeois family intervened at the level of *everyday life* – the management of daily living practices, its quotidian experience, activities, seeming trivialities, its geography of intimacies, sexual and emotional, and its governing strategies and relations of power between men and women, parents and child-ren. One of the most effective ways colonial bourgeois, patri-archal, and heternormative society was able to secure and *reproduce* its familial ideology in the nineteenth and twentieth centuries was through the use of visual technologies of representation. Visual media, along with print culture, in the twentieth century emerged as one of the most powerful social and cultural forces. The colonial photographic archive, for example, constituted a key technology of representation that coincided with the epistemic violence of eugenics and miscegena-tion, forced sterilizations and hysterectomies, and, especially, the coer-cive use of domestic violence and wife battering, rape, and the sexual assault of indigenous male and female children in the residential schools.

In the nineteenth century the rhetoric of civilization dominated the production and reception of European images of a so-called primitive existence in the colonies. Civilization and Empire were key formations in the deployment of a representational violence that was used to regu-late the bourgeois family by producing a representation of itself as nor-mal, natural, and different from its other, the Aboriginal Family.

Michel Foucault's analysis of the relationship between text and author in his essay 'What Is an Author?' provides a point of departure for working through the visual imprint of authority that emerges with the growing importance of the spectacle in twentieth-century colonial technologies of power and rule (Foucault 1994). My interest in re-visiting his essay is twofold. I want to critique the moment in this essay when 'civilization' is re-signified as an authorial marker, hidden in the folds of his analysis, and yet, despite this ideological blind spot, I also want to point out that he is entirely correct when at the conclusion to his essay, following a list of questions related to the inevitable historical change in the meaning of authorship, he states emphatically that 'we would hear hardly anything but the stirring of an indifference; What difference does it make who is speaking?' (222). Interpreting this last remark, however, has proved challenging. If the 'who' in question is a marginal or excluded speaking subject, then, of course, it does matter, but if the 'who' is the speaking subject of authority, then, I would suggest, indifference might prove to be a useful strategy for undoing such authorial power.

Although Foucault is interested in displacing the author function within a European bourgeois literary formation, he nevertheless relocates its power and authority elsewhere. Indeed, I would argue, it is the mark of 'civilization' that comes to reoccupy the author function in Foucault's essay. The re-signification of authority surfaces when, in the following remark, Foucault refers to 'a civilization like our own': 'we could say that in *a civilization like our own* there are a certain number of discourses endowed with the "author function" while others are *deprived* of it' (211, emphasis added). This use of deprivation suggests that those excluded from *a civilization like our own* possess discourses that, without an author function, are, in the end, impoverished.

'*In our civilization*, it has not always been the same types of texts that have required attribution to an author' (212, emphasis added). Indeed, Foucault is careful to mark the 'literary' and its genealogical inheritance to those 'stories, epics, tragedies, comedies' that were 'put into circulation, and valorized without any question about the identity of their author; their anonymity caused no difficulties since their ancientness, whether real or imagined, was regarded as a sufficient guarantee of their status' (212). But what of the contemporary ethnographies compiled when bourgeois literature, and the novel especially, became prominent in the nineteenth century? These texts are full of un-authored myths, accounts, stories, and events. Did these non-authored aspects of the ethnographic account accrue status because of their 'ancient' value? Or were they relegated to the category of the 'de-prived,' without an author function and its complementary civiliza-tional authority – except, of course, that which was credited to the eth-nographer himself?[3] Foucault dabbles in cultural relativism to dance around this problem, and not once but several times: 'the modes of circulation, valorization, attribution, and appropriation of discourses vary with each culture and are modified within each' (212). An innocuous enough statement, but one that fails to acknowledge that such systems of discursive circulation, valorization, attribution, and appropriation vary not just as a dispensation of cultural differences but as a result of imperial and colonial power. One of the effects of such power was how the position of the 'native informant' as a collaborator in the construction of the ethnographic archive was entirely eclipsed. The figure of the native informant is a reminder that the authorial function of civilization maintains its authority, in part, by denying indigenous societies any place in the very construction of its 'discursivity.'

For Foucault, Marx and Freud represent the 'founders of a discursivity' capable of challenging the limits of the authorial function. In order to demonstrate the difference between discursivity and non-discursivity, Foucault explains how Ann Radcliffe's *The Mysteries of Udolpho* or *The Castles of Athlin and Dunbayne* 'made possible the appearance of Gothic horror novels at the beginning of the nineteenth century,' and thus her work represents an example of how 'her author function exceeds her own work' (217). However, Foucault argues, while Radcliffe's 'texts opened the way for a certain number of resemblances and analogies which have their model or principle in her work,' the writings of Marx and Freud 'made possible not only a certain number of analogies but also (and equally important) a certain number of differences. They have created a possibility for something other than their discourse, yet something belonging to what they founded' (217–18). Marx and Freud emerge as heroes of a textuality whose 'work' is characterized by a paradoxical capacity to initiate a 'return to the origin.' As Foucault elaborates, 'This return, which is part of the discursive field itself, never stops modifying it. The return is not a historical supplement that would be added to the discursivity, or merely an ornament; on the contrary, it constitutes an effective and necessary task of transforming the discursive practice itself ... re-examining Freud's texts modifies psychoanalysis itself, just as a reexamination of Marx's would modify Marxism' (219). This distinction between the reproduction of the same in gothic fiction and the generative capabilities of difference in Marx and Freud is produced upon a set of implicit assumptions based on the gendering and racializing of specific literary genres as white, female, or feminine and discursivity as the providence of a white masculine and male productivity. Thus, the juxtaposition of the gothic horror novel, with its attention to domesticity, hysteria, and the racially motivated reproductive regulation of bourgeois women's bodies, to the founding fathers of discursivity also reproduces the nineteenth-century division between private and public spheres of knowledge and communication. Discursivity appears as a generative enterprise far removed from the gendered, racialized, and reproductive bodies of hysterical and gothic domestic fictions. It is as if the biological fiction of female reproductivity has been transposed onto white women's fiction and the symbolic powers of white male productivity have been claimed by Foucault for a particular genre of public discourse with its generative rationalities and real-world significances.

The processes of modification Foucault attributes to discursivity can thus be seen as a process of re-authorization that divides 'writing' into such categories as civilized and savage, or feminine and masculine. Foucault's use, if not dismissal, of domesticity and domestic fiction means that he cannot intervene in the imperial and patriarchal limits of the 'author function' with its attendant bourgeois and patriarchal authority in colonial space. When Foucault asks, 'What if, within a workbook filled with aphorisms, one finds a reference, the notation of a meeting or of an address, or a laundry list: is it a work, or not?' (207) such a question begs to be addressed within a materialist analytical framework that acknowledges the social specificity of 'work' as distinct from 'a work' – at least, as the materialities of the English language would allow for such a distinction. Of special interest here, then, is domesticity and female labour, without which 'discursivity' might never have come into existence to begin with.

This intervention into Foucault's re-authorization of discursivity via the civilizational rhetoric of a domestic – and maternal – apartheid returns 'us' to the question 'What difference does it make who is speaking?' I prefer to interpret Foucault's emphasis toward the indifference of the speaking subject from the perspective of authorial power as opposed to the marginalization of voices. In which case, indifference becomes a vital strategy in which the dispossessed and those who have been violently regulated by the fictive and its 'author function' remain wisely indifferent to authors and authorities. In so doing, it becomes possible to reclaim the empowering capacities of signification, their processes of production, and their modes of reception. Thus, while exercising some indifference toward the authority even of the 'found[ing] [fathers] of discursivity,' I would turn their work to other purposes and introduce strategies in de-signification capable of de-authorizing the power of civilization and its domestic quarters.

The Worlding of Everyday Life

This examination of 'the aboriginal family' looks at how late nine-teenth- and early twentieth-century visual and textual materials were constitutive of the web of colonial power that contributed to making and unmaking the very category of *the Aboriginal*. Having already achieved its economic imperialist agenda to gain control over the land and its resources in the previous two centuries, the violence of repre-sentation in conjunction with scientific and non-scientific knowledges, economically extended a colonial and neocolonial indirect, if not 'medi-ated,' rule over indigenous peoples. In other words, it worked in tan-dem to shift the balance of power from indigenous kinship – governing economies to the public rule of the European capitalist nation. Such a process of radical social change was mediated by techniques and tech-nologies of cultural as well as political re-presentation. It was also mediated by the split between domestic and public rule.

In his critique of everyday life, the French sociologist Henri Lefebvre argued for a shift in historical and political perspectives from the 'higher spheres' of the state, parliament, leaders, and policies to the problems of the everyday in the modern world. It was not simply in order to reinscribe a division between public and private spheres, nor to engage in simple reversals, that Lefebvre reoriented his gaze from the eagle's to the serpent's eye. Rather, it was to underscore the moment of historical rupture when the normativity of the split between public and private is exposed. In Lefebvre's terms, it is what happens when the boundaries of everyday life shatter and life as it is lived surges forth into the domain of history (Lefebvre 2002: 3). At such moments, the arbitrary distinction between high and low, or public and private, spheres, dissolves, and their intimate connectivity is made visible. For Lefebvre the normative boundaries between domestic and public realms created during the emergence of bourgeois capitalism in the nineteenth century could be exposed only during times of revolution-ary change. Ultimately, however, such moments of historical rupture belong to the contradictory forces of history and, thus, may occur as a result of various forms of change or upheaval, even including the op-pressive violence of imperialism, colonization, slavery, and occupation. Such conditions call for a different orientation toward the value of everyday life for historical and political purposes, one in which every-day life can be viewed as an assemblage of representations through which 'the family' was able to operate as a material and institutional force in colonial rule, reconfiguring and transforming the movement across the boundaries of the interdependent and contingent spheres of public/private and Empire/colony.

Decolonization in Canada is generally viewed as a process of negotiation between indigenous organizations and institutions, including First Nations, Métis and Inuit, and the legislative and executive bodies of the nation state. These negotiations take place in an arena of power relations often characterized by a struggle over who or what claims the right to govern indigenous peoples, whether it be from the indigenous perspective of self-governance or the Indian Act, for example. But access to these 'higher levels' of political decision-making is not only uneven and unequal for indigenous people, in general, but for indigenous women and children, in particular, because what counts in the critical framing of decolonization often excludes or minimizes the sphere of everyday life and especially 'the family' as viable political sites of power and transformation.

In Homi Bhabha's essay 'The World and the Home,' alienation in the domestic space is analysed as a psychoanalytical experience that divides 'one' from 'oneself':

> In a feverish stillness, the intimate recesses of the domestic space become sites for history's most intricate invasions. In that displacement, the border between home and world becomes confused; and, uncannily, the private and the public become part of each other, forcing upon us a vision that is as divided as it is disorienting. (Bhabha 1997: 445)

This idea of an alienated experience in the idealized notion of home and hearth is not new to feminist theorizing of the division between private and public (see Landes 1988, 1998). Bhabha uses the word 'unhomely' to distinguish an experience and a category from something that cannot be 'easily accommodated in that familiar division of the social life into private and public spheres' (Bhabha 1997: 445). This familiar division of the private and public is without a doubt a central tenet in feminist theories of domesticity and the institution of the family, and it is intricately, if not intimately, related to the emergence of a radical sexual politics in the 1960s that sought to uncover the specificity of women's oppression, and perhaps their liberation, in questions of sexuality, knowledge and power. Bhabha's turn away from feminist critiques of oppression and 'home' toward the unhomely – a re-signifying of Freud's *Unheimlich*, with its connotation of 'unhoused-ness' – occupies a space in-between the public and private, and between feminism and decolonization (Freud 1995: 121).[4] Thus, his terminology is both useful and unsettling, familiar and disturbing, in the way that it gestures toward feminism and yet simultaneously displaces it, a gesture, I would argue, that is entirely symptomatic of the complicated, if not 'uncanny,' place that feminism occupies in the arena of decolonization. However difficult it may be, it is vital to keep feminism in decolonization; otherwise, the notion of home and, indeed, Bhabha's 'unhomely' is reduced to its merely metonymic value, a distilled essence on which the supposedly larger and more important questions of economic imperialism, territorialization, diasporic migrations, colonization, and globalization can be examined. By limiting analysis to metonymic evaluation, as Bhabha does, questions of sexuality and imperial conquest are in danger of becoming merely a matter of apolitical semiotic interest in the eroticism of colonial conquest and penetration. Consequently, important questions concerning the material force of colonial sexual politics on the bodies of indigenous people, especially women and children, are lost.[5]

Decolonization has been defined as a

> process of revealing and dismantling colonialist power in all its forms. This includes dismantling the hidden aspects of those institutional and cultural forces that had maintained the colonialist power and that remain even after political independence is achieved. Initially, in many places in the colonized world, the process of resistance was conducted in terms or institutions appropriated from the colonizing culture itself. This was only to be expected, since early nationalists had been educated to perceive themselves as potential heirs to European political systems and models of culture. This occurred not only in settler colonies where the white colonial élite was a direct product of the system, but even in colonies of occupation. Macaulay's infamous 1835 Minute on Indian Education had proposed the deliberate creation in India of just such a class of 'brown white men,' educated to value European culture above their own. This is the *locus classicus* of this hegemonic process of control, but there are numerous other examples in the practices of other colonies. (Ashcroft, Griffiths, and Tiffin 2000: 63)

What counts as an 'institution' in the colonial context? Is 'the family' an institution? Is it one of the 'numerous other examples' of how hegemony works to suture the social ruptures that threaten to shift power from the colonizer to the colonized? What is it about 'the family' that makes it so difficult, if not impossible, to see as a space of power and control that may carry on the work of colonization even after official institutions have been decolonized? Decolonization, however, need not be reduced to a proces of shifting power from 'white' elites to 'brown' elites. It may also be the ongoing reality of an *aporia* that exists between officially sanctioned institutions and those institutions that are either unrecognized or emerging, such as the family. I choose to use the term 'decolonization' (rather than the more popular 'postcolonialism') in order to signify such an ongoing process of colonial critique beyond the legislated emergence of postcolonial nation states. The uneven relations between everyday life and decision-making practices, legislated changes in governance, or transformations in economic structures – for indigenous women, youth, and children especially – demand a language that speaks to the micropolitical shifts in daily living, thus making it possible to chart the responses, reactions, resistances, and negotiations that take place in relation to legally or socially sanctioned laws. That we might retain a meaning of decolonization that has not yet sutured closed the gap between official institutional transfers and those who already exist on the margins of, or outside of, those institutional parameters to begin with, is, I think, still a possibility. In other words, *decolonization* might more usefully signify the rupture that occurs between what is socially recognized to be an institution in the first place, and therefore bound to articulate decolonial policies within official constraints, and that which is in the process of becoming recognizable as a locus of power. But because of contigent relations between or among a network of social forces (i.e., racial, biopolitical, patriarchal), those emergent areas of power remain seemingly absent from the historical process of decolonization. It is precisely because of these 'other' contingent sites of transformation that it is entirely possible for so-called decolonial institutions to retain their colonial relations of power even after they have changed hands, so to speak. Discourses of racial and sexual difference rendered the bodies of indigenous people invisible, as in worthless and expendable. Thus, it is necessary to examine what counts as an 'institution' and how the institutional and non-institutionalizations of everyday life impacted upon the exercise of colonial power, especially the use of the domestic sphere and its social spatialization of 'the family' as a key technology of that power. As Andrea Smith notes, 'the analysis of and strategies for addressing gender violence have failed to address the manner in which gender violence is not simply a tool of patriarchal control, but also serves as a tool of racism and colonialism' (Smith 2005: 1). Sexual assault and domestic violence, heterosexuality and the family, and the hierarchical division of public/ private powers are deeply intertwined in the histories of imperialism, colonization, and decolonization.

In his essay 'The World, the Text, and the Critic,' Edward Said argues for a materialist analysis of the literary text from the perspective of its 'worldliness.' By this he means that the text has a specific location both in terms of its 'sensuous particularity' and its 'historical contingency,' and that both 'are considered as being incorporated in the text, an infrangible part of its capacity for conveying and producing meaning' (Said 1983: 39). The notion of worldliness enabled Said to situate canonical texts, such as Jane Austen's *Mansfield Park*, within the broader scope of historical circumstances, particularly nationalism, imperialism, and colonization (Said 1993: 80–96). While everything about European or American culture cannot be reduced to the exigencies of colonalism and empire, it is, nevertheless, disingenuous, Said argued, to ignore how expressive forms of cultural production consolidated the idea of Empire and 'enabled, encouraged, and otherwise assured the West's readiness to assume and enjoy the experience of empire' (Said 1983: 80). Eschewing a simple causality between Europe and the non-European world, Said writes that

> we should try to discern instead a counterpoint between overt patterns in British writing about Britain and representations of the world beyond the British Isles. The inherent mode for this counterpoint is not temporal but spatial. How do writers in the period before the great age of explicit, pro-grammatic colonial expansion – the 'scramble for Africa,' say – situate and see themselves and work in the larger world? We shall find them using striking but careful strategies, many of them derived from expected sources – positive ideas of home, of a nation and its language, of proper order, good behavior, moral values. (Said 1983: 81)

In his attempt to comprehend how humanistic thought in the eighteenth and nineteenth centuries did little to stand in the way of the acceleration of imperial rule, Said postulates that 'perhaps the custom of distinguishing "our" home and order from "theirs" grew into a harsh political rule for accumulating more of "them" to rule, study, and subordinate' (Said 1983: 82). In both these passages, Said attends to the relationship between 'home' and 'nation' in outlining the techniques and strategies deployed in the colonial context. What this suggests is that the temporal and spatial dimensions of imperial rule were not only subject to territorial dispossessions in Europe's colonization of the so-called 'New World,' but that everyday life, ideas of home, and even the architectural imprint of the household were intense sites for the consolidation of colonial rule. I would also suggest that these conceptual and material sites of existence were key spaces in which the West 'enjoy[ed] the experience of Empire.' Enjoyment and the fulfilment of a desire for the things of the earth – especially commodities and women's bodies – were also part of that 'sensuous particularity' essential to the material worlding of the literary text. The geopolitics of imperial rule crossed several cartographic axes, including the division of public and private spheres under nineteenth-century bourgeois governance and the division of empire and colony under imperial rule. It is my contention that the question of the disconnection between the great humanist values promulgated by the liberal mainstream of European society and its imperial enterprise, must be addressed by examining the way in which everyday life, home and household, became key representational spaces precisely for the purpose of mediating the contradictions of imperial violence and the benevolent paternalism of regulatory and apparently non-coercive techniques of colonial rule.

Thus, this book shifts the conventional frames of reference used to examine colonization, such as economic expansion, territorial annexation, the exploitation of natural resources, and the abuse of individual and collective rights, to the everyday living practices of the family. This is not to say that the study of postcolonial and advanced capitalist/colonial states is not vital to our understanding of global relations of violence. M. Jacqui Alexander and Chandra Talpade Mohanty argue, for example, that both states 'organize and reinforce a cathectic structure based in sexual difference (i.e., heterosexuality), which they enforce through a variety of means, including legislation. In almost all instances, however, these states conflate heterosexuality with citizenship and organize a "citizenship machinery" in order to produce a class of loyal heterosexual citizens and a subordinated class of sexualized, nonprocreative, noncitizens, disloyal to the nation, and, therefore, suspect' (Alexander and Mohanty 1997: xxiii). In other words, the production of sexualities in the family is also organized by what the state overtly or covertly sanctions as its citizenry. Bonita Lawrence contends, however, that more focus must be given to how such a 'complex rendition of a global geopolitical process can obscure how these histories come together in the experiences of different Indigenous nations "on the ground." It also obscures the *processes* that enabled colonizers to acquire the land, and the *policies* that were put into place to control the peoples displaced from the land' (Lawrence 2002: 26). Lawrence seeks to make such processes and their effects transparent by attending to the knowledge produced in indigenous communities. Documenting their experiences, according to Lawrence, challenges 'myths about Native savagery and the benefits of European technologies' (Lawrence 2002, 26). Taking into account the importance of attending to processes on the ground and the need to focus on capitalist/colonial statehood, I would suggest that it is in the space between these knowledge categories that the study of technologies of representation can most usefully demonstrate the transnational complicities mediating the 'everyday' and the 'global.' It is these very complicities, as Alexander and Mohanty note, that 'discipline and mobilize the bodies of women – in particular [indigenous] women – in order to consolidate patriarchal and colonizing processes' (Alexander and Mohanty 1997: xxiii). The transactional strategies I use here are ones of de-signification aimed at disclosing the iterative or re-signifying mechanisms used to maintain the hegemony of civilization and savagery or modernity and traditionalism. Such strategies also work simultaneously to instigate a rupture or break in the equilibrium of colonial hegemonic practices.

My intention here is to articulate these transactional strategies with that of a worldiness in everyday life in order to situate the 'sensual particularity' of domesticity as an equally infrangible part of a text's capacity for conveying and producing meaning, and especially so *within* the interwoven contexts of imperialism, colonization, and globalization. In other words, I am interested in a study of the domestic archive and its emergence over the twentieth century as a representative site for mediating the transnational flows of bodies, economies, and powers under colonization, neocolonization, and globalization.

It is the everyday worlding of the domestic sphere, the politics of familial and personal relations, that governs the methodological choices and many of the insights in this text. Here the domains of 'high' and 'low' culture, or civil and domestic culture, are turned upside down. I work outward from governance in domestic life to the politics of ruling in the public domain. I work from ways of knowing and seeing that exist in the rich store of tropes and images in popular literature, film, and other accessible aspects of material culture. This approach is, perhaps, all too symptomatic of a postindustrial materialism, a time in which popular representational technologies dominate the visual landscape of the city and the 'household' in their many shapes and forms, blurring boundaries between home and learning, work and play, labouring and desiring bodies. It is also the effect of the dominance of a culture of commodities that slowly and insistently replaced social diversity throughout the nineteenth-century European imperialist and colonial period. Thus, the commodity form, perhaps in spite of itself, has a certain critical agency in social and cultural analyses. This text, then, does more than take the materials of popular culture as 'objects' or 'fetishes' of critical analysis; rather, it treats those materials as the very substance, method, and content of knowledge about society and culture. Through films, fictions, material objects, and photographic archives, along with psychoanalytical discourses, government reports, legislation, and royal commissions, it is possible to trace how 'the family' was deployed as a material force in the implementation of colonial and neocolonial governance in Canada.

Aboriginality; or, The Search for Origins

The family was one of the most important social apparatuses through which to import various technologies of surveillance to further colonial governance in Canada during the late nineteenth and twentieth centuries. Thus the discourse on the family is an important locus from which to trace the cultural materialist practices of colonization and the biopolitical and biotextual interconnections between and among the domestic sphere, everyday life, and representational violence. Historical and sociological accounts of the family, such as Leonore Davidoff and Catherine Hall's *Family Fortunes: Men and Women of the English Middle Class, 1780–1850*, Michèle Barrett and Mary McIntosh's *The Anti-social Family*, and Mark Poster's *A Critical Theory of the Family*, define and document the emergence of the English bourgeois family and household, its rise to hegemonic status during the nineteenth century, and the powerful effects of familial ideology on the formation of British male and female, bourgeois and working-class, subjects.

While I am primarily focusing here on the bourgeois family as a signifying practice, a site of competing meanings and values produced and reproduced through textual and visual mediation, the historical and sociological scholarship on the family is important to understanding the bourgeois family as an institution, phenomenon, and structure of reality determined by social, political, and economic forces. Writing in the 1980s, the socialist-feminist Michèle Barrett argued that the family was 'the' site of woman's oppression. Moreover, she called for an analysis of an *ideology of familialism* as distinct from examining concrete families: '*Families*, in short, are an achievement of industriousness, respectability and regulation, rather than a pre-given or natural entity, and it was only later that these aggregations of co-residing kin came to be seen as the only natural form of household organization' (Barrett 1989: 203). Interestingly, it is anthropological discourse that provides Barrett with evidence to counteract the supposed uniformity, naturalness, and normativity of the European bourgeois family and its hegemonic place. In one example, citing Ann Oakley's *Sex, Gender and Society*, Barrett writes: 'The universality of mother/child interdependence has been challenged by anthropological evidence of different cultural child-rearing practices' (Barrett 1989: 196). In another, she writes: 'The meaning of kinship ties has varied enormously; indeed any study of anthropology reveals that the social significance of particular kinship links differs dramatically in cross-cultural comparisons' (Barrett 1989: 200). Implicitly, the figure of the aboriginal provides a hidden lever to the ahistoricity of sociological investigations of family structure and meaning. If the aboriginal family provides a strong contestatory ground to the myth of the family's universality, it does so in order to provide a case for the centrality of the European family as an historical figure. European history is thus founded on aboriginality and its representativeness as an indicator of 'cultural difference.'

The argument for historical specificity falls on the heels of a rhetorical ethnocentrism in which 'other' (read colonial) cultures are enlisted, positively, to provide evidence of 'cultural difference.' Such a notion of cultural difference contains the implicit understanding that such other cultures represent Europe's infancy and a state of prefamilial universality; hence, the significance of aboriginal cultures for European *history*. Colonial cultures do not, then, have a history of their own but remain like the category of 'primitive art' in a separate space in the museum, a prehistoric and yet timeless symbol of European history.

On one level, Barrett is entirely aware of the ways in which 'pre-capitalist' societies are deployed in the search for the origins of women's oppression. The term 'pre-capitalist' is often used as a code for so-called primitive or aboriginal cultures, particularly in Engels's *The Origin of the Family, Private Property and the State*. But with reference to the opposition between Engels's thesis that early human societies were matriarchal and Freud's psychoanalytical theory of the Oedipal complex as a primal patriarchal scene, the appropriation of Engels over Freud, Barrett suggests, 'is often a good index of an author's position on the causes of women's oppression, for if you are going to argue the "effect-of-capitalism" approach it helps to evoke either early human society or at least pre-capitalist society as less oppressive of women. This is one reason why it is so difficult to establish the "origins" of women's oppression: historical evidence is not neutral' (Barrett 1989: 191).[6] Both matriarchal and patriarchal theories of the origins of 'the family' deploy the figure of aboriginality to substantiate its European and capitalist historical roots. Barrett's own use of 'other cultures' in her argument for historical specificity is, however, a more recent deployment of the figure of aboriginality, of which Engels's and Freud's usages represent nineteenth- and early-twentieth-century versions. Today it is the rhetoric of cultural difference advanced by anthropological discourse (and underlying much contemporary social policy debates) that dominates the appropriation and deployment of aboriginality. Despite Barrett's emphasis on the disjuncture that exists between supposed 'material' or concrete and 'ideological' claims, such claims are evidently modernist in their historical specification. Colonial cultures or aboriginal peoples provide, on the one hand, a necessarily conservative, static, or traditional basis, a root cause or radical alterity to European modernity, and, on the other, a theoretical or speculative entity, a mythic other to European history. The rhetoric of aboriginality, however, has its own history, from its central position in nineteenth- and early twentieth-century preoccupations with Europe's 'infancy' to its contemporary place as a sign of cultural difference, a Significant Other situated in a hierarchal opposition to the Enlightened Subject.

On the question of racism and 'the family,' Barrett addressed criticism of her work as follows:

> [T]he weight attached to 'the family' as a primary site of oppression has been challenged with regard to the role of the state. Here it is principally, and for good reason, black feminists who have argued that the violence and coercion of a racist state – often explicitly directed against black families as in the implementation of immigration policies – means that it is the state rather than the family that is the oppressor as far as black women are concerned. (Barrett 1989: xx)

When Black feminists in Britain challenged her assumptions on the basis that the state was far more problematic for the Black British diaspora than the family, Barrett admirably reflected on the ethnocentric bias of her research assumptions, although she held firm to her conclusion and argued for greater tolerance and a pluralist approach to the choices people make (Barrett 1989: xxi). Part of what can be learned from this debate is that it is not inherent in the structure of institutions such as 'the family' to guarantee either the exercise of freedom or repression, although they may be such sites at particular historical moments and in particular cultural or social and spatial locations. More analysis is necessary of the ways the colonial state, for example, imposed a model of 'the family' on indigenous societies and through such government policies as the Indian Act systematically attacked kinship relations and the sexual relationships of First Nations women, in particular. It is not, in other words, simply a matter of choice. Rather, I would argue that we should view 'the family' in the twentieth century as a discursive and semiotic apparatus deployed in various instances to regulate, normalize, and naturalize human relations for purposes of extending the biopolitical powers of imperialist transnational states.

Ethnographic Pornography in the Spaces of Representational Violence

In the colonial context, the intertwining of aboriginality, violence, and gender is blatantly mapped onto the female Aboriginal body, as witnessed in a series of murals still displayed on the walls and ceilings of the British Columbia legislative buildings, in Victoria, BC. On 3 July 2002 the Canadian Broadcasting Company (CBC) issued a news item that describes the debate surrounding these murals as follows:

> The murals inside the British Columbia legislature are supposed to depict courage, enterprise, labour and justice – the proud history of the European explorers. But some aboriginal people believe the murals are not something to be proud of. Most of the aboriginal women are depicted bare breasted, shown in what native leaders call subservient positions. Chief Ed John says the murals, painted by a non-aboriginal artist 70 years ago, remind him of how some traders treated First Nations women – not much better than prostitutes. John and others have been trying to get the murals removed for about 20 years. (http://cbc.ca/... /news/2000/07/3/murals0007)

Four images displayed in the lower rotunda of the legislative buildings are titled *Courage, Enterprise, Labour,* and *Justice.* Parts of *Labour* and *Justice* were shown on the CBC news item. The images can also be accessed on the Net, where they are accompanied by written text. *Justice,* for example, appears with the words: 'Judge Begbie is shown, holding court in Clinton during the Cariboo Gold Rush. He walked, rode horseback and canoed over most of British Columbia to bring justice to the mining camps.' Beside *Labour,* the text reads: 'This Mural shows the building of *Fort Victoria*.' In the cases of both *Labour* and *Justice,* the texts stand apart from the image, barely approximating descriptions of visual representation, if not remarkably closed in their lack of reference to Aboriginal/ European relations. In *Justice* an un-named male Indian stands with his hands held behind his back and head bowed. He is the figure of the criminal to whom justice is brought to bear by the white man sitting behind the table, whose name we now know is Judge Begbie, a diligent worker for BC justice. Beside him stands a Native woman, hands crossed in front of her breasts; but, nevertheless, the artist, George H. Southwell, has meticulously painted the left nipple of her beast. In *Labour* three bare-breasted women form the focal point of the painting: one set of eyes gazes directly at the viewer. Another image, *Courage,* is also notable for the naked children that appear in the bottom left-hand corner and the image of a Native woman standing beside a priest's staff, her breasts almost exposed. Along with these paintings in the lower rotunda appear copies of the Magna Carta and, somewhat ironically, the Canadian Charter of Rights and Freedoms (see figures I.2–5).[7]

Knowledge disciplines and organizes the meaning of violence by maintaining boundaries between the real and the imagined, the empirical or physical, the concrete and territorial, as well as the epistemic and representational. For example, during the First World War, masculinity and aboriginality were linked to violence in order to reinvent a centuries-long myth about the superiority of European civilization to aboriginal savagery, thus masking the atrocities of the war caused by the decision-making practices of a governing group of elite European men. The discourses of aboriginality were clearly gendered and paternal, giving rise to ideas about masculinity and manliness in the figure of the noble savage, sexuality and promiscuity in the figure of the wild woman, and infantilism and passivity in the aboriginal child's body.

I.2 *Courage. Meeting of Captains.* Painting by George Southwell, 1940.

I.3 *Enterprise. The Arrival of James Douglas on Vancouver Island.* Painting by George Southwell, 1940.

I.4 *Labour. Building of Fort Victoria*. Painting by George Southwell, 1940.

I.5 *Justice. Judge Begbie Holding Court.* Painting by George Southwell, 1940.

Cultural formations, however, are enormously fluid, hybrid, contradictory, and unstable; hence, the range of representations, practices, and knowledges used to maintain the hegemony of bourgeois colonial culture and the equally diverse strategies of de-signification deployed to decolonize its representational violence.

One of my objectives is to de-signify colonial violence, so that the ethnographic pornography and injustice exhibited in the Victoria legislature buildings, for example, are recognized as a general instrument in constructing, maintaining, and perpetuating colonial domination and governance; and not only historically but in relation to the current problems of domestic violence and sexual assault that indigenous women and children face today and what many indigenous men and women experienced in the residential school system. At issue here is how colonialization is studied and critiqued, or, in-deed, how it is excluded or marginalized from critical debates such as the history of the rise of the British bourgeois nuclear family as a hegemonic formation in the nineteenth century. This history, I would argue, is thoroughly implicated in imperial domination in the colonies, its *re*-presentation of indigenous people as *aboriginal*, and its legislation of indigenous bodies, kinship relations, sexuality, and political agency.

In taking responsibility for the apparitional aboriginal that haunts the 'eternal present,' as Johannes Fabian put it, the anti-racist transnational feminist critic must render visible the *mechanisms* (i.e., the technologies and techniques of representation) by which the past came to be silenced and hidden (Fabian 1983). By addressing material which might have had little or no significance for the historical record and may even be perceived to have no aesthetic or truth value, my intention is to unfold these mechanisms and their material effects, especially on the body. The purpose of this work is to challenge the representational violence toward indigenous people and what stands as its apparent inevitability in colonial and decolonial practices, and to do so by disclosing the articulation of a *silence*:

> Why didn't 'I' – the female body – surface in the text, or was it there all along? In the silence? 'Missing' becomes a metaphor for the silence around the text that omits the woman's s/place. Words crowd her out into silence. Women have, in fact, left their mark on the many silences that surround language – we must, therefore, learn to read those silences. (Philip 2002: 85)

My secret

I am six years old
I happened to be in a house alone with my cousin
She told me to come to her then ordered me to pull my pants down.
She touched my private parts and told me to lie down.
I didn't know what was going on ...
I never told anyone ... She told me not to ...
She would pinch me on my hands or
other parts of my body to keep me silent ... I am hurting ...
this is my secret. (My secret 1991: 1)

For legal scholar Honourable Judge Mary Ellen Turpel-Lafond, the phrase 'domestic violence' carries a double burden: 'To First Nations people, the expressions "culture of violence" and "domestic violence" not only have their customary connotation of violence by men against women but also mean domestic (that is, Canadian State) violence against the First Nations' (Turpel-Lafond 1993: 183). Turpel-Lafond aligns two apparently discontinuous regimes of violence: the domestic sphere and the colonial state. The former is usually perceived as micropolitical in its wielding of power, and the latter macropolitical. It is rare for cultural and social critics to acknowledge that these spheres of violence are mutually dependent and inextricably linked together. When, earlier in the twentieth century, Virginia Woolf argued for an analysis of patriarchal and paternalistic regimes of power in her critical work *Three Guineas*, many readers such as Vita Sackville-West thought that her connection between the rule of the father and that of the fascist dictator was problematic, largely because they felt it undermined the horrifying significance of fascism.[8] Materialist feminist critiques of biopower and the body provide a strong analytical tool with which to understand and critique the shifting and colliding regimes of power affecting the lives of women and children in these related spheres of social and political reality. Turpel-Lafond argues that incidences of domestic violence and sexual assault among First Nations families are related to the colonial policies of the Canadian state, such as the Indian Act, the church-run residential school systems, the imposition of non–First Nations foster parenting, and the exclusion of status Indian women from local governance. Representational violence is an integral part of this vast network of colonial power, power that operated through the discontinuous, yet mutually related, domains of social, cultural, political, economic, and *familial* life. Anti-imperialist feminists such as Turpel-Lafond, Grace Oulette, and Kim Anderson have long been arguing for an intellectual justice that no longer denies the imbrications of colonial state and domestic forms of violence (Ouellette 2003 and Anderson 2000).

I argue that domestic violence must be situated in a matrix of powers that extend from daily living to governmental structures. Furthermore, domestic violence must be understood as a contradictory formation, particularly when it comes to examining the subjects who are interpellated as perpetrators and victims. In her discussion of pre-modern versus modern power in Foucault's work and its relevance to domestic violence, Andrea Westlund argues that, within Foucault's paradigm of power, domestic violence falls into the category of pre-modern, whereas the invasive disciplinary and regulatory techniques introduced through medicine and the law represent non-coercive, modern modes of power and control. She writes that 'battered women ... experience pre-modern and modern forms of power side by side: not only do they have to deal with the instigation of terror of an all-powerful "sovereign," but they are also often compelled to turn for help to modern institutions such as medicine and psychiatry, police, courts, and so on' (Westlund 1999: 1045–6). Although I am uneasy with locating domestic violence within an oppositional debate about the metaphysics of pre-modern versus modern forms of violence, since it conforms to the Euro-logocentrism of savagery/civilization, Westlund is right in noting that such different modes of violence can exist simultaneously. More problematic, however, is her metaphorical reduction of violence to that between sovereign and subjugated. As difficult as it is to comprehend, the figure of the perpetrator of violence in the guise of a sovereign male subject and the implication of victimization as absolute are questionable assumptions, since perpetrators and victims of social, physical, and institutional violence experience contradictory and uneven forms of power and subjection in a patriarchal, racist, homophobic, and class society.[9] Furthermore, Westlund's suggestion that battered women are compelled to turn to 'modern institutions such as medicine and psychiatry, police, courts, and so on' also raises the problem of the contradictory forces of power operating in women's and children's lives, when, because of racial, class, and sexual discrimination, not all women and children have a choice of, or even access, to such institutions of justice, protection, and healing. In other words, there is no simple distinction between coercive and non-coercive forms of violence, for violence is the operation of power which works on the body in many ways to brutalize it, violate it, discipline and regulate it, and environmentally damage it. From plastic surgery to the bruised and battered face, from the raped vagina in the domestic sphere or the war zone or the residential school, the self's body is severally alienated and torn from itself. It is particularly within the context of self-representation that I see the possibilities of decolonizing the family and its violence, of retrieving the self's body and the joy of differentiation in love and pleasure. Self-representation becomes vital not only within one's self but also in connection to other women. In representing and situating our wounded bodies, we connect to a larger arena of transformation in which there is no feminism without decolonization and no decolonization unless it reaches women and the poor. From the gendered power relations between imperialism and indigenous struggles for decolonization to the dialectical relations between feminism and decolonial self-determination and autonomy, a critique of the sexism and racism of colonialism must emerge as a central, constitutive element in the struggle against the oppression of women in a white patriarchal capitalist society. Gendering, Gayatri Spivak maintains, is foundational to colonial exploitation and oppression (Spivak 1995: 202). Failure to acknowledge this inevitably leads to its redeployment in postcolonial criticism.

Colonial Homosociality and 'Race' in Colonial Governance

Colonial ideas about racial superiority and the concept of race must also be situated in relation to indigenous women's bodies, the problematic of human reproduction, and familial relations. In the *History of Sexuality*, Foucault turns toward the affirmation of bourgeois hegemony in the nineteenth century and its biopolitics, the contested history of juridical power in the deployment of familial alliances, and the techniques of power operating in the normalization and regulation of sexuality. Central to Foucault's analysis of the securing of bourgeois hegemony is the idea that the bourgeoisie was creating a '"class" body with its health, hygiene, descent, and race' (Foucault 1978: 142). This affirmation of the bourgeois self's bodily culture eventually led to a contested zone between a 'problematic of relations' and a 'problematic of the "flesh."'

Ann Laura Stoler's *Race and the Education of Desire: Foucault's 'History of Sexuality' and the Colonial Order of Things* opened up new ways of thinking about the links between and among the domestic sphere, race, and colonial/indigenous sexual and familial relations (see Stoler 1989,

2003). In Foucault's schema of things, sexuality, the sensations of the body, its quality of pleasures and knowledge about those pleasures – along with an emphasis on the body that produces and consumes – exist, in a dialectical fashion, in nineteenth-century European bourgeois culture alongside of, in conjunction with, and/or in contradiction to the conventional, if not dominant, discourses of juridical power and the law: the question of alliances and the links between marriage partners, human reproduction, and the economic circulation of wealth. In the deployment of sexuality, with its intensification of the body and its problematic of the flesh, Foucault located processes of desire and power far more complex and difficult to fix than those that had solidified into a problematic of relations. Unique to the nineteenth-century European bourgeois family, Foucault argued, was the convergence of alliances or relations with sexuality: 'The family is the interchange of sexuality and alliance: it conveys the law and the juridical dimension in the deployment of sexuality; and it conveys the economy of pleasure and the intensity of sensations in the regimes of alliance' (Foucault 1978: 108). For Foucault, alliance referred to marriage relations between men and women that consolidated bourgeois economic and political power (Flandrin 1979). I would suggest that the primary significance of alliance lies less with marriage laws and more with the rules of governance between men, a homosocial governmentality. Bourgeois women in marriage functioned as mediations, bodies that existed in that exchange space of difference used to solidify and strengthen male bonds of friendship, equality, and rule otherwise known as fraternity. In the colonial encounter, rules of alliance posed similar and different problems. If, like their European counterparts, indigenous men were suppose to become enlightened citizens of the state, the act of dominating them *like women* posed a problem, if not a danger.

If by alliance we are to understand its significance for governance among men and the desire for fraternity, then contradictory aspects of the colonial/indigenous encounter become intelligible. In other words, it is the problem of 'race,' and not only sexual difference, that will also intervene in the liberal project of 'universal equality' to ensure the continued exclusion of all colonial peoples, men, women, and children included. It is, however, in the final instance, the indigenous female body that will become the historical boundary configuration to determine the values of exclusion/inclusion, civilized/savage, civil/unruly.

The racism of colonial expansion is constitutive, in Foucault's terms, to the biohistory of nineteenth-century European thought that consolidated the notion of 'body as machine' but dialectically situated that body in terms of biological processes, such as propagation, births and mortality, health, life expectancy and longevity. Thus, the nineteenth century introduced regulatory controls centred on 'a biopolitics of the population' and a 'species body' (Foucault 1978: 139). Foucault notes that

> racism took shape at this point (racism in its modern, 'biologizing,' statist form): it was then that a whole politics of settlement (peuplement), family, marriage, education, social hierarchization, and property, accompanied by a long series of permanent interventions at the level of the body, conduct, health, and everyday life, received their colour and their justification from the mythical concern with protecting the purity of the blood and ensuring the triumph of the race. (Foucault 1978: 149)

It is this biohistorical dialectical approach to the body that Foucault deploys in order to account for twentieth-century forms of fascism, and, in particular, Nazism. Stoler extends Foucault's work on the bio-history of race to include the colonial encounter. She astutely observes: 'We have hardly even registered the fact that the writing of colonial history has often been predicated on just the assumption that Foucault attacked; the premise that colonial power relations can be accounted for and explained as a sublimated expression of repressed desires in the West, of desires that resurface in moralizing missions, myths of the 'wild woman,' in a romance with the rural 'primitive,' or in other more violent, virile, substitute forms' (Stoler 1989: 167). More than a repressive or exclusionary function, the discourses and politics of sexuality and desire operated to contain and to rationalize what was perceived to be exorbitant and excessive.

In chapter 1, I set out to render permeable the apparent boundary that lies between imperial and patriarchal regimes of power by examining the imposition of the English bourgeois family in Canadian colonial relations at the turn of the century and its effect on indigenous women. This chapter begins with a discussion of the formation of the European bourgeois family in the late nineteenth and early twentieth centuries in the critical discourses on 'race' and 'biopolitics,' notably in the work of Jacques Donzelot and Anna Davin. Central to the analysis of familial race biopolitics in the Canadian colonial context is, firstly, how familial descent was deployed in late nineteenth-century legislative policies as a way to establish colonial rule, and, secondly, how these early policies in their recent formulation in the *Report of the Royal Commission on Aboriginal Peoples* (1996) re-signify that history for the purposes of advancing decolonization. Not only did state legislation contribute to making and unmaking the figure of the aboriginal family in the early twentieth-century colonial context of Canada, so did reproductive technologies such as film. Robert Flaherty's early-twentieth-century documentary film *Nanook of the North* was a key text in creating the figure of the primordial father, installing his alliance with the European patriarchal male and eventually establishing his subordination to the civilizing power of the white, Euro-patriarchal father. Chapter 2 looks at how *Nanook of the North* represents the desire on the part of a male colonial elite to establish 'contact' with Aboriginal Man on the basis of their shared complicity in patriarchal governance. Flaherty set out to make a friend in Nanook, but this meant that Nanook's 'wives,' his family life in general, would have to be subjected to bourgeois strategies of surveillance. The film underscores the point that colonial history could not do without its Aboriginal Man. Such a figure was indebted   to a nineteenth-century rhetoric of *aboriginality* whose significance lay in its capacity to resolve for patriarchal and imperialist consciousness certain anxieties over patrilineal descent, racial purity, and cultural origins.

Through the use of textual montage and the creation of what I call a biotextual reassemblage, chapter 3 juxtaposes competing discourses on savagery and sexual difference from the late nineteenth and twentieth centuries, including Freud's *Totem and Taboo*, *Tarzan* films and contemporary critical analysis of them, and an 1887 Pears' Soap advertisement that depicts a scene, somewhere in Sudan, of several Arab men facing a rock inscribed with the words 'PEARS' SOAP IS THE BEST.' This reading of the Pears' Soap text includes critical engagement with already existing postcolonial readings of the soap ads in order to re-situate this particular ad in terms of how the visual and textual aspects of such commodity discourses contributed to the commodification of the Aboriginal body itself. The assemblage of these particular texts in this chapter constitutes an image/text/commodity matrix, and seeks to demonstrate how a particular knowledge network was established in order to create the 'threat' of the primordial father as the figure of an original violence from which civilization must be protected. Thus, the justification for colonial rule and the legitimation of *its* violence, especially over indigenous women's bodies, was put into effect by manufacturing this apparently threatening figure.

Not only did the colonial bourgeoisie seek to regulate indigenous kinship relations, but it also sought to regulate itself in order to check the potentially unconscious origins of its own savagery. Controls would need to be exercised over bourgeois and working-class men alike, as witnessed by the struggles that took place over the definitions of manliness in homosocial and homosexual relations during the First World War in England. Pat Barker's *Regeneration* trilogy is a late-twentieth-century work of historical fiction that uses the figures of aboriginality and male homosexuality to explore the definitions of masculinity in operation during this time. Through Barker's anthropological excavation and psychoanalytical re-framing of the early twentieth-century English male subject, chapter 4 analyses the interconnectedness of these figures, how they were used to regulate British bourgeois male relations and to stabilize and define the meanings of masculinity and savagery in the First World War. As Barker's representation of these figures illustrates, the appearance of the feminine in a male body not only created ambivalence, but, more importantly, it was contradictory. It both established the hegemonic equilibrium of colonial, bourgeois patriarchal power by creating the figure of the so-called infantilized and feminized aboriginal, and it was also problematic to maintaining such hegemony when it emerged in the body of the English male homosexual.

Chapter 5 contains a self-reflexive approach to images of the aboriginal family, perhaps because it deals with the photographic archive and, in particular, family photos. The affective response such images stir up can not be overlooked, especially because I grew up with a colonial history on my mother's side that meant I had spent time looking at family photos of bourgeois families, heard about my mother's life in what was then Rhodesia, and, somewhat to my mother's dismay, developed a political critique of these 'personal' and familial historical narratives. Such moments can be instructive for a variety of reasons, but it meant that initially I had to confront my ambivalence towards the colonial photographic archive, and then move on to make use of this experience to understand its intellectual value – how, for example, the archive attempts to organize my reception and knowledge of 'the Aboriginal family.' This chapter examines two very different archival sources: one, an electronic database affiliated with the Royal Museum of British Columbia in Victoria, BC (and available on-line through a BC government archival Web service); and, the other, a photographic collection of a notable female bourgeois traveller of the Canadian Northwest at the beginning of the twentieth century, Mary T.S. Schäffer, held in the Whyte Museum in Banff, Alberta. Through my 'confrontation' with these archives, I learned to negotiate several ways of seeing, as well as critically writing about, colonial photography. From my initial ambivalence and resistances, I moved towards a spectator subject position of 'eye/I witness.' My study of these archives and, especially, my readings of some selected images are intended to be neither programmatic nor methodologically definitive; rather, they are constitutive of a strategy of de-signification designed to open up the complexity of such images as well as to demonstrate the instability of meaning that exists between words and images, including my own, and between and among the specific contexts of colonization, neocolonization, and decolonization.

In chapter 6 I reread a Royal Canadian Mounted Police (RCMP) file from the 1940s concerning the disappearance of an Inuit woman and her children in the Northwest Territories. In an effort to solve the mystery of her disappearance, various interviews were collected from her disease-ridden French-Canadian husband and from local religious authorities. These interviews and the file itself reveal a disturbing set of assumptions about domestic violence, miscegenation, and contagion. The case was carefully scrutinized and monitored by high-ranking RCMP officials in Ottawa who were nowhere in close proximity to the case or people involved, thus demonstrating how colonial power worked across the boundaries of federal and territorial jurisdictions in an effort to regulate familial relations between Inuit and a colonial working class.

Chapter 7 examines *Stolen Life: The Journey of a Cree Woman* and how Rudy Wiebe retells Yvonne Johnson's personal experience of sexual violence, her involvement in a murder, and the subsequent trial and history of her imprisonment. Not only does Wiebe confront the racism of the legal systems in Canada and the United States in this unique auto/biography, but he also makes use of various textual strategies as a non-violent means to bring about *justice* for indigenous people, in general, and Yvonne Johnson, in particular. In this collaborative venture with Johnson, he also takes on the task of disclosing his own political and cultural commitment to working across the borders of colonial, racial, and sexual violence. *Stolen Life* represents a double movement in decolonization, one that involves resistance to existing conditions of legality, and one that generates new ways of looking at the meaning of justice and the legal critique of colonial violence against indigenous women. This chapter engages in the chiasmatic interweaving of the 'law' and 'justice.' Following the important work of indigenous legal scholars and that of Jacques Derrida on the possibility of justice in decolonization, I hope to locate within Johnson's account of her childhood body something, in Derrida's words, affirmatively *un*-deconstructible. The emphasis in this chapter is on the female aboriginal child's body and questions of justice and healing.

Yvonne Johnson's story, like many contemporary works by indigenous writers, critics, community workers, and artists, is actively engaged in decolonizing this history of representational violence and its patriarchal, racist, homophobic, and imperialist semiotics of subjugation, not to mention its continuing legacy in the twenty-first century. In this book, I have focused primarily on the historical emergence of a semiotics of representational violence toward indigenous people during the early twentieth century. Indigenous political organizations are actively engaged in addressing the problems of spousal violence, especially with reference to recent changes in the juridical sphere, where the use of sentencing circles to address intimate violence raises new contradictions and problems for the emergence of legal pluralist solutions. The final chapter looks at how the figure of aboriginality that emerged in the contexts of sexuality and imperialism is radically de-signified and transformed by indigenous writers and film-makers. In juxtaposition to the colonial regulation of heteronormativity and the reproductive heterosexual and aboriginal family represented by such made-for-television films as *Where the Spirit Lives* is Tomson Highway's novel *The Kiss of the Fur Queen*, about two brothers whose experience of sexual violence in the residential school system shapes their sexual, artistic, and colonized identities in radically different ways. Highway uses representational strategies of de-signification to undo the sexualized and familiarized violence of colonization and occupation. This novel makes it possible to think differently about the meaning of political kinship and the value of cultural practices that politicize and transform such relations across a range of liberation movements for social change. Such 'Indian Acts' of de-signification effectively decolonize and *de-familiarize* the very spectacle of colonization. They disrupt the contractual imperatives and patriarchal sequencing of Canadian state legislative practices, thus moving the critique of colonization and current struggles against imperialism beyond the paralytic closure of postcolonial melancholia.

There is, I would venture to say, a counter colonial history to be written from the perspective of those genealogies of aboriginality that focus on the hitherto neglected political formations and experiences of domesticity, the home, kinship relations, and their emotional and corporeal intimacies.

1 An Origin Story of No Origins: Biopolitics and Race in the Geographies of the Maternal Body

The homes I most remember are the ones where my mother scattered her cro-
cheted doilies and rag rugs, painted the rooms with sorrowful lyrics of Kitty
Wells, Hank Williams, and Wolf Carter, hung my grandmother's homemade
curtains, pictures of the Yukon, sepia-coloured photos of her childhood, and
various snapshots of our nomadic tribe captured like prisoners and staring
their contempt from behind dust-covered frames. And always, wherever we
were, Rembrandt's *Man with Golden Helmet* whom Mom called the 'Iron Soldier,' whose strong shadowed features and downcast eyes seemed to watch our
every move, his golden helmet shining victoriously, a beacon of irony that I am
sure spoke to her at the Salvation Army thrift store.

    Gregory Scofield, *Thunder through My Veins: Memories of a Métis Childhood*

In 1781, trying to negotiate a peace treaty, she cried, 'Peace ... let it continue.
This peace must last forever. Let your children be ours. Our children will be
yours. Let your women hear our words.' The idea that differing races could belong to each other in family and love is the most radical of ideas. Did the white
women hear Nanye'hi's words?

    Beth Brant, 'Grandmothers of a New World' in *Writing as Witness*

In order to situate the political significance of the deployment of representational violence, it is necessary to consider the history of Canadian
legislative practices that were geared towards dismantling the political
kinship and economies of First Peoples. Nineteenth-century colonial
policies in Canada attempted to secure colonial authority by establishing the rule of patriarchal descent in the making of an 'aboriginal family.' This was achieved largely by disentitling First Nations women

from decision-making practices and political governance. Defined against the bourgeois ideal of the heterosexual white female body of leisure, romance, and femininity, the Aboriginal Mother emerged as a key figure of biopolitical and imperial rule. She stood in direct conflict to a European patriarchal organization of power.

In Canada, the best-known instrument for excluding indigenous women from political governance is to be found in the Indian Act (1876) and its subsequent amendments up to 1951. The Indian Act is one of the most notorious documents from the nineteenth century to exercise the authority of a nation state to secure political power for the colonial bourgeoisie over indigenous people. The history of sexual abuse in the church-run residential school systems, the removal of children from their families and communities and their placement in non-Native foster homes, and the regulation of status for Indian women who married non-status Indians or non–Indians, are but a few examples of strategies used in the Indian Act to affirm bourgeois colonial power through the subjugation of indigenous children and female bodies.[1] From early on, colonial policies were implemented to regulate the bodies of indigenous women by controlling their sexual, reproductive, and kinship relations. What these policies point to is the centrality of the reproductive body to colonial governance; that the reproductive body had to be regulated and controlled for colonial rule to secure its racial and heterosexual hegemony.[2] This chapter examines these questions with reference to Jacques Donzelot's and Anna Davin's theoretical and historical critiques of the family. Borrowing from the work of Michel Foucault, these theorists acknowledge the significance of the body to regimes of familial power, divisions of the public and domestic spheres, and the role of 'race' and psychoanalysis in mediating between them; yet, in different ways and to different degrees, they fail to understand the larger political scope of governing relations between empire and colony in the constitution of the family: how, for example, the colony became a site for implementing a new regime of sexual-familial politics.

Following this discussion, I examine some early colonial legislation which functioned to tighten the grip of colonial authority through the imposition of ideologies of patriarchal descent, the creation of an 'aboriginal family,' and the disentitlement of indigenous women from political decision-making practices. These early pieces of government legislation are outlined and critiqued in the *Report of the Royal Commission on Aboriginal Peoples,* issued in the 1990s. This report re-narrates these legislative policies in order to show how they were used in the

late nineteenth century to accomplish the aims of the colonial government; in their current narrative form, this discursive history is recontex-
tualized to advance decolonization. These early policies are significant
because of the way they helped define an arena of biopolitical relations
upon which to exercise and deploy ideologies of 'sex' and 'race.' Colonial governance required the micromanaging of such relations along
several intersecting axes, including femininity/masculinity and primi-
tive/civilized as well as public and private, or civic and domestic, divisions of space. The disentitling of indigenous women from governance,
accomplished, in part, by the fraternal links created between indigenous and colonial men in these policies, divided indigenous kinship
relations along hierarchical gender lines and led the way for the implementation of patriarchy and the regulation of 'the aboriginal family' on
a European bourgeois model.

I begin, somewhat arbitrarily, with the question: Is there a geo-historical specificity to the family? It is difficult to write about, let alone examine, this entity known as 'the family' when it is nothing short of a myth
used to naturalize heterosexual reproductive relations. In all its historical and geopolitical specificities, the family is not simply some manifest
reality or necessarily a secure object of historical research. Rather, it is
an uncertain form whose intelligibility, according to Jacques Donzelot,
'can only come from studying the system of relations it maintains with
the sociopolitical level' (Donzelot 1979: xxv). To speak about the family,
then, and its everyday dominion over domesticity, emotions, children,
sexuality, and housework, is to enter into a discussion already circumscribed by the meaning of modern civil society, its public sphere, or the
so-called higher spheres of political power. To study this hierarchical
system of relations between so-called lower and higher spheres, 'requires us,' as Donzelot elaborates, 'to detect all the political mediations
that exist between the two registers, to identify the lines of transformation that are situated in that space of intersections' (xxv). For Donzelot,
psychoanalysis in the early twentieth century represented a key force of
transformation, responsible for a significant reformation of the European bourgeois family. In fact, it was responsible for creating a hybrid-
ization of public and private spaces by narrativizing the private life of
the individual in the public discourse of the professional scientist and
psychoanalyst.

Donzelot argues that what made psychoanalysis effective and powerful as a major force in shaping social life was precisely its capacity to establish itself as a mediating force between public and private spaces. This was possible as a result of the fact that 'while law, medicine, psychiatry, and religion did provide techniques for managing conflictual relations and maladjustments, virtually all of these techniques implied heavy-handed solutions involving direct constraint and hence a high cost in terms of resistance to their application. In contrast, psychoanalysis supplies – directly or indirectly – responses of a regulatory and non-coercive type. Thus, through the role it assigns to parental images in the formation of the individual, and consequently in that of his or her existential or social failures, psychoanalysis makes it possible to displace the question of responsibility into the 'imaginary order" (xxiv). Situating psychoanalysis and its primary object of interrogation, sexuality, at the centre of European social life at the turn of the twentieth century, in the way Donzelot does here, produces an enormously productive set of questions and problems for studies that operate at the threshold of gender and decolonial studies: how, for example, did imperialism serve to maintain the centrality of psychoanalysis as the principal force of mediation between private and public domains and thus a determining agent in the reformation of the family in colonial space? What regulatory and non-coercive responses could psychoanalysis supply to a set of problems such as rape, domestic violence, and sexual assault that were not even acknowledged, let alone dealt with, by the repressive 'heavy-handed' mechanisms of law, medicine, or religion? If the effectiveness of psychoanalysis lay in its capacity to intervene into the otherwise private spaces of everyday life, what role might it have played in continuing to sanction ignorance of domestic violence and sexual abuse in the bourgeois colonial family? At what point could psychoanalysis no longer ignore the reality of domestic violence and sexual assault within the colonized family and, thus, turn its attention to specifying and categorizing its pathologies, as it has done recently with the introduction of such terms as 'residential school syndrome,' modelled on the classification of post-traumatic stress disorder (Janoff-Bulman 1992). This is to raise, of course, historical questions regarding the pathologization of colonial and domestic violence. Clearly, a significant shift occurred in the 1960s and 1970s with the legal recognition of domestic and sexual violence. While radical feminists brought political pressure to bear on the judicial system to recognize the criminality of familial violence by politicizing personal experience, psychoanalysis, as Donzelot's analysis implies, turned the politics of familial oppression into a pathology of victimization. In doing so, this provided the arbiters of social violence with non-coercive and presumably more cost-effective and efficient measures for managing the privatization of violence – thus producing or entering into a new economy of social violence.[3] But the question remains how to take into consideration histories of familial violence that were or are not necessarily visible to the letter of the law, that purportedly fall outside both the heavy-handed mechanisms of repressive apparatuses of power as well as the non-coercive and regulatory practices of psychoanalysis. How do we analyse problems of domestic violence and sexual assault as constitutive aspects of 'the family' at the turn of the twentieth century when they appear to fall outside recognizable codes of familial practices and discourses, not to mention their place in the newly hybridized psychoanlytical space of public and private interests? How do we approach the violent (i.e., coercive) aspects of familial life in relation to the regulatory and normative operations of psychoanalysis?

In reframing the significance of psychoanalysis within the context of colonization and patriarchal oppression, my aim is to create a complex surface of intersecting, if not competing, regimes of knowing and seeing, where the disparate fields of knowledge and vastly different practices of domesticity, violence, colonization, sexuality, and psychoanalysis are seen as discontinuous, however mutually related, aspects of a much larger picture of geo-historical representation. For not only did psychoanalysis destabilize the public/private split, but so did the increasing scientific planning of domesticity, motherhood, reproduction, and child-rearing practices, which, as Anna Davin demonstrates, were aimed at managing the problem of imperialism and motherhood.

Davin's essay 'Imperialism and Motherhood' explores the historical discourse of motherhood and its importance to British imperialism and racial supremacy in the early twentieth century. Her essay also represents a point of departure for some methodological considerations concerning the geo-historical specificity of the colonized family. Davin, like Donzelot, notes the subtle change in the relationship between family and state taking place in the early twentieth century: 'Since parents where bringing up the next generation of citizens, the state had an interest in how they did it. Child rearing was becoming a national duty, not just a moral one: if it was done badly, the state could intervene; if parental intentions were good but there were difficulties, the state should give help; and if it was done well, parents should be rewarded at least by approval for their patriotic contribution ... A powerful ideology of motherhood emerged in relation to these problems of the early twentieth century, though it was firmly rooted, of course, in nineteenth-century assumptions about women, domesticity, and individualism. Motherhood was to be given new dignity: it was the duty and destiny of women to be the "mothers of the race," but also their great reward' (Davin 1997: 91–2). Imperialist wars such as the Boer War and the First World War provide a particular historical context for conceptualizing the ideology of motherhood that emerged at this time; the need, for example, for 'cannon fodder,' as Davin notes, as well as for a healthy workforce and a virile army and navy (123, 138). Another historical frame exists, however, in the imperialism of the female reproductive body enlisted in the service of a scientific approach to social planning. Eugenics, the study of infant mortality and the health of the nation, contraception, and domestic governance formed a complex biopolitical network of knowledge and power. From the biopolitics of reproductive engineering to the domestic politics of everyday life, the female reproductive body – its *reproductive potential*, that is, or the reproductive *hypothesis* in general – were both a target and strategy of a heterosexual subjugation in the imperialist project.

Both Donzelot and Davin recognize 'biopower' as central to identifying a field of practices that were directly responsible for transformating relations between public and private spaces at this time. Donzelot, after Foucault, defines biopolitics as 'the proliferation of political technologies that invested the body, health, modes of subsistence and lodging – the entire space of existence in European countries from the eighteenth century onward. All the techniques that found their unifying pole in what, at the outset, was called *policing*: not understood in the limiting, repressive sense we give the term today, but according to a much broader meaning that encompassed all the methods for developing the quality of the population and the strength of the nation' (Donzelot 1979: 6–7). Davin reframes Foucault's and Donzelot's understanding of biopolitics from a much-needed feminist perspective. She focuses on working- and middle-class British women and how the ideology of motherhood served to manage and regulate their lives in a broader imperialist context dominated by the creation and preservation of a so-called imperial race. Her essay reconstructs the various synchronic lines of mutation that produced an imperialist ideology of motherhood, including science and the study of eugenics, the professionalization of childcare and mothering, socialist support for imperialism (i.e., the

Fabians), and the philanthropic and moralizing mission of bourgeois society. Yet, just as Donzelot remains blind to the imperialist and feminist contextualizations of psychoanalysis, Davin ignores the importance of the colonial context to the racialization of motherhood. For example, she notes that 'motherhood was so powerful a symbol that often class differences disappeared, along with the realities of working-class life. All the individual real mothers were subsumed into one ideal figure, the Queen Bee, protected and fertile, producing the next generation for the good of the hive. The home was "the cradle of the race ... Empire's first line of defence," not a cramped cottage in Merthyr Tydfil or a squalid slum room. The family was such an accepted symbol for the state that its actual disparate identities were forgotten' (Davin 1997: 135). The blurring of class and family/state distinctions through the use of the rhetoric of 'racial motherhood' meant that those disparate identities (i.e., the distinction between working-class and middle-class families) were not only forgotten but also shifted elsewhere, to the colonies, precisely for the purpose of creating a false sense of national, if not class, unity among women within Britain, and in connection to white women in the colonies.[4] The rhetoric of racial motherhood not only repositioned the class subordination of working men and women vis-à-vis the imperial and colonial bourgeoisie, but it also contributed to the justification to colonize the indigenous population by invoking the spectre of miscegenation as a threat to the so-called purity and supremacy of the imperial race. The problem of miscegenation confirmed the British male's rightful disposition to rule over the people, territories, and natural resources of the colonies. Imperial, racist, and gendered narratives were, as Inderpal Grewal notes, part of the lives of all women who lived in England, although varied by class and nationalism (Grewal 1996: 9); they were also part of the lives of women in the colonies, varied not only by class and nationalism, but by the discourses and rhetorics, silences and signs, of sexual and cultural difference, and the colonization of indigenous women's bodies through various regulatory and coercive measures.

The problems that I have raised in Donzelot's and Davin's analyses of the reformation of public and private spaces in Europe in the early twentieth century do not simply stem from their sanctioned ignorance concerning the colonies, its inhabitants and the processes and practices of colonization. Nor is it simply a question of shifting geopolitical paradigms in order to account for the absence of a critique of colonization and indigenous peoples as subjects and agents. The reformation of public and private spaces in Europe in the early twentieth century due to the biopolitics of racial motherhood opens up some important methodological questions about the need for critical frameworks that make it possible to move beyond ideology critique and discourse analysis to conceptualizing the body as a material dimension of biopolitical power, the forces and effects of meaning-production in various cultural systems of representation, including the *oeconomy* of colonial governance – at home and in the colonies.[5]

Pat Barker's novel *Another World* (1998) demonstrates the link between a European representation of 'whiteness' in the nineteenth century and its indebtedness to the colonies as a site of otherness. In this novel, Barker explores the configuration of adolescence, violence, and masculinity in a late-twentieth-century northern English city. When newly settled residents of an old Victorian house start to renovate the living room, they discover under the wallpaper a menacing image painted on the wall decades ago. In the following passage, Barker visually constructs the other world of a bourgeois Victorian family:

> Gradually, the portrait's revealed. A red-haired woman emerges from under Fran's scraper, with the sour expression of someone who's driven a hard bargain and is not contented with the result. Behind her stands a girl with thin ringlets dangling round a frail-looking neck. Huge eyes – her father's eyes – the underlids so prominent it's like one of those trick drawings where the face still looks normal upside-down ... He bends down and peers into the space she's created. An erect penis springs from the unbuttoned flies, as thick and pale as the decaying cabbage stalks in the kitchen garden. Gareth looks across and sniggers ... Gareth's scraping away at the bodice of the seated woman. 'Boobs,' he announces triumphantly. The woman's breasts are great lard-white footballs, covered by a canal system of blue veins ... At the centre of the group, uncovered last, is a small, fair-haired boy, whose outstretched arms, one podgy fist resting on the knee of either parent, forms the base-line of the composition. Patches of wallpaper still cling to the painting like scabs of chicken pox, but even so its power is clear. Victorian paterfamilias, wife and children: two sons, a daughter. Pinned out, exhibited. Even without the exposed penis, the meticulously delineated and hated breasts, you'd have sensed the tension in this family, with the golden-haired toddler at its dark centre. (Barker 1998: 39-40)

The mocking self-image of the Victorian family portrait is a telling indictment of the bourgeois patriarchal family. But it is not only the bourgeois patriarchal family that is being represented here, as the final mention of the 'golden-haired toddler at its dark centre' suggests, and should alert us to, the racial and colonial politics that lie at the core of the bourgeois patriarchal family's regulation of its heterosexuality, 'species body,' and lines of descent. The misogynist representation of the white female body, the reference to 'great lard-white footballs, covered by a canal system of blue veins,' is a racially coded maternal reference – as is the erect penis described as thick and pale – that marks both the sexual domination of the father in the context of Empire and the white colonial rule of the father over a dark primitivism that would threaten to disrupt his control over white bourgeois women's and children's bodies, as well as those of the colony.

Nineteenth- and early-twentieth-century European bourgeois and patriarchal domestic relations, governed by the 'rule of the father,' shaped the very terms of British colonial and indigenous contact and served as the model for British colonial relations with First Nations in Canada. Moreover, those relations structured the proper meaning of 'the family' for First Nations societies. The words of an Inuit woman, recorded anonymously for the *Report of the Royal Commission on Aboriginal Peoples* (1996), describe in striking fashion the ways the administrative and technical machinery of colonial power disrupted existing kinship relations:

My mother talks about how it was for people on the land – I talk more about the people who are the adults in the community right now ... When I got into school, everything changed for me all at once. My parents didn't have a say any more in the way my life went. When I came in off the land, the people with any type of authority were Qallunaat [non-aboriginal]. The teachers were Qallunaat, the principals were Qallunaat, the nurses were Qallunaat, the RCMP [Royal Canadian Mounted Police] were Qallunaat, the administrators were Qallunaat ... They acted like our parents but they weren't our parents. It seemed to us at the time that the administrators ... and whoever else was in authority were talking above our heads, talking about our welfare and not letting us have a say about it. They treated us like we belonged to them, not to our parents. We didn't have a say and our parents and grandparents didn't have a say ... They taught us a new culture, a different culture from our own, they taught us that we have to live like the white people. We had to become like the white people. (*Report* 1996)

This account illustrates the way colonial power made use of the notion of benevolent parenting to transform, radically, indigenous kinship relations by modelling gender inequalities on those of the imperial state. To become 'white' was to become the bourgeois colonial family with the White Father at its head.

This biopolitics of control over the so-called species body became the justification for the exclusion of First Nations women from public arenas of political decision-making and newly formed political institutions. The potential failure of the indigenous kinship to model itself on the bourgeois nation-building family resulted in a divide-and-rule approach to indigenous gender relations, conferring enlightenment candidacy only on indigenous men who could manage, regulate, and govern indigenous women and children.

A geo-historical analysis of the materialism of the body is needed in order to be able to account for the policing and coercive measures used to colonize the reproductive hypothesis of indigenous female bodies; to understand, for example, the political technologies, physical and representational violences, genderings, racial markings, and cultural practices that gave rise to a specific form of biopolitical colonization in the early twentieth century, its continuing legacy and contemporary resistance to it. This requires rethinking bodily configurations, their material practices and effects. It also requires frameworks of understanding in which colonization is recognized as always-already within the critical discourses, practices, and institutions of the Empire – that indigenous subjects were not *essential* in a biologically reductive racial or sexual sense, but nevertheless necessary and essential to the hegemonic representation of 'Englishness' or 'Europeanness,' Empire and civilization.

Cultural Difference? Cultural Essentialism? Cultural Materialism?

Martha Flaherty, president of Pauktuutit, the Inuit Women's Association of Canada, describes the early gender division of labour that formed the basis of everyday political decision-making practices among the Inuit. She writes: 'There is agreement that [Inuit] women were traditionally responsible for decisions about children, food preparation and the running of the camp. While clear divisions of labour along gender lines existed, women's and men's work was equally valued. If a woman was a sloppy sewer, her husband might freeze; a man who was a poor hunter would have a hungry family. Everyone in the camp worked hard and everyone had a specific role based on the age, gender and capabilities' (*Report* 1996). Although the specifics of gender labour relations differ among indigenous people and between First Nations and Inuit, striking similarities are also evident. This description of Inuit gender relations is mirrored among First Nations generally, as in the Honourable Judge Mary Ellen Turpel-Lafond's similar description of the centrality of women's political power among the Cree:

> I should note that the traditional teachings by our Cree Elders instruct us that Cree women are at the centre of the Circle of Life. While you may think of this as a metaphor, it is in fact an important reality in terms of how one perceives the world and how authority is structured in our communities. It is women who give birth both in the physical and in the spiritual sense to the social, political, and cultural life of the community. It is upon women that the focus of the community has historically been placed and it was, not surprisingly, against women that a history of legislative discrimination was directed by the Canadian State. Our communities do not have a history of disentitlement of women from political or productive life. (Turpel-Lafond 1993: 180)

The exercise of political powers among indigenous women and the gender division of labour in which those powers were contextualized contrast starkly to the discrimination indigenous women experienced under colonial patriarchal rule at the end of the nineteenth century. Under European governance, the division of labour and political governance among First Peoples shifted to a hierarchical system, thus creating a power imbalance between public and private, or civic and domestic, realms. Even in the late eighteenth century, so astute a commentator on Indian women's political authority among the Iroquois confederacy as Immanuel Kant could not refrain from couching such divisions of labour in the hierarchical terms of distinct domestic and public spheres:

> Among all savages there are none by whom the feminine sex is held in greater actual regard than by those of Canada. In this they surpass perhaps even our civilized part of the world. It is not as if they paid the women humble respects; those would be mere compliments. No, they actually exercise authority. They assemble and deliberate upon the most important regulations of the nation, even upon the question of war or peace. They thereupon send their deputies to the men's council and generally it is their

voice that determines the decision. But they purchase this privilege dearly enough. They are burdened with all the domestic concerns, and further-more share all the hardships of the men. (Quoted in Eze 1997: 57)

Kant regards the noble 'Canadian savage' as the 'most sublime crea-ture,' truthful, honest, virtuous, and capable of meaningful (i.e., frater-nal) friendship: 'if a lawgiver arose among the Six Nations, one would see a Spartan republic rise in the New World' (Eze 1997: 56). He is equal in his praise for the 'noble squaw,' but only inasmuch as he recognizes that her political authority is 'purchased' at the cost of continued drudgery in the domestic sphere and entrapment in a savage and prim-itive way of life (i.e., 'the hardships of the men'). Kant views indigenous politics within the framework of a European political model that depends upon a strict division of the public and domestic, governing and labouring, spheres where domesticity and labour are held in con-tempt by civilized men, who think and do not work with their hands. Clearly Kant could not accept the political authority of the Indian woman without rendering her a victim of so-called domestic drudgery.

The European bourgeoisie transformed an already existing division of labour among indigenous societies into a hierarchical one and sub-sumed the material values of the domestic sphere under those of the public use of Reason. It is on the basis of the domestic/public opposi-tion and its hierarchical positioning that the disentitlement of indige-nous women from political power succeeded. Indigenous men were also disentitled from political power, but the processes of disempower-ment between First Peoples women and men were unequal, as I intend to demonstrate.

In *Exemplar of Liberty*, Donald Grinde and Bruce Johansen argue that American democracy was, in part, shaped by the examples of the American Indian confederacies that bordered the British colonies (Grinde and Johansen 1991: xx) They demonstrate convincingly the influence of the Indian confederacies on socialist and feminist thought of the nineteenth century, noting, for example, that Matilda Joslyn Gage discussed 'several Iroquois traditions that tended to create checks and balances between the sexes, including descent through the female line, the ability of women to nominate male leaders, the fact that women had a veto power over declarations of war, and the women's supreme authority in the household. Gage also noted that Iroquois women had rights to their property and children after divorce' (226). While the leaders of the American women's movement of the nineteenth century borrowed ideas about universal suffrage for their middle-class constituency from the Iroquois confederacy, their ideas on women's equality did not extend to the originators of this democratic tradition. Seen in this light, was it really a question of 'influence' or of a convenient appropriation that would only add to, rather than alleviate, the oppression of indigenous women by the nation state? It was primarily nineteenth-century ethnography on the Iroquois confederacy that provided the critics of industrial capitalism such as Marx and Engels with the ammunition for a revolutionary overthrow of this legacy. The works of Lewis Henry Morgan supplied a representation of aboriginal societies seemingly in opposition to and untouched by the dominant, uncontested ideas of nineteenth-century European society (Morgan 1877). Nineteenth-century white feminists and socialists appropriated an indigenous mode of governance from such discourses, discourses thoroughly enveloped within a Euro-American ethnocentrism that largely denied the history and realities of First Peoples, and which certainly denied the damage done to indigenous women's 'political authority' by colonization.[6]

In the contemporary discourses of decolonization, this same anthropological discourse serves, in Michel Foucault's terms, as the basis of a 'reverse discourse' in which 'legitimacy or "naturality" [is] acknowledged, often [using] the same vocabulary [and] the same categories' by which First Peoples women, for example, were politically disqualified (Foucault 1978: 101). Ironically, then, Martha Flaherty's and Hon. Judge Turpel-Lafond's use of the language of a gender division of labour dissolves the 'us'/'them' divide, challenging the colonial reader to confront the fact that 'they' are the same as 'us.' Some critics would see this as a form of 'cultural essentialism'; I would argue that it represents a form of 'cultural materialism' to the extent that indigenous women are talking about, in Raymond Williams's terms, 'physical-material existence and processes' expressed in a culturally specific language that seeks to undo the separation and conquest of nature, woman, and indigenous peoples that are the result of colonization (Williams 1980: 108).

Traditionally, Marxian materialist history has never ventured far from the premise that the subject of material history is the history of labour and, in particular, the male labouring body, making and remaking himself through production and reproduction. Both the figural and empirical construction of the male labouring body during the industrial revolution of the nineteenth century established a knowable relation between society and nature. According to Raymond Williams, however, material history was compromised significantly when cultural history 'was made dependent, secondary, "superstructural": a realm of "mere" ideas, beliefs, arts, customs, determined by the basic material history' (Williams 1977: 19). From a feminist perspective, not only was cultural history compromised by its location in the architectonics of 'ideas' and ideology, but, equally important, the reproductive body of women was consigned to material history's significant other. Marxist feminism restored a 'politics of reproduction' and 'domestic labour' to material historiography, but did so by incorporating these new theoretical problematics into its base paradigm as patriarchal capitalist ideology.[7] Women's material history was thereby once again subsumed, implicitly or explicitly, under the material history of male labour as the primary driving force of the economic base.

Recently, a new conception of feminist material history has emerged, influenced, I would say, by a Foucauldian turn toward a genealogy of the body and a feminist analytics of power in everyday life and experience.[8] Feminist materialisms located within this theoretical matrix continue to subscribe to the traditional marxian and marxist feminist ideas about labouring female bodies (although Foucault himself veered away from this) and open up new possibilities for conceiving culture, power, and the body in terms of desire and sexuality. The bodies that matter here are not only those traditionally studied, such as the labouring female body and the biologically reproductive body, but also the desiring and desirable female body, and the machinery of its desire: its productivity, its symbolic and libidinal powers, and its knowledges about desire, consumption, and sex.

This double axis of interrogation of the material realities of female labouring and desiring bodies meets the historical challenge posed by Raymond Williams to create as well as acknowledge the inevitable 'changing materialist content of materialism' (Williams 1980: 122). Part of that change involves the turn toward the materiality of language and other graphemes, with an emphasis on sexuality, culture, and visual and textual fields of expression. This culture of the body has come to occupy an important place from which to theorize and critique the materiality of cultural and symbolic powers.

Intertwined with this material history of labour, desire, and reproduction in the imperialist and colonial contexts is the history of culture, and 'cultural difference' signifies the latest analytical twist in the history of meanings attributed to the category of Culture. As Williams tells this history in *Keywords*, the significance of 'culture' must be situated within the context of the historical rationality of the Enlightenment with its underlying assumption of a progressive and linear development of society, a progression which casts 'traditional' and 'modern' as binary oppositions (Williams 1976). Here the notion of cultural difference serves to draw the boundary between traditional societies or cultures and modern civilizations. However, the notion of 'cultural difference' is also used to signify opposition to the presumed normativeness and universality of a dominant way of life, with its material existence and management of life, its development and representation as 'civilization.' Cultural difference, then, represents dominant values and simultaneously competing truths in defining cultural life.

Although the claims of cultural difference are often represented as idealized forms of resistance on the part of the subjugated, such claims may have more complicated histories and uses. For example, in Kuujjuaq, an Inuit community in the eastern Arctic, an Anglican minister, Iyetsiak Simigak, was charged with four separate counts of sexual abuse and sexual exploitation, 'one for sexual interference with a child under 14 years of age, and three counts of sexual exploitation by a person in a position of trust and authority' (George 1997: 3). In June 1997, Simigak, aged sixty-two, pleaded guilty to all charges. He was sentenced to eight months in jail. In his defence, the Rev. Benjamin Arreak disputed the sentence, stating it does not 'reflect Inuit culture.' The *Nunatsiaq News* reported that Arreak, 'an Anglican minister in Kuujjuaq and a longtime friend of Simigak's, gave evidence on Simigak's behalf at the sentence hearing. Arreak claims that what Simigak did "isn't really a crime" in Inuit culture. "He wasn't really purposefully trying to do sexual abuse," Rev. Arreak said in an interview with *Nunatsiaq News* this week. "He just did it in the old Inuit traditional ways of treating young ladies, to make them proud of their womanhood. In Inuit culture, it isn't really a crime"' (George 1997: 3).

In this example, Inuit men appropriate a mode of cultural essentialism in order to exonerate themselves from sexual abuse and to justify the subjugation of Inuit women. Notable is the uneasy and complicated nature of resistance and freedom narratives when they are reduced to essentializing truths. On the one hand, cultural essentialisms produce effects of the real; they suggest the 'true' and the 'natural,' categories that make for the repressive exclusion or conflation of the relationship between difference and sameness. On the other, indigenous women's cultural materialist analysis that appears consonant with dominant colonial representations also proves threatening both to the dominant colonial order and to patriarchal exclusions of indigenous women from political power in decolonization.

The boundary between 'cultural essentialisms' and 'cultural materialisms' is constantly shifting; thus, it is important for feminist cultural materialists to note the historical deployment of 'cultural essentialisms' in order to track how the (r)use of 'cultural difference' works in a patriarchal imperialist context in support of, as well as in competition with, indigenous women's power and politics.

'Sex' and 'Race' in Nineteenth-Century Canadian Colonial Policy

Because modern patriarchal techniques of power administered and regulated through colonial economic and political structures were profoundly unstable, it was always necessary to attempt to obtain colonial patriarchy through regulatory bodies and juridical and pedagogical strategies, such as those contained in the Indian Act. The discourses of decolonization represented by the *Report of the Royal Commission on Aboriginal Peoples* contain their own contradictions, especially with regards to indigenous women and their struggle to undo bourgeois colonial power by bringing about social change and decolonializing patriarchy in the modern aboriginal family. The *Report* is an event charged with the urgency of the present. It outlines First Nations, Métis, and Inuit recommendations for and strategies of decolonization, including the devolution of government powers to Indigenous nations. What a critical historicism is called upon to do in assessing this document is to account for how it came into existence in its particular discursive form and system of categorization (that system is easily gleaned from the table of contents in each of the five volumes or the CD-ROM format). What disciplinary and interdisciplinary knowledges, epistemologies, and 'pure,' natural, and human sciences were deployed to tell the story of the struggles, survivals, continuities, and resistances of Canada's First Peoples? And what rhetorics, silences, and logics pervade the document's multifarious strategies and tactics? Strategies of subject-exclusion will, of course, be apart of this organization of knowledge; more important, I think, are the strategies of subject-inclusion, incorporation, assimilation, and differentiation that permit this document to do its work.

The *Report* is a political document not simply because it has official government sanction and financial support, but also because it was designed within the fine meshes of the web of power. The document is an instance of micro-logical power become visible. The field of political analysis includes this everyday micro-political level of power, the daily struggles engaged in to produce such a document and to enlist the services of academics, activists, caterers, community organizers, secretaries, elders, youth, women, political leaders, and all the assistants, translators, and researchers – all the players involved in the production of knowledge and bringing with them histories, experiences, and categories of thought.

The section titled 'Women's Perspectives' contains a biohistory of state policies and government interventions that set out to impose a hierarchical gender division of governance, on lands, territories, and housing ownership, accomplished first by legislating a racial and then a bureaucratized or *institutionalized* identity of the Indian. Demographic (re)locations and patrilineal and racialized forms of descent represent their core strategies.[9] This biohistory begins in 1850 with An Act for the Better Protection of the Lands and Property of the Indians in Lower Canada. In this act, lines of descent, questions of Indian blood quanta, and 'intermarriages' between Indian men and non-Indian women, and Indian women and non-Indian men, were used to determine who was legally allowed to reside on a reserve. Non-Indian men who married Indian women could not acquire Indian status, but Indian men who married non-Indian women would retain their status and non-Indian women would acquire it. Because the descendants of both types of marriage would have 'Indian blood,' they were considered Indians. But conflicts began to emerge regarding the 'sexed' and 'racial' identification of 'intermarriage,' which meant that Indian status began to be increasingly associated with a male line of descent. The colonial governments of Upper and Lower Canada initially attempted to identify – in order to be able to dissolve – Indian status through men. In An Act to Encourage the Gradual Civilization of the Indian Tribes in the Province, and to Amend the Laws Respecting Indians (1857), adult male Indians were granted enfranchisement in colonial society and property rights on the reserve in order to facilitate the dissolution of Indian status. The wife and children of an Indian man were automatically enfranchised, thus enforcing European patriarchal laws that subsumed the legal, economic, and political rights of women under their husbands and fathers. Rights of inheritance were granted to the children of an enfranchised man, but not his wife, who, when there were no children to inherit property, would have usufructuary land rights until remarriage or death.

The *Report* documents this pre-Confederation colonial biohistory and its imposition of a patrilineal and racial model of descent on indigenous societies. The Gradual Enfranchisement Act of 1869, the first piece of post-Confederation legislation concerning Indians, furthered the colonial project of civilizing and assimilating Indians by 'marginalizing Indian women: for the first time, Indian women were accorded fewer legal rights than Indian men in their home communities' (*Report* 1996). Indian women were denied the right to vote in band elections (entirely in keeping with the prevailing social and political norms of Victorian England); an Indian woman who married an Indian man from another reserve lost her band status and became a member of her husband's band; and an Indian woman who married a non-Indian man lost her status completely and could be forced off the reserve (which did not apply to Indian men who married non-Indian women). The Indian Act (1876) consolidated and expanded this previous legislation, putting into place patriarchal regulatory measures that went far beyond the determination of Indian descent and identity through the father/husband.

A complex set of problems emerges from this colonial biohistory, both from the historical documents themselves and in how they are recounted in the *Report*. In retelling this history, a constellation of political and material problems emerges that includes the question of identity determined through blood quanta (i.e., 'race') and the status of the parents, gendered indigenous differences in the designation of spousal status (Indian wife/non-Indian husband or Indian husband/non-Indian wife), the institutionalization of gender differences in the distribution of residency (including housing, territory, and reserve rules of ownership), and the implementation of gender differences regarding voting rights.[10] The amendments to the Indian Act in 1951 shifted the discourse of Indian identity from a symbolic system clustered around blood ties to a bureaucratic function of 'registration' which further entrenched gender divisions by introducing section 12(1)(b), whereby Indian women who married non-Indian men were stripped of their status and any other supplementary rights, band benefits, and access to annuities granted to status Indian women by the Enfranchisement Act (1869) and Indian Act (1876). The designation of Indian status, the right to govern, and the control of spaces, including territories, reserve lands, and housing, made up the essential components of this colonial history (Turpel-Lafond 1993). An understanding of the organization of this history around this particular constellation of 'problems' is essential to the understanding of the history and the aftermath of the passing of Bill C-31 in June 1985.[11]

Since the story of Bill C-31 has been told and evaluated elsewhere, I will briefly summarize its significance.[12] Bill C-31 removed the gender discrimination of the Indian Act and reinstated many Indian women who had been previously disbarred from band membership. This came about, in part, because such discrimination contravened the Canadian Charter of Rights and Freedoms, passed in 1982, legislating against the discrimination of women. But the move to reinstate dispossessed Indian women was largely the result of a sustained struggle on the part of individual indigenous women and First Nations women's organizations since the 1970s. Yvonne Bedard brought legal action against her band in a precedent-setting case. She, along with Jeannette Corbière Lavell, challenged the Indian Act, especially its institutionalization of colonial patriarchy in band governance and housing regulations. The *Report* tells her story as follows:

> Yvonne Bedard, from the Six Nations Reserve in southern Ontario, lost her status when she married out in 1964. She separated from her husband in 1970 and returned to the reserve with her two children to live in a house inherited from her mother. In order to live in her family home, Bedard found she had to obtain band council permission to reside on-reserve, as she was no longer a status Indian and therefore no longer legally entitled to inherit property on the reserve. Nor were her children. She was given a year to dispose of the property and later obtained an extension; when it expired, the band council decided she must leave the reserve. Fearing eviction, Bedard brought legal action against the band. (*Report* 1996)

A woman's marital status and her right to inheritance and housing on reserve conjoin in Bedard's experience. Many First Nations organizations fought Bill C-31, arguing that by reinstating the rights of Indian women, the right to determine band membership would rest in an act of the colonial government and not with the bands themselves. The predominantly male First Nations band councils, however, were actively discriminating against Indian women. This discrimination took new forms in the aftermath of Bill C-31, as the following testimonials excerpted from the Royal Commission *Report* show. On 19 November 1992, Mèrilda St Onge, of the Women of the Montagnais Nation, Sept-Îles, Quebec, testified:

> I married a non-Aboriginal person and was discriminated against. In 1985 the act was amended and so I regained my status, along with a number of

other women. And yet the discrimination continued. This is an act which has lasted 125 years, and it is difficult to change something that old because it becomes part of people's lives. It became a habit, a tradition for our Aboriginal people to discriminate against these women. Today we are still suffering this discrimination even though the law has been amended. We speak of discrimination because I returned to my community ... When the time came to apply for housing for the reinstated women, they were always told there was no land. Many excuses were given: 'we have no money,' 'the band councils have no money' ... In my community I had to fight for six years in order to meet with the chiefs ... There are people who cannot return to their communities for the reasons I have given you because the bands do not accept them ... (*Report*, 1996; ellipses in the original)

On 27 May 1993, Michèle Rouleau of the Quebec Native Women's Association, Montreal, Quebec, testified: 'What the Aboriginal leaders are unfortunately applying today, I am not saying all leaders, is the policy of exclusion. In the first years of implementation of Bill C-31, from 1985 to 1987, the approach of some band councils was simply to try to make some rules that would not accept the re-registered women... I think this was extremely regrettable and the government bears a large part of the guilt ... it is obvious that there was very strong opposition to the return of people to the communities because the people have no more houses, the people have no more room ... There is a terrible lack of space so the issue of re-registration is strongly linked to the issue of land' (*Report*, 1996; ellipses in the original).

Since the Indian Act required reserve residency as a precondition for voting on band council decisions, women who were excluded from residency were also excluded from the decision-making process that determined who would and would not get housing. Within this woman/governance/space matrix, indigenous women continued to experience discrimination and oppression. Such is the geopolitical determinism of colonialism that sexual and marital status controlled women's access to relations of governance and the material necessities of housing, home, and community. It seems fairly clear in the *Report* that gender defined in terms of sexual and racial difference is the central contradiction of the colonial, patriarchal history of the Canadian state and, thus, First Nations decolonization.

The commission recommends that the solution to indigenous women's problems 'lies in the process of nation building' (*Report* 1996). Indigenous nation-building involves the important questions of citizenship and identity, which are established through band membership codes. Many First Nations women perceived band membership codes to be unfair and felt they were often used against them. In pointing out this specific problem faced by First Nations women, the *Report* itself underscores their oppression by saying that 'ultimately, any policy that creates distinctions within a group can create division in that group. The amended act establishes a series of distinctions around which disputes can develop: subsection 6(1) versus subsection 6(2) [of the Indian Act in reference to defining the difference between 'status' and 'non-status' Indians], members versus non-members, and Indian versus non-Indian. Even more damaging, these categories have the potential to become the basis for social divisions within First Nations communities. Divisions within a group can be accentuated, and tensions heightened, when resources are scarce' (*Report* 1996).

The irony here, of course, is that gender differences instituted through notions of sexual and racial difference and the resulting sexual discrimination appear to be natural and not constructed categories, such as those of status and non-status Indian, Indian and non-Indian. In the latter case, such distinctions were often made in government policy on the basis of prior and primary distinctions between an Indian woman and an Indian or non-Indian man. The dangers of seeing gender relations as natural rather than socially constructed appears in the commission's statement that 'in the pre-Confederation period, concepts were introduced that were foreign to aboriginal communities and that, wittingly or unwittingly, undermined Aboriginal cultural values. In many cases, the legislation displaced the natural, community-based and self-identification approach to determining membership – which included descent, marriage, residency, adoption and simple voluntary association with a particular group – and thus disrupted complex and interrelated social, economic and kinship structures. Patrilineal descent of the type embodied in the Gradual Civilization Act, for example, was the least common principle of descent in Aboriginal societies, but through these laws, it became predominant' (*Report* 1996). Patrilineal descent is imposed onto a naturalized form of descent, implied as matrilineal. Inadvertently, this unacknowledged notion of 'sexual difference,' which is as much culturally and historically constructed and specific as patriarchy, reinscribes a fundamental aspect of the patriarchal and racial colonial logic that led to and perpetuated the oppression of First Nations women in the first place. Within this framework, matrilineal relations – in opposition to the colonial patrilineal/racial lines of descent imposed through government policy – are regarded as 'natural' and, therefore, as a 'natural basis' for furthering indigenous nationalism.

Earlier I quoted Martha Flaherty's remark that 'while clear divisions of labour along gender lines existed [in pre-Contact times], women's and men's work was equally valued.' The notion of a primal gender equality anticipates something of the dialectician's danger: a return to an imaginary past in which membership in the Indigenous nation is based on a powerful myth of descent through women's creative, generative, and productive body. However, as I will discuss in chapter 5, moments of strategic essentialism have been deployed by indigenous women to further their inclusion in debates on decolonization and nationalism.

In the newly formed Inuit nation, Nunavut, rather than trying to enforce such equality through a return to an idealized past, a political decision was taken to try to implement gender equality in a new system of electoral representation. In a discussion paper released by the Nunavut Implementation Commission on 6 December 1994, entitled *Two-Member Constituencies and Gender Equality: A 'Made in Nunavut' Solution for an Effective and Representative Legislature,* the commission recommended that the Nunavut Legislative Assembly be composed equally of elected male and female representatives from each constituency because the 'most under-represented group in politics – in Nunavut, in Canada, and in much of the world – is women' (Nunavut Implementation Committee 1994: 1). Based on the reformulated liberal notion of 'collective rights' that underscores much of indigenous nationalism, the paper argues that

> collectively, women place greater emphasis on the ways in which public policy impacts on the family and the community. Some individual men and women do, of course, have different opinions ... Canadian society has long recognised that certain groups of people – the Québecois and Francophones outside Québec, for example – should be recognised as having group rights. More recently, Canadian society has recognised the existence of aboriginal rights: the Nunavut Land Claim and the future Government of Nunavut are in fact products of that recognition. The human rights of women can also be understood – and implemented – as a form of group rights. (Nunavut Implementation Committee 1994: 5)

This document reflects the vision articulated by Martha Flaherty, president of the Inuit Women's Association, who writes in the *Report* that 'women have suffered doubly for we lost status in our own society and were subjected to the patriarchal institution born in the south. Until a proper balance is achieved among Inuit men and women, mechanisms must be put into place to ensure that women are equally represented in all decision-making processes and on all decision-making bodies' (*Report* 1996). The discourse of the family emerges as a site of legitimacy and justification for including Inuit women in formal decision-making, and yet the family itself remains the site of their most intense and unrelenting oppression in the forms of sexual abuse and domestic violence.[13] Quoted in a Royal Commission on Aboriginal Peoples Special Report, *Bridging the Cultural Divide: A Report on Aboriginal People and Criminal Justice in Canada,* Honourable Judge Mary Ellen Turpel-Lafond argues for the development of a postcolonial perspective that goes beyond recourse to a mythic past, a pre-colonial regime, especially in the area of justice:

> I find it a great challenge to chart the differences between the Canadian and Aboriginal systems because I am suspicious of simplistic anthropological inquiries, and I am increasingly aware of how dynamic, interacting and undivorced culture is from history, politics and economics. Should we strive to describe a pre-colonial state of affairs? What is the point anyway? Can the pre-colonial regime ever be resurrected? My own view is no, not except as a relic of the past. It cannot be resurrected because we have all been touched by imperialism and colonialism, and there is no simplistic escape to some pre-colonial history except a rhetorical one. In my view, we need to regain control over criminal justice, indeed all justice matters, but in a thoroughly post-colonial fashion ... One cannot erase the history of colonialism, but we must, as an imperative, undo it in a contemporary context ... We have to accept that there are profound social and economic problems in Aboriginal communities today that never existed precolonization and even in the first few hundred years of interaction. Problems of alcohol and solvent abuse, family violence and sexual abuse, and youth crime – these are indications of a fundamental breakdown in the social order in Aboriginal communities of a magnitude never known before. A reform dialogue or proposals in the criminal justice field have to come to grips with this contemporary reality and not just retreat into a pre-colonial situation. (*Report* 1996)

Domestic violence and sexual assault against women are linked to the interrelationships between European colonial and indigenous national politics. Not only do colonial policies foster divided domestic and political spheres, but they also help bring about alliances and complicities between colonial and indigenous male elites through the conjoined oppression of women. This legacy of imperial patriarchy can still be seen in some aspects of indigenous national politics, as in the use of sentencing circles that result in silencing Inuit women both in the home and in the public domain.

At a time when the concept of 'legal pluralism' (the multiple, and sometimes combined, use of Aboriginal customary law and Canadian state law) is gaining ground in the judicial system of Canada, Pauktuutit, the Inuit Women's Association of Canada, initiated a report on sentencing circles out of concern for a situation in which a circle was convened to deal with a man who assaulted his wife. As the report explains, the sentencing circle

> and other community-based justice initiatives have been advanced by individuals and groups throughout Canada struggling to limit the use of incarceration. Their focus has been on reconciliation and rehabilitation as goals for sentencing; broadening sentence alternatives so as to lessen government expenditure and provide for more community participation; and providing a greater role for victims of crime. (Pauktuutit, *Inuit Women and Justice: Progress Report Number One* [n.d.], 23)

The first sentencing circle was held in the spring of 1993 in the Nunavik region of Quebec and was presided over by Judge Jean-Luc Dutil. Importantly, this initial implementation of legal pluralism was in response to a case of spousal violence.

Mary Crnkovich observed this case and submitted a report to the Department of Justice Canada and Pauktuutit. This report and the appendix that contains Crnkovich's summary of the circle clearly indicate that simply changing the form with which to administer justice for Inuit women is not enough. This sentencing circle was turned into another technology of oppression towards women that conveniently ignored the multiple power dynamics between the victim and her abuser, and the Inuit community and the Canadian justice system at large. As Crnkovich explains, the sentencing circle introduced new forms of silencing:

> Aside from the fact that the sentence was based on a proposal presented

by the accused, the victim could hardly, in her position, oppose such a proposal or complain that it was not working ... Not only did the victim have a history of being silenced by her husband, but the sentencing circle may also have imposed an even greater silence. This circle was the first of its kind, being supported by the Judge and Inuit leaders. If she spoke out about further abuses or her dislike of this sentence, what would she be saying about this process everyone supported? Now, in addition to fearing her husband's retribution, she may fear that by speaking out she would be speaking out against the community. The sentence created in this circle is one endorsed not only by the Mayor and other participants, but also by the Judge and a highly respected Inuit politician. The pressure to not speak out against a sentencing alternative supported by so many is great. The victim may be afraid to admit she is being beaten because such an admission, she may fear, may be interpreted as a failure of this process. She may hold herself to blame and once again continue to suffer the silence. (Pauktuutit, *Inuit Women and Justice*, 24)

The Pauktuutit report made specific recommendations to address the use of sentencing circles in cases of sexual assault and wife assault, underscoring the importance of attending to the needs of the victim, which are (1) to be heard and (2) to be protected from further violence.

As this complex situation indicates, cultural difference is the alibi given to re-establish the equilibrium of patriarchal-colonial hegemony. Cultural difference becomes a powerful and contemporary form of representational violence in which elite men who exercise power in colonial and decolonial institutions of governance collude in the continued oppression of First Nations, Métis, and Inuit women, youth and children. This history of collusion emerges in such texts as Robert Flaherty's famous documentary film *Nanook of the North*. The following chapter explores how the film attempts to represent a homosocial bond between colonial and indigenous men. Through its spatial politics, the film transforms Nanook into the patriarchal Father of the 'Eskimo Family,' but the representation does not in the end 'quite fit,' as a subtext of ethnographic pornography emerges and implications of 'perversity' in the figure of polygamy are mobilized to discredit this familial ab-*origin*al story.

2 The Spatial Politics of Homosocial Colonial Desire in Robert Flaherty's *Nanook of the North*

As discussed in chapter 1, colonial policies granted indigenous men power as subjects under Canadian law in exchange for dispossessing indigenous women of decision-making powers, especially in the daily management of the household and children. In such representations as Flaherty's *Nanook of the North*, indigenous men are seen as potential leaders who must form the political alliances necessary with colonial men to further the political expansion of the Canadian state. The eventual exclusion of indigenous women from the network of power relations extending throughout Canada in the eighteeenth, nineteenth, and early twentieth centuries became a necessary precondition to the expansion of colonial rule. Whereas colonial and indigenous men perceived benefits accruing from the historical or economic forces that connected them, indigenous women were placed firmly outside this system of male relations of governance, a system secured through the imposition of a model of the bourgeois family with economic rules and mode of governance characterized by hierarchical domestic/civil relations and separate spheres of private and public activity.

For Michel Foucault the pedagogical function of maintaining and developing the child's body is central to, in the modern instrumentalization of the family, the *post-oeconomy* of the bourgeois family: 'The family is no longer to be just a system of relations inscribed in a social status, a kinship system, a mechanism for the transmission of property. It is to become a dense, saturated, permanent, continuous physical en-vironment which envelops, maintains and develops the child's body ... No doubt [the family] still serves to give rise to two lineages and hence produce a descent, but it serves also to produce – under the best possible conditions – a human being who will live to the state of adulthood ...

The family, seen as a narrow, localised pedagogical apparatus, consolidates itself within the interior of the great traditional family-as- alliance' (Foucault 1980b: 172–3). Foucault overlooks the rule of the patriarchal father over women as well as children and its pedagogical implications in the case of the male child who must fulfil an Oedipal longing to establish the father/son antagonism over the mother's body. This autochthonous narrative suppression of the mother's body is instrumental in developing and maintaining male alliance-building. While earlier British and French mercantile expansion of the fur trade during the seventeenth and eighteenth centuries depended heavily on an imperial sexual politics involving indigenous women and male European fur traders, by the nineteenth century and the implementation of colonization, establishing relations between European governing authorities and an indigenous ruling male elite proved a highly important strategy in British colonial expansion (see Emberley 1993: 100–29).

In the spacing of colonial male alliances, the indigenous female body represents the main obstacle to achieving the colonial rule of the father: it is her body that facilitates the Oedipal mechanism, but must then be discarded. In the colonial encounter, the European child's body is displaced and substituted by the infantilized savage. Since it is the place through which to administer and regulate the indigenous female body, the Aboriginal Family thus becomes an important site for achieving colonial rule and male relations of governance. Indeed, successful governance in the colonial context depends upon successful governance of the Aboriginal Family, including the child.

Infantilization was, as Uday Mehta has noted, a foundational aspect of the liberal ideology underlying British imperial practices in colonial governance during the early twentieth century. In his critique of the purported universality and inclusionary character of nineteenth-century European liberalism, Mehta argues that among the many subjects who were in fact excluded from that characterization were 'colonial peoples, slaves, women,' and, he adds, 'those without sufficient property to exercise either suffrage or real political power' (Mehta 1997: 79–80). This exclusion was accomplished through the deployment of a philosophical anthropology, defined as follows:

What is meant by this is that the universal claims can be made because they derive from certain characteristics that are common to all human being. Central among these anthropological characteristics or foundations for liberal theory are the claims that everyone is naturally free, that they are in the relevant moral respects equal, and finally that they are rational. One might therefore say that the starting point for the political and institutional prescriptions of liberal theory is an anthropological minimum or an anthropological common denominator. (Mehta 1997: 63)

Mehta argues, however, that this anthropological minimum became the means through which liberal ideology could 'configurate the boundary between the politically included and politically excluded' (Mehta 1997: 67). It was particularly the codes of 'inscrutability' and 'civilizational infantilism' that policed such a boundary (Mehta 1997: 60). These codes of exclusion were also inflected, I would argue, by prevailing notions of 'feminization' and 'domestication.' Such complex codes became part of a subtle, and yet foundational, colonial strategy of legitimization with which to justify imperial rule over the colonies. The force of their exclusionary power lay in the fact that they were constitutive of the political ideology underlying the most distinctive feature of European governance during the nineteenth century, namely the division between domestic and public spheres. Nowhere, perhaps, was that boundary of 'the politically included and politically excluded' policed more sharply than in this form of divided rule and the specific ways in which this division was exported to the colonies.

Control over the distribution of goods and wealth in the familial economy and the domination of the father over female reproduction and sexuality were two conditions that had to be met if colonial governance was to succeed in aligning the interests of the familial political sphere with those of the colonial state. Among other things with which the colonial government must be concerned were 'men in their relations, their links, their imbrication with those other things which are wealth, resources, means of subsistence, the territory with its specific qualities, climate, irrigation, fertility, etc.; men in their relation to other kinds of things which are customs, habits, ways of doing and thinking, etc.; lastly, men in their relation to that other kind of things which are accidents and misfortunes such as famine, epidemics, death, etc' (Foucault 1979b: 11). These concerns are constitutive of Foucault's conception of bio-power. In order to achieve the hegemony of biopower, however, the primary thing men must be concerned with is women's bodies and control over the signification of female sexual difference. This difference must be defined solely in terms of its meaning for human reproduction, fertility, and population control – in Foucault's terms, the 'species body' (Foucault 1978: 139). This singular reduction of women's bodies to their reproductive signification justifies the exclusion of women from relations of political power, even as their bodies function as the central biopolitical mechanism for regulating strategies of life and death in colonial space.

In conjunction with the institution of state policies designed to shift the balance of political power within indigenous kinship relations, was the deployment of film and photography as emerging technologies of representation that could be used to further colonial rule by inscribing a homosocial encounter between the colonizer and his noble savage. Relations between bourgeois men and indigenous elites were often romanticized by such cultural practices. This attempt to secure colonial rule through the implementation of a heterosexual and heteronormative construction of sexual difference required not only disentitling indigenous women but replacing the gendered distributions of power among gatherer/hunter societies by the patriarchal and imperial rule of private and public spheres.

Nanook of the North is an early filmic text that demonstrates how 'the family' became a visual screen for colonial power to re-signify Inuit kinship relations within the ideological representation of the English and Euro-American bourgeois family. Such filmic sources were part of the vast network of colonial knowledges, practices, and representations circulating at the time that sought to 'pre-figure' the Aboriginal as an already existing entity in the history of European civilization. The spectre of the primordial father was also a particularly important colonial invention, notably during the First World War, when the need to displace questions of violence elsewhere were pressing.

This chapter examines how the spatial representation of imperial domestic and public governance was reproduced by Robert Flaherty's *Nanook of the North*. Although postcolonial critical evaluations of the film have noted the way the film focuses on the character of Nanook as an 'archetypal Primitive Man' and how the film is indebted to an ethnographic construction of 'Nanook's family,' the naturalization of this 'Family Portrait' still goes relatively unexamined and unchallenged. Even an astute critic such as Fatimah Tobing Rony, in an otherwise important critique of the film as an attempt to create 'authenticity,' acknowledges that 'Flaherty is the father of a men's club of explorer/artists' and that the 'awe ... [Flaherty] is granted emerges from the myth of his relationship with Nanook: it is an ideal perfect relationship between ethnographer and his faithful, loyal, simple subject' (Rony 1996: 126); yet, she nevertheless fails to address how this patriarchal contract and its colonial homosocial relations were produced by the film itself and, furthermore, what their implications were for colonial rule in the North at that time. Shari Huhndorf, on the other hand, examines the subtle strategies that feminize and infantilize Nanook, especially in relation to white men:

> While at the beginning of the film Nanook the brave hunter constitutes a clear counterimage to that of the smiling, feminine Nyla, upon his only encounter with a white man in the film, Nanook is transformed into the 'smiling one' (that is, the childish, happy-go-lucky Eskimo, the other aspect of the stereotype). He is, in a word, feminized in relation to the trader, the sole representative of the European world in the film. At the trading post, we watch Nanook cheerfully bartering for beads and brightly colored candy and, like a young child, showing off his puppies. The trader's manner also suggests the childishness of his guest. He 'entertains' Nanook and 'attempts to explain' to him the workings of the gramophone, described patronizingly as 'how the white man cans his voice.' Nanook's wonderment at this example of European technology – the quintessential marker of Western progress – further suggests its superiority. Moreover, his peculiar reaction in this scene (directed by Flaherty) evokes childishness in a particularly resonant way. Reminiscent of the responses of children presented with new objects, he actually bites the record. (Huhndorf 2000: 136)

The following discussion pays close attention to the gendering of the figure of Primitive Man, not as a archetype who simply reiterates the lost narratives of an ethnographic or vanishing present, but as an ethnographic trope in the Enlightenment construction of the white bourgeois male's historical Other. Such a figure was put into play, I argue, in order to create a patriarchal bourgeois mode of colonial rule in the early twentieth century.

An Origin Story of No Origins, or, When Is Colonial Space Most like the Domestic Sphere?

In a scene from Robert Flaherty's 1922 silent film *Nanook of the North*, Nanook, the Great Hunter, disembarks from his kayak with a young child. Subsequently, a woman emerges from the inside of the kayak with a naked baby, whom she places inside the hood of her *amautik* (women's parka). Then another woman emerges from the inside of the kayak, and finally a puppy named Comock. This scene – a scene I respond to with delight at the incongruity between the apparent narrowness and smallness of the kayak and its ability to give birth to so many people – turns over in my mind repeatedly, and with each revolution new associations spring to life. I read and reread this scene as a screen allegory of filmic representation itself. Like the fecundity of the overflowing kayak, film technology is capable of conjuring up images from its mechanical womb, creating for its audience an apparently immediate experience of The Eskimo Family and The Eskimo Way of Life. This mechanical birth of The Eskimo Family is a hybrid reproduction, conjoining the mythic register of the kayak that gives birth to a family with the technical capacities of image reproduction, thus demonstrating the birth of the family in the age of mechanical reproduction.[1] Once effected, this secular version of the first father of the first family becomes a twentieth-century Origin Story, a masterful Enlightenment narrative of the First Family (i.e., primitive and patriarchal) that rivals its monotheistic other. At least since the seventeenth century, this first family has had its origins in a romantic primitivism and a singular notion of the patriarchal rule of the Father. In the early twentieth century, Inuit are one of a few indigenous societies left to further secure the Euro-American bourgeois family's secular origins – 'Indians' having already been invested with a surplus of salvage imagery like Edward S. Curtis's desolate photograph of the Navaho, 'The Vanishing Race' (1907) (Curtis 1997: 36; Lyman 1982). For Europeans' consciousness, the 'vanishing race' hypothesis of the late nineteenth century triggered the loss of their own historical roots, as that history was conceived in relation to an infantilized 'other.' Ethnographic salvage operations, then, were underscored by European, Euro-Canadian, and Euro-American anxieties over their own 'origins.'

The mythical displacement that occurs when the Kayak 'gives birth' to the Aboriginal Family may momentarily render invisible how ethnographic documentary uses filmic technology to construct its image of an Eskimo Way of Life. At the same time, however, it triggers a fictional dimension within ethno-documentary representation that can no longer contain an active delight in its own constructed-ness. But as I want to argue in this chapter, it is simply not enough to recognize how the film discloses or constructs its reality. If that were so, then we could rest content that Flaherty merely distorts Inuit family life for his own purposes, including its entertainment value. What is at stake, I think, is something far more complex, namely, Flaherty's use of *the family* as a conceptual device with which to anchor the flow of images and narrate the power of the colonial state. His use of the family in this way spurs on other questions, such as why the narrative of familial descent was enlisted in the early twentieth century to do the work of colonial governance in the Canadian North? The answer lies, in part, in the history of the European patriarchal bourgeois family of nineteenth-century invention, and its growing dependency on the colonies as the space within which to test as well as to secure a representation of itself as socially heteronormal, and therefore natural. The Aboriginal Family would become an intense arena of biopolitical control precisely to enable the European bourgeoisie to secure its familial and domestic relations of governance and power over the reproductive female body, its 'naturalness' achieved, in part, in association with the Aboriginal Family.

In the Darwinian tale of evolution applied to human culture, aboriginality signifies the idea that all cultures go through similar stages of cultural development, from the simple to the complex; thus, indigenous societies are made to represent an earlier stage of cultural evolution. Specifically, they represent the roots, if not the infancy, of a mature and progressive (i.e., European) civilization. This nineteenth-century narrative of cultural evolution was both sustained and secured by British empire-building. A further stage in this evolutionary tale from nature to culture involves the transformation of nature's raw material into the artifice and materiality of commodity culture. Within this developmental framework, aboriginality was seen as a primitive form of raw social material with the potential to be transformed by the en-lightened European familial and imperial commodity culture of the late nineteenth century. Thus, the Aboriginal Family would become a site over which to exercise both biopolitical and economic forms of colonial governance. Psychoanalysis would also contribute to narrativizing the civilizing process and its developmental model of the social body. A.A. Brill, in his 'Translator's Introduction' to the English edition of Sigmund Freud's *Totem and Taboo: Resemblances between the Psychic Lives of Savages and Neurotics* (1913), expressed this idea clearly when he wrote:

> Thus the civilized adult is the result of his childhood or the sum total of his early impressions; psychoanalysis thus confirms the old saying: The child is father to the man. It is at this point in the development of psychoanalysis

that the paths gradually broadened until they finally culminated in this work. There were many indications that the childhood of the individual showed a marked resemblance to the primitive history or the childhood of races. The knowledge gained from dream analysis and phantasies, when applied to the productions of racial phantasies, like myths and fairy tales, seemed to indicate that the first impulse to form myths was due to the same emotional striving which produced dreams, fancies and symptoms. (Brill 1918: xiv)

The history of the aboriginal in North America is replete with origins stories, stories marking a temporal battlefield when time began, the time of European contact, the time when a different cartographic imagination came into play and when inscriptions of the earth underwent a dramatic change in their modes of signification. Secular 'origin stories' since the seventeenth century and the birth of reason almost always contain the ideal of the virtuous savage, the noble and infantile roots of Europe's enlightened masculinity. These stories universalize the figure of the aboriginal, removing it from its historical context, and, ironically, rendering the myth of Europe's infancy rootless. Thus, the European imaginary is left with an origin story of no origins, an autochthonous myth of Universal Man coded as Aboriginal Man.

The Oedipal myth occupied a privileged place in late nineteenth-century European stories of lost and reinvented origins. The late nineteenth century trafficked in the exchange of other signs of loss and nostalgia, from antiques to ethnographic objects, and also women's bodies – their reproductive and sexual economies. Women's bodies were, perhaps, the most important site of exchange for locating *the* lost origin, and yet ciphering through it all manner of displacement and difference. Having vacated the female body as a literal bearer of life – if not to radically displace women's flesh in giving birth to new human life – that potentially or already realized sexed female body became the metaphorical bearer of a host of contradictory values, not least of which was the contradiction between the reproductive and sexual; or, put another way, domestic alliances and the politics of pleasure (or political alliances and the domesticity of pleasures). What persists in the Oedipal ideology of an origin story of no origins is the naturalization of feminine sexual difference. Such persistence must inevitably be countered by an equally persistent critique of feminine sexual difference as a founding moment, the origins of history and culture – as if history and culture were great mothers nurturing the sons of power and domination.

Flaherty's mechanical birthing of the Eskimo family is not unlike Lévi-Strauss's structural analysis of the Oedipal myth as a sign of 'the persistence of the autochthonous origin of man' – the story of man giving birth to himself, apparently through the agency of 'nature,' but more often than not, through various technologies and materials of representation.

The Oedipal myth is another secular version of an origin story of no origins. Freud was Flaherty's contemporary. *Totem and Taboo: Resemblances between the Psychic Lives of Savages and Neurotics* was published in 1913, and its English translation appeared in 1918. In *Totem and Taboo*, Freud lays the groundwork for the Oedipal complex as the central mechanism through which to understand the psychic origins of a masculinized and patriarchal Western civilization. Lévi-Strauss's analysis of the Oedipal myth in 'The Structural Study of Myth' focuses on a central tension in the biopolitical sphere of colonial rule, namely an unresolved tension between the overrating and underrating of blood relations. The myth of an autochthonous origin of man attempts, according to Lévi-Strauss, to resolve, albeit unsuccessfully, this tension. Lévi-Strauss concludes his analysis with the summary remark that the myth

> has to do with the inability, for a culture which holds the belief that mankind is autochthonous ... to find a satisfactory transition between this theory and the knowledge that human beings are actually born from the union of man and woman. Although the problem obviously cannot be solved, the Oedipus myth provides a kind of logical tool which relates the original problem – born from one or born from two? – to the derivative problem: born from different or born from same? By a correlation of this type, the overrating of blood relations is to the underrating of blood relations as the attempt to escape autochthony is to the impossibility to succeed in it. Although experience contradicts theory, social life validates cosmology by its similarity of structure. Hence cosmology is true. (Lévi-Strauss 1963b: 216)

If we highlight the derivative problem touched on by Lévi-Strauss – 'born from different or born from same' – it is possible to see that the persistence of the autochthonous myth of man's origins – the origin story of no origins – lies at the crux of a biopolitical struggle in Flaherty's film to establish and secure Inuit and Euro–North American male relations of rule in colonial space.

The narrative of the origin story of no origins serves as a zero degree in the gendering of colonial rule. Consider, for example, its allegorical potency in describing the possible and yet failed relations between indigenous and European men: if, on the one hand, Inuit men, such as Nanook, are 'born from same,' that is, born of the mother's flesh and blood like European men, the justification for colonial rule by a Euro-American male elite would be dangerously challenged for the colonialist, for he would have to recognize the similarity of their human origins, their sameness. If, on the other hand, Inuit men are born from different, born from a Kayak or Mother Nature, then the difference Inuit women's bodies prefigure sets them outside the exchanges of power between Inuit and Euro-North American men. Female bodies figure simply as objects to be governed, and not subjects who govern. Discourses of sexual and racial difference and their representative value for institutionalizing the family as a biopolitical sphere of regulation and control dominated the politics of empire and colonization throughout the nineteenth centry and in the early twentieth century. Flaherty's *Nanook* provides a brilliant example of how the technologies of familial regulation were introduced into colonial space in the early twentieth century and is worth examining here in some detail. Before doing so, however, I would like to situate my analysis of this film.

My analysis of *Nanook* does not set out to investigate the film's visual field for the truth or falsity of its representation of Inuit life; indeed, the use of the homogeneous colonial trope known as 'the Eskimo' makes it difficult, if not questionable, to consider the problem. Rather, what interests me is the way the film produces knowledge, not necessarily about Inuit, but about the Euro-American middle-class family and its sense of itself as socially normal. My question is: how does this ethno-documentary work to install the necessity, rationality, needs and wants of this self-affirming social configuration known as the 'family'? Or, put another way, when is colonial space most like the Euro-American domestic sphere? The ethno-documentary film was one of a range of colonial bourgeois strategies of surveillance deployed to manage, govern, and regulate the Inuit body, and the making of the so-called Eskimo Family was one of its principal objectives.

Ethnographic Aesthetics; or, The Installation of the Real in Feminine Space

Nanook of the North is a famous early example of the genre of documentary film. A prefatory notice to the film informs the viewer of its significance: 'It is generally regarded as the work from which all subsequent efforts to bring real life to the screen have stemmed.' As an ethnographic documentary, Flaherty's film was, and perhaps still is, in the business of creating a seemingly immediate experience for the spectator of the conventions, habits, customs, and manners of that non-Western culture known in the early twentieth century as Eskimo. The science of ethnography combined with early film technology to invent a documentary style that would authorize the West's knowledge of its colonized peoples. Interestingly, many of the early examples of documentary film would be made in the colonies: note, for example, the films *An Arab Knife Grinder at Work* (British, 1897) and *Sunday Morning in Mexico* (U.S., 1897) (Musser 1996: 88). The truth claims assembled by the ethnographic film documentary were not only designed to introduce the Western Spectator to the differential value posed by colonial subjects – and there is a great deal about the film to indicate who it thinks it is positioning as its spectator – but to deploy that differential value in order to affirm the superiority of bourgeois colonial bodily culture, its codes of conduct, its homemaking and child-rearing practices, its hygiene, not to mention its sex, its labour, and its 'race.' The everyday culture of bourgeois colonial life, its micropolitics, takes place in the social sphere of the family. As the notion of 'social sphere' indicates, spatial metaphors organize its micropolitics.

Nanook attempts to secure colonial bourgeois and masculine hegemony by demarcating various spatial frontiers, initially through depictions of a feminine landscape and a masculine hunting ground, and then between the public space of the hunting ground and the 'private' sphere of the igloo, the domestic abode.[2]

An earlier inter-title in the film describes the northern landscape in the following terms:

The mysterious Barren Lands – desolate, boulder-strewn, wind-swept – illimitable spaces which top the world.

And:

The sterility of the soil and the rigour of the climate, no other race could survive: yet here, utterly dependent upon animal life, which is their sole source of food, live the most cheerful people in all the world – the fearless, loveable ... Eskimos.

Barrenness and sterility constitute the metaphorical horizon, and yet these are not simply convenient metaphors, but geopolitical realities of a feminization of space, specifically its reproductive passivity. The bodies that occupy this space are those of the Eskimos, Nanook and 'his family': 'This picture,' the viewer is informed following the above mentioned texts, 'concerns the life of one Nanook (The Bear), his family and little band of followers, "Itivimuits" of Hopewell Sound, Northern Ungava, through whose kindness, faithfulness and patience this film was made.' On the one hand, we have a realization of feminine space, an illimitable space that is barren and sterile. On the other hand, an active, masculine space emerges with reference to the 'hunting ground.' It is the configuration of a masculine space that allows Flaherty to present his audience with an explanatory map. In successive frames, the viewer is shown a map of eastern Canada and the territory surrounding Hudson Bay. The region directly east of the Hudson Bay is Ungava, constituting northern Quebec and Labrador and stretching to the farthest northern frontier. This map is followed by the following inter-title: 'The hunting ground of Nanook and his followers is a little kingdom in size – nearly as large as England, yet occupied by less than three hundred souls.' The gender tropes used to contain the representation of the land in *Nanook* not only create a geopolitical division between imperialist and indigenous uses of the land, but they also reconfigure relations of power between colonial and Inuit men, both of whom reside over a territory of land. The reference to a 'little kingdom ... nearly as large as England' is, of course, a feudal metaphor and links indigenous governance with that of an archaic political form in which a sixteenth-century European sovereign's legitimacy lay, according to Foucault, in his connection to a realm (Foucault 1979b: 10). In addition to creating geopolitical links between European and Aboriginal Man, contemporary colonial and bourgeois politics are elided by this metaphorical slippage.

The feminization and masculinization of particular aspects of indigenous space are enjoined by another metaphorical horizon, one that belongs to European exploration narratives or nineteenth-century travel literatures to Africa and the Near and Far East. Essentially, the northern landscape is described, paradoxically, in terms of the desert: 'The desert interior, if deer hunting fails, is the country of death – for there is no food'; and 'As Arctic snow is dry as sand, the sled runners must be glazed with ice to make them slide easily.' A walrus-hunting scene recalls the safari, in which we are informed that the fierce walrus 'is well called the "tiger of the North."' A reference to 'snow smoking fields of sea and plain' underscores the peculiar reversal of hot and cold imagery. Perhaps it is the sheer geographical scale of the desert and the treeless, snow-covered land that join these metaphorical domains. It seems to me, however, that with this spatial matrix, the desert north, a temporal rupture occurs. The shift to earlier British and French imperial exploration signals a similar point of reference, if not to the landscape per se, then to the historical and geopolitical conditions that gave landscape meaning for imperial expansion – its agricultural or mining potential. Although the North was clearly not destined to become the site of a new fertile crescent, its mineral reserves and deposits were well known, as they were in Mesopotamia (modern-day Iraq) at this time.

During the 1920s relations between Inuit and non-Inuit in the North were largely economic, organized around the white fox fur trade. Interests in mineral deposits were also a priority in northern explorations at this time. The experience of Robert Flaherty (1889–1951) in the North was shaped by his geologist father, whom he accompanied on many excursions into the North. Later, as a mining engineer himself, Flaherty explored the Ungava Peninsula, which became the location for his film, *Nanook of the North*.

The textual descriptions of the desert North, and the film shots of drifting snow and a blinding, windswept landscape, together represent one spatio-temporal axis negotiated by the film. Another temporal dimension unfolds in the film's narrative quest for food and survival, a narrative that follows the movement of environmental change: the seasons, 'summer' and 'winter,' or ice and no ice, morning and night, and the journey to hunting grounds. The narrative of environmental flux masks the historico-geopolitical changes brought about by the economic colonization of the North. The scene at the trading post where Nanook exchanges white fox furs and polar bear skins for 'knives, beads, and bright coloured candy' – sugar, of course, being a primary export commodity from Britain – appears as part of the natural cycle of nomadic movement, incorporated into a predictable and persistent environmental movement. Here we can see how the generative principles of capital displace, mimic, and yet seize hold of the generative principles of nature, its biopower, its reproductive capacities, its bodily flows, circulations, and metabolisms.[3] In the film's construction of cultural otherness, various axes in the cartography of difference are mapped onto one another. The spatial frontiers of north and south, colonized and nationalized, contain and give meaning to the differential values of primitive/civilized and feminine/masculine.

In order to secure the middle-class Eskimo family, it is necessary to create the division between the private and the public, a division that the film organizes spatially in its visual demonstrations of work, leisure, domesticity, and the landscape. The spatial configuration in which these truth claims and boundary markers are rehearsed is an extraordinary phantasmic place called the North, in which Flaherty situates the first father and family, Nanook, Nyla, (another woman named Cunayou), Allegoo, baby, and Comock, the puppy.

When Is Colonial Space Most like the Domestic Sphere?

The twentieth-century process of excluding indigenous women from governance occurs through a biological and spatial segregation. The film distinguishes between a desert North, barren, sterile, passive, and feminine, and a hunting ground, a masculine site, active, productive, life-giving in its capacity to feed and nurture the Eskimo family, to save them from starvation, to provide skins for clothes, oil for fuel, and other essentials necessary to survive in the harsh, northern climate. Nanook overcomes the threat of starvation many times in the film. One notable scene depicts the Christian allegory of Nanook as the fisherman of plenty, drawing out fish after fish from a hole in the ice. The scene concludes with 'Nanook giv[ing] a brother fisherman a lift into shore.' The salvation narrative of Christian thought permeates Flaherty's organization of this scene, thus weaving another myth-making strand into the fabric of the Rousseauian ideal, the European figure of the 'virtuous savage,' the protector of all things feminine, natural, and non-commodifiable.

Flaherty's mechanical birth of the Eskimo family and representation of Nanook as the first father attempt to affirm colonial bourgeois and masculine hegemony by demarcating a spatial frontier between the public and the private, the hunting ground and the igloo, the domestic abode. This opposition is further contained in the illimitable feminine space of the vast, empty, barren, and sterile landscape. The public/private spatial frontier inscribed on this empty landscape works to establish dispositions of masculine virtue, an ethical consciousness of labour, bourgeois moralities, the disciplined body, and the white man's right to govern women, children, and non–Euro-Americans.

The making of the igloo in the film foregrounds the contradiction between the outside status of Inuit and their feminization, and the alliance-making between Flaherty and Nanook. The line between the public and private or domestic life installs the possibility of an alliance. It is rehearsed, yet undone when knowledge about Eskimo private life becomes subject to the very public gaze of ethnographic investigation.

The spectator is introduced to domesticity early in the film in a set of scenes at the trading post. Nyla and her naked baby play with a litter of huskies: 'Nyla, not to be outdone, displays her young huskies too – one rainbow, less than four months old.' This scene is followed by Nanook learning about the technical wonders of the gramophone: 'In deference to Nanook, the great hunter, the trader entertains and attempts to explain the principle – how the white man "cans" his voice.' Next: 'Some of Nanook's children are banqueted by the trader – sea biscuit and lard!' 'But Allegoo indulged to excess, so the trader sent for – castor oil!' These particular scenes draw a distinction between mother/child and man/technology, with Allegoo as the object of bodily excess. Play, entertainment, eating, and socializing constitute essential activities of the leisure class and the making of an 'everyday life.' The notion of everyday life, however, is gender coded to the extent that man's every-day world is circumscribed by a public sphere of leisure and entertain-ment, and woman's everyday world is shaped by the duties and obligations of domesticity, such as child-bearing and -rearing practices. Interestingly, it is the domestic domain, and not the public sphere, where the demands and disciplines of the civilizing process are most notably exercised.

The bodily culture of the domestic sphere is essential to establishing differential values between the civilized and the savage, the civil and the unruly. The development of Europe's civilizing process deployed technologies, practices, and apparatuses of bodily culture that disci-plined and shaped socially acceptable behaviours. The disciplining of bodies, on the home front and in the colonies, depended on the intro-duction of a range of material techniques, encompassing seemingly uneventful activities of everyday life, such as eating, socializing, and dressing as well as political, legal, promotional, educational, and medi-cal practices. Table manners, adornment, 'natural functions,' daily hygiene, and social and sexual interactions constitute aspects of bodily culture that were subject to a civilizing process and mission.

Domesticity is not beyond the reach of the Eskimo, as the igloo-making scene confirms. This series of scenes that demonstrate how to make an igloo foreground the contradiction between the 'exclusionary' status of Inuit as colonial peoples, and the alliance-making between Flaherty and Nanook, what many film critics pointedly call their 'collaboration,' but only, of course, with reference to the aesthetic activity of film-making.

Nanook's making of the igloo is represented as a technological feat, mundane and tedious compared to the excitement of the hunt – making the igloo is, nevertheless, a job that must be done. He labours for a mere hour and in the process constructs the womb-like abode. The highlight of his construction efforts is the ice-window with the square chunk of snow carved out for its placement propped up vertically to the edge of the outside window to maximize the reflection from the little bit of daylight present. How very clever, the urban spectator marvels. 'While father works ...' the text reads, Allegoo plays with a small sled pulled by one of the husky puppies.

Play and pedagogy intermingle with Nanook and Allegoo, who is shown playing and arrow on a seal pup made of snow under the guidance and direction of Nanook. Allegoo's play at hunting occupies an ambiguous terrain, somewhere between 'sport' and 'education.'

These scenes of homemaking, igloo building, play, and education, replete with Nyla performing domestic chores such as cleaning the window from within the home, depict ethnographic fragments of information on objects and micro-technologies of life in an igloo: 'The hearthstone of the Eskimo ... Seal oil for fuel – moss for wicking – a stone pot for melting snow. The temperature within the igloo must be kept below freezing to prevent the dome and walls from melting.' Eskimo commodities are minimal: 'A few robes of bear and deer skin, a stone pot and stone lamps is the list of their household belongings.'

The masculine world of house design and construction, male modes of leisure, play, education, and (ethnographic and/or commodity) knowledge is divided from the feminine world of female labour in the service of male needs, hygiene, and sexual pleasure by the temporal flux of night and day. After the list of household belongings, the Eskimo Family is shown going to bed. Night falls and then the text announces that it is 'MORNING.' The women rise first, and the spectator witnesses the conflation of private space into an ethnographic study of an indigenous domestic sphere.

The ethnographic documentary style in this silent film uses textual material to produce the meaning and the making of the Eskimo Family; and yet, this process of textually asserting the existence of the bourgeois Eskimo family – in the use of phrases such as 'one Nanook (The Bear), his family and little band of followers, "Itivimuits"' – is contradicted by images that destabilize the certainties of monogamous, heterosexual, middle-class life. After the completion of the igloo, for example, the spectator, in the name of scientific ethnographic knowledge, is treated to the public display of the private ritual of going to bed. In this filmic surveillance of an intimate moment, the spectator observes two women sleeping with Nanook and the children. The women undress in front of us, we see their naked torsos, and the ethnographic gaze – that 'study of conventions, habits, customs and manners of non-Western cultures' as Uday Mehta puts it – protects the viewer from confronting her or his own pornographic indulgence. Who is this other woman? A lesbian lover, a second wife to Nanook? Early in the film, Nyla, 'the smiling one,' ostensibly represents Nanook's 'wife.' Only much later in the film does the other woman receive recognition and a name, Cunayou. Visually, this virtual, polygamous family fails to conform to the heteronormative model civilized family. And yet, the uncertainty about Nanook's familial connections, the suggestive sexual excessiveness, and, by early twentieth-century Freudian standards, its *perverseness*, are precisely what makes the film intriguing. The connotations of sexual excess are compounded by shots of Nanook eating raw food with relish. Ironically, then, it is in the failure of Nanook and his virtual family to *realize* itself (i.e., become the reality that is the proper civilized family) that the civilized, bourgeois, heterosexual family is affirmed. To add a further twist to the eroticized narrative of civilization and savagery in the film is the knowledge that emerges in Claude Massot's subsequent documentary *Nanook Revisited* (1988), in which he interviews Inuit from Allakariallak's (Nanook's) community to learn about their responses to the film and its historical legacy within their community. In an interview with Charles Nayoumealuk, whose father was a friend of Allakariallak, the following information is revealed: 'the two women in *Nanook* – Nyla (Alice [?] Nuvalinga) and Cunayoo (whose real name we do not know) – were not Allakariallak's wives, but were in fact common-law wives of Flaherty' (quoted in Rony 1996: 123). Rony does not notice the incongruities in this statement, not only in the way they underscore how the 'ethnographic present' in the film itself is already an eroticized moment that, in Rony's own brilliant words, created a 'peephole into the distant past' (102), but also the layers of irony such knowledge brings forth about Flaherty's own 'polymorphous polygamy' and adultery.

When does Nanook and his company best represent the family? When they are almost, but not quite like it. When they appear to have escaped the trials and tribulations of the family, when they can take it or leave it but are not restricted by it, when they can still be adventurers, explorers, excited about what each day will bring, and nomadic. But ... well ... the tragedy of their lives is obvious. They are innocent, naïve, wild, and happy children playing dangerous games with unbeatable natural forces. Who would willingly choose such a life? Like those situated on the margins of bourgeois society – the criminal, the insane, the poor – the so-called savage are also subject to a dramatic othering, an aboriginality, that renders their way of life irrational. The film, having sufficiently situated the Eskimo outside the realm of any contest for Enlightenment candidacy, will nevertheless do its best to introduce the non-Eskimo/Euro–North American viewer to an informative northern experience. This experience, however, is not without adventure, mystery, comedy, excitement, and all the other important ingredients of a popular and entertaining novel. And yet, what I am trying to demonstrate is that this exclusionary gesture is internally contradictory, in that the attempt to situate Inuit 'outside' the realm of public political governance is undone in Flaherty's attempts to secure a basis of alliance-building between himself or the spectator and Nanook.

The belonging and not-belonging of Nanook's family to Euro-American codes of civilized family life constitute an open visual and textual discontinuity or disturbance in the filmic experience of the colonial spectator. Hence, the Euro-American viewer is called upon to resolve this problem, to choose between his or her own sense of familial knowledge and the alternative presented in the film, and ultimately, of course, to decide in favour of the former while simultaneously feeling pity for the hardships and primitive existence of the Eskimos. The paternalistic feelings the film encourages and supports are, of course, entirely constitutive of the colonial encounter and its philanthropic, civilizing mission. Religion and education have played a significant part in that mission and analyses of it. The bourgeois colonial family and the making of a domestic, private sphere as distinct from a public sphere of political governance and economic control are also very much constitutive of this missionizing spirit, if not the central contradiction that the colonial encounter must seek to resolve if it is to maintain and affirm its disposition to rule and achieve political, economic, and social hegemonic domination.[4]

Subsequent images include daily routines of hygiene and women's child-care responsibilities, such as Nyla cleaning the baby with her own spit and a piece of fur. The spectator is then introduced to a representation of 'rubbing noses,' which is written up on the screen as an 'Eskimo kiss.' For all the intensity of the sexual subtext running throughout the film, here we are explicitly made witness to a childlike and innocent form of sexual pleasure. Hygiene, sex, and menial tasks belong to the realm of Eskimo women and take on a sharp contrast to hunting, labour, and the sexual prowess of the single Eskimo man.

Hunting, family, sexuality, the journey across time and space, ethnographic knowledge, and techniques of everyday living constitute the dominant themes that emerge and work to crystallize the homogenizing aboriginal trope of 'the Eskimo' and Eskimo life in this film. I have intervened in these crystallized moments by mobilizing counter-hegemonic, decolonial, and feminist critiques of the colonial encounter between Euro-American and indigenous men, the representation of Eskimo women as secondary to that encounter, the use of spatio-temporal metaphors that territorialize and gender the land for the southern spectator, and the deployment of a scientific, ethnographic gaze to legitimate an invasion into the private sphere, coded as the domestic domain and, therefore, freely open to interrogation, scrutiny, and penetration by the public eye of the camera. The overlapping of the private and domestic, as distinct from the public realm, is due, of course, to the question of sexuality and pleasure in relation to human reproduction – sexuality being a supposedly private issue, and human reproduction and child-rearing practices, a domestic one. Finally, the making of this domestic realm is intimately connected to indigenous women's bodies and the spatio-temporal dimension of a feminized colonial space. The hierarchical division between the civic and domestic spheres is an important aspect of the dominance of the bourgeois family in the colonial context, where it facilitated fraternal relations among men and disentitled indigenous women from political power.

In the case of *Nanook of the North*, the vast, feminine space of the sterile and barren landscape becomes, then, the site of an exorbitant surplus of sexual potency represented by the film's sexual subtext in its various ambiguous figures, whether through the heteronormativity of polygamy or the so-called perversion of homosexuality. As Ann Laura Stoler notes, 'to be truly European was to cultivate a bourgeois self in which familial and national obligations were the priority and sex was held in check – not by silencing the discussion of sex, but by parcelling out demonstrations of excess to different social groups and thereby exorcising its proximal effects ... persons ruled by their sexual desires were natives and "fictive" Europeans, instantiating their inappropriate disposition to rule' (Stoler 1989: 182–3).[5] *Nanook of the North* was part of the colonial project that was not about locating its repressed sexual desires elsewhere, but about the heteronormative specification of perversion (polygamy, incest, homosexuality, and the Oedipal problematic, in general) in the context of indigenous space and the ethnographics of indigenous life.[6] The success of a racist biopolitics in Europe that reached its zenith with Nazism was highly interdependent, I would suggest, upon the success of regulating human reproduction and sexuality in the colonies during the late nineteenth and early twentieth centuries, principally through indigenous women's bodies. This biopolitics of control over propagation and the 'species body' contributed to, and, in fact, became a major justification for, excluding indigenous women from public arenas of political decision-making practices and newly formed political institutions in the North. Although the film attempts an alliance with 'Nanook' to the exclusion of his female partner or partners, the failure of his 'family' to model itself on the bourgeois nation-building family installs a divide-and-rule approach to indigenous peoples, suggesting that Enlightenment candidacy would only come to Inuit (i.e., Inuit men) on the basis of their ability to manage, regulate, and govern Inuit women and children.

While such forms of homosociality attempted to enfranchise the image of the aboriginal patriarch, it did so in contradiction to European discourses in which a semiotic machinery was put to work to carve out the image of an aggressive, unruly, and lawless nomad roaming the globe and wreaking havoc in the unconscious of civilized man – the primordial father.

In this chapter, I noted how the formation of the aboriginal patriarch in the film *Nanook of the North* both resulted from as well as furthered the romanticization of homosocial relations between men in the colonial context. In addition to – and perhaps in support of – establishing relations between so-called colonial and colonized men was the epistemic production of an aboriginal Other *within* the consciousness of Civilized Man. In Freud's *Totem and Taboo*, for example, the figure of the Primordial Father, drawn from nineteenth-century ethnographic texts, is valorized within the sphere of the sacred as a foundational and originary figure in the psycho-historical development of civilized man. But this figure is represented as essentially violent and the embodiment of a wildness and savagery that threatened to undo the sanctity of the bourgeois family. Polygamy, especially, is a central figure of conflict for the implementation of the civilized family. In Freud's narrative it comes to represent the quintessential 'problem' of the primal horde. The following chapter examines how a range of discourses during the nineteenth and early twentieth centuries were invested in the production and reproduction of the phantasmatic figure of the Primal Father.

3 Originary Violence and the Spectre of the Primordial Father: A Biotextual Reassemblage

Ideologies of sexual and racial difference in the rhetoric of civilization and savagery were produced at the turn of the twentieth century by a diverse assortment of discourses ranging from the new sciences of anthropology and psychiatry to popular novels such as Robert Louis Stevenson's *The Strange Case of Dr. Jekyll and Mr. Hyde* (1886) and the infamous Pears' Soap advertisements. Those rare early twentieth-century texts which competed with this constellation of primitivism, sexuality, and masculinity included British government documents such as the 'Special Report from the Select Committee on Putumayo' (1913) and, especially, Roger Casement's 'Correspondence Respecting the Treatment of British Colonial Subjects and Native Indians Employed in the Collection of Rubber in the Putumayo District' (1912–13), in which Casement condemned the violence done to the Native Indians working in the rubber trade (Taussig 1987). On the other hand, the popular Tarzan novels by Edgar Rice Burroughs and, of course, the later Johnny Weissmuller movies contributed to the fetishization of the so-called savage (Torgovnick 1990). Like a *knowledge network*, these textual and visual practices put into play a series of intertextual migrations that maintained, resisted, and reorganized the equilibrium of colonial, bourgeois hegemony in the early twentieth century. This chapter is about assembling some of the components of that network of intersecting knowledges and representations.

Freud's *Totem and Taboo: Resemblances between the Psychic Lives of Savages and Neurotics* (1913) and Engels's *The Origin of the Family, Private Property, and the State, in the Light of the Researches of Lewis H. Morgan* (1884) represent two key texts that contribute to this nineteenth- and early-twentieth-century genealogy of aboriginality and sexual difference. Texts such as Bronislaw Malinowski's *The Sexual Life of Savages*, Claude Lévi-Strauss's *Tristes tropiques*, and Richard Leakey's more recent *The Origin of Humankind* confirm the enduring significance of this configuration of aboriginal sexual difference to twentieth-century conceptions of the Euro-American middle-class family.[1]

These discursive practices, ranging from authoritative scientific treatises to popular literature and government documents, constituted a language textile of colonial power. Such discourses, to paraphrase Michel Foucault, often intersected with each other, were sometimes juxtaposed, but also knew nothing of one another and, even, excluded one another.[2] Nevertheless, these texts operated within a colonial grid of intelligibility and constitute a discursive *dispositif*, to borrow from Foucault, a way of organizing subjects and the functioning of a 'microphysics of power.'[3] At least two interlocking generalized disciplines at work in this colonial grid of intelligibility, along with sexuality, of course, were gender (including masculinity and femininity) *and* aboriginality.

Body, Interrupted

In the early eighteenth century, a Cree woman named Thanadelthur was enlisted by Governor James Knight to bring about a peace treaty between the Cree and Chipewyan, so that British economic forces could penetrate further into the North and establish Fort Churchill on Hudson Bay. In recycling her story elsewhere, I highlighted the combined rhetorical and physical violence to emerge in Governor Knight's diary excerpts on Thanadelthur as well as the epistemic violence that emerges in the historical and feminist rewritings of Thanadelthur's role in the founding of Churchill (Emberley 1993, chapter 3). The scene of 'domestic violence' described in Knight's journal – not once but twice – in which he recounts his physical brutality toward Thanadelthur triggers the textual iterability of colonial violence in the historical record, with its exclusions and idealistic inclusions of her strategic political role in the colonial fur trade.

The repetitions in Knight's account suggest that the text of imperialism is an unruly script, one that must be written over and over again in order to hold in place, however provisionally, its meaning and significance. As Ann Laura Stoler writes, 'colonialism was not a secure bourgeois project' (1989: 99). At times, it defies linear narration, the sequentiality of language and writing, narrative forms, and closures. It also defies the reductive logics, silences, and rhetorics of professional academic discourse, a discourse that must continually interrupt its claims to knowledge so that the many truths about imperialism, its historical memory, continuing legacy, and after-effects can be heard.

'We are the abused,' writes Yvonne Johnson, 'which does not mean we are stupid. It means in our pain we are always thinking, and always alone' (Wiebe and Johnson 1998: 425).

Body, interrupted is a metaphor for the irreducible wounded body, a body too often anatomized into animal, human, mechanical, and commodified parts. It is my contention that this body is now writing its history and raising the question of its rights, the rights of the wounded, dismembered, and disabled body. Addressing this body requires a different organization of knowledge. It also requires different representational practices. *The book has somehow to be adapted to the body, and at a venture one would say that women's books should be shorter, more concentrated, than those of men, and framed so that they do not need long hours of steady and uninterrupted work. For interruptions there will always be. Again, the nerves that feed the brain would seem to differ in men and women, and if you are going to make them work their best and hardest, you must find out what treatment suits them – whether these hours of lectures, for instance, which the monks devised, presumably, hundreds of years ago, suit them – what alternations of work and rest they need, interpreting rest not as doing nothing but as doing something but something that is different; and what should that difference be?* (Woolf 1981: 78). If there is a significant change to semiotic materialist practices today, it is to be found in the body as concept and metaphor for reading, writing, visualizing, and enacting a critique of the physico-material existences and processes of violence and emancipation. My own rewriting practices have thus tended toward *biotextual reassemblage*, a transactional strategy that allows for various materials to come into contact with each other in order to disrupt their apparent regimes of knowing and seeing. Sometimes this leads to the juxtaposition of disparate elements, a montage effect of readings, materials, arguments, and poetics that permits a diffuse look at the technologies and techniques deployed in the service of colonial governance and its educational, juridical, and medical institutions. *We have been witnessing throughout history that battles for human rights have always been battles carried out because of the way meanings are imposed and perpetuated. Hence, the need to question the fixity of these meanings as well as the way they are construed, appropriated, and naturalized, defined on terms other than our own or the ones we would like to explore* (Trinh 1999: 61).

Biotextual reassemblage facilitates the examination of multiple frames of meaning, thus challenging the reductivity of a monotheistic scientific method that works to forge a vast and expansive amount of knowledge into a singular mold. It de-disciplines the normal writing technology of the essay form and the bodily economies that distribute its energies and productivities.[4] Economies of writing, their institutional locations, whether in education or the military, discipline the text and body, its utility, rationality, definitions of excess and obedience to proper forms. The economy of the male soldiering body during the First World War was always one of scarcity, as if the war functioned by a logic of a political economy of market forces in which soldiering bodies were manufactured to meet the demands of the front line. Like the disciplining of labouring bodies to assembly-line manufacturing, the male soldiering body was subjected to a serial production of death and to the collective daily subjection of a micrological distribution of power in military governance. The economy of bodies, their uses and exchanges in the direction of the gaze, the timbre of the voice, or the echo in the tympanum, in the touch, smell, desire, and labour of their consumption, pleasure, and pain – it is these material bodies and their sensory experiences that are ordered by various pathologies and physiologies, and by other medical, juridical, and pedagogical practices, representations, disciplines, and everyday knowledges. Textual montage displays the various ways the economies of bodies circulate at certain moments in history and across certain geopolitical spaces.

In the following section, focusing primarily on Freud's *Totem and Taboo*, I use a somewhat promiscuous method of citation. I am purposefully transgressing the rules of scholarly decorum here by citing bits and pieces of Freud's text (in italics) and weaving those fragments into my own text in a way that disintegrates and distorts the original. This sacrilegious act goes to the heart of an academic taboo. But why, I ask, must we fear the authority of our intellectual fathers? Why must we behave as children in the house of learning and reproduce that authority in our pedagogical practices by citing the original faithfully and without adultery? Why do we treat the original text like a taboo fetish, as if it contained the spirit of our ancestors? *But it must not be forgotten that even the most primitive and conservative* academics *are, in a certain sense, old, and have a long period behind them during which whatsoever was* [ab]original *with them has undergone much development and distortion. Thus among those* academics *who still evince it, we find* pedagogical authority *today in the most manifold states of decay and disintegration; we observe that fragments of it have passed over to other social and* professional *institutions; or it may exist in fixed forms but far removed from its original nature. The difficulty then consists in the fact that it is not altogether easy to decide what in the actual conditions is to be taken as a faithful copy of the* original academy *and what is to be considered as a secondary distortion of it.* I have dropped the use of quotation marks and substituted the use of italics so as not to interrupt the flow of my sentences but to mark, nevertheless, the counterfeit words that echo throughout my syntax.

Part One: Promiscuity in the Germ Cell of Civilization

In *Totem and Taboo* Freud works very hard at attempting to secure an authoritative place for the bourgeois father in the governance of the household, the European nation, and its colonial outposts. The figure of the primordial father, coded as Aboriginal Man, is key to obtaining this illusion of uncontested political power. Aboriginal Man is Bourgeois Man's significant other, at once his wild child who has not yet been domesticated and his uncharted unconscious that holds desires and longings that must be organized and classified, mapped and shaped, in specific ways for an imperialist capitalist society, coded as Civilization, to function and flourish. This fragment sets out to show how Freud deploys infantilism and feminine inscrutability into his psychoanalytical conceptual field in order to render transparent the self-perceived superiority of white bourgeois masculinity, its Oedipal formation, and the rule of the European Father over the colonies.

In his quest for scientific knowledge about the psychic life of savages and the primitive origins of neuroses, Freud treads a fine line between known territory and the unexplored: *But it must not be forgotten that even the most primitive and conservative races are, in a certain sense, old, and have a long period behind them during which whatsoever was aboriginal with them has undergone much development and distortion. Thus among those races who still evince it, we find totemism today in the most manifold states of decay and disintegration; we observe that fragments of it have passed over to other social and religious institutions; or it may exist in fixed forms but far removed from its original nature. The difficulty then consists in the fact that it is not altogether easy to decide what in the actual conditions is to be taken as a faithful copy of the significant past and what is to be considered as a secondary distortion of it.* In the last chapter, Freud repeats himself: *It must not be forgotten that primitive races are not young races but really are as old as the most civilized, and that we have no right to expect that they have preserved their original ideas and institutions for our information without any evolution or*

distortion. It is certain, on the contrary, that far-reaching changes in all direc-
tions have taken place among primitive races, so that we can never unhesitat-
ingly decide which of their present conditions and opinions have preserved the
original past, having remained petrified, as it were, and which represent a dis-
tortion and change of the original. It is due to this that one meets the many dis-
putes among authors as to what proportion of the peculiarities of a primitive
culture is to be taken as a primary, and what as a later and secondary manifes-
tation. To establish the original conditions, therefore, always remains a matter
of construction. Finally, it is not easy to adapt oneself to the ways of thinking of
primitive races. For like children, we easily misunderstand them, and are
always inclined to interpret their acts and feelings according to our own psy-
chic constellations.

The similarity between the two passages is remarkable, as is the
injunction to the reader: *it must not be forgotten* that primitive races are
not young races. They have been subject to evolution, development and
distortion, even degeneration and decay – the point being that so-called
primitive cultures cannot be found in their authentic or original form.
They are, in a word, *a*boriginal: *originating from* some now inaccessible
point of origin, some 'original nature' or 'original past.' The remarkable
similarity between these passages, or to word it differently, the distortions in Freud's re-presentation of his original thesis from one reference
to another, signals an ongoing tension throughout the text in its capacity to be faithful to an original form, to be able to tell the difference
between the original and a copy, between secondary and primary manifestations, between footnote and text – and to resist infantile recurrence, the tendency to mimicry and repetition. In what can only be
described in pedagogical terms as an act of interpretative control and
regulation of the meaning and significance of totemism and taboo in
modern society, Freud, the scientist, sets out to civilize the student of
psychoanalysis, to tame and domesticate any propensity in his implied
reader toward 'wild readings' or any other sort of textual promiscuity.

Freud's narrative relationship to his subject matter and to his reader-
ship is not unlike that of the Oedipal father to his potentially unruly
son, not to mention the child's wayward mother. Totem and taboo are
the original heterosexual Judeo-Christian couple, Adam and Eve.
Indeed, Freud argues, these aboriginal figures constitute the basis of a
modern Judeo-Christian European religion. Borrowing from anthropology, Freud follows a tripartite structure of epistemological development in the history of humankind: from totemism, to religion, and
finally, science. In the scientific scheme of things, totem and taboo have

metamorphosed into the psychoanalytical configuration of Oedipal father and mother. The savage and the neurotic are their respective offspring. *The totem is an animal. The totem knows and spares its children. The totem is hereditary either through the maternal or paternal line (maternal transmission probably always preceded and was only later supplanted by the paternal).* Like property, the totem descends through the bloodline. Infantile, animalistic, and feminine, the aboriginal, metonymically displaced by the totem in Freud's discourse, is everything but the European, and yet the aboriginal is Europe's childhood and her children. Europe is, thus, *far removed from its original nature.* The totem is the first father, the benevolent father who spares his unruly children and protects them from the horrors of degeneration and decay. Thou shall not kill the totem, the first father. The original taboo is, of course, incest between mother and son. By the conclusion to *Totem and Taboo*, Freud has reduced a diverse and varied set of ethnographic material on aboriginal kinship relations to its primal, essential, kernel of truth: the monogamous nuclear Oedipal bourgeois family.

Mark Poster argues that Freud's theory of the Oedipus complex reproduces the main conditions of the bourgeois family: 'It reproduces the social insecurity of the bourgeoisie, since it creates a deep emotional need to become like the father, to be "successful," and it marshals the child's emotional energy through the guardian super-ego toward achievement in work, toward deferred gratification. Oedipus instills a sexual displacement, an economics of the libido that can only find satisfaction in the economics of capital accumulation, at the direct expense of bodily gratification. After all far from being natural man, homo economicus is a rare and strange species' (Poster 1978, 22–23). It is in the following passage that Freud's position on the family and his own social insecurities about its dissolution can be seen: *The psychological premises on which [communism] is based are an untenable illusion. In abolishing private property we deprive the human love of aggression of one of its instruments ... Aggressiveness was not created by property ... If we do away with personal rights over material wealth, there still remains prerogative in the field of sexual relationships, which is bound to become the source of the strongest dislike and the most violent hostility among men who in other respects are on an equal footing. If we were to remove this factor too, by allowing complete freedom of sexual life and thus abolishing the family, the germ-cell of civilization, we cannot, it is true, easily foresee what new paths the development of civilization could take; but one thing we can expect, and that is that this indestructible feature of human nature will follow it there.* Freud is clearly politically opposed to the emerging currents of socialism and communism in England and Europe in the early twentieth century. His opposition to this, and perhaps other, burgeoning political movements at this time – suffragism, for example – suggests that the social insecurity of the bourgeois male lay in the different ways these revolutionary forces threatened the patriarchal, nuclear family form, its rule of the father, monogamous sexual practices, patrilineal inheritance, and knowledge about paternal origins; in short, the private property rights of the father over the monies and bodies of his wife and children. In order to secure bourgeois masculinity and the rule of the bourgeois male, Freud reconstructs early twentieth-century ethnography on Primitive Man in the context of psychoanalysis and the figure of the neurotic.[5] The figure of the savage becomes for Freud an ideal place to locate the 'domestic' insecurities, and neuroses, of the European nation and to launch an attack on the socialist, feminist, and anti-imperialist ideas of his time.

Why is Freud so concerned to fix the meaning of Aboriginal Man at this time? I think the answer lies in his fear of communism as a possible site for the dissolution of the bourgeois family, a political structure of power that he was obviously heavily invested in. That communism sought the dissolution, if not the abolition, of the family, was not news. Consider Marx and Engels's initial ironic disclaimer and succinct analysis in *The Communist Manifesto* (1848):

> Abolition of the family! Even the most radical flare up at this infamous proposal of the Communists.
>
> On what foundation is today's family, the bourgeois family, based? On capital, on private gain. Fully developed, it exists only among the bourgeoisie; but it finds its complement in the lack of family imposed on proletarians and in public prostitution.
>
> The bourgeois family will vanish as a matter of course when this its complement vanishes, and both will vanish with the vanishing of capital. (Findlay 2004: 78)

In his work of materialist historiography, *The Origin of the Family, Private Property, and the State*, Engels drew the conclusion that 'the overthrow of mother-right was the *world-historical defeat of the female sex*' (Engels 1972: 120). His evidence relied upon the Swiss jurist and historian Johann J. Bachofen's *Das Mutterrecht* (Mother Right, 1861), and the work of the anthropologist Lewis Henry Morgan and his discussion of the Iroquois confederacy in *Ancient Society* (1877), in which Morgan describes the formation of a 'primitive communistic household' based in matrilineal descent and a matriarchal kinship formation as the material basis of political and social relations: 'The communistic household ... is the material foundation of that supremacy of the women which was general in primitive time, and which it is Bachofen's third great merit to have discovered' (Engels 1972: 113). For Engels, primitive communism stood in a critical relation to nineteenth-century monogamy and prostitution: non-monogamy (i.e., the abolition of the family) would do away with sexual ownership, which included the reduction of wives to domestic slavery as well as the invention of prostitution as a criminal and morally bankrupt activity. But Engels's use of primitive societies for providing evidence for the remaking of communism itself conformed to a general infantilization and femininization that were always already constitutive to aboriginality:

> The gentile constitution in its best days, as we saw it in America, presupposed an extremely undeveloped state of production and therefore an extremely sparse population over a wide area. Man's attitude to nature was therefore one of almost complete subjection to a strange incomprehensible power, as is reflected in his childish religious conceptions. Man was bounded by his tribe, both in relation to strangers from outside the tribe and to himself; the tribe, the gens, and their institutions were sacred and inviolable, a higher power established by nature to which the individual subjected himself unconditionally in feeling, thought, and action. However impressive the people of this epoch appear to us, they are completely undifferentiated from one another; as Marx says, they are still attached to the navel string of the primitive community. The power of this primitive community had to be broken, and it was broken. But it was broken by influences which from the very start appear as a degradation, a fall from the simple moral greatness of the old gentile society. The lowest interests – base greed, brutal appetites, sordid avarice, selfish robbery of the common wealth – inaugurate the new, civilized, class society. It is by the vilest means – theft, violence, fraud, treason – that the old classless gentile society is undermined and overthrown. And the new society itself during all the 2,500 years of its existence has never been anything else but the development of the small minority at the expense of the great exploited and oppressed majority; today it is so more than ever before. (Engels 1972: 160–1)

Perhaps revealing the weakest aspect of his argument for historical purposes, Engels does not consider the effects of European imperialism and colonization on the destruction of contemporary indigenous societies but sees their demise as a product of internal degradation.

For Freud's historical unfolding from primitivism through religion to science, as for Marx and Engels's historical narrative from savagery through barbarism to civilization, the proximity between the savage and the neurotic, between the savage and the communistic family, must be close enough to establish the developmental relationship from infancy to adulthood, from the roots of European civilization to its fully constituted realization in 'the family'; and yet, distant enough to secure European man's superiority over his aboriginal ancestor, the Primal Father or the Primal Mother, and contemporary colonized subject.

First, I want to examine the fault lines in Freud's own construction of the aboriginal and the mythical relationship between the savage and the neurotic, which, ironically, re-presents the figures of the original and its distorted, if not – and in keeping with the racial rhetoric of degeneracy in the scientific discourses during the nineteenth century – degenerate, copy. Then I will draw a different picture of Freud's deployment of the Aboriginal as a figural manipulation designed to retrieve this figure for his own purpose, which is to establish his Oedipal theory of psycho-sexual formation as the transformative and essential truth of bourgeois society – and not communism.

Although the Oedipal myth attempts to secure a history of continuity for the bourgeois nuclear family by recreating its origins in the Primitive Family, the universalization of the Oedipal complex does not, in the end, historicize kinship or bourgeois family structures. Freud has neither an historical nor a comparative method; he has a myth constructed on the basis of a dualistic structure. The concept of *historical development* evades Freud's aboriginal. While European civilization advances from *primitive man* and an *early stage of our own development*, the aboriginal, the subject of *legends, myths, and fairy tales*; decays and disintegrates from his original existence, his authenticity, and his integrity. And yet, without the aboriginal myth there is no European history. *Their psychic life assumes a peculiar interest for us, for we can recognize in their psychic life a well-preserved, early stage of our own development*. The fact that the degeneration of the aboriginal *must not be forgotten* is a sign of its historical significance to European memory. The fact that *we observe* the fragmentary existence of totemism in *other social and religious institutions* is a sign of the aboriginal's *originary* place in the history of Europe's institutions – and not the 'institutions' of aboriginal society.

Like the natural scientist, *we* can *observe* such phenomena as if *we* were *observing* Australian fauna.

Freud does not construct historical continuities or discontinuities in the history of humankind; he constructs an imaginary primal scene, its distorted copy (the figure of the savage), and the proper, fully constituted realization or re-presentation of a modern, scientific primitivism conceptualized in the figure of the 'compulsive neurotic' through the rhetoric of civilization and ethnographic discourse.

[...]

It is easy to play with Freud's text: to ravage it, pull it apart, commit all sorts of distortions. It is as if the shelf life of *Totem and Taboo* has begun to decay, with a half-life of ninety years or so. It is impossible to reconstruct the original text faithfully; even quotes and citations will not maintain their integrity. The Author of the Original Text clearly sees himself as a totemic figure, one who contains the spirit of our ancestors; He asks that you, the son, do not kill the father, the original totem, in an effort to put an end to the patriarchal violence of the father. And if I take in Freud's text, digest it, there is a danger that my cannibalistic epiphanies will be punished with disciplinary backlash. I may choose to love the text, to eat up its words, to spit them out, or guard them as my own special *turds of the fancy. He was moved by urgings that he had never sensed before. He was impelled to bury his teeth in the raw flesh and gorge himself. He realised that this was partially the result of gnawing hunger; but yet it seemed deeper, something primitive and bestial that always had been a part of him but that never before had had occasion to come to the surface. He knew in that brief instant the feeling of the wild beast for its kill* (Burroughs 1915: 30). Why? Because I would rather be a promiscuous savage than a member of Freud's family? But if I do so, I pay a price: an outburst of *violent hostility among men, aggressiveness,* that *indestructible feature of human nature, will follow.* The threat is always there.

Dora was a wild thing: *When the time for the procession approached, he asked the girl to wait for him at the door which opened on to the staircase leading to the upper storey, while he pulled down the outside shutters. He then came back and, instead of going out by the open door, suddenly clasped the girl to him and pressed a kiss upon her lips.* The scene is like something out of a

Harlequin romance or film noir. *This was surely just the situation to call up a distinct feeling of sexual excitement in a girl of fourteen who had never before been approached. But Dora had at that moment a violent feeling of disgust, tore herself free from the man, and hurried past him to the staircase and from there to the street door.* The melodrama does not end here. Freud's prognosis: *In this scene ... the behaviour of this child of fourteen was already entirely and completely hysterical. I should without question consider a person hysterical in whom an occasion for sexual excitement elicited feelings that were preponderantly or exclusively unpleasurable ... The elucidation of the mechanism of this reversal of affect is one of the most important and at the same time one of the most difficult problems in the psychology of the neuroses.*[6] Why is it so difficult for Freud to understand that Dora rejected Herr K? *Instead of the genital sensation which would certainly have been felt by a healthy girl in such circumstances, Dora was overcome by the unpleasurable feeling which is proper to the tract of mucous membrane at the entrance to the alimentary canal – that is by disgust.* In Freud's family, Dora was suppose to find Herr K's sexual advances pleasurable. That she does not defines her as hysterical. What renders Dora 'hysterical' is the psychoanalytical interpretative schema that does not name sexual violence (on the so-called 'reversal of affect,' Freud is apparently unable to achieve certainty and plenitude in his interpretation) and, therefore, confuses 'romance' with 'rape' and affection with exchange. *When she was feeling embittered she used to be overcome by the idea that she had been handed over to Herr K. as the price of his tolerating the relations between her father and his wife; and her rage at the father's making such a use of her was visible behind her affection for him. At other times she was quite well aware that she had been guilty of exaggeration in talking like this. The two men had of course never made a formal agreement in which she was treated as an object for barter ... But as a matter of fact things were in a position in which each of the two men avoided drawing any conclusions from the other's behaviour which would have been awkward for his own plans. It was possible for Herr K to send Dora flowers every day for a whole year while he was in the neighbourhood, to take every opportunity of giving her valuable presents, and to spend all his spare time in her company, without her parents noticing anything in his behaviour that was characteristic of love-making*[7] ... that was characteristic of stalking.

A historical observation: By 1896 Freud had abandoned his theory of the father's seduction of the daughter. He shifted from an analysis of father/daughter incest and its effect in the condition of hysteria to the mother/son Oedipal relationship of unfulfilled incestuous longing desublimated into a realm of fantasy and neurosis. Jeffrey M. Masson, in his important book *The Assault on Truth: Freud's Suppression of the Seduc-tion Theory* (1984), writes that by 'shifting the emphasis from an actual world of sadness, misery, and cruelty to an internal stage on which actors performed invented dramas for an invisible audience, Freud began a trend away from the real world that, it seems to me, is at the root of the present-day sterility of psychoanalysis and psychiatry throughout the world' (quoted in Showalter 1997: 41). In his research into the Freud archive, Masson concluded that the historical record of Freud's inquiry and his shift from 'hysteria' to a theory of 'Oedipal' psycho-sexual development was distorted to cover up Freud's profes-sional cowardice in his refusal to pursue the truth of sexual abuse and incest in the patriarchal bourgeois imperial family: in other words, who, really, was its perpetrator and who were its victims?

Is *Totem and Taboo*, published sometime after Freud's denunciation of the realities of father/daughter incest, another attempt on Freud's part to further justify this denunciation by reconfiguring Oedipal in-cestuous fantasies in relation to a so-called primitive past? European civilization had emerged from privitivism and yet, in the course of its 'progressive' unfolding toward Civilization, had apparently eradicated the savage urge of incest. The continuing struggle on Freud's part to shift the conceptual frames of what constitutes the Real and Fantasy is entirely evident in the text and materializes in consanguineous and non-consanguineous relations. *Almost everywhere the totem prevails there also exists the law that the members of the same totem are not allowed to enter into sexual relations with each other; that is, that they cannot marry each other. This represents the exogamy which is associated with the totem.*

Freud asserts that savages demonstrate an excessive concern over incest. *In fact their whole social organization seems to serve this object or to have been brought into relation with its attainment.* But that is because *sav-ages who, according to our standard, are ... very immoral. Accordingly we may always safely assume that crimes forbidden by law are crimes which men have a natural propensity to commit.* What distinguishes the savage from the civilized for Freud is that '*in the beginning was the deed.*' These are Freud's concluding remarks, written to declare that primitive man committed patricide and that this foundational event, the murder of the Primordial Father, initiates the guilt upon which society (i.e., fraternal relations among men) emerges. The death of the Primordial Father occurs due to Oedipal incest, the son kills the father in order to have, sexually, the mother. The Oedipal complex is a fantasy of incestuous longing, the guilt from which becomes the foundation of European bourgeois patriarchal familial social organization, taken to be and affirmed by Freud as universal. The savage committed the deed, and civilization emerged from the expatiation of this originary guilt. This is the Freudian model of psycho-social cultural development.

There is, however, a moment in Freud's text when he must assert the dominance of mother/son incest over father/daughter incest as the model of cultural as well as individual development. He does so through the ethnographic work of J.G. Frazer and his four-volume work *Totemism and Exogamy. As the totem is hereditary and is not changed by marriage, the results of the prohibition, for instance in the case of maternal heredity, are easily perceived. If, for example, the man belongs to a clan with the totem of the Kangaroo and marries a woman of the Emu totem, the children, both boys and girls, are all Emu. According to the totem law incestuous relations with his mother and his sister, who are Emu like himself, are therefore made impossible for a son of this marriage.* Freud will now resort to a footnote in order to reassert the significance of this information for the history of the Oedipal complex:

> But the father, who is a Kangaroo, is free – at least under prohibition – to commit incest with his daughters, who are Emu. In the case of paternal inheritance of the totem the father would be Kangaroo as well as the children; then incest with the daughters would be forbidden to the father and incest with the mother would be left open to the son. These consequences of the totem prohibition seem to indicate that the maternal inheritance is older than the paternal one, for there are grounds for assuming that the totem prohibitions are directed first of all against the incestuous desires of the son. (Freud 1918: 9)

Incest between father and daughter is less significant than incest between mother and son; thus, *maternal inheritance is older than the paternal one. There are grounds for assuming that the totem prohibitions are directed first of all against the incestuous desires of the son.* What those 'grounds' are 'we,' the readers, are not privy to. Freud has located in the ethnographic record of 'mother-right' further support for his claim to the Oedipal complex as the foundation of psycho-sexual development. In so doing, however, he has engaged in an extraordinary production of the figure of 'the savage,' who, in the early twentieth century, and especially after the First World War, was a significant figure through which to justify all sorts of truth claims regarding the origins of violence, sexuality, and need for imperial governance.

How does Freud produce the savage in his text; how does he appropriate the ethnographic knowledge of the so-called savages, and to what end? There are many interests, as I intend to show, at stake in Freud's deployment of this figure. For example, by representing taboo as 'incomprehensible' and 'irrational,' he thus confirms the savages' indisposition to rule, a political indisposition to rule for any form of primitivism, including that put forward by Karl Marx, Friedrick Engels, and other socialists interests in communal models of political organization. Freud confers a transparent and invisible power on the European scientist to take available social and political knowledge and manipulate it for his purposes, which are, in part, to support his own seemingly 'incomprehensible and irrational' move away from the realities of sexual abuse to the unconscious fantasies of Oedipal sublimation *and* to challenge other appropriations of the so-called Primitive which were also making use of this figure for the purposes of advancing alternative political economies to the dominant imperial capitalism currently operating in Europe in the early twentieth century. To redeploy the figure of the primitive to curb the political challenges mounted by suffragism and socialism at this time was a decidedly political and conservative move designed to maintain a patriarchal and imperialist political economy; it was to conserve a racist one as well, which, given the violent realities of anti-Semitism at this time, is perhaps the basis for understanding what I perceive to be Freud's 'ambivalence' toward the so-called savage, a point to which I will return. In some respects, the very edifice of psychoanalysis, with its metaphors and metonymies of Oedipal fantasy and the infantilized and primitivized neurotic, serves to shield from sight the real conflicts of human antagonisms produced not only within and by the bourgeois patriarchal family but also the bourgeois imperial nation, and, importantly, their interdependence. We have here a form of mythic re-signification.

Freud makes use of infantilization and the notion of 'infantile recurrence' to establish the link between the compulsive neurotic and the savage ... *for the incest dread of savages has long been known as such, and is in need of no further interpretation. What we can add to the further appreciation of incest dread is the statement that it is a subtle infantile trait and is in striking agreement with the psychic life of the neurotic. Psychoanalysis has taught us that the first object selection of the boy is of an incestuous nature and that it is directed to the forbidden objects, the mother and the sister; psychoanalysis has taught us also the methods through which the maturing individual frees himself from these incestuous attractions. The neurotic, however, regularly presents to us a piece of psychic infantilism; he has either not been able to free himself from the childlike conditions of psycho-sexuality, or else he has returned to them (inhibited development and regression). Hence the incestuous fixations of the libido still play or again are playing the main role in his unconscious psychic life. We have gone so far as to declare that the relation to the parents instigated by incestuous longings is the central complex of the neurosis. This discovery of the significance of incest for the neurosis naturally meets with the most general incredulity on the part of the grown-up, normal man; a similar rejection will also meet the researches of Otto Rank, which show in even larger scope to what extent the incest theme stands in the centre of poetical interest and how it forms the material of poetry in countless variations and distortions. We are forced to believe that such a rejection is above all the product of man's deep aversion to his former incest wishes which have since succumbed to repression. It is therefore of importance to us to be able to show that man's incest wishes, which later are destined to become unconscious, are still felt to be dangerous by savage races, who consider them worthy of the most severe defensive measures.*

Infantile and primitive; unable to comprehend *their* sexual excesses; *unrestrained intercourse; they* are ungovernable; *they* must be governed.

While taboo is recognized by Freud as 'the oldest unwritten code of law of humanity,' taboo prohibitions *lack all justification and are of unknown origin. Though incomprehensible to us they are taken as a matter of course by those who are under their dominance.* And yet, *the taboo of Polynesian savages is after all not so remote from us as we were at first inclined to believe; the moral and customary prohibitions which we ourselves obey may have some essential relation to this primitive taboo the explanation of which may in the end throw light upon the dark origins of our own 'categorical imperative.'* Taboo is comprehensible as the dark origins of the Kantian notion of an absolute and unconditional command of the moral law, defined in the *Oxford English Dictionary* as 'a law given by pure reason, and binding universally on every rational will,' and yet taboo is incomprehensible and of unknown origins *to the savages themselves*. This ambivalent disposition toward taboo as the basis of law and a juridical social system for Europeans, but not for Primitives, reveals Freud's political bias toward colonization as a justifiable mode of European domination and rule. Freud will mystify taboo as a form of superstitious magic. He will refuse to recognize it as a juridical system designed to check the accumulation of power and prestige. In chapter 2, 'Taboo and the Ambivalence of Emotions,' Freud constructs an argument in which the ambivalent response on the part of primitives toward their chiefs, entailing both tenderness and hostility, provides an explanation for taboo prohibitions and restrictions: chiefs *must both be guarded and be guarded against. The savage Kings are endowed with a wealth of power and an ability to bestow happiness only gods possess; certainly in later stages of civilization none but the most servile courtiers would play the hypocrite.* The power of indigenous male elites is compared to a mode of European monarchial governance. Female leadership is completely obliterated from Freud's account of ambivalence toward the chief. This distortion of the political organization of some indigenous societies, along with his refusal to recognize taboo as a critical force in the administration of social power conforms to European colonial violence and its self-appointed justification to rule over 'the natives' because they apparently have no political and juridical modes of governance at their disposal. *They* engage in superstitious modes of projection. *For primitive men say it themselves and, as far as the totemic system is still in effect today, the totem is called ancestor and primal father.* Freud's developmental model of social development, from primitive myth to religion to science, is another direct challenge to the representation of different systems of governance, especially those that can be used to represent the benefits of communism. It also affirms the exercise of imperial power over the indigenous peoples of the so-called colonies.

Taboo is for Freud defined by 'ambivalence.' This notion of ambivalence straddles oppositions between 'clean' and 'unclean,' as well as tenderness and hostility. The female body emerges as an implicit referent in this schema along with the chief's body, both bodies being generative sites of power over life and death. I want to suggest that this notion of ambivalence in Freud's text constitutes an opening out of his own negative political hallucination toward indigenous society as virtually non-existent to a certain awareness of a non-European Other; even an awareness of how the aboriginal becomes an Other within European consciousness, so that what emerges from Freud's text is a more general form of colonial ambivalence toward indigenous societies. Colonial ambivalence would thus contain its tenderness via its infantilization of indigenous peoples as childlike, simple, and innocent, and yet also produce hostility toward indigenous peoples both as the essential embodiment of a violence that must be eradicated from so-called civilized bourgeois society and as a representative figure of communism. Why this ambivalent production of affective responses to, and partial and contradictory dispositions toward, the aboriginal? Hostility because they refuse to vanish, to become an ancestral heritage from which European bourgeois consciousness can establish and re-establish its hegemony; or because of a displaced antagonism on Freud's part toward socialist theories of communal life in which indigenous societies represent a refusal of the fraternal powers of the patriarchal state, and thus pose a serious challenge to imperial rule and its foundational premises of 'fraternity' and bourgeois equality – they would, in Marx and Engels's terms, bring about the 'vanishing of capital.' Such premises must have seemed even more in need of rethinking during the First World War, with the massive, if not traumatic, loss of life among young men. Such a traumatic experience of loss in European history begged to be filled with a significant Other, both by way of defending the current order of violence and, perhaps, finding blame for it elsewhere.

The science of psychoanalysis was one method of sacrificing the history of a people to a conservative and imperial knowledge and, in so doing, committing a form of epistemic genocide in which real indigenous societies are completely eradicated and denied historical and ontological autonomy. Rather, indigenous societies become a reductive non-embodiment of a non-European Other in which to locate the traumatic effect of the violence of the European bourgeois state.

Trauma has a repetitive impulse, and it should come as no surprise that following *Totem and Taboo*, Freud engaged in another process of trying to account for a moment of originary violence, the collective murder of the primordial father, in the figure of Moses in *Moses and Monotheism*. In his essay *Freud and the Non-European*, Edward Said reads this text in the context of Freud's relationship to the emergence of Zionism in Europe and his own Jewish identity. What interests Said in *Moses and Monotheism* is Freud's figuration of Moses as Egyptian: 'Like Beethoven's late works, Freud's *Spätwerk* is obsessed with returning not just to the problem of Moses's identity – which, of course, is at the very core of the treatise – but to the very elements of identity itself, as if that issue so crucial to psychoanalysis, the very heart of the science, could be returned to in the way that Beethoven's late work returns to such basics as tonality and rhythm' (Said 2003: 29). Freud is quite clear, even adamant according to Said, that 'Moses was an Egyptian, and was therefore different from the people who adopted him as their leader – people, that is, who became the Jews whom Moses seems to have later created as *his* people' (Said 2003: 35). This striking feature of *Moses and Monotheism* becomes for Said a significant textual revelation in the contemporary context of the formation of the Israeli state in 1948. Said goes on to explain what for him is significant about Moses' identity to the latter historical event:

> Palestinians who lived in pre-1948 Palestine can neither return (in the case of the refugees) nor have access to land as Jews can. Quite differently from the spirit of Freud's deliberately provocative reminders that Judaism's founder was a non-Jew, and that Judaism begins in the realm of Egyptian, non-Jewish monotheism, Israeli legislation countervenes, represses, and even cancels Freud's carefully maintained opening out of Jewish identity towards its non-Jewish background. The complex layers of the past, so to speak, have been eliminated by official Israel. So – as I read him in the setting of Israel's ideologically conscious policies – Freud, by contrast, had left considerable room to accommodate Judaism's non-Jewish antecedents and contemporaries ... This other non-Jewish, non-European history has now been erased, no longer to be found in so far as an official Jewish identity is concerned. (Said 2003: 44)

Freud's reading of Moses as a 'foreigner,' a non-Jew, is for Said, and for Jacqueline Rose in her afterword to Said's essay, also a recognition of the non-European within Freud's Europe, a Europe that was consolidating its anti-Semitism into the soon-to-be-realized tragic violence of the Holocaust. In response to Said's claim 'that Freud mobilized the non-European past in order to undermine any doctrinal attempt that might be made to put Jewish identity on a sound foundational basis,' Rose adds that 'we could almost remove the "and" from the title of this lecture, "Freud *and* the Non-European," and read it instead as "Freud *the* Non-European." Or – to put it another way – through this complex, ambivalent relationship to his own Jewish identity, Freud, precisely as outsider, was able to tear away the façade of European perfectibility long before the horrors of the Second World War and the violence of anti-colonial struggle would bring it crashing to the ground' (Said 2003: 70). Interestingly, Rose draws attention to anti-colonial struggle and follows this acknowledgment with a passage from Freud's preface to the 1930 Hebrew edition of *Totem and Taboo* in which he declares both his distance from Judaism as a religion and yet the importance of his identity as Jewish. She also makes what I think is an important connection between these two texts. *Moses and Monotheism*, she writes,

> offers the thesis, already adumbrated in *Totem and Taboo*, that an act of murder is constitutive of the social tie. In fact monotheism, together with

the 'advance in intellectuality' that is said to accompany it, takes hold only because of the bloody deed which resided over its birth. As has often been pointed out, you can reject the flawed historical argument of both these texts while accepting the underlying thesis that there is no sociality without violence, that peoples are most powerfully and effectively united by what they agree to hate. What binds the people to each other and to their God is that they killed him. (Said 2003: 75)

Although Rose admires Said's reading of Freud's text as an opening up to the question of the instability of identity, she reads Freud's text as a violent one, in that the 'Jewish people kill their leader.' Rose suggests that there is another side to the story of how the conflictual strains on identity manifest: 'For trauma, far from generating freedom, openness to others as well as to the divided and unresolved fragments of a self, leads to a very different kind of fragmentation – one which is, in Freud's own words, "devastating," and causes identities to batten down, to go exactly the other way: towards dogma, the dangers of coercive and coercing forms of faith. Are we at risk of idealizing the flaws and fissures of identity? Fragmentation can engender petrification, just as it can be a consequence of historical alienation that a people, far from dispersing themselves, start digging for a history to legitimate the violence of the state' (Said 2003: 75–6). For Rose, then, it is the repetition of violence in the consolidations of identity as a consequence of historical trauma that is in question; while, for Said, it is still a question of how to write the condition of the politics of diaspora in which the instabilities of identity are a normal way of life.

The debate between Rose and Said over the fragmentation of identity opens up further questions regarding the inevitability of violence, or the notion that an act of violence is the inevitable spur to the constitution of sociality and society in general. Rose puts this idea forward when she notes that it has often been pointed out that there is 'no sociality without violence, that peoples are most powerfully and effectively united by what they agree to hate.' René Girard supports her thesis in *Violence and the Sacred*, especially his chapter devoted to rereading Freud's *Totem and Taboo*. For Girard, the importance of this text lies in Freud's recognition of an originary and collective murder of the primordial father: 'For what after all is the subject of *Totem and Taboo*? Is Freud not dealing with the father, the father of the primitive tribe who was destined to be murdered? Freud's subject is patricide – the very crime Freud believed he had discovered at the heart of Greek tradegy, a crime projected by the criminals onto their victims' (Girard 1977: 208). The victim here, or in Girard's specific terms, the 'surrogate victim,' is the object of Girard's interest; in particular, he sees in *Totem and Taboo* a 'general theory of sacrifice.'

In all modern crises, 'like all sacrificial crises,' according to Girard, the making of the surrogate victim is a result of a specific process defined by 'the elimination of differences':

> The interplay of antagonism actually does the eliminating, without ever being recognized for what it truly is: the increasingly feeble, increasingly tragic interventions of an enfeebled difference. This difference appears to be always growing, but it fades away whenever someone tries to appropriate it. Each faction is mystified by the isolated restructurings, increasingly fragile and transitory, which lend their support to each of the antagonists in turn. The final degradation of the mythic element takes the form of a proliferation of rival and mutually destructive forms whose relationship to the myth itself is highly ambiguous. These forms are demystifying as well as mythic; that is they are mythic in the very nature of their demystification, which is never illusory, to be sure, but is always restricted to the *other* myth. The myths of demystification cling to the great collective myth and draw nourishment from it, rather like worms feeding on a corpse. (Girard 1977: 206)

The notion that the surrogate victim can be a figure both mythic and demystifying fits well with Freud's use of indigenous societies as the originary and therefore mythic site of the realization of an Oedipal murder. Thus, this 'mystifying demystification,' as Girard terms it, can be seen to emerge in Freud in his appropriation of the figure of the Aboriginal as a way of laying bare the apparent cause and reality of an originary and collective murder; I would argue, however, that Freud's deployment of this mythic story of collective murder, apparently evidenced by primitive forms of taboo, attempts to cast doubt on the political legitimacy of communism. Both theories of human social and individual development, communism versus bourgeois capitalist familialism, appropriate the figure of the Aboriginal. Marx and Engels appropriate it for the purposes of demystifying the alienation and exploitation of labouring bodies under a capitalist mode of production. Freud, however, appropriates aboriginality to further mystify this figure of demystification through a tale of mythic origins in which aboriginality is characterized as essentially violent and, somewhat ironically for the colonial mind, 'ungovernable,' and therefore – and here is the key – unable to provide a model of governance (one that is based on distributive and dispersed modes of power) that could significantly challenge the hierarchical division of powers under the rise of bourgeois capitalism in the nineteenth century. Girard reproduces his ethnocentric bias toward the inevitability of violence among so-called primitives in the following: 'the prohibitions of primitive peoples display a knowledge of violence and its ways that surpasses our modern comprehension. The reason is clear; the prohibitions were dictated by violence itself, by the violent manifestations of a previous crisis, and they are fixed in place as a bulwark against similar outbursts' (Girard 1977: 219). And yet, as I discuss in the following chapter with reference to Pat Barker's *Regeneration* trilogy, the First World War provided a display of violence that in its techno-military superiority surpassed any previous modern comprehension. To what lengths will European bourgeois consciousness go to legitimate its own horrific violence, its genocides and collective murders?

In between the oppositional argument outlined in Said's and Rose's discussion on the consolidations and instabilities of identity enters another figure, that of the Aboriginal, who along with the Jew, the Arab, the Mother, and the Homosexual, constitutes a figure whose shared partiality lies in the various ways it has been sacrificed to the subject of knowledge in the early to mid-twentieth century, and not without real consequences for those *identified* as such. Trauma is, as Rose acknowledges, repetitious, but more interesting is the problem of the reiterative capacities of trauma such that a new object of violence is often created in order to supersede its predecessor, and the internalization of historical trauma reproduces violence, yet again, that does not *return* to those who have the power to bring it about in the first place, but moves toward an other Other. Such an argument goes against the notion of the supposed inevitability of violence as the condition of an unacknowledged 'primitivism.' And this, in turn, has specific implications for theories of sexual violence. In Girard, there is again the dispensation toward reappropriating the mythic figure of the aboriginal to articulate the inevitability of sexual violence as another condition of primitivism:

All the evidence seems to confirm the proposal, set forth at the outset of this work, that sexuality is part of the larger problem of violence and the sacred. Sexual prohibitions, like all other prohibitions, are sacrificial in nature; and all legitimate sexuality is sacrificial. Strictly speaking, between members of the same community, legitimate sexuality exists no more than legitimate violence in the community. The prohibitions involving [mother/son] incest and those directed against murder or ritual killing among members of the same community [of the Father] have a common origin and function. That is why they resemble one another and why in many cases, as Robertson Smith has pointed out, they cover exactly the same ground. (Girard 1977: 219)

Not surprisingly, Freud's theory of the *savage* origins of Oedipal desire contains an extraordinary amount of violence toward women. In order to prove the significance of the prohibitions against sexual relations between members of the same totem, he recounts, by way of Frazer, a narrative of the severity of the punishment for this particular transgression. Quoting Frazer on the Ta-Ta-thi tribe of New South Wales, the reader learns that a man is killed and *a woman is only beaten or speared, or both, till she is nearly dead; the reason given for not actually killing her being that she was probably coerced.* The savagery of the savage is established by *his* capacity for violence towards women. Primitive man may exhibit an Oedipal structure of sexual relations by ensuring that son/mother sexual relations are prohibited, but that is where the similarity between the savage and the European man ends. After all, the savage represents a primitive state that has progressed, advanced, and developed into the adult European and civilized male. Primitive instincts may still erupt in the European male, but only in those who belong to the uncivilized classes or 'semi-savage races.' And although totemic descent through the matrilineal line ensures against son/mother incest, it does not prohibit father/daughter incest, as already noted. In this single regard, the savage is better than the European because *he* has managed to prohibit son/mother incest, but the cost is high in savagery toward women. In other words, matrilineal descent and *mother* rights of inheritance, ironically and perversely, do not ensure the physical safety of *daughters*; it does not protect them from coercion, sexual assault, rape, and incest. In other words, the apparent power of the mother opens the daughter to oppression and domination.

The nuclear *family* of single dwelling, heterosexual marriage coded as *blood relations*, is Freud's metaphor for the totem prohibition against incest with *the mother or the sisters. It also makes it impossible for the man to have sexual union with all the women of his own group, with a number of females, therefore, who are not consanguineously related to him, by treating all these women like blood relations ... Everybody descended from the same totem is consanguineous, that is, of one family; and in this family the most distant grades of relationship are recognized as an absolute obstacle to sexual union.* And yet, he turns his metaphor inside out when he writes *of substituting the totem relationship for the real blood relationship.* Reality rests in blood relations, which are really marriage relations because the only *blood relation* that exists is between mother and child. It is the blood in the umbilical cord that constitutes a *blood relation.* Thus, the notion of a *blood relation* is a metaphor for *family relations,* which is a metaphor for the *totem relationship.* Always already the site of a natural, biological filiation, the *blood relation* is continually displaced by the patriarchal family form and the savagery of the totemic system. The blood relation becomes the irreducible biopolitical conception of *the family* and thus lies at the heart of *familial ideology,* its disjuncture from *desire* and acceptance of *violence toward women* originating, instinctively, with so-called *primitive man.*

The family has now become, in Freud's scheme of the things, the natural state and the totemic system a substitution for it, a substitution that effaces monogamous marital relations *between two individuals* by constituting the relationship *between an individual and his group.* In violation of *the exclusive conjugal right of a man to a woman,* the natural order of things is substituted, incorrectly, by what the anthropologist Lewis Henry Morgan – in a direct critique of Marx and Engels's key anthropological source – called a *'classifying system.'* Unnatural, of course, the reference appears in quotation marks to underscore its difference from the natural speech of the family and the exclusive conjugal right of a man to a woman. As noted earlier, Mark Poster critiques Freud's *individualism* and demonstrates Freud's contempt for *the group,* especially the commune or the communistic potential of the group. As Poster writes, with the abolition of the family, 'Oedipus, the super-ego, the anal character, the traits of masculinity and femininity, the extreme form of sex-role differentiation in the nuclear family, might also depart' (Poster 1978: 28–9). What would also vanish is the exclusive ownership of women by men, the privatization of such property relations, and the consumption of female desire and reproductivity. In the bourgeois capitalist family, the generative female body is owned by a single male. In Morgan's unnatural classifying system, *a man calls not only his begetter 'father' but also every other man who, according to the tribal regulations, might have married his mother and thus become his father.* With false logic and an equally false sense of analogy, Freud continues: *he calls 'mother' not only the woman who bore him but also every other woman who might have become his mother without violation of the tribal laws.* It is an enormous challenge to speculate the latter and yet so easy to understand the former situation regarding the father. Here, the anxiety over paternal origins and the desire to preserve bourgeois male ownership of female bodies trouble the reduction of Freud's use of aboriginality as only an attack on communism and his desire to elaborate a theoretical construction of individualism.

Totemic relations constitute a false family for Freud, whereas the European bourgeois family is the natural state of things. The indiscriminate naming of 'fathers,' 'mothers,' 'brothers,' and 'sisters' among the tribal peoples *signifies much more the social than the physical relations.* The dangers of this social custom do appear in the bourgeois nursery *when the child is induced to greet every male and female friend of the parents as 'uncle' and 'aunt,' or it may be found in a transferred sense when we speak of 'Brothers in Apollo,' or 'Sisters in Christ.'* Strictly speaking, the savages' use of the names of 'father,' 'mother,' 'brother,' and 'sister' is only metaphorical, an approximation of real consanguineous family relations. It is a quaint tradition, like the one that takes place in the nursery, but it is no match for the seriousness, reverence, and naturalness of the father/mother/child bond of the bourgeois nuclear family.

It is not just the communist group arrangement that disturbs Freud, but group marriage. Freud defines *group marriage* specifically as *a number of men exercising conjugal rights over a number of women. The children of this group marriage would then rightly look upon each other as brothers and sisters although not born of the same mother, and would take all the men of the group for their fathers.* Again, it is the loss of the single father, the true individual who remains undifferentiated from his paternal lineage through ownership of his wife's body, that strikes at the core of Freud's analysis. This single father is the First Father of the First Family of Man. It is only later that Freud will acknowledge that it is not only *restriction on the marriage choice* that concerns him but also *restriction on sexual freedom.* This is the price that must be paid to ensure the single paternal line of descent. The reproductive female body must take the dominant position over the sexual female body, a body that must be restricted and curbed. So, too, the aboriginal body is prone to a licentiousness that must also be held in check: *We must say that these savages are even more sensitive to incest than we, perhaps because they are more subject to temptations than we are, and hence require more extensive protection against it.* Only the individual bourgeois man occupies the correct moral position in familial relations, which is a restricted or monogamous heterosexuality. The bourgeois woman, the aboriginal, the lesbian, and the homosexual represent those whose sexuality must be restricted. The aboriginal is then the bourgeois man's imaginary *homo*-other – the phantasmatic excess who threatens to undo the work of bourgeois men to maintain control and power over bourgeois women and children: *To hear that these savages hold sacred orgies in which persons of just these forbidden degrees of kinship [i.e., bother and sister] seek sexual union would seem still more peculiar to us, if we did not prefer to make use of this contradiction to explain the prohibition instead of being astonished at it.*

The Dutch missionary who reported these customs added that unfortunately he had to consider them well founded. It is assumed without question by these races that a man and a woman left alone together will indulge in the most extreme intimacy, and as they expect all kinds of punishments and evil consequences from consanguineous intercourse they do quite right to avoid all temptations by means of such prohibitions.

There is little that is repressive about this and a lot that is voyeuristic and ethno-pornographic. The savage is European bourgeois man's unconscious and infantile state. He is excess, promiscuity, uncontrollable sexual desire, polygamous, multiple, un-individuated, communistic, orgiastic, and homosexual. He is also the law, the legislator, the regulator, the rule, the jury, judge, and the one who punishes, in short, the First Father, individual, adult, and child. Father, Son, and ... so on and so forth. I'd still rather be a promiscuous savage, *à la Marx and Engels*, than a member of Freud's family.

Part Two: Tarzan (and Jane); or, Savagery (and Civilization)

Even the movie titles elide the existence of the petty-bourgeois female heroine, 'Jane.' In the Metro-Goldwyn-Mayer production of Tarzan movies in the 1930s and 1940s, starring Johnny Weissmuller and Maureen O'Sullivan, Tarzan, the white wild man of the African jungle, always appears solo in the title. As with all the titles of all Tarzan films, including *Tarzan and His Mate* (1934) and *Tarzan Finds a Son!* (1939), 'Jane,' the proper name, is conspicuously absent.[8]

In *Tarzan and His Mate* Maureen O'Sullivan appears on screen in a long lamé evening dress straight from Paris and wearing French perfume. She soon drops the impractical bourgeois female attire for a scanty two-piece leather number held together by strings. Predating the 'string bikini,' this outfit nevertheless conjures up perverse desires

that those skinny threads will snap at any moment and leave Jane stark
naked swinging through the jungle. It's actually the French number
that Tarzan pulls off with little effort. The underwater shots of Jane's
naked body swimming with Tarzan – or, rather, Weissmuller the Olym-
pic-class swimmer – are somewhat surprisingly risqué and pornographic. In *Tarzan Finds a Son!* Jane becomes 'mother,' and her thigh-
baring string sampot is toned down. She now dons a decent pair of
leather shorts. Sexually enticing, exotic, and erotic, Jane is the archetypal playmate to Tarzan, the wild and singularly possessive male
primitive. As the adopted mother of Tarzan's son in *Tarzan Finds a Son!*
Jane is the dutiful mother. They now live in a fancy sub-jungle two storey walk-up, with a set that looks to contemporary audiences like
something out of a cross between the *Flintstones* and *Gilligan's Island*: a
mechanical elevator pulled up by Timba the pet elephant, an indoor
cooling fan operated by Cheetah, the pet monkey, clay dinner plates,
and a fire in the kitchen for cooking pterodactyl-size eggs. Jane is the
perfect bourgeois hostess, bringing in cut flowers to adorn the dinner
table, bathing baby in warm water and feeding him from a bottle made
from hollowed-out bamboo shoots. When the colonial expedition
arrives to retrieve their son, 'Boy,' as the lost heir to the Greystoke fortune, Jane invites them for lunch and teaches her husband, Tarzan, the
importance of being civilized. In the struggle to preserve the Primitive
Family, Jane makes one fatal mistake after another. It is Tarzan and his
always impeccable instincts that save the day – and save Boy from his
evil money-grubbing relatives. Tarzan rules over the wilds of Africa, its
frightening animals and tribesmen, the irrationality of bourgeois
women, and the uncivil behaviour of greedy middle-class opportun-
ists; it is Tarzan who saves the Bourgeois Family from itself. The Oedipal trauma of the lost father is finally overcome when Tarzan is
returned to his rightful place as heir to Lord Greystoke's fortune, only
to give it up momentarily for one last foray into the wild and unfettered
domain of his youth and fancy, once again proving that the freedom
narrative of the colonial nomad is a rich man's dream.

The importance of domesticity as the mark of civility and civilization
is evidenced by such remarkable passages as the following from the
notable late-nineteenth-century work on English etiquette, *Mrs. Beeton's Book of Household Management*:

It is equally true that some races of men do not dine any more than the
tiger or the vulture. It is not a dinner at which sits the aboriginal Austra-

lian, who gnaws his bone half bare and then flings it behind to his squaw.
And the native of Terra-del-Fuego does not dine when he gets his morsel
of red clay. Dining is the privilege of civilization. The rank which a people
occupy in the grand scale may be measured by their way of taking their
meals, as well as by their way of treating their women. The nation which
knows how to dine has learnt the leading lesson of progress. It implies
both the will and the skill to reduce to order, and surround the idealisms
and graces, the more material conditions of human experience; and wherever that will and that skill exist, life cannot be wholly ignoble. (Beeton
1960: 905)

To treat women well in a civilized state meant to allow them the authority of managing the domestic sphere, a form of 'local governance,' from
which to civilize the children and 'the natives.'

Demonstrating the centrality of popular culture to contemporary
myths and ideologies, Eric Cheyfitz examines Edgar Rice Burroughs's
popular 1912 adventure romance *Tarzan of the Apes* as the definitive
model of the foreign policy of the United States toward the Third World
in the twentieth century, with the novel's racial and class politics a figural translation of the contemporary rhetoric of civilization. From
Shakespeare's *The Tempest* to Burroughs's Tarzan novels, Cheyfitz brilliantly elaborates 'a primal scene from classical rhetoric: the scene in
which an orator through the power of eloquence "civilizes" "savage"
humanity' (Cheyfitz 1991: xxvi). What Cheyfitz overlooks in both these
'high' and 'low' literary references is that the civilizing force is, in fact,
largely feminine and female.

Cheyfitz's Marxist literary analysis of *Tarzan of the Apes* demonstrates
the centrality of the ideology of individualism to the adventure
romance genre. For Cheyfitz, the *Tarzan* series represents a 'romance of
identity' or individualism that seeks 'to erase the cultural or ideological
basis of racial and class identity' (Cheyfitz 1991: 14–15). In explicating
the translation of nation into self, nationalism into identity, Cheyfitz
argues that 'the cultural function of *Tarzan* is radically to reduce or
homogenize domestic political complexities [such as those of poverty
and homelessness] by displacing them onto a foreign scene [such as
those of territorial dispossession in South Africa, for example], whose
own political complexities are thereby radically homogenized in the
vision of the romance' (Cheyfitz 1991: 15). Relations between foreign
and domestic are mediated by the figure of 'homelessness' for Cheyfitz.
He writes, 'To turn our attention obsessively as we have in the United

States to that radically decontextualized figure the "terrorist" (a modern version of that other European projection, the "cannibal," or Caliban) is a way of forgetting our homeless people, for example, by forgetting that what we call terrorism in the Middle East is itself the result of the political struggle against homelessness. The terrorist is the demonized specter of our own homeless people, just as Caliban, that "born devil, on whose nature / Nurture can never stick" [IV.i.188–9], is the demonized specter of Europe's lower classes, who were themselves beset by the violence of homelessness at the time of *The Tempest*' (Cheyfitz 1991: 15). Elaborating on the theme of translation, which is the main conceptual metaphor of Cheyfitz's text, he concludes: 'Following this pattern of transfiguring the domestic and the foreign in terms of one another, so that ironically, the differential connections between them are repressed in a particular ideological representation of the foreign, the romance of racial, or national, identity that has dominated U.S. foreign policy (toward other than European peoples) throughout its history is inevitably a romance of translation, in which, like the Indians in the Marshall Court's decisions, the other is translated into the terms of the self in order to be alienated from those terms. We might say that at the heart of every imperial fiction (the heart of darkness) there is a fiction of translation' (Cheyfitz 1991: 15).

Although excellent on the intersections of race and class, Cheyfitz does not deal adequately with gender in examining an imperialist ideology of individualism that, I would argue, is decidedly marked by ideas about masculinity and male/female, parent/child relations in the domestic sphere and bourgeois family. Tarzan is not only British, white, noble, and no doubt Christian, he is also male. His figure belongs to a long history of literary and rhetorical tropes that not only includes Caliban, Tarzan, and the Middle Eastern 'terrorist' but also Rousseau's noble savage, Frankenstein's monster, Dr Hyde's Mr Jekyl, and even Freud's savage in *Totem and Taboo* – to name a few intertextual references in the historical transposition of this violent figure of 'Aboriginal Man.'

In his analysis of the class and race politics in *Tarzan the Ape Man*, Cheyfitz quotes the following passage from the beginning of the novel: 'I have come across the ages out of the dim and distant past from the lair of the primeval man to claim you – for your sake I have become a civilized man – for your sake I have crossed oceans and continents – for your sake I will be whatever you will me to be.' Cheyfitz goes on to say that these 'are the words of Tarzan's marriage proposal to Jane Porter, the Baltimore woman who with her "delicate ... snowy skin" holds the most powerful sway over Tarzan, representing for him, like Miranda for that archetypal imperialist Prospero, everything in "civilization" that must be protected from the apes and black Africans, latter-day Calibans, who, in addition to two gangs of mutinous sailors (defined by their speech as conspicuously lower class), are the villains of the novel. Indeed, these "ignorant, half-brute" sailors, representative of the working class in the novel, along with Jane's black maid, Esmeralda, who is also portrayed, though for comic relief, as an ignorant half-brute, are relegated to the realm of the foreign inhabited by the apes and the Africans' (Cheyfitz 1991: 11). It is Tarzan's impending domestication into the bourgeois Oedipal family that precipitates his will to submit to civilization. In the case of Jane's black domestic servant, the foreign is incorporated into the domestic, the harlequin romance displaces the adventure romance, and 'homelessness' is shown to be the domestic and bourgeois metaphor of place and property that it truly is.

The crux of Cheyfitz's discussion of *Tarzan the Ape Man* centres on the question of paternal origins, and the bringing back of the father's body to narrative consciousness that allows for the rightful inheritance of the Greystoke fortune. It is the discrepancy between, in Cheyfitz's words, the dead baby in a crib who is buried with Tarzan's biological parents and 'the baby in the text' whose fingerprints in his father's African diary lead to the true identity of Tarzan, that resolves Tarzan's ambiguous racial, species, and class origins (Cheyfitz 1991: 11–12).

As the story goes, a baby was found in the crib along with Tarzan's biological parents and buried with them. This baby, it turns out, was the mother ape's dead child. She replaced her dead child with the living child, Tarzan. The baby ape is displaced by the white child of noble ancestry. The savagery of nature, the baby in the crib, with its brutality and the constant reminder of death, is displaced by civilization, the baby in the text, who grabbed his father's pen when writing his diary and left his indelible mark in the form of fingerprints that would later be identified as Tarzan's. When Tarzan learns to speak, he clearly articulates that 'he was a M-A-N, they were A-P-E-S' (Burroughs 1912: 39). The gap that opens up between speech, and gibberish, civilization and savagery, is sutured closed by the work of reason, science, and investigation. But there is a cost to the acquisition of the civilization of speech which is the supposed 'natural love' of the mother, the ape-mother, in particular: 'That the huge, fierce brute loved this child of another race is beyond question, and he, too, gave to the great, hairy beast all the affection that would have belonged to his fair young mother had she lived' (quoted in Cheyfitz 1991: 20). Cheyfitz writes: 'What can translate across racial boundaries, apparently, is the "natural" love of mother and child; the principal male apes on the other hand are entirely brutal to the child. This kind of sentimentality, which is a simultaneous universalization and alienation of races according to gender, typifies racist discourse' (Cheyfitz 1991: 20). Cheyfitz further analyses this displacement of the child in the crib by the child in the text as an instance of the violent displacement that occurs in the process of translation. 'This scene, in which Kala grabs the infant Lord Greystoke from his crib, displacing him with her own dead baby and transferring the living child lovingly into her arms, is neither a mark of the evolutionary difference between ape and human nor of their primal evolutionary identity as embodied in the mother, but a figure for the process of translation that, underwriting U.S. foreign policy, civilized the other in order to savage her' (Cheyfitz 1991: 21). In the end, it is the female figure of savagery that stands as the raw and unruly aspect of nature that must be civilized. It is the figure of mother in the Oedipal drama and bourgeois family who will tame nature into civilization and raise the son to replace her husband and father. The limit of civilization is the bourgeois family, its Aboriginal Mother and Primordial Father.

It is not my intention here to deploy the category of gender to displace race and class categories; but, rather, to demonstrate the intersection of multiple partialities that further challenges and troubles a dualistic logic of 'either/or.' We need to take the social categories of race, class, and gender as spatial coordinates along several intersecting axes. These conceptual terms combine and recombine in a multitude of ways, and it is the work of a social literary criticism to analyse and understand the complexity of relations among these historical experiences and conceptual categories. In terms of a gender analysis of Tarzan and the racial and class politics of domestic/foreign relations, this means attending to, among other things, the white European female body as the site of racial fantasies, including fears of miscegenation and desires for racial and Christian purity. It also means attending to the bodily culture and civilizational rhetoric of the bourgeois family with its emphasis on hygiene, proper manners, and cleanliness, and configurations of disease, sexuality, and degeneration. The sphere of domesticity and its spatial frontiers of the inside or the internal are the very basis of a nineteenth-century imperialist discourse that attempted to *naturalize* social relations by regulating and governing the very meaning of

Nature in the oppositional structure of the bourgeois white female body and the aboriginal mother.

Part Three: Entering the Image/Text/Commodity Matrix

In the summer of 1997, I travelled to London, England, from a remote northern town, Prince George, in British Columbia, to track down an archive, then called the Mansell Collection. My reason for doing so was to examine Pears' Soap advertisements, the ones I had seen in Eric Hobsbawm's *The Age of Empire, 1875–1914* and that were discussed by Anne McClintock in *Imperial Leather* and Thomas Richards in *The Commodity Culture of Victorian Britain* (Hobsbawm 1987; McClintock 1995; Richards 1990), and to compare this collection with my own private one. I discovered, however, that the majority of the archive had been bought by Time Inc. and shipped to Manhattan, where it was currently housed, appropriately enough, in a building on the Avenue of the Americas. The discarded remnants where left with a 'sister' company in London, called Katz Pictures Ltd in Zetland House. When I arrived at Katz Picture Ltd, I was shown to a corner of a large open-concept office in which a series of filing cabinets had been somewhat chaotically arranged. Clearly, there were other cabinets in storage somewhere – from piecing together some semblance of an alphabetical sequence among the existing cabinets, it appeared that they ended at around 'T.' No one in this corporate office knew where the other cabinets were. I had intended to read the Mansell Collection as a supply of images made available to the scholarly researcher (my bias, I admit) for the purpose of transforming such 'images' to 'cultural artifacts' through the contextual and disciplinary demands of the discourses of social, literary, and cultural history. What I found in this catalogued series of visual documents was an old world populated by spirits and phantasms, an impossible world that held out an extraordinary temptation to get lost in its inexhaustible treasure, its prodigious reserve of artifactual chimeras that invited unconfined reveries – full as it was of scenes of violence, desire, power, and the nightmares and barbarisms of history.

The positivity of the archive, the rigorous production of a system of categories in which to contain and justify the dispersion of images, is extensive. I began looking through the printed index of the Mansell Collection, making a note of the categories that interested me. Generally, systems of categorization, taxonomies, denote enclosure, regulation, rules of practice, and normative formations. In this list, however, I found very little continuity; indeed, my attempts to cite only those categories relevant to my immediate research interest (or what I thought that was at the time) were undermined both by the fascination which certain categories conjured up (what's in that folder, I wonder?) and by the seemingly endless transformations and digressions exhibited by the shear number of categories listed. Dispersion, rather than containment, informed my actual experience, delimited as it was by a desire to find, and a reaching out toward otherness and difference: a difference (that an imperial) history makes.

My memories of my experience of this archive subsequently have been filtered through the lens of Foucault's essay 'Fantasia of the Library.' In this essay, Foucault argues that in the nineteenth century a new imaginative space opened up in the writer's experience of the fantastic. With reference to Flaubert's novel *The Temptation of St Anthony*, Foucault writes that the domain of phantasms now 'arises from the black and white surface of printed signs, from the closed and dusty volume that opens with a flight of forgotten words; fantasies are carefully deployed in the hushed library, with its columns of books, with its titles aligned on shelves to form a tight enclosure, but within confines that also liberate impossible worlds. The imaginary now resides between the book and the lamp' (Foucault 1977a: 90–1). The play of illumination on a black and white surface also incorporates the visual sign with the textual, as well as the interchange between image and text. For Foucault, Flaubert provides an example of the play of repetition and difference that would altogether transform the relation between the body and nature, the self and reality, to one dominated by the 'reproduction of reproductions.' 'The imaginary,' he writes, 'is not formed in opposition to reality as its denial or compensation; it grows among signs, from book to book, in the interstice of repetitions and commentaries; it is born and takes shape in the interval between books. It is a phenomenon of the library' (Foucault 1977a: 90–1). Similarly, the visual archive produces its own imaginary space, one that mimics, perhaps, more the experience of television viewing than reading and the subsequent reproduction of fantasies and images. The imaginary now resides between the TV set and the couch, between the computer screen and its illumination from within, between advertising and the symbolic knowledge of signs and trademarks, in the in-between of the image/ text relationship.

Foucault does not provide a materialist analysis as to why this transition to a world of repeatable signs secures its hold on the production of imaginary forces in the nineteenth century. Indeed, Foucault is quite clear that the problem of industrialization and the accumulation of wealth analysed by political economists, including Marx, was not the central mechanism or relation of power to dominate during this period of time. Rather, it was the techniques of power (mobilized by various institutional bodies such as medicine, psychiatry, and the law, and deployed by the bourgeoisie in order to establish their ruling authority) that Foucault valorizes in, for example, *The History of Sexuality*. Foucault, however, underestimates the symbolic production of commodity discourses, such as advertising and fashion supplements, as one of the foremost technologies of power invented by the bourgeoisie to secure its disposition to rule. In particular, it is the symbolic power of commodity discourses – as a structure of desire – that contributed to the bourgeoisie's capacity to rule over women, children, and non-Europeans. Anne McClintock's discussion of Pears' Soap ads notes the significance of the commodity's symbolic power in their promotion of *commodity racism*: 'Commodity racism – in the specifically Victorian forms of advertising and photography, the imperial Expositions and the museum movement – converted the narrative of imperial progress into mass-produced *consumer spectacle*' (McClintock 1995: 33). The narrative of imperial progress, however, could not have been written without the trade in commodities and weapons. The commodity spectacle is a very important part of what I am calling the image/text/commodity matrix. It is a component of it, but not its only value-laden site of exchange. The bodies in the images, as I will discuss, are also 'commodified,' or reduced to commodification, their use value constituted by, in part, their visual quality as subjects for the camera or the illustrator's pen. And let's not forget the empirical reality of the commodities sold in these advertisements. The commodity discourses of advertising and fashion supplements, the bodies depicted in these discourses, and the trade in commodities, all of these are part of the apparatus of the commodity's *manufacture and symbolic production*.

An 1887 advertisement for Pears' Soap depicts a scene, somewhere in Sudan, of several black Arab men facing a rock inscribed with the words 'PEARS' SOAP IS THE BEST.' Notice the man pointing to the words, his head turned toward his companions as if in debate with them over the meaning of this sign. A fourth man kneels on the ground, his hands raised either in horror and fear of this portent or in supplication, a prime example of fetishistic worship of the word.[9] According to the caption below, this etched drawing was inspired by the words of a war

3.1 Pears' Soap newspaper advertisement, 1887.

correspondent in Sudan, who was quoted as saying in the *Daily Tele-graph* (London) in 1884: 'Even if our invasion of the Soudan has done nothing else it has at any rate left the Arab something to puzzle his fuzzy head over, for the legend PEARS' SOAP IS THE BEST *inscribed in huge white characters on the rock which marks the farthest point of our advance toward Berber*, will tax all the wits of the Dervishes of the Desert to trans-late.' These words underscore the image along with the title caption, 'PEARS' SOAP IN THE SOUDAN.'

The white characters inscribed in stone allegorize the indelible mark of a British presence in Sudan that, ironically, will not be simply washed away by the scrub of a brush and a good soap. The British were in Sudan to further Egyptian, but primarily British, interests. British rule extended into Sudan because of the Nile valley, with its fertile agri-cultural soil and irrigation possibilities for growing cotton. Albert Hourani explains that 'the explicit reason for [British expansion into Sudan] was the rise of a religious movement, that of Muhammad Ahmad (1844–85), regarded by his follows as the *mahdi* [Messiah], with the aim of restoring the rule of Islamic justice. Egyptian rule over the country was ended by 1884, and an Islamic form of government was created, but it was not so much the fear of its expansion as fear of other European governments moving in that led to an Anglo-Egyptian occupation which destroyed the Islamic state and in 1899 set up a new system of government, formally an Anglo-Egyptian "condominium," but in fact with a mainly British administration' (Hourani 1991: 284). Ahmad led successful campaigns in 1883 and 1885 against British forces. As Erskine B.Childers notes, however, 'The killing of Gordon and his men at Khartoum by the "whirling dervishes" of the "Mad Mohammadan Mahdi" drove home an impression in the British public mind that was to last for decades' (Childers 1962: 46). Ahmad's death in 1885 meant the overthrow of the Mahdist state by British-Egyptian forces in 1889. Sudan was to remain under joint Egyptian-British rule until it gained independence on 1 January 1956.

The expansion of the commodity form under British imperialism clearly knew no boundaries. Pears' Soap, an indelible sign of capitalist expansion masquerading as the cleansing agent necessary to the advance of civilization, finds its way to the farthest reaches of British military incursion. But according to the soap ad, its presence in Sudan would appear to be confusing to the inhabitants; those white characters written on a rock 'will tax all the wits of the Dervishes of the Desert to translate.' The late-nineteenth-century British reader of this image is encouraged to view the black male bodies as empty of consciousness – lacking subjective experience as well as intelligence – and therefore the British consumer, who is also a reader, must take up the burden of endowing meaning and consciousness where it is lacking in the men. Thus, the British 'authority on the skin,' Professor Sir Erasmus Wilson, F.R.S., is said to have written in the *Journal of Cutaneous Medicine* that 'Pears is a name engraven [*sic*] on the memory of the oldest inhabitant [of England].' The English inhabitant has the necessary substance of memory and can therefore 'translate' the meaning of the white characters for the confused black inhabitants of 'the Soudan.' For their confusion is not simply an issue of language in the narrow sense (i.e., the translation from English to Arabic), but a philosophical problem of translating ignorance into knowledge. Here is the philosophical problem enunciated by Pears' Soap: 'but the Public have not the requisite knowledge of the manufacture of Soap to guide them to a proper selection, so a pretty box, a pretty colour, or an agreeable perfume too frequently outweighs the more important consideration, viz.: *the Composition of the Soap itself,* and thus many a good complexion is spoiled which would be enhanced by proper care.'[10] The 'bright, clear complexion, and a soft skin,' promoted by Pears' Soap are merely the outer signs of an inner cleanliness. The superficiality of external markers – a pretty box, a pretty colour, or an agreeable perfume – masks the real issue of the inner composition of the product. Here we have a context for understanding the header to this advertisement. It reads: 'The Formula of British Conquest.'

Interestingly, the textual component of this advertisement directs the consumer not to be taken in by mere appearances, not to be deceived by artifice, by the gaze, but to look beneath the surface of things to their real composition, for that is where the true nature of a thing can be discerned – when it comes to things, commodities, that is. People are a different matter all together. For the dangers of artifice do not translate to the colonized body. This body is without substance; it is a body empty of the capacity to produce meaning, empty of memory and consciousness, and composed of very little. This body cannot translate the inner to the outer. This body is only ever shell-like without the remote possibility of achieving substance. Thus, illiterate black male bodies are devoid of the capacity to understand the significance of Pears' Soap – their capacity for comprehension might not extend beyond the obvious function of soap as a cleaning agent. A Pears' Soap advertisement from 1891 makes a strident effort to release the consumer from a superficial knowledge of its product: 'Civilization by Soap is only skin-deep directly; but indirectly there is no limit to it ... But what does cleanliness lead to? It leads to a wholesome body and mind; to clean thoughts; to the habit of health; to manly and womanly beauty ... Civilization by soap, pure soap, Pears' Soap, that has no alkali in it – nothing but soap – is more than skin-deep.' In other words, what the colonized body cannot absorb, what the enlightened consumer must understand, is that Pears' Soap *is the best.* This level of connotation can only be understood by the educated consumer, the superior consumer, the British imperial consumer. In one Pears' Soap advertisement, it is clear that the commodity market for soap was not restricted to England, but also included British subjects in the colonies and the indigenous elite of the colonies. The copy of the ad reads: 'Highest Awards Everywhere! London, Paris, Philadelphia, Boston, Sydney, Melbourne, Santiago, Adelaide, Edinburgh, &c.' Another ad for Vaissier's Congo Soap, a competitor in the international market, also signals its appeal to an elite international set of consumers with its reference to the 'Soap des Princes du Congo.'

A notable feature of Pears' Soap is that its composition produces a transparent effect. Such is the screen allegory of this Pears' Soap advertisement that to the British imperial reader, the supremacy of Pears' Soap renders transparent the supremacy of British civilization, where hygiene marks the distinction between a superficial clean white skin and the inherent cleansing agent of civilization's unfolding at the end of the nineteenth century, otherwise known, in reference to North America's aboriginal population, as the 'vanishing race' hypothesis. In another Pears' Soap advertisement, a white cherubic female child gently, lovingly, cleans the face of a black woman lying in a passive position recalling fine art images of odalisques. The caption reads: 'For the complexion.'[11]

The Pears' Soap advertisements that appeared in newsprint in Britain at the end of the nineteenth century not only illuminate a gendered and racialized civilizing process, but they are also events that contributed to its development and advancement. These image/text materials produce a discourse of enlightened commodification by establishing a superior consciousness among British readers who can comprehend or translate the significance of the sign written on the colonized landscape, a significance that points to the superiority of their nation. Indigenous male subjects are figured as illiterate, and indigenous female subjects are corporeal. Both are fetishized and rendered silent – figures who are inappropriate to rule.

Ann Laura Stoler notes that the apparent opposition set up between knowledge and ignorance by Enlightenment discourse masked the real battle 'over which forms of knowledge could lay claims to truth values and the contemporary social order' (Stoler 1989: 77). That the Orient, and in particular the Ottoman Empire, had to be figured as having an 'inappropriate disposition to rule' testifies to the long-standing threat the Ottoman Empire posed for Europe and England and France's persistent rivalry with it. The nineteenth century witnessed a major shift in power from the Ottoman Empire to the dominance of Western Europe, made possible by the industrial revolution and the expansion of commodity production. The Middle East and the Maghreb, along with the Indian subcontinent, became major suppliers of raw materials: Tunisian olive oil for soap; Lebanese silk for the factories of Lyon; Egyptian and Sudanese cotton for the mills of Lancashire; wool and hides from the Maghreb; Tunisian phosphates; foodstuffs, such as oranges, from Palestine; and wine from Algeria. Albert Hourani notes that 'British exports to the eastern Mediterranean countries increased 800 per cent in value between 1815 and 1850; by that time beduin in the Syrian desert were wearing shirts made of Lancashire cotton.' Along with textiles, metal goods, tea, coffee, and sugar were exported from Western Europe to the Middle East and the Maghreb (Hourani 1991: 267, 286).

Signs of power, like the stigmata of gender and race, are written on the body and in the codes of commerce and commodity production. They represent congealed social values. The Pears' Soap advertisements make use of those specific values developed through a centuries old 'civilizing process,' to borrow from Norbert Elias, in which values of cleanliness, sanitation, and brightness shape the metaphorical exteriority of the human condition (Elias 1994). Their metaphoricity is forgotten, however, and they become unquestioned indicators of what it means to be human, their metaphorical powers transferred into a moral rhetoric of Christian purity (the cleanliness of the soul) or Enlightenment rationality: sanity (sanitation) and intelligence (brightness). The discourse of advertising is itself produced by the limits of the commodity form. It turns the use values produced in the white mythologies of the civilizing process into exchange values that signify 'human-ness.' What is exchanged with the commodity, Pears' Soap, at the end of the nineteenth century is an imperialist consciousness: a subjective awareness on the part of imperial consumers that their superior place in the empire rests upon a non-human entity, the colonized Others, who can do no better, in the imperialist imagination, than secure their status as virtuous savage or exotic beauty.

The Pears' Soap advertisements constitute cultural artifacts. They are also part of the discourse of the commodity's symbolic production of meanings and values. The transition of the 'pictorial archive' from a storage house of cultural, national, and imperial artifacts to corporate-owned private warehouses of images foregrounds the already existing commodity potential of the archive in general. Archival usage of the Mansell Collection, presumably since 1840, has ensured its scholarly and journalistic values. With Time Inc.'s purchase of the collection, those values easily convert into the exchange space of pictorial information. In other words, we can already find within the nineteenth-century industrial pictorial archive the existence of processes of commodity valuation, already constitutive of an image/text/commodity matrix. Time Inc.'s acquisition of the Mansell Collection will no doubt bring new mechanisms of dispersion in information exchange into play.[12] It does appear, for example, that under the ownership of Time Inc. and their telecommunications system of dissemination and access, these images have an increased fetishistic quality, an independent existence; that they circulate freely, removed from labour and other body-relations, both with respect to the production of the images and the peoples depicted in them. The image in the age of telecommunication ownership introduces new techniques of power, governance, and states of domination.

In January 1997, Time Inc. announced in a press release on the Web their recent acquisition of the Mansell Collection, 'one of London's oldest and most respected picture libraries, containing over 1 million images and illustrations.' It also advertised the following information: 'The Time Inc. Picture Collection is an asset of Time Inc., America's largest magazine publisher and one of the world's largest book publishers. Time Inc. is a wholly owned subsidiary of Time Warner Inc., the world's leading media company' ('Time Inc. Acquires Mansell Collection,' press release, *Time Inc. and the Mansell Collection*). The press release is an interesting document for plotting the ever-increasing and cannibalizing tendencies of transnational capital expansion. Through a sequence of carefully constructed paragraphs, the reader is taken down a passageway that is like a walk through a corridor in an estate where pictures of family members and/or historical personalities hang on the wall. Each paragraph, each picture, frames a family portrait of the transnational enterprise, Time Inc. First we are introduced to the Mansell Collection:

> The Mansell Collection's photographs date from the beginnings of the medium in the 1840s through World War II, and include work by such famous photographers as E.O. Hoppe, Felix Bonfils, Francis Bedford, and Mathew Brady. The pictures depict a vast range of scenics, important news events, and historical personalities, with a special emphasis on art and architecture. In addition, the Collection includes extraordinary holdings of engraved illustrations, lithographs, and drawings predating the advent of photographic imaging.

Then we are introduced to the Time Inc. Picture Collection, in which the Mansell Collection will be 'integrated' like an adopted member of the family, its one million images incorporated into the larger population. The Time Inc. Picture Collection contains more than twenty-one million images, 'gathered from Time Inc.'s family of publications, including Time, Life, People, Sports Illustrated, Fortune and Time-Life Books.'

Although text-based publishing may be as outdated as the nuclear family, it is clearly still economically viable as a commercial enterprise, and 'the family' is still its best consumer, or the best metonymic for representing the proper consumer body and nation. In the year 2000 if you had clicked onto the '*LIFE* Gallery of Photography' on the Web, you would have found a series of categories: 'Great Photographers,' 'People,' 'Places,' 'Popular Culture,' 'Science,' 'Nature,' 'Sports,' 'War.' Next, click onto the 'Popular Culture Gallery,' where you would find a series of images. The first is 'Family Outing, Birmingham, Alabama, 1956,' by Ed Clark/LIFE, copyright Time Inc. The image is readily reminiscent of Quaker State Oil advertisements from the 1950s, with there depiction of the white family picnic that included, like this photo, white adults, white children, and that essential sign of familial bonding, the white and black dog, positioned against a backdrop of the central commodity reflex, in this case, a white car.[13]

The next image is that of a series on intersecting freeways, the 'Harbor, Hollywood, San Bernadino, Santa Ana and Pasadena Freeways, Los Angeles, 1959,' Ralph Crane/LIFE, copyright Time Inc. Anne McClintock writes of the road that 'for both communism and capitalism, progress was both a journey forward and the beginning of a return; for as in all narratives of progress, to travel the road of progress was to cover, once again, a road already travelled. The metaphor of the "road" or "railway" guaranteed that progress was a fait accompli. The journey was possible because the road had already been made (by God, the Dialectic, the Weltgeist, the Cunning of History, the Law of the Market, Scientific Materialism)' (McClintock 1995: 395). The great icon of American mobility and freedom, the 'freeway' is the way of transportation and commodity flows. The third image is of a metropolis, the great engine of consumer activity, the shops, the selling, the buying, the stealing, the everyday world of a future consumer paradise, a colony amidst a sea of waste and ugliness.

The proper body is also female. Time Inc. circulates within a 1950s feminine consumer culture, where the feminine codification of corporate and consumer relations is used in the reference to Time Inc.'s 'sister Time Warner companies.' The middle-class consumer body is still dominated by a feminine phantasmatic space that is always 'accessible,' fecund, nurturing, and endlessly reproductive: Beth Zarcone, director of the Picture Collection, is quoted as saying, 'The addition of the Mansell Collective opens up a whole new world of opportunities, including our ability to better help our editors and outside clients illustrate stories across all of human history and across global cultures.' The

missionary spirit of the capital enterprise knows no limit, the better to
care for the unrepresented, for all of human history and across global
cultures. The Foster Parent Plan of Time Inc. will nurture our pictorial
needs and collective fantasies of integration into the great circuitry and
simulacra of all corporations, CNN. And it will protect and guard the
images that have been put in its care with all the aggressiveness of the
mother-instinct. Incidentally, you cannot go and leisurely browse
through these images. The Mansell Collection is now part of an exclusive buyer's market; like the archive before it, with its aura of intellectual and scholarly exclusivity, the Time Inc. Picture Collection contains
valuable image-objects inaccessible to the general public. If you want a
particular image, or if you provide the workers at Time Life Syndica-
tion with a topic, they will research it for you. Whereas the Mansell
archive, although privately owned, regulated accessibility through an
implicit educational status, the Time Inc. Picture Collection, also privately owned, will regulate accessibility through the spatial networks
of telecommunications and corporate status: 'Many of the Mansell
images, along with the best of the Collection's current content, will
soon be accessible electronically through the company's state-of-the-art
on-line database system.'

In the privacy of the family, the virginal image is protected, just like
all female children, from the brutality and violence of baser instincts.
Corporations protect their products, through copyright, from the violent appropriations of other corporations, just like men protect their
wives and children from the violence, rape, and brutality of other men:
'George Anderson, the previous owner and I [Graham Howe] are
delighted that these extraordinarily rich works will now be under the
stewardship of Time Inc., with its long tradition of photojournalism
and respect for photography.' The press release is its own version of a
textually fetishized commodity form, where the images are anthropo-
morphized and given a family, a life of their own. Images become historical agents; they desire, dream, and do the work of capitalism. The
previously British-based Mansell Collection is a foster child in a much
larger set of kinship relations – the family, here, an alibi for the integrated circuit of transnational relations.

The last picture-paragraph in this small but ever-expanding corporate gallery is the one I quoted earlier: 'The Time Inc. Picture Collection
is an asset of Time Inc., America's largest magazine publisher and one
of the world's largest book publishers. Time Inc. is a wholly owned subsidiary of Time Warner Inc., the world's leading media company.' Following this worlding of Time Inc. is, perhaps not surprisingly, a

copyright notice: 'Photographs are available upon request. This press release includes copyright material; nevertheless, a limited license is granted to reproduce the available photographs or any portion of this press release in connection with the review or coverage of this event only.' For all the bliss this portrait provides with its nationalist nostalgia for the American nuclear family, transfigured into the united images of Time Inc., modelled, perhaps, on the all too familiar United Colors of Benetton, in the final instance we are dealing with a money-making enterprise, where images are commodities for sale or hire, where Time Inc. functions as a visual broker mediating transactional exchanges of memory, history, time, life, and people.

As a truth-making device for 'worlding' the significance of Time Inc., this press release is constitutive of an image/text/commodity matrix, a particular formation in the transcapital exchange of symbolic representation. Can we call these new image-warehouses archives, or are they stores that sell things, and that 'thing' happens to be a photograph or etching, with its only criterion for inclusion its pictorial value? If we have left the world of the 'scholarly archive' behind – which will put a lot of people, including academics, out of work – and we are now in the domain of a corporate-based pictorial informatics and the monetary exchange of visual knowledge, just what kind of image/text/commodity matrix is emerging? Who or what is being exploited, in whose interest and at what cost?

The image/text/commodity matrix is a complex configuration of overlapping, indeterminate, and interdependent historical relations and experiences. The symbolic production of the meanings and values contained and reproduced in advertising discourses is an important site of critical investigation within the commodity matrix, linked to commodity producers, trade routes of commodity exchange, and the history of economic, as well as military, ecological, libidinal, and territorial imperialisms. The discontinuities between the phantasmatic quality of commodity discourses and the gendered and racialized human relations and bodies depicted by them constitute arenas of contestation, commodification, and technologies of exclusion for the purposes of attempting to secure the hegemonic disposition to rule for the once British, and now American, bourgeoisie.

In the following chapter, Pat Barker's *Regeneration* trilogy marks a point of departure for critically examining how sexuality, gender, and the figure of Aboriginal Man were deployed at the turn of the century in order to recentre the crisis in English colonial and domestic rule, and, in particular, how this crisis was articulated in the gendered language about what it meant to be a 'man.' My interest in Barker's historical fiction is in how her trilogy makes it possible to question the historical narrative of European civilization, largely written without acknowledging its continuities and discontinuities with the colonies, and indigenous peoples especially. The early part of the twentieth century came with a wealth of ethnographic and psychoanalytical discourses that lie at the centre, and not the margins, of so-called European history. Barker's fictional trilogy makes this unwritten dimension of the multiplicities of modern British histories visible.

4 Post/Colonial Masculinities:
The Primitive Duality of 'ma, ma, man' in Pat Barker's *Regeneration* Trilogy

It was on the moral side, and in my own person, that I learned to recognize the thorough and primitive duality of man; I saw that, of the two natures that contended in the field of my consciousness, even if I could rightly be said to be either, it was only because I was radically both.

Robert Louis Stevenson, *The Strange Case of Dr. Jekyll and Mr. Hyde* (1886)

'I don't see you as a *father*, you know.' Looking up from the rug in front of the fire. Laughing. 'More a sort of ... *male mother*' ... Why should he remember that? ... He disliked the term 'male mother.' He thought he could remember disliking it even at the time. He distrusted the implication that nurturing, even when done by a man, remains female, as if the ability were in some way borrowed, or even stolen, from women – a sort of moral equivalent of the *couvade*. If that were true, then there was really very little hope.

Pat Barker, *Regeneration*

The words, 'ma, ma, man,' stutter across the page like one of Pat Barker's 'shell-shocked' characters in her *Regeneration* trilogy, a series of novels in which she explores the birth of a modern pathology, war neuroses, during the First World War. The series includes *Regeneration* (1991), *The Eye in the Door* (1993), and *The Ghost Road* (1995). When the patient with war neurosis stammers or stutters, it is as if the breakdown in his capacity for speech symptomatically mimics the fragmentation of the soldiering body, blown apart and dismembered in story after story about the atrocities of warfare. In his history of shell shock Anthony Babington remarks that a 'soldier soon becomes used to the sight of dead bodies, but he seldom grows accustomed to the sight of the hideously wounded' (Babington 1997: 51). To demonstrate his point, Babington tells the following anecdote: 'An orderly in a Causality Clearing Station described a man being carried in with his face covered by a bandage. "When the bandage was off," he said, "we saw the man had no eyes, no nose, no chin, no mouth – and he was alive." The doctor-in-charge told the orderly to give him four times the usual dose of morphine. This achieved the obvious intention and the man died' (Babington 1997: 51). The hideously wounded male body is an inarticulate body, one that cannot speak and one that must be removed from the sight of those for whom it represents an unspeakable event. Babington wrote his history of shell shock primarily because during the First World War several young men were court-martialled for cowardice and desertion, sentenced to death, and promptly executed. It was later revealed that many of these men had suffered from war neurosis and been sent back to the front. The military tribunals, however, did not acknowledge war neurosis, let alone the possibility of its recurrence under the repetitive strain of trench warfare. These men, too, were silenced. Like the rhetorical figure of the stutterer, the body in pain tries to articulate an experience that, as Elaine Scarry writes, 'half emerges into speech and then quickly recedes once more. Invisible in part because of its resistance to language, [the body in pain] is also invisible because its own powerfulness ensures its isolation, ensures that it will not be seen in the context of other events, that it will fall back from its new arrival in language and remain devastating. Its absolute claim for acknowledgment contributes to its being ultimately unacknowledged' (Scarry 1985: 60–1). Whether by military execution or mercy killing, silencing the power of the mutilated male body represents, as Scarry observes, a refusal to see it in the context of other events.

Barker's *Regeneration* trilogy, although based in real-life events and on some real-life persons, such as the psychotherapist and anthropologist W.H.R. Rivers, is a work of historical fiction and not a representative text of historical truth. This is an important point because of how Barker's novels bring into focus the play of feminine difference in the figures of the homosexual and the aboriginal. It is the circumstances of late twentieth-century new social movements, such as feminist, anti-imperialist, and pro-sex lesbian and gay movements, that make such interconnections possible; however, I would also argue that her novels, precisely because of their fictional dimension, make it possible to question the historical narrative itself and its own indebtedness to origin stories, such as those of heteronormative primitive man.

Barker's trilogy resituates the wounded male body in representational and historical contexts, ensuring that it will, indeed, be 'seen in the context of other events,' in at least two interesting ways. First, the trilogy focuses on gender formation, in particular the transformation of the meanings and values attributed to masculinity and male homosocial relations; second, it situates masculinity and male homosocial relations within the larger context of British imperialism and colonization. Of particular significance to the latter is the role Barker ascribes to the disciplinary knowledges of anthropology and psychiatry in providing counter-discourses to the violence and oppression experienced by British soldiers and gay men as a result of Britain's role in the imperial wars. It is primarily through the representation of masculinity and male relations that Barker's novels give voice to a wounded European male body. These relations, which include psychiatrist and patient in the treatment of war neuroses, and anthropologist and Native informant in the colonial context of Melanesia, are organized around a series of underlying assumptions about homosexuality, the figure of Aboriginal Man, and British colonial and domestic modes of governance and authority. While other literary critics have explored questions of masculinity and war in Barker's novels, this discussion focuses on the multiplicities of masculinities articulated through and by various discursive regimes (see Harris 1998), including British imperialism and colonialism.

Barker's anthropological excavation of the British male subject deploys the figure of Aboriginal Man as Universal Man's significant Other. As we've seen in the previous two chapters, this figure occupied a significant role in securing bourgeois masculinity, its gender and sexuality, through the opposition of civilization and savagery. The following section examines the discourse of masculinity in an effort to bring to the fore some of the contradictions of current collusions and mobilizations of cultural difference.

The Critical Discourse on 'Masculinity'

Barker's novels engage in an historical transposition. They revisit the early twentieth century through the current lens of masculinity studies and, in so doing, reconstruct a history of gender and war. Barker's trilogy is indebted to many historical and literary sources, which she faithfully acknowledges in a postscript to each novel. Elaine Showalter's chapter 'Male Hysteria: W.H.R. Rivers and the Lessons of Shellshock,' in her book *The Female Malady: Women, Madness, and English Culture, 1830–1930*, is a particularly relevant citation. Much of what Showalter discusses and alludes to in her chapter finds its way into Barker's creative representation, notably, the considerable attention to the case of Siegfried Sassoon, the electroshock therapies of Lewis R. Yealland, and the figure of W.H.R. Rivers.

Regeneration retells the story of the wartime poet Siegfried Sassoon, a real-life literary figure who protested the continuance of the war.[1] Barker begins the novel by quoting the full text of Sassoon's letter of protest, dated July 1917. It contains the following contentious words: 'I am making this statement as an act of wilful defiance of military authority, because I believe the war is being deliberately prolonged by those who have the power to end it ... I believe that this war, upon which I entered as a war of defense and liberation, has now become a war of aggression and conquest ... I have seen and endured the suffering of the troops, and I can no longer be a party to prolong these sufferings for ends which I believe to be evil and unjust. I am not protesting against the conduct of the war, but against the political errors and insincerities for which the fighting men are being sacrificed' (Barker 1991: 3). Although the military establishment ignored the medical discourse on war neuroses in court-martialling offenders for cowardice and desertion, in the real-life case of Sassoon, 'shell shock' was used strategically on the part of his friend Robert Graves to avoid court martial for other reasons. Against his wishes, Sassoon was brought up in front of a Special Medical Board instead of a military tribunal. Graves used his influence to have Sassoon sent to the military asylum Craiglockhart in Scotland and placed in the care of a Dr W.H.R. Rivers, FRS (1864–1922), a renowned anthropologist and psychoanalyst.[2]

According to Joanna Bourke, the First World War clearly represents a break with previous ideas about manliness and the emergence of a modern conception of 'masculinity' (Bourke 1996). The discourse on masculinity and war is sometimes couched in terms of loss or a sense of lack. In *Masculinities and Identities*, David Buchbinder characterizes the significance of the First World War to changing conceptions of masculinity in terms of a loss of traditional masculinity. 'World War I (1914–18) was a major blow to the traditional imagery of war as heroic, glorious and especially as befitting young men. During this Great War, more young men died than in any previous war, and a generation of potentially brilliant writers, thinkers, and scientists was grievously decimated. War, as fought in the trenches in the driving rain or snow of a European winter, was inglorious and dehumanizing; mustard gas and other kinds of chemical warfare cut at the very heart of the idea of a chivalrous enemy whom one could see and with whom one could fight directly, as, indeed, also did the development of the submarine and the Zeppelin. In addition, the new phenomenon of shell-shock left men witless, amnesiac, nervous, prone to break down at the least noise or stress' (Buchbinder 1994: 9). Buchbinder's reduction of 'shell shock' to a form of silly feminine nervousness, combined with his lament for the loss of that 'generation of potentially brilliant writers, thinkers, and scientists,' betrays his nostalgia for the Victorian ideal of the white, bourgeois, male hero. This loss of the heroic ideal is, of course, the loss of the colonial adventurer who finds his place in the nineteenth-century imperial wars and restores his masculine prowess in colonial governance (Rutherford 1997). He is a figure caught in the web of that vast geopolitical imaginary of imperial conquest, with its narratives of freedom and escape from the restrictions and tiresome self-regulatory practices of bourgeois family life.

Where Buchbinder implicates the domestic sphere in his critique of masculinity, Showalter explicitly links her critique to Victorian domesticity. She argues that war neuroses were 'femininized' forms of illness because the medical analysis of the condition was based primarily on theories of 'female hysteria.' She concludes that 'these accounts of male hysteria – a rare phenomenon – suggest that it is a feminine kind of behavior in male subjects. And this feminine aspect is a recurrent theme in the discussion of war neuroses. When military doctors and psychiatrists dismissed shell-shock patients as cowards, they were often hinting at effeminacy or homosexuality. Karl Abraham, a hard-line Freudian, was one who argued that war neurotics were passive, narcissistic, and impotent men to begin with, whose latent homosexuality was brought to the surface by the all-male environment' (Showalter 1985: 172). Showalter's critical assessment of shell shock is framed almost exclusively in relation to an ideology of femininity and the history of a psychoanalytic modernism grounded in the female body and experience of domesticity. For example, Showalter cites favourably Susan Gilbert's 1983 essay 'Soldier's Heart: Literary Men, Literary Women, and the Great War,' in which Gilbert makes the analogy between the constriction of the trenches and the tight domestic, vocational, and sexual spaces allotted to nineteenth-century women: 'paradoxially, in fact, the war to which so many men had gone in hope of becoming heroes, ended up emasculating them ... confining them as closely as any Victorian Woman had been confined' (as quoted in Showalter 1985: 173–4).

As part of an emerging feminist discourse on masculinity and the representation of homosocial relations, Gilbert's and Showalter's analyses ran the risk of reproducing a representation of masculinity that was 'non-male,' one whose use was only to be found in a recentring of bourgeois femininity and an imperial conception of female experience. Showalter's primary focus is on the distribution of gender in the psychiatric medicalization of the female body, the restrictiveness of femininity, and bourgeois women's resistance to it. By analogy she argues that 'if the essence of maniliness was not to complain, then shell-shock was the body language of masculine complaint, a disguised male protest not only against the war but against the concept of "manliness" itself' (Showalter 1985: 172). Equally problematic, here, is Showalter's representation of gender as an autonomous site of resistance disconnected from other relations of power and domination. Lynne Segal provides an excellent model for the feminist study of masculinities in her book *Slow Motion*, where she examines the differences between masculinities in the nineteenth and twentieth centuries, the emergence of common-sense perceptions of masculinity, and the competing definitions that threatened to undo those perceptions. She explores, for example, the rise of the 'ideal Victorian male,' with its 'increasing glorification of a more muscular, militaristic masculinity in alliance with British imperialist expansion in the late Victorian era' (Segal 1990: 106–7). She also examines the regulatory practices designed to contain and fix the meaning of homosexuality and the racialized inscriptions of savagery and animalistic passions in the image of the 'white man's black man.' Thus, any attempt to construct a genealogy of masculinity must map out a complex web of contested and conflicting meanings interrelated with several axes of power and discourse that cut across the categories of 'race,' class, gender, and sexuality. Furthermore, this genealogy must attend to the historical conditions of emergence in order to make visible, for example, the ways in which masculine gender and sexuality were *mobilized* at the turn of the twentieth century to bring into existence a new form of individuality for middle-class English white men.

Eve Kosofsky Sedgwick observes that at the turn of the century 'both the power relations between the genders and the relations of nationalism and imperialism, *for instance*, were in highly visible crisis' (Sedgwick 1990: 2; emphasis added). She goes on to insist that under patriarchal conditions or 'inequality and contest between genders,' same-sex bonds cannot 'fail to be a site of intensive regulation that intersects virtually every issue of power and gender.' A shift in sexual discourse, Sedgwick continues, cannot be circumscribed 'within some proper domain of sexuality (whatever that might be),' reduced or contained, in other words, by sexuality itself. Taking as axiomatic Foucault's hypothesis that sexuality is a distinctively privileged discourse in the construction of individuality, its truth, knowledge, and identity, Sedgwick argues that 'it becomes truer and truer that the language of sexuality not only intersects with but transforms the other languages and relations by which we know' (Sedgwick 1990: 2–3). Thus, for Sedgwick, gender relations, nationalism, and imperialism represent particular sites of intersection and transformation, as well as contested and formative discourses, at this particular historical moment. In fact, discourses of masculine gender and sexuality were deployed at the turn of the century in order to maintain the hegemonic equilibrium of state power, to secure national, military, and imperial dominance, and to counteract, if not dissipate, the rise of an anti-war and anti-imperialist politics. The emergence of a new subject, truth, and knowledge of individuality was clearly masculine and imperial in its construction.

Questions of imperialism, decolonization, homosexuality, and homosociality represent key areas of power, domination, and resistance that make up this early twentieth-century genealogy of 'Man.' More than what Showalter called its 'trial of the Victorian masculine ideal,' this genealogy of Man is about the regulation of sexual and national, as well as gender, differences. It traces an intricate web of intersecting and interlocking determinations that figure in the precarious struggles of the bourgeoisie to maintain an equilibrium of power and control, and to do so especially within the bourgeois family, its heteronormative and heterosexual values and practices as well as parent-child relations, and in the public institutions of schooling, the state, and colonial modes of governance.[3]

Conceptions of masculinity, femininity, homosexuality, heterosexuality, and parentism were deployed in uneven and unequal ways precisely to secure the hegemony of the bourgeois Oedipal family and its representation as socially normal and, therefore, natural. The masculine gender and heterosexuality that emerged with this hegemony of the bourgeois family was quite useful in dealing with the crisis of nationalism and imperialism at the turn of the century. Whereas in the nineteenth century the patriarchal dominance of the father secured the rule of the bourgeois family, at the turn of the century a heterosexist patriarchal regime of power, with its specific ideal of civilized Universal Man, was deployed in the context of state power both to negotiate the rationality of violence needed to mount the war and to extend and perpetuate the war itself.

Masculinity, then, was not simply about men and their identity, lost, resistant, or otherwise. It was about maintaining national power and formulating the rationality needed to combat a growing resistance on the part of those experiencing the horror and irrationality of war. Masculinity, its gender formation and interlocking sexual practices, was deployed to manage the crisis of the war, resulting in a great deal of representational violence done to perceptions of maleness, homosociality, and homosexual relations. Homosexuality, for instance, was framed by the limits of a feminine passivity, powerlessness, and weakness, or its obverse, a brute and irrational sadism. In the colonies, masculinity also became essential to the rationalization of imperialist and patriarchal modes of governance. The feminist historian Mrinalini Sinha argues, for example, that the feminizing as well as infantilizing of Bengali men were central to colonial rule (Sinha 1995). As gender identity, masculinity became the code of fraternal relations needed to maintain patriarchal complicities and powers of domination on many 'domestic' fronts – at home, in the colonies, and among European nation states, including what came to be known as the 'alliance [read: fraternal] system,' often regarded as the cause of the First World War.[4]

Gendered Violence and Aboriginality

The title of the first novel, *Regeneration*, is meant to signal the scientific experiments carried out by Rivers and his colleague Henry Head on the regeneration of nerve endings. These experiments involved severing and then suturing the nerve supply to Head's left forearm. Like modern-day Frankensteins, Rivers and Head put Head's body back together, not at the level of joints, bone, and muscle, but at the site of the body's inner workings, its nerves, its mental as much as its physical properties. The regeneration of nerves, the physical suturing together of severed threads, serves as a metonym for the lost body of man, his self and identity, the victim of war neuroses who has apparently 'lost his nerve.' Freudian therapy, the talking cure, will suture his mind back together again and regenerate the meaning of his life, identity, and experience.

In a pivotal passage in *The Eye in the Door*, Rivers explains the nerve regeneration process, which had taken place in two phases:

> The first was characterized by a high threshold of sensation, though when the sensation was finally evoked it was, to use Head's own word, 'extreme.' In addition to this all-or-nothing quality, the sensation was diffi-cult to localize. Sitting blindfold at the table, Head had been unable to locate the stimulus that was causing him such severe pain. This primitive form of innervation they called the protopathic. The second phase of regeneration –which they called the epicritic – followed some months later, and was characterized by the ability to make graduated responses and to locate the source of a stimulus precisely, as the epicritic level of innervation was restored, the lower, or protopathic, level was partially integrated with it and partially suppressed, so that the epicritic system carried out two functions: one, to help the organism adapt to its environ-ment by supplying it with accurate information; the other, to suppress the protopathic, to keep the animal within leashed. Inevitably, as time went on, both words had acquired broader meanings, so that 'epicritic' came to stand for everything rational, ordered, cerebral, objective, while 'proto-pathic' referred to the emotional, the sensual, the chaotic, the primitive. In this way the experiment both reflected Rivers's internal divisions and sup-plied him with a vocabulary in which to express them. (Barker 1993: 142)

I quote this passage at length because it is key to unlocking 'the eye in the door,' focusing, as it does, on self-inflicted pain as a metonym for the self-regulation of pain, violence, and terror and an internalization of the panoptic gaze, essential to the regulating and normalizing of civi-lized man. Not only does the scientific experiment reflect the dualism that sustains a bourgeois masculine ideal of civilization, but it is also a spur to reconciling the competing aspects of the divided imperial male subject.

Rivers's internal divisions are represented through the anthropologi-cal rationality of cultural relativism: 'He looked up, at the blue, empty sky, and realized that their view of *his* society was neither more nor less valid than his of theirs. No bearded elderly white man looked down on them, endorsing one set of values and condemning the other. And with that realization, the whole frame of social and moral rules that keeps individuals imprisoned – and sane – collapsed, and for a while he was in the same position as these drifting, dispossessed people' (Barker 1995: 118). The freedom narrative associated with a nomadic way of life, without possessions, without boundaries or borders, without the restrictions and regulations of family and state, must also be free of the 'bearded elderly white man,' the father who governs, rationalizes, and regulates bourgeois family, institutional, religious, and state life. In the colonies, however, this figure is hardly non-existent: 'Look, you know what the penalities are,' says Rivers to his co-fieldworker, Hocart. 'If they [Njiru's people] go on a [headhunting] raid there's no way the British Commissioner isn't going to hear about it. And then you've got a gunboat off the coast, villages on fire, trees cut down, crops destroyed, pigs killed. Screaming women and children driven into the bush. You *know* what happens. "Makes you proud to be British, doesn't it?" "No," Tight-lipped. "Good. When these people were taking heads they virtually depopulated Ysabel. It *had* to be stopped"' (Barker 1995: 185–6).

Rivers and his colleague are concerned about an illegal headhunting operation, since the chief has died and as a result his widow has been placed in a sort of cage from which she can be released only by the taking of a head. A male child is taken into captivity and there is an unspoken assumption that it is this child's head that will be offered up in sacrifice. Barker juxtaposes Rivers account of the tensions fulminating over the restrictions on headhunting and a possible transgression of British law with that of an officer, Billy Prior, and his image of a decapitated head taken from the Western European tradition: 'And I started thinking – there's a lot of time to think on marches – about Father Mackenzie's church, the huge shadowy crucifix on the rood screen dominating everything, a sheaf of holly hocks lying in the chancel waiting to be arranged, their long stems scrawling wet across the floor. And behind every altar, blood, torture, death. St John's head on a platter, Salome offering it to Herodias, the women's white arms a sort of cage around the severed head with its glazed eyes' (Barker 1995: 176). These headhunting images culminate in the final depiction of a soldier named Hallet and his fatal head injury. Prior writes in his diary:

We fell into the trench, Hallet on top of us. I got something damp on my face that wasn't mud, and brushing it away found a gob of Hallet's brain between my fingertips. Because he'd gone quiet on the last stretch I expected to find him unconscious or dead, but he was neither. I gave him a drink of water. I had to press my hand against his face to get it down, because otherwise it slopped out of the hole. And all the time I was doing it I was thinking, Die can't you? For God's sake, man, just *die*. But he didn't. (Barker 1995: 197)

Eventually Hallet is sent to the London hospital where Rivers works. Like the mercy killing by the doctor retold by Babington, dealing with such violence and dismemberment would seem to demand what Rivers calls a 'suspension of empathy.' And yet, Rivers reflects, 'The same suspension of empathy that was so necessary a part of the physician's task was also, in other contexts, the root of all monstrosity. Not merely the soldier, but the torturer also, practices the same suspension' (Barker 1993: 164). Rivers cannot maintain this form of dissociation at the conclusion of the novel with Hallet. Before he dies in the hospital, Hallet desperately tries to articulate something that no one in his family seems to be able to understand: '"*Shotvarfet, Shotvarfet*"' (Barker 1995: 274). He dies of his own accord, but not after Rivers understands the fragments of sound to mean 'it's not worth it.' In a state of half-dreaming, half-awakening, Rivers hears Njiru repeating the words of the exorcism of Ave, the destroyer of peoples. Njiru appears with the words: '*There is an end of men, an end of chiefs, an end of chieftains' wives, an end of chiefs' children – then go down and depart. Do not yearn for us, the fingerless, the crippled, the broken. Go down and depart, oh, oh, oh*' (Barker 1995: 276). In other words, do not desire your own disfiguration and put an end to the culture of dismemberment, and the rationalities of violence that sustain it.

The kidnapped boy in Melanesia is not decapitated but given the job of becoming the keeper of the skulls. The ghosts, all the ghosts of the lost boys of empire, are stuck in never-never land, a no-man's-land of phantoms and memories that can only be restored by children's fictions like *Peter Pan*. These ghosts are also the ones contained in the skull houses of the headhunters, a phantasmatic display of death matched only by the image of the savagery of European wars: Hallet's skull seeping its life from a hole in his head.

In retelling this aspect of Barker's novel, I want to situate her use of the figure of Aboriginal Man, which she uses to construct a fraternal relationship between Njiru and Rivers, thus providing an instance of colonial homosociality that is highly problematic.

In *The Ghost Road*, Barker turns from an exploration of the making of wounded male bodies to their recovery and healing. Through the mutual recognition of their physical deformations, male bonding occurs, between Rivers and his patient Billy Prior, an officer from a working-class background who has internalized an abject image of himself as a brutish creature capable only of animalistic passions and violence, and between the anthropologist Rivers and his Native informant, the shaman Njiru, a member of a headhunting tribe whose activities were banned by the British government (Barker 1995: 185). For Rivers, the wound occurred in his childhood, when his father gave him a lesson in manhood, teaching him that it is unacceptable to cry in the face of horror and pain. Njiru's body is physically deformed, and his deformation signifies physical pain and wounding. Rivers rediscovers his wounded body through the memory-scape of his fieldwork in Melanesia, where he shares an intense experience of fear and terror with Njiru when a huge mass of bats collectively fly over them in the confined space of a cave. Rivers is reborn in this shared experience of nature's terror with Njiru, an event that becomes the possibility of transformation. Michael Taussig writes that the 'space of death is preeminently a space of transformation ... through the experience of coming close to death there well may be a more vivid sense of life; through fear there can come not only a growth in self-consciousness but also fragmentation, then loss of self conforming to authority ...' (Taussig 1987: 7). The friendship between Rivers and Njiru is established through the mutual recognition of their wounded bodies. But more than the physical manifestation of a wounded body is the history of British imperialism and its use of force to destroy the real practice of headhunting. At different levels of patriarchal governance in the family, colony, and Empire, man's body is subjected to the rule of the White Father.

On a metaphorical level, the headhunter Njiru is the primitive legacy of Rivers the modern-day headhunter, the psychiatrist. The figure of the primitive made it possible to construct a new totality of Civilized Man, a composite figure made up anatomical elements and sensorial experiences as in Rivers's and Head's nerve-regeneration experiments. This composite figure combined the ambiguous sensations and pleasures that ranged from the exoticism of romance, travel, and exploration to the terror, sadism, and ethnographic pornography of colonial violence. Textual practices from scientific treatises to popular literature created new ways of organizing people and knowledges under the category of 'primitive,' be they working-class, homosexual, indigenous, or colonialized subjects. It was especially the case that primitivism became fundamental to the identity of the bourgeois male individual and intersected with that other great fictitious unity of the nineteenth century outlined by Foucault, 'sex.' (Foucault 1978). Thus, the representational violence of aboriginality came to occupy a significant place in the discourse of masculinity and the meaning of manliness. The homosexual, Foucault writes, became a type, almost a 'species' (Foucault 1978: 139). So, too, did the Aboriginal, and perhaps even more so.

Crucial to these fictitious unities of 'sex' and 'aboriginality' is how a certain reversal takes place in which these ideas, initially created from a variety of phenomena, then come to be seen as the very *cause* of those phenomena. Thus, while primitivism is defined, for example, by British colonial discourses on headhunting or Rivers's notion of the proto-pathic composed of 'the emotional, the sensual, the chaotic, the primitive,' aboriginality eventually comes to be seen as the very cause of such violent, savage, and uncivilized behaviour. In other words, the roots of Prior's 'warrior double' or Rivers's 'suspension of empathy' are seen as the cause of something identified as primitive, something that, in the end, must be recognized as part of the meaning of being a man – a civilized man, that is. Barker attempts to counteract the violence of primitivism that threatens the basis of colonial male relations by creating a fraternal bond between Rivers and Njiru through this link of the 'ma, ma, man.' Significantly, Rivers also stutters. He, too, is a 'ma, ma, man,' portrayed, not as an authority figure, but as a nurturer, a sort of surrogate victim wounded by a sadistic father. The fact remains, however, that this exploration of fraternal relations takes place in the larger context of British colonialism and imperialism and its different effects on male and female indigenous bodies.

The fraternity between Rivers and Njiru, while cause for celebration in the context of European liberalism, also brings into question male colonial/indigenous relations, how they are established across patriarchal and heterosexual lines of power, and the kinds of complicities in the oppression of women that result from such alliances. For example, in his genealogical research, Rivers runs into a huge problem with his Native informant Rinambesi, the oldest man on the island and, thus, the best resource for recording the islanders' genealogies. He is, however, subject to a taboo, explained in the following terms:

Sexual intercourse between unmarried young people was very free, though 'free' was perhaps the wrong word, since every act had to be preceded by a payment of shells by the young man to the girl's parents. After marriage complete fidelity was required, and one expression of this was that one must never utter the name of an ex-lover.

All the women's names in Rinambesi's generation had to be left blank. Looking at the row of cards in front of him, Rivers turned to Njiru. 'This fellow make fuck-fuck *all* women?'

A gleam of amusement. 'Yes.'

Rivers threw the pencil down. Rinambesi, grinning toothlessly, was making a deeply unsuccessful attempt to look modest. Rivers started to laugh and after a moment Njiru joined in, a curious moment of kinship across the gulf of culture. (Barker 1995: 129–30)

A playful allusion to masculine prowess; and yet, female bodies suture the gap of that seemingly unbridgeable instance of cultural difference.

The Ritual Effacement of Man

At the conclusion to *The Order of Things*, Foucault impresses on the reader's mind an image of the dissolution of Man: 'Man,' he writes, 'is an invention easily shown by the archaeology of our thought to be of recent date. And whose end is, perhaps, nigh ... We can readily wager that man will be effaced, like a face traced in the sand at the edge of the sea' (as quoted in Macey 1993: 169).[5] Barker's novels situate the dissolution of Man in close proximity to the threat or existence of physical and psychological dismemberment. A genealogy of Man must include these forms of violent dismemberment as well as the knowledges and reasoning about violence – the basis of a 'violent reason' that organizes and divides subjects into savage and civilized categories.

According to Elaine Showalter, 'shell shock' represents a conflict between instinct and reason. It is 'an emotional disturbance produced by warfare itself, by chronic conditions of fear, tension, horror, disgust, and grief'; war neurosis was 'an escape from an intolerable situation,' a compromise negotiated by the psyche between the instinct of self-pres-ervation and the prohibitions against deception or flight, which were 'rendered impossible by ideals of duty, patriotism, and honor' (Show-alter 1985: 170). This constellation of 'ideals' – not to mention the added fear of courtmartial for desertion and possible execution as a result – belonged to a general mode of rationality deployed to render the subal-tern body susceptible to the violence of new military technologies such as the machine gun and chemicals, and fragile in its capacity to resist the forces and powers that would discipline it to stay put.

Constitutive to this disciplining of the soldiering body was the figure of Universal Man, a figure of plenitude, of a whole body and the fullness of speech, language, and meaning. At the turn of the century, this ideal figure was not without his significant Other, the figure of Aboriginal Man or the savage, sometimes noble, more often brutal and uncivilized. The most striking example of this Universal/Primitive split male subject is to be found in Robert Louis Stevenson's *The Strange Case of Dr. Jekyll and Mr. Hyde*. A diverse set of discursive practices at the turn of the century contributed to the emergence of this divided Man. When Burroughs writes of Tarzan, 'He was a M-A-N, they were A-P-E-S,' we immediately identify the evolutionary narrative of humankind's progress that bolstered man's sense of his essential difference and superiority from other species (Burroughs 1912: 39). Darwin's scientific theories of evolution and psychoanalytical texts such as Richard von Krafft-Ebing's *Pyschopathia Sexualis*, along with the prodigious output of ethnographies and anthropological monographs during the nineteenth century, collectively constituted a representation of Universal Man and his significant Primitive Other. Legislative documents such as Canada's Indian Act of 1876 and other acts of colonial policy are similarly significant, in that they produced a range of distinctions and discriminations between status and non-status, Indian men and women, Métis and Indian, and so on and so forth. If Krafft-Ebing's *Pyschopathia Sexualis* was responsible for institutionalizing and legalizing the identity of the homosexual, the Indian Act can also be said to have institutionalized a bureaucratic, government-sanctioned, and legal identity of 'the Indian' – ironically, although perhaps not incidentally, at a time when Edward Curtis's famous photograph proclaimed a 'Vanishing Race.' In colonial policies, the European metaphor of Universal Man and his significant Other impacted on the realities of indigenous people as colonial men attempted to secure alliances with indigenous men by regulating Indian women's lives through the imposition of a European biopolitics of racist, patriarchal, and heterosexual gender norms.

The figure of Universal Man in this colonial *dispositif* underscored the dominance of bourgeois male governance at home and in the colonies. Ironically, however, these same works also documented the dissolution of this figure. Whether it was an evolutionary tale of human progress, the invention of 'the human race' or an 'unconscious,' or the myth of Primitive Man as the root of European civilization, these rhetorical 'missing links' made it impossible for Universal Man to continue to thrive in the singularity and uniqueness of a bourgeois ideology of masculine individualism, structured on such hidden oppositions as man and animal, colonizer and colonized, neurotic and savage.

In her trilogy, Barker creates a fractured space of masculine identity. Her narrative technique, a form of *narrative dissociation*, breaks down the very meaning of Universal Man, as conventional boundaries between narrative voice and character consciousness, between psychiatrist and patient, become increasingly fluid and mutually interrelated. In the place of Universal Man, and out of the images of mutilated bodies, fragmented experiences, and broken language, emerges a complex masculine identity, one with a history, a gender, a sex, a class, a religion, a nation, and a mother. By focusing on the question of masculinity, Barker's trilogy represents a radical departure from what was once an identifiable body of 'women's writing,' including her own previous novels such as *Union Street* and *Blow Your House Down*.[6] Her central characters are men, and her thematic interest in masculinity and war is very different from, say, Virginia Woolf's critical work *Three Guineas* (1938), her novel *Mrs. Dalloway* (1925), or Rebecca West's *The Return of the Soldier* (1918). In another sense, then, her novels also fracture the supposedly unified space of gender identity, representation, and authorship. And yet, surprisingly, these texts are entirely relevant to a feminist decolonial criticism, to unravelling the threads that make up this turn-of-the-century tapestry of violence, gender, rationality, and the ends of Man. Any discussion of Barker's trilogy must attend to the discontinuous, and yet mutually contingent, practices of gender formation, sexuality, and colonialism through a critical examination of the discourse of 'masculinity' and its significance to the rationality of violence, aboriginality, and national power that prevailed in the early twentieth century.

Masculinity was part of a colonial grid of intelligibility and the apparatuses of power working to secure Britain's national, militaristic, and imperial dominance at the turn of the century. Interestingly, it was in the very structure of a discontinuity, a break with the figure of 'Universal Man,' that the notion of a 'masculine identity' emerged, holding out the possibility of a view of male subjectivity that was non-sovereign and non-imperial. Yet, at the moment of its birth, the masculine individual was deployed as part of a new rationality and truth on the necessity of state violence, of national, domestic, and colonial powers. Primitivism became the causal link suturing together violence, sadism, and masculinity.

The dream of the plenitude of the father's body and his return (Captain James Cook, for example) was replaced by the dream of fraternity, alliances between men whose relations were falsely viewed across cultures and time as the kinship equivalent of a shared social contract. Taussig puts its brilliantly in his discussion of the economy of terror in the Putumayo when he writes: 'I do not understand the power the traders had over the Indians. Most everything said on this topic is saturated with fantasy and wildly contradictory to boot. On the one hand is the strident emphasis on conquest as the ultimate sweaty *macho* affirmation of civilization unfurled on the frontier, penetrating the wild. On the other hand is a quite contrary picture, that of a sort of social contract between like-minded traders, Indians, and whites, complementing each other's needs in the fastness of the forest, docile Indians and maternal, nurturing white men' (Taussig 1987: 24). Taussig ably puts into play the split-gendering of colonial governance, the split between masculine and feminine or civilized and domestic scenes of regulation and control, the one through brute force, the other through an ideology of benevolent parenting. The limits of 'ma, ma, man,' then, must also be circumscribed by this colonial rationality of violence, in which the sadistic father and male nurturer are viewed as flip sides of the same coin, part of a genealogy of masculinity deployed to intervene at the site of colonial relations of governance among men. A genealogy of Man must include the range of institutional practices from psychiatric medicine to anthropological fieldwork, from popular culture to visual and literary culture, that gave meaning and shape to those complicitous homosocial relations as the final acceptance of so-called civilized man's ab/original duality.

5 The Family in the Age of Mechanical Reproduction: Aboriginality in the Photographic Archive

[The archive] deprives us of our continuities; it dissipates that temporal identity in which we are pleased to look at ourselves when we wish to exorcise the discontinuities of history; it breaks the thread of transcendental teleologies; and where anthropological thought once questioned man's being or subjectivity, it now bursts open the other, and the outside. In this sense, the diagnosis does not establish the fact of our identity by the play of distinctions. It establishes that we are difference, that our reason is the difference of discourses, our history the difference of times, our selves the difference of masks. That difference, far from being the forgotten and recovered origin, is this dispersion that we are and make.

Michel Foucault, *The Archaeology of Knowledge*

Like other biographical texts, the photographic family album tells a story, a narrative of familial and familiar relations, of filiations that blend and develop over time, that start off small and grow bigger and bigger with each passing day, year, and generation. The family portrait is sometimes the product of a formal event, a holiday, a staged production in the studio, an accident of time and place, and other moments that are made to stand for one's auto-visual-biography. The images themselves are framed by the formal limits of the eye of the camera and then reframed by how they are situated in relation to other images and texts, or to the places in which they are located or found. Further to the formal frame of the photograph and its material location are the sociohistorical contexts which, writes Mieke Bal, 'limit the possible meanings' of the image – the meanings that emerge in the act of reading and spill out chaotically and randomly onto the page (Bal 1996: x). The family album is a particular visual frame of representation and the subject of Jo Spence and Patricia Holland's edited volume *Family Snaps: The Meaning of Domestic Photography*. This important book in photographic studies stages the instability of meaning in the family album by compiling a series of essays, interventions, and explorations that denaturalize the formal and contextual assumptions that create and re-create this seemingly transparent and innocent genre. The book stages various acts of *reframing* in order to rupture the family portrait out of its apparent coherency, its predictability and familiarity. As Holland writes in her introduction, 'Blurring the boundaries between personal reminiscence, cultural comment and social history, paying attention to the overlap between history and fantasy, using popular entertainment, reading official histories between the lines and against the grain, these exploratory styles fit easily with the *bricolage* and loose ends of the family album' (Spence and Holland 1991: 9). The family album is perhaps not as secure a site of meaning as we would like to believe. Throughout the family album, the spectator is confronted by the familiarity of faces and names but their unmistakable differences as well. The chatter, the noise, and the conversations around the images sometimes contradict memories and experiences. Uneasiness and ambivalence rise up as one tries to align subjective memory with the exterior image and stabilize the relationship between meaning and event; thus the spectator is confronted with the difficulty of keeping still the significance of the image even if it remains so on the page. Sometimes the image becomes dislocated, even lost, but leaves its shadow-mark nevertheless. Resistance erupts within the family album's disposition of truth.

In an autobiographical sketch titled 'Biography of a Dress,' the Carribean-American writer Jamaica Kincaid tells a story about a yellow smocked dress that was made by her mother for her second birthday. More importantly, the dress was made because Kincaid's mother wanted to have her photographed in this dress for her birthday. One of the meanings attributed to the dress by Kincaid's mother lay in its value for this photographic representation. For Kincaid, however, the dress signals a painful memory and the realization that her mother was trying to reconstruct an image of Jamaica as a white child. This is how Kincaid remembers the experience:

My skin was not the colour of cream in the process of spoiling, my hair was not the texture of silk and the colour of flax, my eyes did not gleam like blue jewels in a crown, the afternoons in which I sat watching my mother make me this dress were not cool, and verdant lawns and pastures and hills and dales did not stretch out before me; but it was the picture of such a girl at two years old – a girl whose skin was the colour of cream in the process of spoiling, whose hair was the texture of silk and the colour of flax, a girl whose eyes gleamed like blue jewels in a crown, a girl whose afternoons (and mornings and nights) were cool, and before whom stretched verdant lawns and pastures and hills and dales – that my mother saw, a picture on an almanac advertising a particularly fine and scented soap (a soap she could not afford to buy then but I can now), and this picture of this girl wearing a yellow dress with smocking on the front bodice perhaps created in my mother the desire to have a daughter who looked like that or perhaps created the desire in my mother to try and make the daughter she already had look like that. (Kincaid 1992: 96–7).

The image of a white, blond, and blue-eyed girl in an advertising image powerfully shaped the meaning of being female, feminine, and civilized for Kincaid's mother. Kincaid's narrative elaborates the meanings of femininity, not only in a gendered inscriptional space connected to the world of appearances, clothing, and hygiene, but in a racialized inscriptional space in which the body, the colour of skin, hair, eyes, and even the beauty of natural scenery are also seen to be part of the meanings attributed to a European and colonial definition of civilization and white femininity. It is interesting that Kincaid calls this story 'Biography of a Dress' and not, for example, 'Autobiography of Her Second Birthday.' The emphasis on the dress and the advertising image draws attention to the object of the gaze, and not the subject, or the person looking. It is as if Kincaid is remembering the way in which her child's body was being treated by her mother, as if it were an object too, something that could be or should be changed like a dress.

Origin stories in the discourse of fashion assume that skin colour and clothing belong equally to the world of appearances; to be fashionable, feminine, and hence female is to be able to transform oneself into a white, middle-class woman. Even critical books on fashion assume that body painting and tattooing are original instances of 'fashion,' as examples of 'bodily adornment.' *Adorned in Dreams: Fashion and Modernity* begins with a sixteenth-century watercolour of a Native-American woman by the British painter John White, titled *A Woman of Florida* (Wilson 1985: 4). This representation of an indigenous woman is underscored by the caption 'The widespread human desire to change the human body: in this case by body painting or tattooing' (Wilson 1985:

5). Skin is prefigured as clothing and as a site of exhibition and display. In the figure of the white, middle-class woman, however, the colour of her skin remains transparent. It is the Other skin colours that are marked and re-marked upon as 'like' an article of clothing. Kincaid foregrounds this chromatic inversion by placing the emphasis on the yellow dress, the object of her subjective experience. Kincaid's 'Biography of a Dress' is a *petit récit* that disrupts the colonial gaze and its phantasmatic production of aboriginal female difference. Kincaid's text is published with the photograph in question, ruptured from its familial framing in the normative and naturalized narrative of the unobtainable bourgeois ideal.

In this chapter, I am interested in confronting the colonial photographic archive and how it organizes my reception and knowledge of a general cultural formation known as 'the Aboriginal family.' The archives include an electronic database affiliated with the Royal Museum of British Columbia in Victoria, BC (and available on-line through a BC government archival Web service) and a photographic archival collection of the notable female bourgeois traveller of the Canadian Northwest in the early twentieth century, Mary T.S. Schäffer, held in the Whyte Museum in Banff, Alberta. My confrontation with these archives produced a series of ambivalent responses and resistances to the way they both organized and policed a colonial spectatorship. Although my study of these archives, and especially my readings of some selected images, are intended to be neither programmatic nor methodologically definitive, nevertheless, they are constitutive of a process of re-signification that, while attempting to open the complexity of such images, can do little more than demonstrate the instability of meanings that exist between words and images in the contexts of colonization and decolonization. I am left as an eye/I witness to history.

In the following passage from Ralph Ellison's novel *Invisible Man*, the invisible narrator witnesses the eviction of an elderly Black couple from their home in Harlem:

> I turned aside and looked at the clutter of household objects which the two men continued to pile on the walk. And as the crowd pushed me I looked

down to see looking out of an oval frame a portrait of the old couple when young, seeing the sad, stiff dignity of the faces there; feeling strange memories awakening that began an echoing in my head like that of a hysterical voice stuttering in a dark street ... And in a basket I saw a straightening comb, switches of false hair, a curling iron, a card with silvery letters against a background of dark red velvet, reading 'God Bless Our Home' ... I watched the white men put down a basket in which I saw a whiskey bottle filled with rock candy and camphor, a small Ethiopian flag, a faded tintype of Abraham Lincoln, and the smiling image of a Hollywood star torn from a magazine. And on a pillow several badly cracked pieces of delicate china, a commemorative plate celebrating the St. Louis World's Fair. (Ellison 1952: 271)

In the several pages Ellison devotes to this eviction narrative, the reader, along with the invisible narrator, becomes implicated in a scene, a witness to the utter despair and angst felt by the dislocation of everyday objects and their expulsion from the 'comfort of home.' The catalogue of objects reads like an unruly archaeological archive, its troubling effect due to the fact that these objects represent a symbolic displacement of the surplus of emotional life that inhabits the dank and dusky odour of everyday living. In the final instance, of course, these dispossessed objects represent the lives of the couple evicted from their home. While white men toss cheap commodities and personal artifacts onto the street, the invisible man feels nauseated; his stomach turns as personal and historical memories of racism and slavery collide with each other and the present: 'In my hand I held three lapsed life insurance policies with perforated seals stamped "Void": a yellowing newspaper portrait of a huge black man with the caption: Marcus Garvey Deported ... and my finger closed upon something resting in a frozen footstep: a fragile paper, coming apart with age, written in black ink grown yellow. I read: FREE PAPERS. *Be it known to all men that my negro, Primus Provo, has been freed by me this sixth day of August, 1859. Signed: John Samuels. Macon* ... I folded it quickly ...' (Ellison 1952: 272). In this dramatic scene of eviction and dislocation, the humble artifacts of personal life become a public museum of everyday living, and the reader along with the narrator become intrusive spectators to the disruptive force of personal experience invading the public sphere. The increasing porosity between the private sphere of accumulation and the public domain of commodity exchange and jurisprudence destabilizes the ordinary significance attached to these objects. The mixture of things haphazardly thrown on the sidewalk represents a wild profusion of the real and the imaginary, the concrete and the ephemeral, the present and the memorial, people and things. These everyday things signify world historical events, slavery, exile, deportation, and eviction, and they become, in the narrator's words, textualized by 'remembered words, ... linked verbal echoes, [and] images heard even when not listening at home' (Ellison 1952: 273). This dangerous mixture of history and everyday living, of words, people, and things, threatens to break up the epistemic and geopolitical borders between the so-called higher spheres – the Nation, Empire, governance, leaders, policies – and everyday life with its mundane matters of domesticity, sentiment, childhood, sexuality, and household labour. In contrast to the multiple realities and existential affectivities of everyday life and its debris stands the orderly depiction of photographic images in the archive.

Resistance on the part of the spectator may range from psychoanalytical disavowal to a kind of political action, from the fear of interrogating family photos too closely for what they may reveal about personal experiences, histories, and memories, to a politics of resistance toward the use and abuse of personal images in struggles for power and domination. Adeola Solanke, in her postcolonial critique of photographic representations of her parents and grandparents in Nigeria, writes that 'the *images* representing the public soul of pre-colonial Africa are themselves in need of independence' (Solanke 1991: 138). Resistance often leads to a process of resignification in which the photographic 'text,' its visual, coded, and written dimensions, offers up opportunities for redefinition and the production of other meanings. Marianne Hirsch points out that 'getting beneath the surface or around the frame of conventional family photographs can make space for resistances or revisions of social roles and positions in vastly different cultural contexts – of conventions upheld through photographic practice' (Hirsch 1997: 193). Thus the spectator can experience and participate in negotiating several forms of resistance and resignification: resistance to the evidentiary claims and referential power of the photographic family portrait; and ambivalence toward the use, or abuse, of the family portrait in official historical accounts. In the historical contexts of colonization and imperialism, slavery and diaspora, the tensions between the spectator and the family photograph are further complicated by the discontinuous, yet mutually related, intersections of the personal and the political.

In the idealized version of the middle-class photographic family album, photos are organized according to a developmental sequence characteristic of an Oedipal narrative about the growth of the family from its marital beginnings by civil or religious contract to compulsory child-bearing, from the original heterosexual couple to the multiple lineages of genealogical descent. In the public archive, however, family portraits are ruptured from the seemingly normal and natural domain of everyday domestic life. In the case of the digital archive in the Royal Museum of British Columbia, images of family portraits are scanned into computer databases. The website offers a number of prescribed subject headings, as well as providing viewers with the opportunity to search their own. I click the subject heading 'Family Groups.' What comes forth is a disparate set of images, images that lack the familiar teleological framing of the family album. These images occupy a different representational space that, in turn, delimits the image and transforms it into a discrete space of representation.

Questions such as how this new electronic organization of family photographs transforms the meanings ascribed to the family portrait, what new techniques of *framing* emerge in this context and how they reframe or limit the possibilities of readings, and how the spectator reads intertextually for 'the family portrait' within the family portrait – where conflicts arise between the perception of the proper family, its possible historical significance, and its lived realities – require an approach that can situate the formal limits of mechanical reproduction in relation to the contextual limits of the family photograph (i.e., its all too easily taken-for-granted socio-historical framework). Such a dialectical materialist approach is necessary in order to understand how images become *representative* in colonial history – what, indeed, it is that they represent or are made to represent. Further to the question of representability are the epistemic principles, systematicities, methodologies, and disciplines that organize the possible reading(s) of the family photographic image.

While examining the digital archive at the Royal Museum of British Columbia in April of 2003, I click onto the prescribed subject heading 'Family Groups,' and the database produces 620 matches. I'm given the option to choose up to nine images at a time in order to construct a 'Contact Sheet,' a visual grid containing nine boxes. The visual grid simulates a classificatory paradigm of intelligibility. The symmetry of the frames – their formal regularity – creates the illusion that some essential unity transcending time and place links these distinct images. In part, this formal iterability produces, both materially and ideologically, the supposed universality of 'the family.'

In the traditional family album, the sequential narrative is never 'uncomplicated,' as Marianne Hirsch puts it. She writes, it 'does not forget to reassert its boundaries of difference at certain strategic moments.' So, too, a content analysis of the 620 matches reveals a principle of inclusivity and the deployment of 'diversity' as familiarity (Hirsch 1997: 47). The category, 'Family Groups,' succeeds in creating certain anxieties of belonging, while it also establishes its apparent 'universality' by demonstrating the scope of its existence. As if the computer database were mimicking the representational logic of the famous 1955 Museum of Modern Art exhibition titled 'The Family of Man,' curated by Edward Steichen, in which hundreds of family photos were displayed precisely in order to exemplify *diversity* as a family-oriented objective, my content analysis of the digital archive revealed nothing surprising. Of the 620 matches there were four 'Indian Families,' one 'Chinese Family,' and one 'Japanese Canadian Family' displayed in the first 150 entries, most of which consisted, as did the following 250 images, of white, middle-class families. Several 'Indian Families' appeared in the early 400s and mid-500s range, approximately thirty in all. A couple more of the Chinese Family and Japanese Family appeared, along with a few photos of orphanages at the end of the numerical list, including one of Chinese children called the 'Oriental Home Family.' There was one Black family, number 612 (out of 620). This website, owned and operated by the provincial government, is ostensibly for use by a 'public' interested in examining family genealogies. It is one way the Royal Museum remains accountable to its provincial taxpayers.

If the placements of these images has anything to tell us, it is that the assumed spectatorship for this database is predominantly white, middle-class, and 'English.' The rules that govern cataloguing procedures for the Library of Congress, for example, explicitly state that initial entries will be most representative of the subject heading in question, and those entries that are 'other' are included at the end. The instances of 'visible minority-ness' or visible difference that can be determined through identity signifiers such as bodies and clothes reinforce English-ness as a code of normativity in relation to which visible difference comes to signify the desire to mimic it. Some 'differences,' however, are not containable in the same way but become incorporated into the colonial archive by way of 'Other' hegemonic practices. For example, some images include within the 'family group' governesses and farm labourers, those whose links to the family are based on class, gender, and 'race' hierarchies of labour exploitation and oppression (see figures 5.1 to 5.8).

Contact Sheet: 5.1 'Harold Alfred and Family,' Alert Bay, B.C.,' n.d. 5.2 'Bear Lake Tom and Family,' c. 1913. Photographer: Frank C. Swannell, 1880–1969. 5.3 'Lord and Lady Aberdeen with Their Children, and Miss Witterman, Governess, at Their Coldstream Home, in 1895.' 5.4 'Ahousat. Chief Ketla and Family,' 189_.

For all the differences signified within these photos, I would suggest that it is more difficult to unpack the power dynamics between and among the categories of 'men' and 'women, ' 'parents' and 'children,' within the institution of the nuclear family. Such an examination reveals that patriarchal governance is a constitutive feature of its 'familiarity.' It is not the case, of course, that patriarchal gender relations are universal and global; rather, they are made to appear universal across cultures, so that the presentation of a 'Japanese Family' or an 'Aboriginal Family' is framed by its conformity, not just to the photographic

5.5 'William Ketlo and Family, Nechako Road.' Photographer: Frank Swannell, 1912. 5.6 'Japanese Family, Victoria; on left Matsura Uyenabe; on right, Fumi Uyenabe,' c. 1900. 5.7 'East Indian (Sikh) Farm Labourers and Members of the Burrell Family,' 190_. 5.8 'Mr. Robinson with His Family,' 191_.

conventions of 'the family portrait,' but to its colonial governing practices and relations of patriarchal power.

Those relations and practices of power also include the universalizing of 'the family' in terms of its 'whiteness' and 'Englishness,' specifically linked to the bodies of white, bourgeois women. Thus, it is important to interrogate closely the naturalization of 'the family' in the photographic portrait as something that occurs as a result of the representation of colonial patriarchal alliances across national boundaries *and* racialized gender codes of alterity and difference. These intersecting representations of sameness and difference, identity and alterity, in the family portrait are entirely constitutive of a colonial web of power and its many governing practices and modes of representational classification.

The archival assemblage of family portraits produces and reproduces, as it does on the actual computer screen, a normative grid of intelligibility, a set of conventions by which it is possible to understand the very meaning of the family through its composition, the positioning of bodies, their physicality, and their arrangement vis-à-vis each other. The constitutive elements of the family appear to be engraved in stone, immutable, and transparent. W.H.R. Rivers, in what is acknowledged to be a seminal work in early twentieth-century anthropological studies of kinship and social organization, writes in his *Genealogical Method of Anthropological Enquiry*: 'I begin with the method of collecting the pedigrees which furnish the basis of the method. The first point to be attended to is that, owing to the great difference between the systems of relationship of savage and civilized peoples, it is desirable to use as few terms denoting kinship as possible, and complete pedigrees can be obtained when the terms are limited to the following: father, mother, child, husband and wife' (Rivers 1968: 97). The components of the family are delineated as universal precisely because they can be applied to both 'savage and civilized peoples' regardless of the 'great difference between the systems of relationship.' The universality Rivers attributes to such terminology belongs, however, to an established discourse in which the European bourgeois family figures as *the* representative, and hence universal, family structure. This so-called universality is achieved, in part, by the reproducibility of the image and the discursive iterability of a particular set of codes: father, mother, child, husband, and wife. These codes, the product of mechanical reproduction and technical classification, must also, however, be mobilized within particular orders of regularity created, historically and politically, by the oppositional logics of colonial power. Thus, each photo in the BC digital archive can be enlarged and isolated from the set so as to study or make contact with its own particular order of regularity: the mobilization of dualities such as nature/artifice and civilization/savagery and the use of differential signs and figures, including but not limited to the Orient, aboriginality, and femininity.

In the image titled simply 'Lord Aberdeen' (fig. 5.9), the bodies circle around the figure of the mother, the biological core at the centre of its surrounding filiations; and yet the circle is disrupted by a vertical line cut by the figures of the mother and father. One child, the youngest, still touches his mother's body. It is by virtue of his status as the youngest

5.9 'Lord Aberdeen,' c. 1896.

that he is still allowed to occupy this proximity to the mother's body – and such proximity to the maternal figure signifies his place as the last born. The eldest son stands beside his father. The eldest daughter places her hand on the middle boy's shoulder, suturing the bond between brother and sister. There exists in this visual field a series of relations that are gendered, generational, and geopolitical. The clothing of the male children in traditional Scottish kilts connotes the colonial link to Empire and the role of Scotland's indigenous elite in carrying out the duties and obligations of the Empire in the Canadian colonial context. There is the luxurious texture of velvet in the women's clothes, the silk bow around the dog's neck, the oriental carpet, and the painted backdrop of a sculptured staircase ornament and candelabra. The delicate folds of the lace collars and trim on the women's clothing contrast with the large crimped folds of the boys' white vests made from a heavier cotton or linen fabric. The starched upright collar against the sturdy tweed suit marks the evolutionary power of the male upright body, standing tall and erect, his eyes gazing off into the distance as if he were in his mind's eye and not in the eye looking at the bland wall of a photographic studio. In his essay 'The Suit and the Photograph,' John Berger examined the visual discontinuity of European peasants dressed in bourgeois male clothing. He coined the phrase *sedentary power* to describe the symbolic value of the suit: 'Almost anonymous as a uniform, it was the first ruling costume to idealize purely *sedentary* power, the power of the administrator and conference table' (Berger 1980: 38). Similarly, in *Three Guineas*, Virginia Woolf noted how other forms of male attire connoted symbolic power, especially military uniforms and the fur-trimmed gowns worn by magistrates or university professors at Oxford and Cambridge (Woolf 1938). Lord Aberdeen's ruling status in the family and in the colony as governor general of Canada from 1893 to 1898 is represented in the photograph in the way his clothes are differentiated from those of the women and the children, who appear in feminine artifice or traditional costume. Only Lord Aberdeen appears to be dressed in his normal and perfectly natural everyday clothes.

The conventions of the staged family portrait perform their own kind of sedentary power – the posed and self-imposed immobility of bodies in a spatio-temporal dimension signifying the solid immutability of 'the white bourgeois family,' its patriarchal rule, racial supremacy, and centrality to colonial governance. But such symbolic powers are also achieved in the representational space of this photograph through the oppositional logic of artifice/nature and tradition/primitive. For example, the power of feminine artifice is signified by the luxurious clothing, the painted oriental backdrop, the bourgeois woman's feminine beauty, and the staging of the bodies along with the traditional costume worn by the boys that naturalize Lord Aberdeen's status and position of colonial authority. In the constantly shifting borders between nature and artifice in imperial and colonial contexts, here femininity re-presents artifice and deception in opposition to nature, the bearer of truth, brute fact, and authenticity. In this colonial context, symbolic powers are naturalized, and nature itself becomes the passive repository of all that must be made to stand outside the colonial spheres of influence, authority, and power. Thus, the location of feminine artifice in colonial space functions as a particular technique of power designed to differentiate nature, the wild, the frontier, and the bush from bourgeois civilization. It also works to uphold 'bourgeois civilization' as the proper domain for the bourgeois mother. Lady Ishbel Aberdeen was the first president of the newly founded National Council of Women of Canada (1897). This organization and others have come to represent for feminist historiography a form of 'maternal feminism' in Canada's history of white middle-class women. In this case, the National Council of Women, following in the footsteps of the American organization of the same name, was built upon the philanthropic heritage of bourgeois women and their concern for the 'underprivileged,' such as women prisoners, women factory workers, and women immigrants.[1] Such organizations also served to establish and maintain the hegemony of colonial state power in Canada, a point I will return to with the photographic work of Mary Schäffer.

The micropolitical dimension of body-powers consisting of posture, clothing, surrounding furniture, objects, and landscape, as well as the spatial coordination of bodies in relation to one another represent some of the clues that make it possible to trace the contested meanings of familial ideology in colonial space. The staging of the family scene in photographic images produces these body-powers, and the image of 'the family,' in turn, becomes a representational effect of its micropolitical powers.

Within the representational space of the bourgeois colonial family portrait emerges, then, this figure of the civilized family. But it is not only the iterability of these images that brings the figure of the bourgeois colonial family into view in this archival collection; it is also the

5.10 'Group Picture with Indian Family.' Photographer unknown, n.d.

fact that among all these many images of the wealthy colonial elite of Victoria, British Columbia, some images appear to stand out in stark contrast to the majority, such as the image with the caption 'Group Picture with Indian Family' (fig. 5.10). The picture is blurry, taken outdoors on a riverbank. It contains an array of women and children, its sameness or regularity contained by the woman/child configuration, its difference by the lack of any male figures, not to mention the anomalous figure of the white child to the far right. This image is differentiated from the preceding ones in its representation of the 'Other': the poor and uncivilized, non-bourgeois family. Now the preceding images take on a new mode of signification: the bourgeois family is enlisted in the pictographic colonial archive as an agent of imperial and patriarchal conquest.

The double axis of sameness and difference, apparent in the materiality of mechanical reproduction and its ideological codification, does the hegemonic cultural work necessary in British colonization in late nineteenth- and early twentieth-century Canada: (1) to regulate gender, class, and 'race' relations within the colonial bourgeois family; (2) establish the white colonial bourgeois family as a global phenomenon; and (3) create practices of looking and knowing that teach 'imperial spectatorship,' the sanctioned knowledge with which to identify who is civilized and who is not.

5.11 'Samson Beaver and His Family' (postcard description); 'Sampson Beaver, His Squaw, and Little Frances Louise' (caption in *Old Indian Trails*). Photographer: Mary Schäffer, 1907.

Madonnas Roughing It in the Bush

Mary T.S. Schäffer is the author of the early twentieth-century travelogue *Old Indian Trails: Incidents of Camp and Trail Life, Covering Two Years' Exploration through the Rocky Mountains of Canada* (1911). Her account contains photographs she took of two expeditions carried out with her companion Mary W. Adams in 1907 and 1908. A photo of a Native mother, father, and child appears in her book and has been popularized on a contemporary postcard (see fig. 5.11). It is available at major tourist sites in Alberta, including Banff, where the Whyte Museum, which holds Schäffer's archive, is located. The postcard description reads: 'Samson Beaver and His Family. This lovely photograph of Stoney Indian Samson Beaver was taken by Mary Schäffer in 1906. She was a writer, naturalist, photographer and explorer who lived and worked in the Rockies for many years.' In *Old Indian Trails* the caption reads: 'Sampson Beaver, His Squaw, and Little Frances Louise.'

In addition to Schäffer's representation of the so-called Aboriginal Family in this image and others, she also had a particular fascination with the mother/child configuration. Schäffer took many photos of what she herself called 'the Indian Madonna.' The iterability of this figure crossed the religious as well as the anthropological frontiers of the bourgeois family, framing indigenous kinship relations within the figural limits of the Christian bourgeois family. Before discussing her work in greater detail, I want first to situate it within a colonial geography of the maternal body.

The all too familiar 'feminization' of colonial space made it possible for bourgeois women to find a very specific location in the colonial project. Colonial space could easily become a site of intense identification with the oppressed. Thus the philanthropic ideal of the bourgeois woman, who always appears grammatically in the singular due to her apparent individuality and uniqueness as compared to the working masses, tribes, or natives, permitted 'her' the opportunity to regulate her identity in a paternalistic guise. The British woman's journal *The Imperial Colonialist* (1902–27) was created so as to provide female working-class domestic and factory labour to the colonies, especially New Zealand, Palestine, and Canada in the early twentieth century. The philanthropic work of English bourgeois women contributed to colonial governance and was a particularly gendered strategy that allowed such women to transfer their skills in the management of the home and children to colonial space.

The history of British bourgeois women travellers in the nineteenth and twentieth centuries suggests that colonial travel for leisure or business offered these women the opportunity to realize an unprecedented freedom from the confines of domesticity and access to new and interesting knowledge and experience, and to new and different relations of power. Colonization opened up travel to bourgeois women. It also, however, brought new problems in gender and sexual relations: new alliances between colonial and indigenous male elites, new objects of sexual desire for colonial men and women, and new relations of power within the bourgeois home among husbands, wives, youth, and servants; in short, it gave rise to a new sexual politics in the colonial bourgeois household. Given the tenuous situation of bourgeois women's hold on their physical-material existence in the nineteenth and early twentieth centuries, for which they depended on husbands, fathers, or brothers, the newly emerging sexual and gender alliances between men were, needless to say, threatening, and thus a catalyst to further secure bourgeois hegemony through the support and involvement of bourgeois women in the colonial civilizing mission – most notably through the figure of Christian motherhood.

In the geo-historical trilectics of space, body, and power, the figure of the Aboriginal Mother came to occupy a significant place for colonial bourgeois woman. Her body stands at the juncture of a multitude of colonial practices and representations that sought to regulate and dominate the lives of indigenous people territorially, administratively, governmentally, and economically. Indigenous mothers suffered the real effects of colonial policies. Their sexuality and bodies were subject to regulations for the purposes of establishing and reaffirming racial purity and patriarchal governance in the family – its rule of women and children. The Indian Act (1876), as well as other nineteenth-century Canadian legislation discussed in chapter 1, enabled colonial powers to exercise control over the maternal body, a body that was the biopolitical agent of demographic control, racial regulation, the supply of physical labour power, the role of the bourgeois citizen, and the constitution of the nation. This repositioning of kinship relations reconfigured the power dynamics between indigenous men and women, the jobs assigned to their bodies and the spaces they occupied.

As the Aboriginal 'poster family,' Schäffer's image of Sampson Beaver and his family conforms to the Universal familial configuration. Sampson Beaver is the head of his family, and in both Schäffer's caption as well as the one attached to the postcard, it is only his name and that of the child that appear. The mother, Leah Sampson, is referred to, possessively and derogatorily, as 'His Squaw.' The caption situates Sampson Beaver as the patriarchal father, as if this representation were the most natural of social formations: either it is the family itself that conforms to nature, or it is the (ab)original family in nature, the always already origins of the European bourgeois family, that is depicted. Interestingly their clothes combine European styles, dresses for women and the little girl, pants and vest for the man. They wear jewellery and beaded moccasins. The syntax of the body positions, read from left to right, also signifies the patriarchal domination of the First Father. Interestingly, the image I received from the archive reversed this syntax, and after numerous queries I was informed that this was how the image should be printed. Whatever Schäffer's original intentions may have been, the reversal signifies the instability of a colonial-patriarchal syntax that can be so easily undone. And perhaps, even, a political unconscious at work.

In Schäffer's book, nature is circumscribed in her narrative by aesthetic interests: 'I often wonder when passing an Indian camp-ground, be it ancient or modern, if ever for an instant the natural beauty of a location consciously appeals to them. I have seen not one but many of their camps and seldom or never have they failed to be artistic in their setting, and this one was no exception' (Schäffer 1911: 174). Nature is so natural to the Indian that its artistic possibilities remain unconscious or go unnoticed. So, too, is the Aboriginal family a product of nature's raw materiality and not its artificially understood 'natural beauty.' Little Frances Louise is not the only child of Sampson Beaver and His Squaw. She is one of many, but, importantly, she is Schäffer's favourite:

> She had been my little favorite when last we were among the Indians, accepting my advances with a sweet baby womanliness quite unlike the other children, for which I had rewarded her by presenting her with a doll I had constructed from an old table-napkin stuffed with newspaper, and whose features were made visible to the naked eye by the judicious use of a lead-pencil. Necessity constructed that doll, love blinded the little mother's eyes to any imperfections, and the gift gave me a spot of my own in the memory of the forest baby; to call her name was to introduce myself. (175)

Little Frances Louise is nature's mythical 'forest baby,' a wild child tamed into domesticity and motherhood with the introduction of a makeshift doll and bourgeois feminine sentimentality in her appropriate emotional response to Schäffer's 'advances.' But nature's rough earthliness, its ultimate savagery, is hard to shake off: 'In an instant her little face appeared at the tepee-flap, just as solemn, just as sweet, and just as dirty as ever.' Hygiene is central to the civilizing process of bourgeois domesticity: 'She turned and spoke to some one inside, and in a moment out came three smiling, dirty squaws, who looked as though wash-days were not over numerous ... ' Indian women represent the 'essence' of nature – raw, dirty and animalistic: 'Such grimy paws, but such shapely ones they were, so small and dainty, with tapering fingers, that their white sister, bending from her saddle, envied them' (176).

The 'essence' of a feminized nature is a class-conscious stereotype of the labouring woman, a figure that Schäffer's text takes for granted. Her figuration of the aboriginal woman in the guise of the bourgeois woman of vanity, however, is constructed with ironic pleasure and deployed to counter the male stereotype of 'the sullen, stupid Indian':

> When I hear those 'who know,' speak of the sullen, stupid Indian, I wish they could have been on hand the afternoon the white squaws visited the red ones with their cameras. There were no men to disturb the peace, the women quickly caught our ideas, entered the spirit of the game, and with musical laughter and little giggles, allowed themselves to be hauled about and pushed and posed in a fashion to turn an artist green with envy. The children forgot their rabbit-like shyness, and copied their elders in posing for us ... Yahe-Weha [Stoney name for Schäffer that means Mountain Woman] might photograph to her heart's content. She had promised pictures the year before, and had kept the promise, and she might have as many photographs now as she wanted.
>
> ...
>
> Personal experience has shown me that the Indian has the vanity of his white brethren, but he is not going to pose for nothing. I have no belief in their superstitious dread of photography, at least so far as the Plains Indians are concerned; it is simply a matter of fair trade. (176, 178)

'The Indian Madonna' (fig. 5.12) appears at this point in Schäffer's text (181).

Schäffer further challenges the image of the sullen and stupid Indian in her remark that 'it is so hard to associate jokes with Indians whom most of us have only met in books.' Not only does she challenge this myth, she also makes fun of her own missionary zeal in attempting to reorient male/female relations among the Indians:

> Beginning, I said: 'Silas, do you really let your squaw saddle and pack your horses?' 'Sure.' (How well he had learned English!) 'And let her fix the tepee-poles and put up the tepee?' 'Yes.' 'And get the wood, and cook, and tan the skins?' 'Yes, sure!' (He was growing impatient at so much quizzing.) The time seemed ripe for some missionary work which was perceptibly needed along more lines than one, and every one else had stopped to listen. 'Now, Silas,' I said impressively, 'you should be like the white men, you should do the work for your squaw. *We* do not put up our tepees or pack our horses or cut the wood, our men do that.' Taking his

5.12 'The Indian Madonna.' Photographer: Mary Schäffer, 1907.

pipe from his mouth and inspecting me from head to foot leisurely, he said, 'You lazy!'

...

The missionary effort went to the floor with a bang and every one burst out laughing (at the missionary, of course) and she only recovered herself enough to say, 'And what do you do while your squaw works?' 'This,' and he folded his arms, closed his eyes, and puffed away at his pipe. But the rest of them need not have laughed, his look of contempt had swept round and included every man who had so demeaned himself as to be placed in such straits by a woman. (180, 181)

Schäffer's photograph of Sampson Beaver and his family appears in the interstices of this text. Thus, her commentary on acceptable gender-labour relations is also constructed in the image of the proper Aboriginal bourgeois family.[2]

Constitutive to the proper aboriginal bourgeois family is the ideal relationship between Mother and Child. For Schäffer that ideal representation is the Christian image of Madonna and Child, which appears in her travelogue *Old Indian Trails*, as noted above. It is also a remarkable feature of her larger photographic archive, as well as of that of other notable photographers of the West, such as Byron Harmon. The work of both Schäffer and Harmon includes many more such images (see figs. 5.13 and 5.14).

Schäffer's photographs of the (ab)original family in Nature self-consciously follow the Rousseauian ideal of the noble savage as head of the First Family. This Aboriginal family, the First Family, the Primitive Family, constitutes a particular Enlightenment deployment against which an emerging bourgeois and patriarchal family was to define itself. It was also the mythical foundation of European civilization's unidentified past time, which ironically, was still in existence in the colonies of contemporary nineteenth-century Europe. Against this mythical construction stands the historical formation of the nineteenth-century bourgeois family. This latter family belongs to the realm of historical truth, whereas the (ab)original family belongs to the realm of myth. If the primitive family is born of nature and the natural world of flesh and procreation, then the bourgeois family is the product of artifice, commodity formation, and femininity; and yet both are overdetermined by patriarchal lines of descent.

The power of Schäffer's postcard image of the Aboriginal Family is stunning and seductive, no less because it was colourized, giving it aes-

5.13 'Indian Woman with Papoose.' Photographer: Mary Schäffer, 1908.

5.14 'Indian Woman and Child.' Photographer: Byron Harmon, 1913.

thetic value for inclusion in her book. Caught up in the compelling draw of this image, the cultural critic Lucy Lippard writes that

> for all its socially enforced static quality, and for all I've read into it, Mary Schaffer's photograph of Sampson, Leah, and Frances Louise Beaver is 'merely' the image of an ephemeral moment. I am first and foremost touched by its peace and freshness. I can feel the ground and grass, warm and damp beneath the people sitting 'here' in an Indian Summer after disaster had struck but before almost all was lost. Despite years of critical analysis, seeing is still believing to some extent – as those who control the dominant culture (and those who ban it from Native contexts) know all too well. In works like this one, some of the barriers are down, or invisible, and we have the illusion of seeing for ourselves, the way we never would see for ourselves, which is what communication is about. (Lippard 1992: 43)

And yet Lippard's momentary experience of disalienation in her encounter with this image unwittingly reinstates the colonial violence that sought to radically undo indigenous kinship relations and replace them with something else.

In her book *Tender Violence: Domestic Visions in an Age of U.S. Imperialism*, Laura Wexler examines, among other things, a series of photographs by the late-nineteenth-century American portrait photographer Gertude Käsebier. Käsebier is well known for her photographs of what Wexler calls 'white motherhood,' especially images of her own daughter and granddaughter. Wexler argues that in Käsebier's images of the mother/child configuration, the white bourgeois female photographer takes on the role of *'universal* mother,' bringing forth the birth of domestic civilization through her photographic reproduction (Wexler 2000: 188). Wexler's discussion of Käsebier's images also focuses on her portraits of male Sioux leadership. These two distinct aspects of Käsebier's work serve to demonstrate her failure, according to Wexler, to acknowledge the Aboriginal mother and to use her photographic work as a way of building alliances between 'white' and Native American women. 'Everything that Käsebier felt about herself and her own daughter and "white" motherhood in general depended upon the fact that for Käsebier, and for the culture she represented, *Indian* motherhood could have no similar heritage' (Wexler 2000: 206). Wexler concludes that Käsebier's work and that of similar middle-class female photographers at this time signal that the 'defeat of cross-racial empathy is the ultimate failure of these women's work. They might have risen to the occasion as women in political alliance with the "Other," and who knows what visions they might then have shared, but they decided as photographers instead to interpret the occasion according to the wishes of the strongmen of empire' (208). In addressing how the colonial bourgeois family and its reproduction of mother/child relations were deeply enmeshed in the codes of aboriginality, Wexler nevertheless assumes, mistakenly, that the mother/child configuration of bourgeois civilization is a transcultural model. I have no quarrel with Wexler's call for political alliances between indigenous and non-indigenous women, a point to which I will return; however, Schäffer's representations of Indian motherhood, which contain their own particular fantasy of cross-cultural female homosociality, should at least alert cultural critics to how the institution and representation of 'the family' do the work of colonial power and governance to regulate and alter indigenous political and social relations through the body of the Aboriginal Mother. Representations of colonial and aboriginal male elites created the illusion of 'cross-cultural' male homosociality, which is more accurately described as a form of complicity among men produced by the conjoined patriarchal oppression of women. One way in which indigenous women were divested of their social and political power was through criticism directed toward the labouring aboriginal female body, 'the squaw,' a body that needed to be radically subjected to a gender process of *embourgeoisement* in order to render such a body feminine, infantile, vulnerable, and powerless.

An additional problem with Wexler's analysis is that she privileges the visual object and its diachronic four-century-long production of the image of the Virgin Mary and Child in several media, a history already discussed, as Wexler notes, by Julia Kristeva in her essay 'Motherhood According to Giovanni Bellini.' Rather than locating this image in the differing historical and geopolitical contexts of European nation and colony, Wexler deploys the image itself as a visual universal equivalent, put up for exchange in a grossly oversimplified chromatic-based notion of 'whiteness' in a Western symbolic economy. It is more important, I would argue, to discuss this image in such contexts in order to track the links between its meaning production and its institutional locations, whether they be religious, educational, racial, or *familial*. In *The Birth of the Clinic*, Michel Foucault demonstrated that the link between discourse and institutional contexts was a constitutive aspect of late nineteenth- to mid-twentieth-century productions of power and knowledge. Moreover, I would suggest that 'the family' during this period of time must be recognized as a subjugated institutional apparatus within which and through which colonial power amassed both knowledge and representation in the Canadian context. What is at stake, therefore, is not achieving 'cross-cultural empathy' based on the apparent universal equivalency of the figure of mother and child, but a careful exploration of the use of such images as part of the techniques of power designed to institutionalize subjects of representation for the purposes of subjugating them as economically as possible. With the rise of film and photography, the deployment of representational, in addition to physical and/ or epistemic, modes of violence became not only increasingly possible but importantly cost-effective as a result of mechanical reproduction.

Eye/I Witnessing

What would it mean to become an eye/I witness to the colonial photographic archive, to move from the imperial spectator examining how the colonial archive classifies 'the family' in the service of normalizing and naturalizing the bourgeois family through its *aboriginal* genealogy to becoming a witness to indigenous histories of domicide and the dissolution of kinship relations and their social, political, and economic realities?[3] In her essay 'Writing as Witness,' Beth Brant defines witnessing with respect to First Nations as an act of historical remembering that leads to renewal. Remembering involves a sense of vision that 'is not just a perception of what is possible, it is a window to the knowledge of what *has* happened and what *is* happening ... Witness to what has been and what is to be. Knowing what has transpired and dreaming of what will come. Listening to the stories brought to us by other beings. Renewing ourselves in the midst of chaos' (Brant 1994: 72, 74). Knowing the history of colonization is part of the process of 'witnessing.' Changing such histories are the processes of witnessing and de-signification that emerge in Brant's storytelling and by the work of artists such as Jane Ash Poitras.

In *Transparent Parents Singing Hearts* (fig. 5.15), Poitras de-signifies the history of colonial domicide by producing an ironic image of the photographic boundaries that separate a bourgeois white mother and her children from a group of aboriginal men. As if the lines on the bottom signalled textual modes of censorship, the relationship between these images calls into question the historical censorship or denial toward the varied kinship histories of the early twentieth century. Poitras's artistic

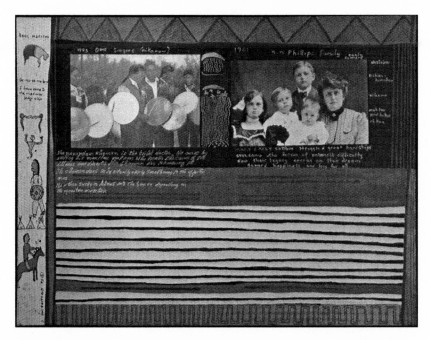

5.15 Jane Ash Poitras, *Transparent Parents Singing Hearts* (1998), mixed media on canvas, 36″ x 48″.

work moves beyond the salvage operations of colonial bourgeois society that sought to fix the Aboriginal in a prehistoric past and thus inscribe indigenous societies within the purist rhetoric of a vanishing race. Using a mixed media format of photographs, texts, and painting, Poitras stirs up the representational violence of colonial history, visually citing it and simultaneously breaking with it by reframing the photographic subject matter within her own larger frame – and decolonial framework – created through painting and intense coloration techniques.

To 'unlearn' and to learn as a non-Native to be a witness to colonial history and to speak to that history of representational violence means to make visible the *mechanisms* (i.e., the technologies and classificatory techniques of representation) that produce and reproduce its violence. This is a twofold process, which, on the one hand, involves unlocking those mechanisms by addressing material which might have had little or no significance for the historical record and may even be perceived to have no aesthetic or truth value, such as family photographs; and, on the other, declassifying these photographs from their bourgeois genealogical framing in the Royal Museum's database and from the Christian mother/child imperative in Schäffer's archive by resituating them in the discontinuous, however mutually related, context of the legislative violence of the state.

Such decolonial processes de-signify the cultural genocide outline by Gerald McMaster in his study of a residential school photograph. In his essay 'Colonial Alchemy: Reading the Boarding School Experience,' he writes:

> The participation of the churches in European imperialism has contributed immensely to alcoholism, family breakdown, and numerous other problems that torment Native communities across Canada and the United States. Today the boarding school is all but non-existent in its original form – that is, administered by religious denominations for the sole purpose of conversion and assimilation. Many of Canada's original boarding school buildings exist, some still operating as schools, albeit usually Indian-controlled ... With so many repulsive stories about boarding school experience emerging from Native communities all across Canada and the United States, it would be more appropriate to turn them into historical sites, comparable to Alcatraz and Auschwitz, as reminders of the legalized atrocities of man against man. (McMaster 1992: 85)

De-signification discloses colonial representational and epistemic violences as neither inevitable nor immutable, but as constitutive realities of historical contestation. Through the act of eye/I witnessing, and a critical re-evaluation of the historical practices of mechanical reproduction and digital simulation, the history of representational colonial violence is transformed. Its benevolent simulations of the Aboriginal family are decolonized. They change from being signs of subjugation in the use and abuse of such images for purposes of cultural genocide to renewed sites of resistance in the palimpsest of decolonization.

6 Inuit Mother Disappeared: The Police in the Archive, 1940–1949

> The secret functions as the subjective practice in which oppositions of private/public, inside/outside, subject/object are established, and the sanctity of their first term kept inviolate. And the phenomenon of the 'open secret' does not, as one might think, bring about the collapse of those binarisms and their ideological effects, but rather attests to their fantasmatic recovery.
>
> D.A. Miller, *The Novel and the Police*

During the 1940s in the Eastern sector of the Northwest Territories an investigation of a French-Canadian trapper (hereafter referred to as A.) took place. The death of two of his children through separate drowning incidents and the disappearance of his Inuit wife and three-month-old son aroused the suspicion of the Royal Canadian Mounted Police (RCMP). The investigation is contained in a series of RCMP records submitted by local subdivision police inspectors at Eskimo Point, territorial and provincial commanding officers in Manitoba and Saskatchewan, and the commissioner of the Criminal Investigations Branch Headquarters in Ottawa, Ontario.[1] Out of the various missives exchanged among these men, exemplary of the colonial symbolic order, over a period of ten years (the reports begin 4 July 1940 and end 5 September 1950) emerges a story of tragic proportions involving deaths, insanity, exhumed bodies, a disappearing wife, and drowned, burned, lost, and cannibalized children: all the compelling subject matter of a good detective novel.

The Logics of Discovery

The story I am about to unfold, however, is not a work of fiction – as in

the narrow sense of when we understand fiction to signify an oppositional value of 'non-truth.' It is a textual formation designed to follow a
logic of discovery: hypotheses, speculations, and presuppositions are
put forth, all aimed at constructing, while seemingly in the process of
discovering, the 'truth' about A.'s 'doings,' if not wrong-doings, in the
North. In an effort to gather evidence in order to find a just cause to
arrest A., the RCMP exhume the bodies of the drowned children. In one
particular case, a mutilated body comes to occupy a significant place as
a site of evidence. But when contested testimony as to the biological sex
of this exhumed body leads to a crisis of unresolvability, the written
inquiry ends. After ten years of investigation, resolved only that they
will never sufficiently construct the truth about the mysterious disappearance of A.'s wife and child and the 'true' sex of one of the exhumed
bodies, the federal Criminal Investigations Branch commissioner, without explanation, deems further investigation unwarranted. Case closed.

This chapter closely examines this RCMP document as an authoritative discourse that generates its investigative procedures through a
process of negotiating the significance of the 'disappeared' Inuit
woman's body and the corpse of a child's sex-undifferentiated body.
Hillary Leone and Jennifer Macdonald describe the process of negotiating the significance of a corpse in the following useful terms:

> The corpse, like the book, must be seen as a product of 'progress'; as such,
> authorities – medical, ethical, judicial, religious – are charged with the task
> of negotiating its borders. They determine the moment at which body
> becomes corpse; they debate how and when and under what circum-
> stances we should employ or deny life-prolonging medical technologies;
> they make fine distinctions between the living and the dead. The authori-
> ties provide answers, albeit conflicting ones. (Leone and Macdonald 1992:
> 596–7)

In the case of the RCMP document, the bodies of the absent Inuit
woman and the sex-undifferentiated corpse are subject to the conflicts
and trials of a definitive search for truth as to the cause of death. But
when a body is subject to the inscriptions of an authoritative discourse,
it becomes a 'written body' capable of producing significations that cut
against the grain of the meanings and values ascribed by an authoritative framing.[2] Not only do authorities negotiate the borders of the
living/dead body and, indeed, determine how the body will signify its
corporeal status, the written body itself can signify a multiplicity of

conflicts and contradictions that extend beyond those borders. I would suggest that for bodies caught in the contestatory field of decolonization, they may deploy hitherto unrecognized significations, geopolitical in their scope, and discontinuous from the normative word-mappings of an authoritative border negotiation.

Furthermore, this discontinuity is located, politically and historically, in the struggles of indigenous peoples in Canada. And it is to those struggles that I must turn, briefly, if the colonial cultural politics of this RCMP document are to be understood in their historical and transcultural specificity. There are two points I wish to make.

Firstly, it is important to note that during the period in which this document was written, the Canadian federal government actively set out to substantiate its borders in the North and lay claim to its sovereignty over potential American or Russian interests. The Inuit who occupied this vast territory were subject to a range of governmental strategies to aid the process, such as the introduction of religious, governmental, policing, and/or military presences as well as a series of disastrous 'relocations' that resulted in extraordinary hardship for the Inuit, including, in some cases, mass starvation and death (see Tester and Kulchyski 1994). The RCMP document represents a small if not minor event in the context of this larger historical struggle, yet as a minor discourse it has the advantage of drawing our attention to the micrological texture of power, the site at which truth and reason can be seen to mediate the larger and seemingly ungraspable complexity of the macrological relations between 'postcolonial nations,' such as First Nations, Métis, and Inuit in Canada, and the nation state of 'Canada' itself.

The second issue concerns the contemporary scene of indigenous women's movement in Canada and its relationship to feminist theoretical debates over the continuing value of 'sexual difference' as a conceptual category for transnational feminist analysis. Without this brief excursus into indigenous women's politics of decolonization, it would not be possible to understand how the current political situation has brought pressure to bear on feminist scholars in Canada to rethink not only current theoretical practices but also ways of reading the past.

When, in 1980s feminist theory, 'sexual difference' came to function as a metonymic code with which to decipher the libidinal investments of global transactions, postcolonial feminists argued that the value placed on 'sexual difference' as an organizing principle with which to analyse the situation of women in a cross-global context contributed

more to exacerbating the contradictions of neocolonialism than furthering our understanding of the intersections of gender, power, and
knowledge in the struggles for decolonization (Mohanty 1994; and Spivak 1986). Nevertheless, this exacerbation of the contradictions of neocolonialism created a productive tension in that our awareness as to the
political stakes involved when sexual differentiation enters the macrological debates of decolonization is dramatically heightened. Take, for
example, the challenge by the Native Women's Association of Canada
(NWAC) and the Women of the Métis Nation (WMN) to the Canadian
constitutional reform debates culminating in the Charlottetown Accord
in 1992. NWAC, supported by the WMN, appealed to the federal court
for their right to political representation in the constitutional negotiations, which included four nationally recognized indigenous political
organizations: the Assembly of First Nations (representing status Indians), the Inuit Tapirisat of Canada (representing Inuit), the National
Métis Council (representing Métis), and the Native Council of Canada
(representing non-status Indians).[3] The challenge, which they won on
appeal, was based on the Charter of Rights and Freedoms, passed as
part of the Constitution Act of 1982 (although it did not take effect until
April of 1985) (*NWAC et al. v. Her Majesty et al.*, 1992). The Charter of
Rights and Freedoms, which guaranteed equality to women, already
played a significant legislative role in the passing of Bill C-31 (1985),
which removed those sections of the Indian Act (1876) and subsequent
amendments (especially in 1951) explicitly discriminating against (status) Native women, as discussed in detail in chapter 1. In the case of Bill
C-31, indigenous women were opposed by several indigenous political
organizations, which argued that Native women's challenge to the
Indian Act was of secondary importance to the greater question of the
Indian Act as a whole and the Canadian state's control over determining who is and is not an Indian. In other words, the supposedly larger
and more important 'collective rights' of First Peoples took precedence
over the 'individual rights' of indigenous women guaranteed under the
Charter of Rights and Freedoms. In the more recent conflict over indigenous women's right to participate in the constitutional reforms, the
same issue of competing collective-versus-individual rights stood at
the crux of the problem. What is strikingly clear is that the notion of
'collective rights' excluded First Nations women.

This brief narrative of the history of the indigenous women's movement would seem to indicate that this political struggle constitutes part
of the women's movement generally referred to as 'the struggle for

equal rights.' Such would be the case if it were not for the transcultural discourse indigenous women deployed in order to legitimate their place in the political arena. This discourse is one that emphasizes matrilineal descent, a gendered division of responsibilities, a metaphorical displacement in the 'mother' as 'mother-earth,' and metonymic associations between body parts and functions and attributes of healing (breast-feeding), life-giving (the womb), etc. I cite the following words by Marlyn Kane and Sylvia Maracle from a special issue of *Canadian Woman Studies / Les Cahiers de la femme*, edited by indigenous women, as an example:

> In our community, the woman was defined as nourisher, and the man, protector, and as protector, he had the role of helper. He only reacted; she acted. She was responsible for the establishment of all of the norms – whether they were political, economic, social, or spiritual. She lived in a very co-operative environment, where power needed not be lorded over.
> ...
> In our Nation, while there is no question that the woman is the central figure in the scheme of things, our official government leaders are still men. That is how our government was given to us, and that is what is in our KAIANERE'KO:WA (great law). They are called ROTIANE, the best translation being 'good men' ... These positions cannot be confused with the elected 'Chiefs' positions as prescribed by the *Indian Act*. Too often we hear men protesting women's attempts to gain these positions by reminding us that, in our ways, the 'Chiefs' are men. I, for one, have promoted women becoming involved in the Band Council system, not because I think it is a good one that should be perpetuated, and not because I think there should be 'equal' representation of women to men. Rather I believe that women have a responsibility to make sure that we don't lose any more, that we don't do any more damage, while we work on getting our original government system back in good working order. (Kane and Maracle 1989: 12, 14)

It is tempting to view this reinvention of tradition as an instance of naïve essentialism. As one critic sees it, this is an instance of the essentialist voice of indigenous women's political discourse: 'While male [Aboriginal] leadership goals emulate the masculinist nation-state (despite expressing a counterhegemonic resistance to state authority), female leadership imagines a neotraditional community for which essentialist womanhood stands as a metaphor. Whereas women conceive of a community in which the womb is to the nation as the heart is to the body, men envision an Indigenous nation whose drum beat radiates from the quasi-powers of a "third order of government"' (Fiske 1994). A simple distinction between a masculine nation and female leadership is untenable, particularly if we consider that Rosmarie Kuptana, past president of the Inuit Tapirisat of Canada, herself opposed the court challenge led by the Native Women's Association in favour of the creation of a 'third order of government.' More to the point are the dangers of falling into the trap of attributing essentialism to indigenous women's politics when what we may be witnessing is an example of a newly emerging decolonial and gendered material reality. If, as Diana Fuss suggests, 'the political investments of the sign "essence" are predicated on the subject's complex positioning in a particular social field, and that the appraisal of this investment depends not on any interior values intrinsic to the sign itself but rather on the shifting and determinative discursive relations which produced it,' then this emergent materiality can best be understood in the context of the discursive history of colonialization, in particular the effects of the Indian Act, which explicitly stated, as one of its discriminatory clauses, that the government would recognize only an elected band council composed of and elected by adult males (Fuss 1989, 20). When, in the above statement, Marlyn Kane and Sylvia Maracle argue for women's participation on band councils, they are fighting back against an oppressive colonial political system created by the Indian Act that at all levels of government denied indigenous women any form of political representation, not to mention its refusal to recognize their already existing political power.

The macrological legislative and constitutionally based struggle for equal rights and the reinvention of a traditional discourse on sexual difference at the micrological level co-exist in indigenous women's political discourse. The simultaneous, and yet discontinuous, relation between these inscriptional spaces represents a contradictory moment in the indigenous women's movement from which to clear a space in order to establish their decolonial positioning as gendered political subjects within their bands as well as at the level of constitutional decision-making practices. Thus, I would maintain that the discourse of indigenous women cannot be understood without a thorough knowledge of the history of colonial discourse. As agents of their own historical making, such gendered materialities – rather than an essentially 'sexualized' division of labour – are not without political and historical efficacy.

What the legal struggle over equal rights for indigenous women and their discursive inscription of tradition tell us, is that any attempt to contain the meanings and values attributed to their bodies will be subject to contestation, particularly when the authorities who are negotiating those bodies include not only the policing apparatus or the bureaucratic policy-makers of the state but also feminist scholars, where anti-racist feminism represents another interest which brings conflicting pressures to the struggle for decolonization. My discussion of an Inuit woman's body and her child's corpse, therefore, will undoubtedly bear the marks of the current contradictions of (de)colonialism, even as I try to mobilize both the critical limits of the concept of 'sexual difference' and those written bodies which signify subjugation as well as gendered resistance to the imperial project in Canada.

The Inquiry

Keeping in mind the limits of the trope of sexual difference for articulating the logics of discovery, I will now reconstruct the story of an inquiry into the Eastern Arctic during the 1940s. By disclosing the gendered character of the textual strategies deployed in this investigation, it is possible to de-naturalize some of the colonial assumptions at work in the narrative structure of the Canadian state's policing apparatus: in particular, those assumptions which, firstly, create a phantasmatic representation of an Inuit woman – the disappearing wife – and turn the moment of her vanishing into the central motivation for investigation; and, secondly, transform the contested terrain of a body's sex into an objective phantom of displaced imperial relations among the Inuit, the state, and a French-Canadian trapper. The disappearing Inuit woman, whose body is never discovered, and the mutilated body of one of the drowned children, whose biological sex is subject to dispute, constitute an ideological terrain of contested meanings. Questions emerge concerning the ethnographic alibis recalled to support a savage and demeaning representation of the lives of this trapper, an Inuit woman, and their children.

A summary description of this decade of police files includes mention of the deaths of four children; two from drowning; one, twelve hours after birth; and still another disappearing with his mother. There are several notable events involving (1) serious burns inflicted to the head and hands of a baby, resulting in amputation and some minor head surgery, both of which took place in a remote cabin and were performed by the child's father; (2) the father's discovery of his son's drowned body a month later with parts of its face and limbs eaten by wolves; (3) A.'s self-described insanity, potentially due to syphilis; (4) a series of grave exhumations, the contents of which bring to the fore a discrepancy between A.'s testimony and a pathologist's laboratory report as to the sex of one of the bodies; and, finally, (5) the mysterious disappearance of A.'s wife, consistently referred to as Mrs A., her Inuit name never given. The vanishing wife initially raises the suspicion of the RCMP that A. has committed an act of foul play. This suspicion comes to structure a broader terrain of distrust from which follows an allegation that not only did A. murder his missing wife and child, but he also killed the two children who purportedly died from drowning accidents.

The following four sections provide a detailed analysis of the investigative report. Since the text I am working with is not readily accessible, I find it necessary to reproduce as much of the original text as possible in order to preserve its narrative continuity. However, the following reconstruction is not without its own ideological investments in disclosing the phallo-ethnocentric assumptions taken on the part of the investigators toward their object(s) of analysis. My point here is precisely to demonstrate the constructedness of the narrative along these ideological lines, after which follows an irreducible process of deconstruction through a series of virtual displacements.

The Fire Sermon

The case built up against A. is massive. The first three documents of the file, each entitled 'Infant daughter of A. (Trapper) – Burned in tent fire,' contain information about a small female infant who received severe burns to her hands and face when the pipes from a camp stove collapsed on the inside of the tent. In the first two documents, A. is said to have requested medical aid to be sent to his remote campsite but, unable to wait for the arrival of a Hudson's Bay Exploration Co. plane some days later, returned to his camp with the injured child and performed his own surgical operations (4 July 1940, 29 August 1940). The third report, dated some nine months after the incident, summarizes the event and A.'s emergency surgery:

> It appears that the pipes from a camp stove collapsed on the inside of the tent and fell over on to the bed upon which the child was laying, together with a bundle of dish cloths which also caught fire. This burning mass dropped directly on top of the child and she was burned severely about the

head and arms and hands necessitating the removal of the index finger at
the first joint and the middle finger at the second joint (by A.) of the right
hand and not the left as previously reported on. A. stated he used disinfec-
tant after snipping the flesh of the fingers off with a pair of scissors, after
having first twisted the fingers off at the joints and that no complications
had set in afterwards, the stumps of the fingers healing perfectly.

A small piece of bone was also removed from the forehead of the infant
sometime after the accident, this piece of bone being approx. 1" x 1/4",
and at this time the spot where the bone was removed is hardly noticeable,
having healed very nicely. (21 April 1941)

The fourth document in the file, dated 29 November 1947 (almost seven
and a half years after the 'Burned in the tent fire' incident), begins a
series of sixteen documents entitled 'Bertha A. – Padlei, N.W.T. – Death
by Drowning.' This report contains a radiogram sent from the Padlei
trading post to the nearest RCMP detachment at Eskimo Point. The
radiogram documents that the same child burned in the tent accident,
Bertha, drowned 13 September 1947 when she fell through the ice while
A. and his wife were absent hunting. (Subsequent reports conclude that
the drowning occurred on 30 September.) Aside from a note to defer an
official account of the incident until an inspector can be detached to A.'s
camp, this report also mentions the cancellation of family allowance
payments in the name of this child.

In the fifth document (2 September 1948), dated almost a year later
and entitled 'A. and Two Children – Eskimo Point, N.W.T. Sick and
Destitute – Churchill, Man,' A. is reported to have left his camp and
taken his two remaining children to Churchill, Manitoba, ostensibly to
receive medical treatment for what he claims is a deteriorating nervous
condition due to syphilis. According to A., his illness renders him
unable to care for his children, and he requests that they be placed in an
orphanage. After a Wassermann test produces a negative result for
syphilis, A. is diagnosed with anxiety neurosis, given an ounce of Castor Oil and an enema, and discharged. The end of the report contains a
brief mention that the mother of the children died last spring, the
spring of 1948.

Death by Water

Documents six (8 September 1948) and seven (11 October 1948) return
to the death by drowning incident. These documents record A.'s statements about how the drowning occurred, as well as information about

where the body was buried, information which will take on a great deal more significance in later reports. It is in the context of these reports that a separate file is opened to investigate the disappearance of Mrs. A. Document eight (9 November 1948), entitled 'Mrs. A. and Small Son Paul J.A. – Padlei District, N.W.T. *Enquiry Re: Disappearance of:*' is the first of another major series of documents. This series plus the 'Death by Drowning' documents comprise the bulk of the file on A., with the exception of a pathologist's autopsy report on a body exhumed from A.'s camp.

The remaining twenty-nine documents date from 8 January 1949 to 5 September 1950. By the ninth document, the mystery has begun to consolidate itself as such. Suspicion of foul play is openly acknowledged in the tenth document (14 April 1949), and the RCMP begin their investigation in earnest. It is interesting to note that suspicion does not arise from the local detachment at Eskimo Point; rather, it is the commanding officer at the Criminal Investigations Branch in Ottawa who voices the first note of suspicion: 'We have grave suspicions, as the result of recent investigations by Cst. C— of our Eskimo Point detachment that the woman and her son met with foul play and suspect that A. is responsible. These are only suspicions so far' (14 April 1949). Further to this declaration of suspicion, the terrain of distrust is immediately expanded to include what were previously held to be accidental drownings of both Bertha and another child named John, whose death in 1942 was never officially reported: 'Two other children of this family, namely, one girl named Bertha was drowned or allegedly drowned on September 30, 1947 ... Another named John, is said to have been drowned somewhere near their cabin in 1942 being 9 years of age at the time.' This drowning of John A. was never reported by the constable in charge of the Eskimo Point detachment at the time (14 April 1949). What were initially thought to be *accidental* drownings now constitute allegedly *intentional* drownings.[4]

In an effort to consolidate the RCMP's suspicions, a process of ethnographic reconstruction begins to take place: facts are dissected from the body of information gathered and then reconstituted into a representation of A.'s life as barbaric and savage. The discursive construction of A.'s savage existence emerges in two interviews held by the RCMP in order to gather more information regarding A.'s relationship to his partner and why she mysteriously vanished. The story of Mrs A.'s disappearance is recounted by the sub/registrar of vital statistics, Mr H. Voisey, at Padlei. Voisey testifies that A. arrived at his place in the afternoon of 18 May 1948 to inform him that his wife had been missing for four days:

> Apparently Mrs. A. had left their Cabin on May 14th. to take the Mail to Padley [*sic*] some 25 miles distance. She had taken a team of Seven Dogs and a tobogan [*sic*] and their small Son with her. A. went on to say, Mr. Voisey stated, that soon after his wife left for Padlei a snow storm accompanied with high winds came up. He had been worried, he stated, regarding his Wife and Child but thought she would have no trouble. He gave her until the 17th. of May – three days – to return from Padlei. When she did not return at this time he started into Padlei to look for her. (4 January 1949)

The RCMP conduct interviews with two individuals who were perhaps the last people outside of her immediate family to see Mrs A. before she disappeared. One interview was taken from an woman referred to as 'P— E.—,' an Inuit midwife who helped in the delivery Mrs A.'s last child in the spring of 1948.[5] She is reported as saying the following:

> Upon being asked P— stated that she had been present at A.'s Camp when the baby was born, sometime in the Spring of 1948 she thought. (Baby was born March 18th. 1948) She stated that a few days after the baby was born she told Mrs. A. that she had to leave to go home. Mr. A. was not in the Cabin at the time. Mrs. A. immediately started to cry and asked her not to go. She stated that she was afraid to stay alone with A. as he might do something to her. Upon being further questioned P— stated that she had never seen A. strike or beat Mrs. A. and she did not know why Mrs. A. should be afraid to stay with Mr. A. P— went on to say that Mr. A. himself had not spoken to her (P—) since she arrived at his place just before the Baby was born. P— stayed at A.'s Cabin three days after the baby was born and then returned home. (4 January 1949)

In a second interview with Father D— of the Roman Catholic Mission, the following information is also gathered:

> During one visit approximately two years ago, [Father D—] stated, Mrs. A. was at home alone when he arrived. When he tried to talk to her in the Eskimo language – which he had done many times previous – she would not answer or talk to him. When A. came home that evening Father D— learned that he, A., had forbiden [*sic*] his wife to talk to anyone, not even

Eskimos. That night, while he stayed in the Cabin, Father D— stated that A. treated his Wife somewhat like a dog. He would not let her eat at the table but made her sit in a corner of the room and he threw scraps of food at her. – Father D— left the Cabin the following day. – Being further questioned Father D— stated that A. had told him in the Summer of 1947 that he would like to leave the North Country now as he had enough but he couldn't do this as he was 'tied down' with an Eskimo Wife and Children. (4 January 1949)

Both interviews confirm A.'s mistreatment of his wife: however, P—'s testimony appears as a somewhat unsympathetic response to Mrs A.'s fearfulness, and Father D—'s represents the voice of a sympathetic and objective observer who, although concerned to communicate with Mrs A., does not intervene on her behalf to put an end to A.'s abusive treatment towards her.

As the narrative unfolds, it is clear that the RCMP are engaged in a process of deductive reasoning designed to confirm their already presumed, however hypothetical, suspicions that A. has committed some acts of murder. On the basis of the interviews with P— and Father D—, Constable C— of Eskimo Point draws the following conclusion:

From the foregoing it is quite apparent and possible that A. may have disposed of his Wife and Child by foul play. There is no conclusive evidence of this fact however at the present time. Bertha A., who was badly scarred by being burned was the first Child to die after A. had stated he would like to leave the North. Then A.'s Wife and Child disappeared. Here again it seems rather odd that A. should suddenly let his Wife go to Padley [sic] when previously he had forbiden [sic] her to leave the Cabin grounds, and even forbid her to talk to other people. (4 January 1949)

In an effort to prove their hypotheses about the legal crimes of murder A. has committed, the RCMP investigators reconstruct the testimonies in a manner that overlooks and thereby sanctions the unrecognized crimes of 'domestic violence' A. commits against his wife and family. Nevertheless, these scenes of brutality play an important role not only in validating suspician against A. but also in validating the conditions of his life generally that would give him a motive: 'he would like to leave the North Country now as he had enough but he couldn't do this as he ... was "tied down" with an Eskimo Wife and Children.' It is this latter statement on which the RCMP attribute a motive to A.'s actions. I would suggest that there exists an assumed disposition on the part of the investigators that corroborates A.'s reasons for wanting to leave: the 'savage' life of the North Country. Indeed, the two interviews taken are as important for their representation of this 'savage' existence as for the information they depart. If solving the legal crime of murder is at stake, the RCMP must reconstruct the viable conditions on which murder would be likely to occur. I am not convinced that it is solely A.'s mistreatment of his wife that gives the RCMP cause to suspect murder; rather, it is the brutal conditions under which he lives that sanction his desire to kill. Those brutal conditions are figured in the body of the Inuit woman as both the victim of a brutality that does not constitute a 'legal crime' and as the body that signifies brutality itself in being that victim. In other words, the figuration of the Inuit woman as a passive victim and helpless 'dog-like' creature who submits to A.'s violence creates the very figure of savagery the RCMP are looking for in order to legitimate their suspicion of murder. The savagery of A. as an individual capable of murder is cathected through the othering of his wife as the authentic savage figure.

In P—'s testimony, the emphasis is on visual, and hence, 'objective proof' as to A.'s treatment of Mrs A. In the recorded interview, it is only '[u]pon being further questioned' that P— states 'she had never seen A. strike or beat Mrs. A.' The sentence continues: 'and she did not know why Mrs. A. should be afraid to stay with Mr. A.' Since there is no visible proof to corroborate the (unacknowledged) crime of domestic violence, that violence itself becomes unknowable. This is one way in which the set-up of the interview allows the RCMP to dismiss the domestic violence as the site of evidence on which to convict A. Domestic violence is not the crime under investigation. Indeed, it does not constitute criminal behaviour at all within the discursive make-up of the inquiry. It is the textual modes of representation of the testimonies which delimit the field of criminality, thereby constituting the active relationship between the crime and the criminal. The information about A.'s treatment of his wife only serves to confirm his murderous intentions and the barbarity of his alleged criminal behaviour. I would also suggest that A. is implicitly being held guilty of another sort of crime, an ethnographic crime of miscegenation, a 'racially mixed marriage' between a French Canadian and Inuit woman and, as the RCMP refer to them, his 'half-breed' children (17 August 1949): a marriage and family A. distances himself from in an effort to escape the difficulties of his life in the North.

The two interviews also tell us that Mrs A. received no support from her own people because A. denied her access to them. Father D—'s support is well intentioned, however limited to sanctioning the violence of a religio-patriarchal control in the 'privacy' of the domestic sphere. Finally, and perhaps most importantly, the RCMP, from whom she also received no help, are only interested in her after her disappearance. The textual construction of these interviews inscribes a phallocentric ethnography and discloses the following contradiction: the colonial man, the French-Canadian trapper, is held in an active and civil opposition of criminality and legitimation, while the Inuit woman, as a figure of savagery, mediates the hierarchical status of this individual man for the state's policing apparatus. The Inuit woman's textual position as the disappearing wife – if not the disappearing referent – adds to her construction as an ideological phantasm, there to breach the gap between the colonial state and the uncontrollable forces of nature, between the commanding officer at the Criminal Investigations Branch in Ottawa and the margins of Canada's northern territory, which the RCMP are designated to assert and protect.

The Burial of the Dead

Another instance of phantasmatic aboriginality occurs following the RCMP's decision that the only way to gather sufficient evidence to convict A. must involve exhuming one of the bodies buried near his camp. The decision to investigate the contents of one particular grave emerges as a result of conflicting reports about the whereabouts of Bertha's grave. Initially A. stated that he buried the body 'on a small hill fifty yards N.W. of the cabin' (8 September 1948). According to a police patrol sent to A.'s cabin on 12 December 1948, Bertha's grave had been moved from its original site:

> Two graves were located some distance from the cabin. One grave was small and apparently belonged to John A., A.'s son who was drowned in 1942. The other grave was very large and was apparently not there when Cst. B— and S/Cst. G— had visited the Cabin in May of 1948 [just after the disappearance of Mrs. A. and her son], according to S/Cst. G—. S/Cst. G— stated that Bertha A. had been buried closer to the Cabin and an old Canoe had been turned over the grave and partially covered with sand and rocks. This grave in question was not there at this time. It had apparently been moved by someone – the canoe was not present either.

As. A. is presently in Churchill no reason could be found at this time as to why Bertha A.'s body should be moved from one place to another. (4 January 1949)

This new and larger grave was located closer to 200 yards away from the cabin and not 50 yards as originally stated by A. (as noted in a subsequent document dated 16 August 1949). The above report continues with: 'It is not known who might be buried there. It is exceptionally large – approximately twice as large as any other grave the writer has seen in the N.W.T.' (4 January 1949).

When RCMP attempts to exhume the body in the middle of an arctic winter prove futile – the hard frozen sand and rocks making the task impossible – instructions are then given to return the following September when the ground has thawed. (Another attempt was made 7 May 1949.) When the body was finally exhumed in August of 1949, Dr M—, the local coroner, noted 'suspicious signs to warrant pathologist investigation' (17 August 1949). M— describes the body thus:

[S]mall headless corps [sic], lying on abdomen, legs flexed on thighs and crossed on each other. Arms were not apparent but body was not moved to see if they were present under. Trunk and limbs were clothed. A stick was used to tear the rotten clothing down the back in order to note injuries, no wound was made with this. In the right scapular region near the vertebral column a hole was noted, and the ribs had detached from the spinal cord. The shoulder was jammed up against the top of the box and no head was in evidence in its normal position. Lying in the region of the upper right shoulder was the mandible which was attached to the ma[x]illa [jawbone]. The maxilla had been detached from the base of skull with some apparent fracturing. The temporal boned [sic] were lying separated in the box. The upper skull was lying on its dome about the middle of the back. There appeared to be an old bandage in the cranial cavity but no soft tissue. What appeared to be one of the forearm bones was lying on the right side – it was fractured at one end with parts missing.

Impressions: – Maxillary, and basal fractures of skull –teeth missing Scalp or hair not present, skull and arm bones in peculiar position, indicate the possibilities of foul play. Due to degeneration it was decided to leave the determination up to a pathologist. (16 August 1949)

Having determined that Mrs A. and her son were not buried in this grave, the RCMP then turn toward the mutilated body as potential evidence of A.'s wrong-doing. The official laboratory report contains the following summary:

> Remains of human child, approximate age nine to ten years. Sex – female. In a fairly good state of nutrition at time of death. Remains show almost complete adipocere formation. Cause of death cannot be definitely stated. There is no evidence however, of any injury to the body skeleton with the exception of what apparently is post mortem destruction, of the right arm as noted, by some carnivora. There are what appear to be tool marks appearing on the right humerus. Date of death can be approximated as at least or over one year. (Laboratory Report, 2 September 1949)

Surprisingly, the pathologist concludes that 'there is no evidence in the remains that is contrary to death by natural means, for example, by drowning' (2 September 1949). On the basis of the pathologist's report, the mutilated body of the young Bertha provides the RCMP with little evidence that might resolve the question of Mrs A.'s disappearance, nor does the pathologist's findings lead to any further illumination as to the nature of A.'s suspicious conduct.[6]

The Return of Elsewhere

The results of the pathologist's report would seem to suggest that the suspicions against A. are insubstantial if not unwarranted. There are, however, two remaining threads dangling in the minds of the RCMP: the case of the drowned boy, whose death was never officially reported to the RCMP, and the reason why Bertha A.'s body was removed from its original site and reburied *elsewhere*.

In order to tie up the details of his son's death, A., who, up until this point, has remained at Churchill and, unbeknownst to him, been under the surveillance of the RCMP, is interviewed in connection with the death by drowning of his son John.[7] In a sworn statement given by A. of the events leading up to his son's death, he recounts a canoeing accident which results in his three-and-a-half-year-old-son not being recovered, although A. managed to rescue his wife, Bertha, and another daughter, Dianna. A. describes how he found the body a month later, by chance:

> [I] could not find John, I searched the river and the lake, about a month later, I dont [sic] remember if I was looking for John or one of my dogs that

had gone away from camp, when I noticed a head and then the body, it had been mauled, both arms were eat [*sic*] off and the face had been eating [*sic*] away, I took the boy to my cabin, where I buried him. (17 October 1949)[8]

Initially, the only apparent discrepancy noticed by the RCMP in A.'s statement concerns the age of the boy. A. says in his report that the child was three and a half years old, whereas the information recorded by an RCMP officer in a report dated 11 October 1948 is that John A. was born in 1933. At the time of his drowning in 1942, this would make him nine years old (1 November 1949).

In response to why Bertha's body was moved, the RCMP hypothesize that in view of the tooth marks noted on the body's bones, perhaps the body could have been dug up by wolves, in which case, A. had to rebury it. This speculation is not merely inspired by the story of the mauled body of John A., but the suggestion is soon put forth that perhaps the body exhumed was, indeed, that of John A. and not Bertha. Subsequent discussions with A. reveal the following:

[D]uring a visit with A. the subject of his Wife's disappearance came up during the course of the conversation, when A. stated he wished the Police could find his wife's body or what would be left of it, as he A. would feel much better if it were found, from there the conversation was discreetly led around to the graves behind his cabin and in this connection the following information was ascertained; Bertha was buried about 3/4 way up the hill behind the cabin and in Deerskins (caribou) and that the grave is marked with a stone at the head and feet and that the body has never been removed. John was buried at the top of the hill in a somewhat larger grave, and that he put John's body in his tool box as it had been badly decomposed and mauled by dogs or wolves and had been decapitated and that he, A. had gathered up John's remains with old rags which he put in the tool box with the body and the head he placed on top of the body, closed the box up and buried same on top of the hill behind his cabin.

...

It would appear from this report that the body examined was that of John A. and not that of Bertha A., as first suspected. (6 December 1949)

The statements by A. concerning the death by drowning of his son would indeed seem to confirm that the body exhumed was that of John and not Bertha. Only one small problem remains: the discrepancy between A.'s description of John's burial and the conclusion of the pathologist's report that the sex of the body exhumed is female.

The pathologist's report clearly states: 'On examination of perineal region there is no evidence of the scrotum or penis. The vaginal opening measures 1/2" in length by 1/16th" in width. The labia minora and labia majora are well defined and what appears to be the urethal [*sic*] opening can be seen' (Laboratory Report, 2 September 1949). In the face of such certainty, the RCMP insist that the exhumed body is 'definitely that of a female' and that A. is 'either lying or has forgotten details in respect to the mode of burial of his son John and his daughter Bertha, or has become confused as between the two.' The report goes on to suggest the latter speculation is not unreasonable since A. 'was in a state of Mental unbalance and he may have been in that mental state for some considerable time during the last year or so of his life in the cabin near Padlei' (21 December 1949).

It is now the mystery of the sex of the dead body that needs to be solved, and the RCMP, already demonstrating their superior skills of deduction and still holding to the infallibility of the Crime Detection Laboratory results, decide that the only way to resolve the case of the dead body's sex is to dig up the other grave site. On 23 August 1950 another grave was opened up:

> The body was covered with deerskins and when the deerskins were removed it was quite plain the [*sic*] see the body was that of Bertha A. She was positively identified by two Eskimos who were present. These Eskimos had known her personally. The Eskimos are S/Cst. G— E.— and K— E.—. The body was in an almost perfect state of preservation and the writer could quite plainly see the scars on the girl's face where she had been burned as a child. Her nose too was partly burned off. There were no visible signs to show that death had been due to foul play. (5 September 1950)

The officer in Eskimo Point who wrote this report concludes by saying that he is of the opinion that Bertha's body should also be sent to the Crime Detection Lab in order to clear up the matter once and for all. The response from the commissioner in Ottawa (suffering, no doubt, from a major attack of castration anxiety) deems further investigation unwarranted, and the case is closed (21 September 1950).

There are at least two essential truths in need of confirmation in the text of the RCMP reports: the true biological sex of a mutilated corpse; and the truth about the disappearance of A.'s wife, an Inuit woman and the mother of the sex-undifferentiated, although presumed female, corpse. In the former truth, not only must a sexed-body be determined, but the logical conditions of necessity for differentiating a body along the male/female biological continuum must be established and put into practice. Following Nietzsche, Michel Foucault tells us that 'truth is undoubtedly the sort of error that cannot be refuted because it was hardened into an unalterable form in the long baking process of history' (Foucault 1977b: 144). Likewise, due to the intensity of freezing temperatures, the relatively well-preserved condition of the dead body could also be said to preserve the physiological and metaphysical conditions for a hardened irrefutability in the pursuit of truth this body will be made to effect and produce. But if we believe that 'the body obeys the exclusive laws of physiology and that it escapes the influence of history,' then, Foucault warns, we continue to err on the side of undeniable falsity (Foucault 1977b: 153). For, according to Foucault, 'the body is molded by a great many distinct regimes; it is broken down by the rhythms of work, rest, and holidays; it is poisoned by food or values, through eating habits or moral laws, it constructs resistances' (Foucault 1977b: 153). In the RCMP text, the corpse does indeed become a site of resistance brought about by the crisis of uncertainty in the determination of its essentially sexed nature, which no amount of autopsic dissection and post-mortem dismemberment will be able, finally, to resolve. Not only will the corpse resist the certainty of a biologically formulated, sexed differentiation for the medico-juridical powers of scientific interpretation, as in a pathologist's report, but it will also resist the feminist investigating subject's attempt to solve this enigma within the metonymically prescribed terms of (hetero)sexual difference. To position the female body as the necessary ground on which to lay solid foundations for a critical investigation will only exacerbate a serious displacement: to borrow Gayatri Spivak's dissociative phrasing, 'the woman's body is the last instance, it is elsewhere' (Spivak 1992b: 101).

The other truth in question is the account of A.'s wife's disappearance, the woman's body that, in the final instance, *is elsewhere*. It is this phantasmatic body which foregrounds the limits of a critical investigation based upon a paradigmatic subject of (hetero)sexual difference. The Inuk woman's vanishing and her subsequent re-discovery as a textual phantasm point to the degree of visible indifference on the part of the juridical investigators towards the indigenous female subject; although the issue of sexual differentiation with reference to the mutilated corpse noticeably dominates the RCMP reports' construction of the case against A., also worth noting is the indifference manifested toward the brutality of the Inuit woman's treatment at the hands of A., recorded and documented in the two interviews. It is important that a feminist reading of this visibly indifferent space remain attuned to the potential problem of reproducing the fetishistic investments of (het-ero)sexual difference for the culture of imperialism. Equally important for feminist criticism is its contribution to decolonizing the genealogy of this conceptual figure 'sexual difference': a project to be furthered through a sustained engagement with the material effects of language – its truth games and logics of discovery – on the bodies of imperialized subjects.

An Epistemology of the Grave

Constitutive to the logic of discovery in the scientific mode of investiga-tion is what Evelyn Fox Keller identifies as 'the urge to fathom the secrets of nature' (Keller 1992: 40). In her discussion of the place secrecy occupies in mapping out the interpretive domain of the discourse of science, Keller notes that 'secrets function to articulate a boundary: an interior not visible to outsiders, the demarcation of a separate domain, a sphere of autonomous power' (Keller 1992: 40). The idea of an interior space that must be brought to the surface, as it were, in order to disclose for examination that which has hitherto remained unexamined, is, as Fox argues, conditioned by the gender hierarchy:

> The ferreting out of nature's secrets, understood as the illumination of a female interior, or the tearing of Nature's veil, may be seen as expressing one of the most unembarrassedly stereotypic impulses of the scientific project. In this interpretation, the task of scientific enlightenment – the illu-mination of the reality behind appearances – is an inversion of surface and interior, an interchange between visible and invisible, that effectively routs the last vestiges of archaic, subterranean female power. (Keller 1992: 41)

The logic of scientific discovery, predicated as it is on an interpretive methodology 'for "undoing" nature's secrets,' succeeds, in the patholo-gist's report, in mapping itself onto the logic of a medico-juridical con-struction of truth (Keller 1992: 41). What is discovered in the process is that the contours of these scientific and legal investigations are demar-cated by the physiological imperatives of an aboriginal/woman/body, defined first and foremost on the foundational premise of a heterosex-ual difference.

Here we can begin to understand the perils of an unexamined essentialist discourse in the RCMP document that places an indigenous female body as the signifier of interiority that must be exteriorized if a definitive meaning of that body is to be extracted. This body must be exhumed from the grave, cut open, and subjected to examination. As in the case of the interviews, the assumptions made on the part of the RCMP about the 'savage nature' of northern life are mediated in all their graphic depictions of violence and dismembered bodies primarily through the body of a woman and the determination of her biological sex: the savage dismemberment of the body in the name of scientific certainty displaced onto a virtual savagery of northern, Inuit existence. The body resists, however, as does the metaphorical displacement in the figure of mother earth, who, in her permafrost state, will not disclose her interiority, that 'archaic, subterranean female power,' without a fight.

The body, writes Foucault, 'and everything that touches it: diet, climate, and soil – is the domain of the *Herkunft* [descent]. The body manifests the stigmata of past experience and also gives rise to desires, failings, and errors. These elements may join in a body where they achieve a sudden expression, but as often, their encounter is an engagement in which they efface each other, where the body becomes the pretext of their insurmountable conflict' (Foucault 1977b: 148). Foucault's inscription of the body as a *pretext* to insurmountable social and cultural antagonism is one site of contest Judith Butler can be said to problematize when she criticizes Foucault's genealogical history for positing a prediscursive notion of the body which assumes 'a materiality prior to signification and form' (Butler 1990: 130). If history for Foucault is quintessentially 'the creation of values and meanings by a signifying practice that requires the subjection of the body,' in the final instance, Butler argues, the body can only be figured 'as the medium which must be destroyed and transfigured in order for "culture" to emerge' (Butler 1990: 13). With specific reference to the sexed body, Butler suggests, the 'production of sex *as* the prediscursive ought to be understood as the effect of the apparatus of cultural construction designated by *gender*' (Butler 1990: 7; Butler's emphasis). In other words, the shape of the body, its figural deployment as a sexed entity, constitutes a terrain of contested meanings and values that are not necessarily pregiven to a sacrificial act of destruction in the name of cultural sovereignty. The idea that the body must be offered up to a mode of sacrificial dismemberment in order for 'culture' to emerge is itself a product of a gendered configuration of bodily regulation: one that awaits 'the inscription-as-incision of the masculine signifier for entrance into language and culture' (Butler 1990: 147–8). The body may indeed subvert a formation of knowledge that, in Foucault's words, 'is not made for understanding; it is made for cutting' (Foucault 1977b: 154).

Cutting allows for dissassemblage and reassemblage, not unlike the very process involved in reconstructing this archival document on my computer screen. The cursor traverses the textual terrain, slicing into it at the appropriate moment, extracting a segment and pasting it elsewhere. The menu on my screen directs me to 'cut,' 'copy,' or 'paste.' As I simulate a critical examination of this minor discourse and read it as a metonymic displacement of a macrological crisis of power, I engage in a storytelling technology that bespeaks the limits of its own certainty: Who controls the means of producing reality? Who polices the beginning and the end of the narrative? In the following section, I discuss the lost ground of heterosexual difference. This discussion is generated by another kind of storytelling event, and one that I recognize risks perpetuating a radical alterity in our reception of cultural (dis)similitude even as I wish to cross the border between the sex/gender dichotomy and the borders of feminist academic discourse.

A Skeleton in the Closet

The definitive identification of the second exhumed corpse as that of Bertha A. plays a dual function of closure within the RCMP text. On the one hand, positive identification makes it possible for the RCMP to close the case; on the other hand, the second exhumed corpse solves the confusion of gender the first body comes to signify precisely because a positive ID can be made. The ability to restore truth to the domain of a positive identity quickly displaces the anxiety of gender unresolvability assigned to the first exhumed body. Positive physiological identification substantiates any metaphysical uncertainty that might otherwise disrupt a definitive reading of the female-sexed status of the body. On both the physiological and metaphysical levels, the positively identified, female-sexed body of Bertha settles the problem of uncertainty the very logic of discovery sets out to resolve. What remains unresolved, of course, is the discrepancy between the pathologist's report of a female-sexed body in reference to the first exhumed body and A.'s own account as to this body's sex, or should I say gender? For the difficulty of positively identifying the originally exhumed body lies in the very understanding of gender difference as a symmetrical mark of sexual identity.

The unidentifiable, if not undecidable, body in this police inquiry marks an unstable continuity between the categories of sex and gender. Just why, when the unidentified-sexed body resists the authorities' attempt to definitively negotiate its borders, a crisis of unresolvability occurs in the RCMP's investigative procedures, is open to speculation. A colleague once mentioned that while visiting an Inuit family, he noticed that one of a pair of twin boys was dressed as a girl.[9] When he inquired as to why one child was dressed as a girl and the other a boy when their biological sex was male, the older brother to the children explained that the female child was named for his eleven-year-old sister who died shortly before the twins were born; hence, the child bears her name. Well trained, as most of us are, in the protocols of heterosexual sex/gender symmetry, my friend asked an obvious question: what happens when the child gets older? He was informed that when the child is old enough, he/she could decide as to whether to keep his/her older sister's name and identity or take a male name and identity for her/himself. The point is that the child will decide who he/she wants to be. In some indigenous cultures, transvestism acts as a spiritual force for transformation often linked to the desire for dissimilitude. For example, the ethnologist Valérie Chaussonnet discusses transvestism among Native peoples of the North Pacific as an agent of spiritual transformation between the human and the animal as well as between gender identities: 'Both men and women wore jewelry, although the styles were not necessarily identical. Bogoras noted that many Chukchi men wore women's earrings, generally by the order of a shaman. By direction of the shaman, Chukchi men also wore women's-style boots on occasion. This transvestism was a ploy to hide and protect the person from evil spirits, in the same way that sick people had their faces blackened so that the evil spirit would not recognize them as human. Transvestism in the shaman's garments represented his or her position between the male and female worlds ... The passage between gender identities and other passages throughout the lives and deaths of Siberian people were marked on clothing with the same care that the Alaskan Eskimo represented the transformational relationship with the animal world' (Chaussonet 1988: 225–6).[10] It is a compelling thought that A. may not have known the gender possibilities underlying his own children's sexual status. It certainly did not occur to the RCMP officers to investigate the possibility and implications of 'transvestism' within the spiritual and naming practices of the Inuit among A.'s and his partner's children.

At the same time the Canadian state sets out to bring the North under its sovereignty and, hence, establish a borderland, it must cope with Inuit geopolitical borders already in existence, borders the Canadian state does not wish to traverse or incorporate so much as obliterate: to make of Inuit culture a paper 'cut-out,' something that can be reduced to paper, to the storytelling technologies of police documents and pathologist's reports. The living bodies of the Inuit fail to obtain a corporeal status in these textual negotiations of a corpse and missing woman, as do the Inuit, in general, for the Canadian state. Nevertheless, the written bodies of this minor discourse continue to produce resistance to the ordering principles of what constitutes a sanctioned subject before the law and the state.

Northern Exposure

In the encounters between European/Euro-Canadian and indigenous people, writing plays a significant role: merchants have kept books, governors have kept diaries, ships' captains have kept logs, RCMP officers have kept reports. Inscription upon inscription inscribes many thousands of non-European people into a universal equivalent for the world's trade in people. Those records, reports, acts, and logs not only document particular events, but as a minor discourse they also constitute a micrological historical narrative and act as a material force partially shaping the lives of people who are subjects of and to history: history, written history of this sort, is the law, one kind of representational violence working with its repressive cohort: the coercive arm of the state: the military: the police force.[11]

As the legal arm of the state, the RCMP exists to maintain the state's national directives to bring the territories of the North under its jurisdiction. Unfortunately for the Canadian state, the Inuit live on these territories. Cultural incorporation is neither desired nor contemplated; only assimilation, the obliteration of all traces of a different mode of social, economic, and political life, is acceptable. Within this legal discourse, we can trace the phantasmatic aboriginality which places a 'mixed body' at the site of an immutable and intrinsic ideology of sexual difference. 'Sexual difference' operates for the RCMP as a signifier of certainty in an otherwise uncertain realm of biological instabilities where the code of 'racial difference' is taken as a symmetrical map of cultural difference. The undifferentiated-sexed body resists positive identification, teaching us not only that sex is not a ground from which to understand the presumed transparency of gender difference, but also that race is not a ground for comprehending the representational violence of cultural difference. Both these foundational categories permeate the micrological textures of powers. In either case, the trap of essentialism is an easy one to fall into unless we perpetually mobilize the metaphorical and metonymic forces at work in the micrological text. To divest the macrologies of the power of their legally sanctioned desire to oppress might actually involve going elsewhere, to a place where the physical and metaphysical are neither frozen in time nor thawing into a sea of indistinguishable elements, what Jane Gallop aptly refers to as 'the oceanic passivity of undifferentiation.' At the very least, we would do well to resist a futile attempt to exhume a body in the middle of an arctic winter, when the ground is frozen solid.

Post Script

In this reading of the colonial archive, I demonstrated the power of the written body to deconstruct the limits of its own logics of discovery. The case is itself notably productive of its own failure to constitute a certain gender and cultural identity in what is nevertheless an identifiably sex-undifferentiated corpse. My point here is to refuse a false synthesis of the dialectics of representation into a 'politics of identity' or the subversive critique thereof. Representational politics are not only productive of legitimate sites of subjectivity before the law and the state (qua Foucault and Butler), but they also produce fields of legitimacy that are at odds with the state and the law; indeed, they can shore up the state and the law's legitimacy as it is predicated on a refusal to recognize 'justice for women.' In legal-speak, I would say that this is evident in the example of the violence done toward the disappearing Inuit woman. The crime is murder, not the act of violence toward women. The problem here is not the recognition of a legal or legitimate subject, but the recognition of what constitutes an act of criminality that, in turn, designates the difference between a criminal and non-criminal (i.e., legal subject).

The subversion of gender identity is important to the fluidity of movement that gender construction itself makes possible: a fluidity, I would argue, that is essential to the front-line bodies of the women's movements, transnationally. But while Judith Butler's critique of iden-

tity politics is useful and important to the performative aspects of representation, I cannot altogether translate that critique into a transcultural context where indigenous women are taking the gender of decolonization with its effects on the politics of representation seriously as a
material strategy for social change. I would end here on a somewhat
polemical note by saying that when Butler deploys the critique of universality in the designation of a category 'woman' for cross-cultural
lines of solidarity, she follows from this critique toward a general criticism of the dangers of the universality of gender politics *in toto*.[12] This
move is in danger of eliding the actual transnational feminist politics
that currently exist here and elsewhere. It seems ironic that at the
moment a transnational feminist movement becomes conceivable, Butler insists that the instability of the category of gender makes such political engagement problematic – philosophically speaking. Does Butler's
feminist philosophy explain the current shifts in transnational feminist
materialities, or is her knowledge production potentially contributing
to the obstruction of a project for social change that the critique of the
imperial category of 'woman' was designed to further? The subversion
of an identity politics belongs to the realm of a performative mode of representation. Without a dialectical engagement with the politics of representation and the materialities of embodiment, we will have no social
movement; likewise, destabilizing the heterosexual matrix of gender
differentiation is just as important in order to inject fluidity into the
new social movements so that bodies are not rendered immobile by the
militaristic and regulatory practices of the heteronormative state and its
policing representatives. Thus, I am suggesting that the problem is not
only a theoretical one, but that the dialectical movement between performative modes of re-presentation (including the very writing of a
feminist philosophy) and a political assembly of representatives (such
as the First Nations women's movement) makes the formation of any
'ground,' be it frozen or otherwise, impossible to maintain.

7 The Possibility of Justice in the Child's Body: Rudy Wiebe and Yvonne Johnson's *Stolen Life: The Journey of a Cree Woman*

Dad stands beside me, crying. A man who looks like a doctor bends over me. He opens my mouth. He says to anybody who is listening, 'How do you sew up a tongue?'

Rudy Wiebe and Yvonne Johnson, *Stolen Life: The Journey of a Cree Woman*

Images of Innocence and Experience

In *Stolen Life: The Journey of a Cree Woman*, Rudy Wiebe narrates the life of Yvonne Johnson, who until 2001 was serving a life sentence for murder in the Okimaw Ohci Healing Lodge for Federally Sentenced Aboriginal Women in south Saskatchewan.[1] Wiebe, a well-known Canadian fiction writer, historian, and cultural critic, reconstructs, at Johnson's request, her life story. The result is, in part, a serious indictment of racism and the legal systems in Canada and the United States, including their policing operations. In addition to challenging juridical institutions and colonization, their book also raises important questions about the meaning of justice. Yvonne Johnson's life story foregrounds the problem of how the legal system can respond meaningfully to the specificity of First Nations women's and children's experience of sexualized and domestic colonial violence.[2]

In 'Force of Law: "The Mystical Foundation of Authority,"' Jacques Derrida usefully distinguishes law from justice. He writes that law (*droit*) 'is not justice. Law is the element of calculation, and it is just that there be law, but justice is incalculable, it requires us to calculate with the incalculable; and aporetic experiences are the experiences, as improbable as they are necessary, of justice, that is to say of moments in

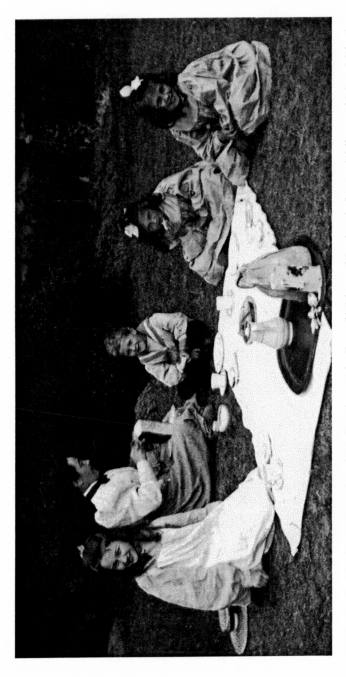

7.1 'Tea in the Garden at Pentrelew, 1201 Fort Street; the Four Children of Frederick George Walker and Mary Maberley Crease with Their Aunt, Josephine Crease.' Photographer unknown, 1897.

7.2 'Stoney Children, Banff Indian Days, 1929.' Photographer unknown. Tom Wilson, in the stetson, was an originator of the Banff Festival.

which the decision between just and unjust is never insured by a rule' (Derrida 1992: 16). As the title of his essay indicates, the law is about force. It is the domain for arbitrating violence and what constitutes its legitimate or illegitimate use. Justice, on the other hand, is not about the administration or calculation of violence; rather, it seeks to do away with it, if not exceed it. While the force of law is concerned with the application of violence, justice concerns itself with judging violence *itself*. This utopian dimension to justice is such that we can only ever wait for it. Justice, writes Derrida, is 'to come', *à venir* (Derrida 1992: 27).

If, however, justice remains only a desiring space on the horizon of experience, what of a critique and transformation of the multiple forms of violence in indigenous women's and children's lives? Waiting for justice to come to the legal system for indigenous peoples is a long and arduous journey; nevertheless, Derrida insists that the risk must be taken: 'incalculable justice *requires* us to calculate ... Not only *must* we calculate, negotiate the relation between the calculable and the incalculable, and negotiate without the sort of rule that wouldn't have to be reinvented there where we are cast, there where we find ourselves; but we *must* take it as far as possible, beyond the place we find ourselves and beyond the already identifiable zones of morality or politics or law, beyond the distinction between national and international, public and private, and so on' because, as Derrida continues, 'each advance in politicization obliges one to reconsider, and so to reinterpret the very foundations of law such as they had previously been calculated or delimited' (Derrida 1992: 28). Derrida situates his discussion of justice in the historical context of fascism and the Holocaust. Here I want to borrow, partially, his critique for the purposes of examining another historical but related context of violence and genocide: imperialism and colonization. Of particular importance here is how the colonial spectacle of the aboriginal family sacrificed the indigenous child's body to imperial rule.

Stolen Life advances decolonization in at least two ways: on the one hand, it unmasks existing conditions of legality, the racism of the legal system, for example; and, on the other, it creates new ways of looking at the meaning of justice in the context of colonial and neocolonial violence toward First Nations women and children, thus further creating the conditions upon which it is possible to recalculate the foundations of the law in light of the specific form of colonial domination toward women and children, including sexual abuse, rape, and domestic violence.

How, we might ask, did the indigenous child's body become such an intensive site for coercive and non-coercive (i.e., regulatory) forms of colonial power and domination? Although legislative policies implemented the ways and means to carry out the colonization of the indigenous child's body, what was also needed for such policies to come into effect were knowledges about and representations of 'the aboriginal child.' The infantilization of the colonized Native, discussed earlier with reference to *Nanook of the North*, in which the aboriginal was created as never quite civilized, mature, enlightened, and thus incapable of self-governance, was constitutive of such epistemic and representational practices. Similarly, the pathologization of the Native in the current use of the notion of 'residential school syndrome' is being used to explain the negative consequences of residential schooling such as 'low self-esteem, alcoholism, somatic disorders, violent tendencies, and other symptoms of psychological distress,' (Chrisjohn et al. 1997: 1). But, as Roland Chrisjohn, Sherri Young, and Michael Maraun insist, this 'present-day symptomatology found in Aboriginal Peoples and societies does not constitute a distinct psychological condition, but is the well known and long-studied response of human beings living under conditions of severe and prolonged oppression' (Chrisjohn et al. 1997: 4).

In January 1993, six twelve-to-fourteen-year-old Innu (also known as Montagnais-Naskapi) youth of Davis Inlet attempted suicide by inhaling gasoline fumes from plastic bags. When they were discovered, the youths refused to stop, screaming that they wanted to die (see Canadian Press 1993a, 1993b). The attempted suicides of these six Innu youth also demand to be contextualized within the history of colonization and its sacrifice of indigenous children and youth to the imperial subject of knowledge and representation.

Anne McGillivray and Brenda Comaskey maintain that colonialism 'shaped the nature, severity and rate of intimate violence in indigenous communities. It has influenced internal and external evaluation of the violence and created an environment in which it thrives as learned behaviour, transmitted across generations, silenced by culture. The reduction of women's roles in tribal economies and politics, the "decentring" of motherhood in mission schooling, and the patriarchy embedded in the Indian Act, in its regulation of band membership and electoral privileges, are entwined with the targeting of childhood for "civilization." Residential schooling and out-group adoption separated children from mother, clan, and culture. This past continues to speak in the dynamics of intimate violence in Aboriginal communities' (McGillivray and Comaskey 1999: 22; see also Proulx and Perrault 2000). Johnson's life story provides a unique opportunity to interrogate the limits of the indigenous child's body – as in the boundaries that circumscribe its representation as well as the limitations or inadequacies of such representations – as an object of sexualized colonial violence, thus pointedly demonstrating 'the targeting of childhood for "civilization."'

The overwhelming attention given to the discussion of violence in First Nations lives, as Patricia Monture-Angus notes, rarely amounts to a sufficient analysis of the problem. In fact, more often than not, it ends up naturalizing the violence further as a seemingly inevitable condition of their lives (Monture-Angus 1995). Nowhere, perhaps, is this more true than in the context of sexual violence toward indigenous women and children, where justice, as in the case of the death of Helen Betty Osborne, can take almost twenty years to come to the light of day. Racial violence is also at the root of the problem of justice, as Sherene Razack points out in her discussion of the murder of Pamela George, a woman of the Saulteaux (Ojibway) nation and a mother of two young children, who was murdered in April 1995 in Regina, Saskatchewan. Razack argues that the confluence of racism, sexual violence, and spatiality created conditions for de-racing the violence done to George in the legal account of what happened to her. Razack argues that

> while it is certainly patriarchy that produces men whose sense of identity is achieved through brutalizing a woman, the men's and the courts' capacity to dehumanize Pamela George came from their understanding of her as the (gendered) racial Other whose degradation confirmed their own identities as white – that is, as men entitled to the land and the full benefits of citizenship. (Razack 2002: 126)

The experience of intimate violence by indigenous women, youth, and children questions the historical and spatial narrative of colonial violence in many ways. Rather than establishing one category such as race, gender, or sexuality as the fundamental cause of such violence, I argue for a chiasmatic understanding of the law in relation to justice in which multiple experiences and identity markers are recognized as neither universal nor static but mobile signs deployed against specific bodies, spaces, and institutions in order to stabilize or de-stabilize colonial power. In other words, it is not the identity of the indigenous body that determines its experience of social, political, and economic violence, but how it is inscribed by and within colonial institutions to maintain the equilibrium of imperial power. The colonial narrative has also been, and continues to be, written in terms of the dispossession of the land or territory and not in terms of the dispossession of the body in language, kinship, and home.[3] In the cases of Helen Betty Osborne and Pamela George, imperial power determined the inscriptions of their bodies as objects of racial, gendered, and sexual violence. Moreover, the forms of colonial dispossession to which they were subjected included the expropriation and commodification of land *and* the dehumanization of their bodies as objects of exchange and exploitation. Both forms of dispossession must be taken into account if decolonization is to reach women, children, and the poor.

While Wiebe's construction of Johnson's 'stolen life' focuses on the existence of neocolonial racism in the judicial system, I argue that Johnson's traumatic experience of sexual violence lies at the core of her experience of colonization and that until this form of colonial domination is recognized as such, the narrative containment of her story cannot bring about the justice desired by Wiebe in his effort to account for Johnson's 'stolen life.' The trauma of her experience of violence is, in fact, reproduced through another form of violence, the violence of writing and the 'law of narrative' that insist upon imposing on her fragments of memory a sequential and apparently coherent narrative form.[4] If justice is to come, it must be newly defined through the indigenous child's body and the material realities of its self-expression.

Not All Vaginas Speak Equally

Stolen Life draws attention to the problem of collaboration and the difficulties that emerge in relation in a text written between, in Antonio Gramsci's useful terms, 'subaltern' and 'intellectual.' In her reading of Gramsci's philosophy of praxis in 'Can the Subaltern Speak?' Gayatri Spivak situates the tension between 'subaltern' and 'intellectual' in relation to the poststructural move toward a politics of desire. Spivak is critical of how Michel Foucault, Felix Guattari, and Gilles Deleuze ignore the ideological significance of textual mediations in the construction of emancipatory 'figures of desire' such as the working class. In her concern to articulate the position of the female subaltern, Spivak examines the multiple layers of discourse on *sati* or 'widow sacrifice' in Hindu and colonial writings.[5] She demonstrates the limits of how *sati* was read as a sign of Indian woman's victimage for the purposes of advancing a paternalistic colonial ideology; thus, the female subaltern was transformed from victim to the equally problematic positioning of the 'Indian woman' as an emancipatory ideal, a figure to be saved in the narratives of decolonial nationalism and independence. By way of exceeding the calculation of violence toward 'the female subaltern,' Spivak turns toward a figure of articulated silence in the female body, the unspeakable and unspeaking vagina. At the conclusion to her essay, Spivak's recalls an image of the suspended body of a female suicide, Bhubaneswari Bhaduri, who hanged herself in 1926. Spivak writes: 'The suicide was a puzzle since, as Bhubaneswari was menstruating at the time, it was clearly not a case of illicit pregnancy. Nearly a decade later, it was discovered, in a letter she had left for her elder sister, that she was a member of one of the many groups involved in the armed struggle for Indian independence. She had been entrusted with a political assassination. Unable to confront the task and yet aware of the practical need for trust, she killed herself' (Spivak 1999: 307). What Spivak 'politicizes' in Bhaduri's death is the use of menstrual blood to signify the limits of the flows and blocks of colonial and neocolonial politics. Her death should not be read as a signifier of female subjection, as it is in the example of *sati*, but as a complex signifier of unspoken desire and the need to transform female oppression in the struggle for national independence from British colonial rule. In the face of evidence to the contrary, Bhaduri's family nevertheless attempted to explain away her suicide on the basis of an illicit pregnancy, and only later had to face the reality of her political longings. In this case, it becomes clear that her very reproductive body (as distinct from her desiring political body) stood at the crux of the problem of decolonization. In Spivak's analysis, the hitherto supplementary status of the potentially reproductive body, essentialized as Woman, is materially transformed into a *general sign of imperialist and anti-imperialist violence*. It is this figure of the unspeakable vagina as sign of a failed decolonial political praxis that Spivak animates for transnational feminisms and that I wish to carry over into the narrative construction of Yvonne Johnson's life story.

In a witness statement Yvonne Johnson wrote and signed on 2 November 1992, witnessed by Detective Linda Billings of the Child Abuse Unit, Edmonton Police Service, Johnson recounts her first memory of sexual abuse at the age of two:

My first attack happened when I was between two to three-years old. We lived in a pink house, next door to a two-storey house and down from the railroad tracks ... The attack on me was by a grown man, by my brother Leon [eight and a half years old at that time], and later on by three other boys, one was tall with red hair. And one boy was our neighbour, and would be in later years as well.

What started my rape was our babysitter [the grown man] caught Leon messing around with me behind the fridge in the kitchen. The man told him, in other words, Leon was not doing it right. I was placed on the kitchen table and the bottom half of my body stripped. He was pointing things out to Leon, saying things like this is this, and this is this. And this is where you put your prick.

...

I cry and try to crawl off the table. The man would yell at me and slap my ass. At first. And put me on my back. He hurt me I think by putting his finger up my cunt. I'd cry and try to get away as I was crawling off the table, then he started to poke my ass as well. He yelled at Leon for letting me get away.

...

If anyone tried to come in the kitchen, like other kids, he'd get Leon to give them a sucker and chase them away. The guy beat me to shut me up, he banged my head on the table. Then when someone came he'd put his cock in my mouth and almost kill me. But also, he'd bend my feet, to where I swear he broke them, to spread my legs and poke at me. I think he went to put lard or oil on his hands, and then Leon would bend my feet. (Wiebe and Johnson 1998: 334–5)

Wiebe's account of Yvonne Johnson's traumatic experience of sexual abuse represents a scar on the surface of late colonization. It marks a time and place when and where the child's body was penetrated, both materially and metaphorically, with significance for colonial power. It would be tempting to try to suture this body back together. But like Mary Shelley's monster in *Frankenstein*, although the pieces come from apparently normal and whole bodies, the reassembled body is never quite the same, never quite right; rather, it appears as an unharmonious and inelegant form riddled with unruly, infantile, and violent impulses. Neither representation of an idealized wholeness nor abject Other is sufficient to understanding the material realities of colonial violence inscribed on the indigenous child's body.

In the case of sexual violence, body-knowledge is often fragmented and disassembled. This partial knowledge has become a way of identifying – and to a large extent dismissing – the knowledge of women's memories of childhood abuse. Thus, representational strategies that seek to tell the truth of the body's pain, suffering, joy, and pleasure must re-member knowledge of the body as well as dis-member officially sanctioned knowledges. Such representational strategies hold out the possibility of dissimulating different knowledges through the body's representational capacities, a point I will return to with reference to Augusto Boal's *Theatre of the Oppressed* and its pedagogical significance for my own teaching of *Stolen Life*.

The material processes of re-membering and dis-membering constitute what I would call *an analytics of dis/memberment* and serve as a methodological framework for the following discussion of the significance of Yvonne Johnson's body to Rudy Wiebe's construction of the history of colonial injustice to indigenous peoples. Johnson's birth with a cleft palate, her numerous surgeries, cosmetic as well as life-preserving, represent a problematic in the narrative of coming face to face with the body of the indigenous woman as the formative contradiction of colonial power.

Early in the text, in a chapter titled 'My Eyes Became My Voice,' Wiebe skilfully weaves his first face-to-face encounter with Johnson in June of 1993 at P4W, the then federal prison for women in Kingston, Ontario, into the fabric of her autobiographical narratives of childhood spent in Butte, Montana.[6] Wiebe separates his textual reconstruction of this initial interview from Johnson's autobiographical narratives by inserting 'Yvonne' in bold print at the beginning of her excerpts. Although Wiebe will construct his own voice, as it were, as the voice of the author, the back and forth dialogue between Wiebe's account of this meeting and Johnson's journal entries will question the foundations of this authorial and authoritative position. Initially, Wiebe's retelling of Yvonne Johnson's 'story' is a way of bringing order to the chaos that has been her life. Writing becomes the means to establish coherency and thus to make sense of the violence that has been done to Johnson as well as the violence she participated in: 'She's smiling at me; she has sent me tapes and videos as well, but they are so difficult to organize, her memories are so interwoven and intersnarled, that I've begged her to write only, however it comes and she remembers, but write it down; write, please' (11). Eventually, however, Wiebe will situate Johnson's 'voice' as the counter-narrative to *the law of narrative*. Johnson says: 'I guess when I talk I express myself like I listened, story form ... I tell little stories so you can see, live, feel what I am trying to explain to you. Like I'm figuring it out, out loud. I'm always all over the place. People say I can't stay on one topic; sometimes when I just say things head-on, point blank, it drives them crazy to have to listen to me ... But the Elders say that story-telling is a gift too. If a person with a story can go deep, where people are angry, sad, where they're hiding thoughts and emotions, raise the past they've maybe forgotten and can't really recognize any more, push them to spirit-walk into themselves – to do that with a story is a gift' (11–12). While the remnants of his determination to stick to the written word linger on the margins of this dialogue – 'if she wants to tell her story, her words must be on paper' (22) – Wiebe will eventually submit to the limits posed by his knowledge of writing: 'After forty years of work at writing, I think I know a bit about making stories, but I don't grasp the impossibilities of this one; not yet' (24). Of course, it is the book, *Stolen Life,* that will bring Johnson's story into the light of day, but Wiebe cannot tell such a story without signalling the *impossibilities* of doing so. He tries, for example, to correct the swerves and swings of Yvonne's narrative: 'I try to bring her back to her original subject: Cecilia in psychiatric care after Earl's death. And she shifts instantly, as sharp as all her memories are. In details they can be as precise as a photograph' (85). And yet, Yvonne cannot remember faces. 'Why did the Creator give me these intricate memories, this photographic mind, and yet allows me only bits and pieces of my past? So many tiny, exact snapshots branded on me. Why can't I see who the person was?' (99). To tell *her* story, to *write* her story, cannot be anything but difficult, given the realities of oppression Johnson has experienced; nevertheless, Johnson does have access to the oral and visual articulation of her experience. 'If I have a visual memory, I don't doubt myself. I don't doubt the houses I lived in, in Butte, Montana' (25).

Her early childhood memories are divided between two rental houses: the Pink house, close to the open mine where her father and mother worked, and the White house, a grand house vacated by its wealthy owners and yet affordable due to the downward-bound economic conditions of the time. Johnson's notion of 'visual memory' is entirely linked to these spatial orientations. Deliberately, the pink and white codification of Yvonne's memories of poverty and pseudo-grandeur fall within their respective race- and class-coded boundaries, not to mention the significance of the White house to colonial governance. Whatever upward mobility the White house may represent, the spatial frontiers of her working-class family's economic situation remain firmly intact. Johnson's visual memory, along with her capacity to spirit walk through these modes of visual, spatial, corporeal, and spiritual mediations, becomes a source of healing-knowledge for breaking the silence about her oppression and for releasing her incarcerated voice. Breaking that silence, however, must be mediated through language, through the history of how Johnson's body became inscribed with value and meaning, and how she resignifies a historico-corporeality to re-member her life.

In recounting her early childhood during the late fifties and early sixties, Johnson examines how the duality of 'predators and victims' governed relationships both inside and outside the home. Alcohol, drug abuse, and the explosive, frightening fights that break out as a result lead Johnson to fear for her body within the house and family. Making use of her visual and spatial memory, she interprets two family photographs from the perspectives of this domestic violence threatening herself and, by contrast, of the very different sort of violence to which her older brother, Earl, will be subjected. In one photo, she describes herself sitting on her brother, Leon's, lap, 'me with my little bare legs parted,' and in another black and white photo she writes that it was 'taken in the yard [and] shows only us kids and the Butte landscape ... and finally me, the littlest, smiling so desperately, with my arms wrapped tight around my chest, holding myself together ... and beside [Leon], tallest of all, my handsome brother Earl. He's going on fifteen, smiling, his heavy hair greased down in a curl on the right side of his face – he spent a lot of time getting the flip in his hair just so before he left for school – leaning forward a little like a Cree peering at you, his hands behind his back, and wearing a white T-shirt with a dark horizontal band. It looks like a wide rope cinched tight around his chest' (27–8). Yvonne's images of the vulnerability of her female child-body and Earl's chest bound by rope anticipate the main events that will irrevocably shape Yvonne Johnson's life: her experience of sexual violence and the death of Earl in prison, the victim of police brutality and racial violence, covered up as suicide. It is this heteronormative logic, in which the indigenous female body is coded as sexual object and the indigenous male body is reduced to a representation of primitive male aggression, that determines Wiebe's representation of Yvonne's and Earl Johnson's bodies as objects of colonial violence.[7] Within this oppositional logic of sexual difference, domestic violence and sexual violence are not part of the official narrative of colonial injustice. Rather, Yvonne's body and her experience of sexual violence will come to supplement the representation of the official and unofficial narratives of Earl's death.

The tension between the writerly power of the professional class that Wiebe embodies and the oral and visual power of Johnson's account of her dispossession informs the back and forth motion of the text, its interruptions, its narrative dissociations between past and present, its humour, surrealities, and the jarring distance between places and people: 'And Yvonne is talking; truly talking. Sometimes it has to come from behind the black curtain of her hair, but she talks; her amazing, unstoppable, now utterable words trigger one memory after another and she follows that spoor like a track leading deeper and deeper into a dark forest' (31). Wiebe's romantic metaphor of the 'dark forest' elides the integral realities of Yvonne's body and its inscriptions of an economically depressed city of Butte, Montana, as the site of her spatial memories and their reconstruction. Her words are *like* spoors, which are *like a track*, like a map to guide Wiebe into the 'dark forest' that is her life, the dark continent that is her landscape of memory and dispossession. Once again the female body is in danger of being reduced to nature; there to figure as a metonymic code for the land and territorial dispossession, rather than subject to dispossession itself.

An Anatomy of Pain

Yvonne Johnson was born with a severe abnormality, an open palate: 'where my nose, top lip, gums, and roof of my mouth should have been, there was only folded tissue that left a gap in my upper mouth' (29), and during her childhood she received numerous reconstructive surgeries. The disfigurement of Johnson's childhood face becomes a metonymic reminder of her struggle to learn how to talk. But when Johnson says that 'learning to talk took years,' Wiebe's framing of her narratives produces a double layer of meaning that trans-codes her physical challenge into an analytical one (35). The chapter titled 'A Killing in the Family,' in which Wiebe narrates Earl's death, as told from the perspective of his father, Clarence, begins with his response to Yvonne's birth defect: 'double cleft lip and palate, the doctor called it. There was just blood in the middle of her face; he had to clean it out before he could make her breathe' (52). Clarence shows Wiebe a photo from the clinic of Yvonne's tiny face: 'A month after birth, eyes squeezed shut above the unrecognizable center of a tiny countenance, labeled on the back "Uncorrected." Then, six months later, "Beginning Correction," after the first surgery. The long, excruciating "correction" of a "mistake" – made by whom? – the unaware irony of medical terms' (52). Correcting a mistake becomes one of the text's unspoken, yet guiding, tropes, as in to correct the mistaken assumption that Earl committed suicide. Rather, his death, according to Clarence, was doctored-up to look like suicide. The mistake in Yvonne's body, however, is result of natural causes; it is hereditary. The oppositional logic of artifice and nature is realigned in relation to another opposition, savagery and civilization. Yvonne's face is coded as natural and bloody, whereas Earl's death is figured as an effect of deception, lies, and cover-ups. Although Yvonne's body can be altered and fixed by medical surgery, its meaning nevertheless remains immutable, an original 'mistake' tied to Nature's authorship and its unrelenting power over the determination of the human form. As such, Yvonne's body becomes a conduit for telling the truth of Earl's death, as if his story must be discharged through this immutable body if the 'truth' concerning his death is to come to light. Not surprisingly, Johnson writes: 'I am like a conductor, not a human being' (41).

In another instance in which Johnson's body is made to occupy a position of mediation, Wiebe describes her sitting on her mom's lap driving 'into the woods' and playing with forming spit in her mouth: 'But I was stubborn even then when I really wanted something, and I practiced and practiced what would be so easy for any ordinary kid – to hang out of the truck window in the rushing air and try to gather a big gob of spit together into the tip of my mouth behind my lips and let if fly out just right, sail round and full and aimed so exactly to carry on the wind and bounce big off the back duals. And, finally, I did it!' (54). The discharge from Yvonne's mouth, from the gaping, bloody hole of orality, will be the trail from which Earl's story will emerge. The issues from her body will fill up the gaps and holes of memory, the empty spaces that for Wiebe represent poison: 'And the Pink House where Yvonne's first memories emerge is suspended somewhere in the invisible air over that black lake, an infected space for memory only. But as indelible as poison to her ... Every house Yvonne lived in in Butte is now nothing but space' (55, 56). But this is not a nothing space; it is the domesticated space of her life and her material experience of violence, a space that held her body and rendered it vulnerable to sexual violence.

It is within the space of the same page that Wiebe narrates Clarence's memory of domestic violence and Earl's death. Domestic violence, however, is downplayed in relation to Earl's death. Clarence sees himself as the 'victim' of the judicial system and refuses to pay the fine set by the judge as a result of his domestic violence toward Cecilia. He would rather stay in jail. Cecilia has a full-time job, however, and needs Clarence to watch the children while she goes to work: 'I said no, it was me got assaulted. I'd stay my time. So she brought the judge over, he told me he'd go easy on the fine. So I came out' (57).

Clarence has chosen to remain living alone in Butte in order to unravel the truth of Earl's death, collecting newspaper articles and information in order to prove, over and over again, the injustice of it. The most plausible account Clarence gives for Earl's death is that he was being threatened by a man with whom he was once friends: they stole some cigarettes together, and Earl confessed; but his testimony indicted his 'best buddy.' His friend then went to Vietnam and had 'a very rough time.' He returned to Butte 'vowing, according to rumours floating around the bars, to get even with Earl' (67). Wiebe, however, includes a speculative, if not mysterious, comment by Johnson on a moment of flight that takes place just before Earl's death. It hints at something that remains unsaid and unacknowledged precisely because Johnson cannot remember or did not know the 'reason' for this act of flight:

> Clarence offers no reason for this trip to Saskatchewan. Yvonne tells me she still cannot understand why they made that ten- to twelve-hour drive north when there was no school break for the four girls. It must have been a 'spur of the moment' decision, but just before they left she remembers Earl was trying to explain something to Clarence and he couldn't – or wouldn't – understand what Earl meant. They argued until Earl got up, furious, and stormed out of the house; within an hour, parents and all four girls were heading for Canada. (61)

What Johnson does remember about Earl's death appears in the form of an inexplicable and mysterious event. Although she is hundreds of miles away from Earl at the time of his death, she feels something like an electrical jolt to her body that throws her off her feet. The chapter concludes with Yvonne telling her mother that Earl's shadow follows her on the walls of the porch and plays hide and seek with her in the forest. In the shadow world of the outdoors and nature, Yvonne communes with Earl's discontented spirit, which, like her ancestor Big Bear, as Wiebe notes, also suffered to be hanged in prison due to colonial injustice. Johnson's inability to re-member why the family made the trip to Canada contains, if not justifies, the narrative absence of an

Other story. Furthermore, this narrative absence is then supplemented by Johnson's mystical experience of Earl's death.

What comes through in Wiebe's reconstruction of Clarence's account of Earl's death is that it was 'the family' that was somehow being threatened, and that their family was ultimately destroyed by Earl's death. But what exactly that threat was we don't know.

The greatest threats to the patriarchal family and its integrity are incest and pedaphilia. Not surprisingly, the other discourse intimated in Wiebe's recounting of Earl's death is the primordial narrative of incest. Clarence's rewriting of Earl's death becomes a sort of protective prophylactic against the contamination of incest that threatens the foundation of the family.

The chapter ends with Clarence and Wiebe crying together over the inexplicable death of Earl – the consolation of fraternal bonding over the melancholic mourning for a lost son – and the Other narrative of incest suggestively woven into the text of Earl's death hangs like a series of loose threads until Johnson picks them up later in order to bring legal charges against her father for sexual abuse.

The official narrative event of Earl's death and Clarence's unofficial rewriting of that narrative set up a seemingly never-ending cycle of competing truths. And the reader is drawn into the gap left between the official story and its counter-narrative only to find herself still listening to a conversation between Wiebe and his Other Author, but unable to complete the speech act. 'I have endless memories without faces. Random, separate memories with no story line, but sprinkled with possible truth' (75). 'It took years for the words with which I could explain or defend myself to be gradually, and with great pain, carved and sewn into my face' (78). Yvonne Johnson's birth defect and corrective surgeries bring a material textuality to her experience of silence. Like the fusing of her lips in a radical surgical procedure designed as a corrective measure which will eventually lead to her obtaining speech, Johnson's capacity to overcome the limits of her physical reality are undone by the metonymic use of her body to act as a silent conduit for Earl's death due to colonial and racial violence. The specificity of the material reality of Yvonne's embodied experience under the same regime of colonial and racial violence is discounted, however, by her role as the 'conductor' of Earl's death.

In the subsequent chapter to Wiebe and Clarence's conversation, narratives of sexual abuse, rape, and incest rupture the narrative to the point that this chapter remains 'unfocused,' as it were. There is still the residue of Earl's death clinging to memories of the family: 'Earl's death remains like a mountain divide in the collective memory of the entire family; at any moment of speech or writing Yvonne will swing to that time, detailed incidents leaping into consciousness' (92). The interventions entitled 'When did this happen? How?' that preface Yvonne's narrative accounts of sexual abuse add to the *confusion* – the lack of coherency, the fragments, the bits and pieces. 'This was my childhood: the world even in my home is uncontrollable and can at any moment burst into violence. I can only react. If I do get caught, I was either careless or asking for it. I am always guilty'; 'never sit with your legs apart, never forget to wear long pants under your dress or they'll see your panties if you forget yourself and play as a child will play, never talk back ... be always alert and ready to outmaneuver danger before it's close enough to catch you' (78). Wiebe intervenes: 'As Yvonne and I struggle together with notebooks, letters, public records, and phone calls to find some order of chronology and fact in her past life, we need to begin again – she sees so much of her life, and consequently memory, as contained in the circle of repetition – we must begin again with her childhood place: Butte, Montana' (80).

After Earl's death, Cecilia commits herself to a psychiatric ward (84). She then becomes the first and only woman truck driver at the mine (87). Another 'after shock' related to Earl's death is Leon's attempt to hang himself. Yvonne's text: 'sometimes I think there might have been some kind of connection between Earl's death and Leon ... perhaps that would explain why Mom became so obsessed with protecting Leon. Even to the point of selling me out, as it sometimes seemed to me – I don't know – or maybe I already do know and just can't remember enough to understand, but no one now, neither Mom nor Leon nor my sisters, will talk to me about this. Only Kathy says she believes I believe what I'm looking for is true – but then she cries, she won't tell me what she remembers. Dad visits and supports me as he can, but he won't, or just can't, try to explain anything about this either' (93).

Both Clarence and Leon are implicated in sexual violence toward Yvonne. Earl saves her life in one horrifying incident when she is almost murdered. The question of time is important here; hence 'When did this happen? How?' Did these events take place, for example, just before Earl's death, and is his death related to them?

Yvonne remembers how Leon delivered her to an old man who sexually abuses her with the help of the babysitter, and she recounts another episode of Leon bringing home lots of money and some clothes which Cecilia throws in the wood stove and burns, except for a plaid skirt that she gives to Kathy, who is later brought home, bleeding, after having been attacked by a gang of boys: 'Kathy disappears, she is shrieking as they beat and grab at her; some of the bigger guys crowding around are opening their pants. They are clawing at her, hands everywhere as she screams, and two of them leap up above the crowd; they are trying to jump on top of her' (88–9). Yvonne fights back with a wooden plank and the boys disperse (89). These stories are woven into the history of Cecilia's involvement with the American Indian Movement (AIM) and the Trail of Broken Treaties trek to Washington in 1972, which she took up in order to deal with Earl's death (105). AIM wants to mount a campaign in protest of Earl's death in Butte, but Clarence, strangely enough, is opposed (102–3). And finally, these unevenly remembered events end with Earl rescuing Yvonne from a violent episode in which she is brutally beaten and placed on a sawmill belt 'that carries the bark from the logs up to the top of the trash cone that smokes all the time.' She falls crashing to the ground and is taken to hospital, where she remembers the doctor saying, 'How do you sew up a tongue?' (109).

These fragments of sexual abuse and the politics of AIM seem oddly disconnected from one another, divided by a semiotics of sexual difference trans-coded onto public and private spaces where men do real politics, or 'real politics' are owned by masculinity in men or women like Cecilia, and feminine women and female children stay at home to be done in by racism, street violence, and domestic violence. Why do these 'worlds' appear so utterly disconnected and disarticulated in Wiebe's narrative frame? Why does Johnson's body only serve as a container of violence and for the discharge of the truth of Earl's death through its own silence, through the absence of its tongue?

Although Wiebe may have set out to write a coherent narrative and impose the law of narrative, he fails precisely because there is a secondary order of trauma that must be overcome, which is the trauma Johnson experiences in attempting to write her story to begin with. For justice to come and, along with it, for healing to take place, the originary violence of incest and sexual abuse must first be acknowledged. It is this textual component of the repetitive element of trauma that Wiebe, as a writer, must confront if he is to participate in the process of telling Johnson's story.

To Spirit Walk the Letter and the Law

Although Wiebe writes that 'there are so many people in your life, no story, is ever only yours alone' (24), just how others become part of our stories is a complicated process, fraught with contradictions and the overdeterminations of historical forces such as imperialism and colonial occupation. Stories are themselves part of communication systems of exchange and as such are subject to allowable transactions that take place under political and economic structures. Under colonial patriarchy, the material realities that emerge in the stories told by women of sexual violence and abuse are not generally recognized as having authorial power and the legitimacy of transacting knowledge. Instead, such materialities of sexualized violence under colonialism are rendered invisible and become mystical remainders at the mythic ends of humanity.

Within Wiebe's text, Johnson emerges as a counter-figure, a phantom storyteller whose relationship to language and literature – the law of narrative – will have to be settled if her story is to be told in the biographical form. As someone victimized by a racist, colonial, and patriarchal legal system, Johnson emerges not only as a perpetrator of a violent crime but, as her case history reveals, someone who has also experienced the racism of the legal system in Canada. Thus, Johnson is framed by Wiebe's narrative as a figure who will question the letter of the law as well as the law of narrative. She will emerge in a contradictory representational space as someone who commits violence (in life and language) and as someone who is the object of it (also in life and language). Wiebe states in his editorial preface that 'the selection, compiling, and arrangement of events and details in this book were done in a manner *the two authors* believe to be honest and accurate. Public documents are quoted selectively, but with every attempt at fairness and accuracy' (xii, emphasis added). The reader assumes, of course, that Wiebe is one author and Johnson the other. But this Other Author is, I think, far more ambiguous than might initially appear, in part, because Johnson does not figure as an 'author' in a conventional way. Rather, this Other Author is a mythical, if not transcendent, one, the *spirit* of the text and of the law – and embodied in Johnson. It is this mystical author who guides Wiebe's desire for a non-violent, rational, and textual resolution to colonial violence. When I write that Yvonne Johnson does not figure as a conventional author, I am not saying that she is not recognizable as a co-writer, but it is Wiebe who put her narrative threads together and carefully crafted the book as a whole. A more interesting project, perhaps, is not to try to situate Johnson as an author of *Stolen Life*, in order to respond to established notions of authority claimed through identity and representation, but to seek to understand how her textual contributions de-authorize and de-mystify the violence that is constitutive of the colonial law of narrative and the narrative force of colonial law.[8]

For Wiebe, Yvonne Johnson occupies the spirit of the letter in a complicated text of desire, power, and interest that attempts to make a coherent narrative of a violent history of colonization. In the particular instance of Earl's death, for example, Yvonne Johnson's body comes to suture the fraternal gap of that historical violence between Clarence and Wiebe. She is the spirit of the law, and as the apparitional aboriginal, she comes to supplement a rational and discursive solution to the failure of the law to defend the subjects most in need of justice. 'To mark the moment when not only a civil but a good society is born out of domestic confusion, singular events that break the letter of the law to instill its spirit are often invoked. The protection of women by men often provides such an event' (Spivak 1988: 298). In Yvonne's case, the man who could have, and did, protect and save Yvonne's life, Earl, is dead. Thus, Wiebe steps in to become the defender of her legal rights. This does not mean that Wiebe turns himself into the hero of Yvonne Johnson's story. He does not ride in like a white knight, there to save 'brown women from brown men.' As Gayatri Spivik has invited us to consider in another context: 'Can the subaltern speak? and Can the subaltern (as woman) speak? our efforts to give the subaltern a voice in history will be doubly open to the dangers run by Freud's discourse. As a product of these considerations, I have put together the sentence "White men are saving brown women from brown men" in a spirit not unlike the one to be encountered in Freud's investigations of the sentence "A child is being beaten"' (Spivak 1988: 296). His integrity as a collaborator is demonstrated on many levels. Firstly, he is acutely aware of his physical presence: 'We hug, quick and loose because for her the arms of men have mostly been dangerous, often terrible' (6); secondly, he demonstrates his intellectual integrity in his rigorous research into the legal implications of Johnson's life and case history; thirdly, his emotional integrity manifests in his friendship with Yvonne, the respect he has for her and her story, and in his numerous interviews and encounters with various members of her family; fourthly, and lastly, he acknowledges the spiritual knowledge Johnson carries with her of the ceremony performed by her Grandma Flora on her child's body to heal her from her trauma of sexual abuse:

> I could see her do this, as if she was walking around inside me looking, it seemed her spirit was mine and she was looking for things I could not hide even if I knew what they were, and I felt I was outside myself, like

watching from a distance. She asked what I had seen, and I couldn't say, though I knew in my spirit what had happened. She spoke and spoke as she unwrapped me, and I knew she was saying to me, 'Now, look at yourself, see, you are all better' ... And I looked at Grandma. With surprise and awe, and I felt her pride about an act well done. She peered at me as if she was walking inside me, looking inside me, looking around to see if all was well, and she saw my spirit was well. (431)

Indeed, in collaboration with Johnson, Wiebe may have put on the record one of the few known accounts of such a ceremony, the benefits of which, Johnson anticipates, could be far-reaching: 'A child doesn't know how to protect itself, either its body or its spirit. Grandma Flora saved my spirit from being damaged beyond restoration by helping me forget, but now the Creator is again letting me remember. My question is, why?' (426). Nevertheless, Wiebe's corporeal integrity stands in direct contrast to Johnson's dis-membered recollection of her life and experience.

Affirmative justice may in fact lie in healing the violence of colonial conquest, rather than in waiting for justice to arrive in a colonial judicial system. Wiebe and Johnson's text makes an important contribution to the question of justice in decolonization, but how it does so is neither self-evident nor entirely obscure. An affirmative justice exists in the folds of its narrative, somewhere in-between two acts of colonial violence and their narrative re-presentation: Earl's death and the rape of Yvonne Johnson's childhood body, the imposition of narrative and Johnson's disassembled story.

While Wiebe testifies to the impossibility of the position he places himself in, his text is most clearly a victory of sorts because it retells the story of the law and justifies the juridical aspect of decolonization that looks to its reformation and restoration within the institutions of the law themselves, including the emergence of legal pluralism, a critique of the incarceration of Native women in Canada, and the racism of the judicial system. The 'law,' however, is heterogeneous and includes the letter of the law and the law of narrative. What his text does not do, and where the warning flags come up, is that it does not speak *to* the law but *from* it, and as a result it fails to perceive that other law at work in Johnson's life, which is Law of the Father under patriarchy, that is, the Oedipal law of incest. In the specific case of Yvonne Johnson, the Law of the Father is called into existence by the crime of 'pedophilia,' the sexualized paternal and colonial conquest of the indigenous female child's body. Yvonne Johnson participated in the murder of a man whom she maintained she had reason to fear, especially with respect to the safety of her children, because she believed him to be a pedophile. She thus took the law (of the Father) into her own hands and participated in his murder.

Humans without Justice

An aboriginality haunts Derrida's essay 'Force of Law' in its return to a mythic violence, incest, and the rule of the Primordial Father. In the Oedipal incest narrative, the Primordial Father's power over female reproduction attempts to ensure the paternal origin of the child, and yet the (male) child is that which most threatens to usurp the father's power. The 'foundations of law' as they appear in Wiebe and Johnson's text, as well as Derrida's essay, are not only the effect of colonial legislative practices, but are also historically rooted in other nineteenth-century European techniques of colonial conquest, specifically the use of disciplines of knowledge such as ethnography and psychopathology to arbitrate the legitimate or illegitimate use of violence toward the (ab)Original child's body. Freud's *Totem and Taboo* (1913) represented the culmination of this work, which took up the narrative of incest and the figure of the primordial father to draw the line between the illegitimacy of incestuous violence and the legitimation of imposing civilization on the 'savages.' Ethnographic psychopathology, which purportedly examined the rule of patriarchy as a mechanism of protection again incest or sexual violence, established sexual violence as the basis of aboriginal cultural formations; thus sexual violence came to define aboriginality, and in turn, created the epistemic conditions on which to rationalize European governance over the so-called savage.

The spirit of the law that 'co-authors' Wiebe's text appeals to a third party, a suspended ideal of justice located in the lost childhood of Yvonne Johnson. But what constitutes the 'stolen life' that entitles this biography? It is Johnson's childhood that has been 'stolen' from her, the innocence and vulnerability of that childhood female body, undone by sexual violence. Derrida restores to the philosophy of experience the lost childhood that as a result of various forms of violence – pedagogical, familial, sexual, Oedipal, epistemic – must be recuperated for the subject to gain justice. But the developmental imperatives of imperialism persistently err in trying to locate the 'childhood of man' in the lost origins of aboriginality.

Derrida mediates the lost childhood of 'Man' through the human/ animal distinction: 'injustice supposes that the other, the victim of the language's injustice, is capable of a language in general, is man as a speaking animal, in the sense that we, men, give to this word language. Moreover, there was a time, not long ago and not yet over, in which "we, men" meant "we adult white male Europeans, carnivorous and capable of sacrifice"' (Derrida 1992: 18). He reiterates that 'one would not speak of injustice or violence toward an animal ... What we confusedly call "animal," the living thing as living and nothing else, is not a subject of the law or of law (*droit*)' (Derrida 1992: 18).[9] As Derrida works through the animal/man problematic, he eventually arrives at the significance that underlies the categorical distinction between them. What is at stake is nothing less than the 'boundaries that institute the human subject (preferably and paradigmatically the adult male, rather than the woman, child or animal) as the measure of the just and the unjust, [and that] does not necessarily lead to injustice, nor to the effacement of an opposition between just and unjust but may, in the name of a demand more insatiable than justice, lead to a reinterpretation of the whole apparatus of boundaries within which a history and a culture have been able to confine their criteriology' (19). The history of imperialism and colonial conquest has been and continues to be critiqued on the basis of how certain bodies are animalized and others humanized at their expense, in slavery, human reproduction, domesticity and other modes of forced labour and incarceration. At one point, Derrida had hoped to 'leave these problems aside ... along with affinity between carnivorous sacrifice, at the basis of our culture and our law, and all the cannibalisms, symbolic or not, that structure intersubjectivity in nursing, love, mourning and, in truth, in all symbolic or linguistic appropriations,' but he is unable to do so. The violence of the metonymic appropriations in the chain of displacements 'woman, child or animal' comes to haunt the adult white male European, who secures his position of discursive institutional power over the question of justice through symbolic appropriations in order to determine who will govern and who will not, who will administer the law and who will not. The child who commits a cannibalistic sacrifice in the act of 'nursing' further raises the spectre of the male child who 'sacrifices' not simply 'the woman' but 'the mother' to the metonymic codes of patriarchal violence, to, in Derrida's terms, a carno-phallogocentrism.

The figure of 'the adult male,' or 'we adult white male Europeans, carnivorous and capable of sacrifice,' overturns the conventional figure of savagery, the ignoble savage, the primitive man, and the primordial father, who lies suspended in Derrida's text between the healing power of ceremony and ceremonial justice. On the animalistic drive to war, Derrida writes:

> In so-called primitive societies, where these meanings would be more clearly brought out, the peace settlement shows very well that war was not a natural phenomenon. No peace is settled without the symbolic phenomenon of a ceremonial. It recalls the fact that there was already ceremony in war. War, then, did not simply amount to a clash of two interests or of two purely physical forces. Here an important parenthesis emphasizes that, to be sure, in the pair war/peace, the peace ceremonial recalls the fact that the war was also an unnatural phenomenon. (39)

In this deconstruction of the mythic and primordial roots of violence, Derrida engages in an ethnographic controversy over the origins of violence in the history of nineteenth- and twentieth-century Europe and its imperial wars. The ceremonial act suspends the essentialist meaning of violence, and its patrilineal descent through the apparent transmission of male violence especially. But as a dimension of conflict resolution, it must be noted that 'ceremony' belongs to the realm of 'performativity' which, according to Derrida, is its own kind of violence ('The very emergence of justice and law, the founding and justifying moment that institutes law implies a performative force, which is always an interpretative force ...' [13]). In order to distinguish the non-violence of the nominal 'savage' from the violence of civility and civilization, Derrida situates its 'performativity' within the reciprocal exchange of the ceremony. Thus, the ceremony is rendered a more innocent and primitive form of performance.

Derrida coins the phrase *'différentielle contamination'* to address the impurities in Walter Benjamin's distinction between natural and positive law. Such a distinction falsifies the existence of the so-called natural law of incest that still operates within Wiebe's conception of the history of injustice in the law toward First Nations. But this phrase, this notion of *'différentielle contamination,'* while citing the racist discourse of degeneracy also obliterates the female body as the bloody site of its transmission, even in Derrida's anti-phallogocentric philosophy. The degenerate figuration of the female body as the material site of contamination cannot be overlooked in the specificity of violence done toward the female aboriginal, nor can the issue from that body be denied. If deconstruction is justice, its 'affirmative' condition must lie in recognizing that the possibility of justice lies in articulating that body to an experience of violence that is nameable and, as such, deconstructable. For the bastard child is only a bastard in relation to the rule of the father. The maternal child, on the other hand, is another sort of (ab)original child, a 'gift without exchange, without circulation, without recognition or gratitude, without economic circularity, without calculation and without rules, without reason and without rationality' (25). What marks the shift from mysticism to reason, from the mystical foundations of paternal authority to the law, is, of course, the birth of the child, and it is this birth that Derrida invokes as 'madness.' Why must human reproduction mark the boundary between reason and mysticism, science and religion? Because the 'criteriology' of a carno-phallogocentrism classifies 'women' and 'children' as animals to be consumed and sacrificed, and 'adult white male Europeans' as the transparent S/subject of the nation, the law, and the legitimate user of violence. Thus, it is not only the law that must be calculated but justice that must be articulated.

Wiebe's account of Johnson's participation in the murder of Chuck Skwarok, her treatment by the legal system, and its failure to treat her without prejudice represents a positive approach to the law, one that in Walter Benjamin's words, 'demands of all violence a proof of its historical origin, which under certain conditions, is declared legal, sanctioned' (Benjamin 1978: 280). As Benjamin explains, the idea of positive law stands in opposition to 'natural law':

> The exclusion of this more precise critical approach is perhaps the predominant feature of a main current of legal philosophy: natural law. It perceives in the use of violent means to just ends no greater problem than a man sees as his 'right' to move his body in the direction of a desired goal. According to this view (for which the terrorism of the French Revolution provided an ideological foundation), violence is a product of nature, as it were, a raw material, the use of which is in no way problematical, unless force is misused for unjust ends ... This thesis of natural law that regards violence as a natural datum is diametrically opposed to that of positive law, which sees violence as a product of history. (Benjamin 1978: 278)

Natural law, the violence of incest that must be subject to the Law of the Father to prohibit it, underlies the justification of domestic violence and sexual assault because it allows 'a man [to] see as his "right" to move his body in the direction of a desired goal,' the right to violence as an appropriate measure to the naturalized and legitimized 'ends' of domination. Thus, the 'ends of man' are the desired goals of conquest, domination, power, exploitation, and control, sanctioned by the natural law of the father. Positive law, on the other hand, focuses on the means, rather than the ends, and demands that violence must be historically acknowledged as falling within the distinction between sanctioned violence and unsanctioned violence. In the case of Johnson, the question of violence and its means is located by Wiebe in the historical acknowledgment of the originary violence of colonial dispossession: the story of Big Bear.[10] Earl's death is acknowledged *de jure* as constitutive of this history of violence. But what of the other crime that haunts the spaces on the margins of this text: the crime that appears in the title but is never sufficiently solved, Yvonne Johnson's *stolen life*? How was *her* life stolen and by whom? Is Wiebe's text, with its emphasis on positive law and the question of what constitutes sanctioned or unsanctioned violence in relation to colonization, an alibi that resurrects the natural law of incest, thus providing liberal consciousness with a screen through which to filter the unpleasant realities of sexualized colonial violence toward the female indigenous child's body? What of the historical acknowledgment of the violence of sexual abuse? For Wiebe and the liberal consciousness of postcolonialism, Yvonne Johnson's stolen life becomes, once again, an allegory of colonial territorial dispossession.

Sexual violence toward indigenous women must be attended to as a fact that in and of itself is general to the history of imperialism, colonization, and globalization, neither supplementary nor apparitional.

Postscript

When I taught this book to a group of Native and non-Native undergraduate students in a course on theories of the body, I had them learn some of the performance techniques from Augusto Boal's *Theatre of the Oppressed*, so that when it came time to read and discuss this book, we could use that material to do another sort of body work, a momentary performance, that might make reading and teaching such a text and its subject matter intelligible and perhaps even justifiable. The students made up a performance, the crux of which was a confrontation between the official discourse of the medical profession and alternative medical practices, neither of which, the students concluded, provided the necessary materials for healing. Alternative narratives, the students' performance suggested, do not necessarily create justice. Rather, justice would seem to lie elsewhere, in articulating what counts *as violence* and not as some seeming inevitability in people's lives.

While the law adjudicates violence, something it already assumes to know, and its legitimate or illegitimate use, as Derrida argues, justice comes with a qualitatively different understanding of violence in its unexpected forms – such as images and writing, sites, too, of an unexpected healing in Yvonne Johnson's case. Whereas Wiebe struggles with his writing, Johnson writes through the impasse of the violence of language and writing that Wiebe inadvertently criticizes her with. However, she does write her story through the mediation of Wiebe, the author, and she does arrive at a place of healing. She disowns her shame and brings charges against her father for sexual abuse. Thus, the originary violence of sexual abuse, is both re-presented and re-valued in her writing through her overcoming of the secondary violence of representation in language and signification. The representation of the healing ceremony and the intense feeling of suffocation Johnson describes as arising from the burning sweet grass, re-enacts the trauma of her breathing difficulties due to her cleft palette, as well as reconfigures the violence of a history of signification that also suffocates the capacity of the self to emerge, transform, and grow beyond being fixed by both the intimate and political histories of colonial violence. Thus, healing is about justice and comes with the acknowledgment of the material limits of representational violence. As the story of Grandma Flora's healing ceremony attests, genealogies of healing through the maternal body are neither legitimate nor illegitimate, but belong to a different materiality and materialization of justice.

8 Genealogies of Difference: *Revamping* the Em*pire*? or, Queering Kinship in a Transnational Decolonial Frame

Except, this time, the Trickster representing God [is] a woman, a goddess in fur. Like in this picture. I've always thought that, ever since we were little kids. I mean, if Native languages have no gender, then why should we? And why, for that matter, should God?

Tomson Highway, *Kiss of the Fur Queen*

Thus, the straight mind continues to affirm that incest, and not homosexuality, represents its major interdiction.

Monique Wittig, 'The Straight Mind'

'The family' is simultaneously a practice, a set of knowledges, and a semiotic apparatus for the production of subjectivities and relationalities, as well as an ideological formation with all its commonsensical baggage and worn-out clichés. Its existence depends upon the seamless interaction of domestic spaces and genealogical temporalities in the production of domesticated subjects possessed of knowledges, practices, and representations with which to produce and reproduce 'the family.' Whenever this seamlessness is threatened, however, violence and contestation erupt. In the interdependency between postmodernity and globalization, the space of domesticity can no longer be seen as a site which harbours 'the family' but, rather, as the site of its productions and re-productions. The production of 'the family' as an institution of human relations is constitutive of the very geography of intimacies and affectivities that are determined by the division of public and domestic governing regimes, however unevenly distributed across Empire and colony. For colonies are built in bourgeois homes, as much as in legislative buildings; colonies are built in the imagination, as much as they are built in real-world practices; and colonies are built in allegedly private or intimate places, as much as they are built in the public domain and its institutions of governance, justice, education, and health care.

Political kinships, constituted on the basis of disparate, yet mutually interested, affiliations, and including but not limited to feminist, anti-racist, lesbian, gay, bi-sexual and transgender, and anti-poverty movements, provide a counter-hegemonic network of affinities capable of cutting across the epistemic and representational frontiers of cultural and sexual difference, thus challenging colonial and capitalist determinations as to who will and will not have access to material well-being and who will and will not have a rightful disposition to govern. Such an organization of political affinities would make for a queer configuration, a provisional embrace demanded by the times and events, that might respond meaningfully to the crisis precipitated when the boundaries of everyday life shatter and life as it is lived surges forth into the domain of history.

In the following polemical charge against 'the family,' Donna Haraway criticizes its essentialist and reductive filiations based on blood ties and origin stories:

> I am sick to death of bonding through kinship and 'the family,' and I long for models of solidarity and human unity and difference rooted in friendship, work, partially shared purposes, intractable collective pain, inescapable mortality, and persistent hope. It is time to theorize an 'unfamiliar' unconscious, a different primal scene, where everything does not stem from the dramas of identity and reproduction. Ties through blood – including blood recast in the coin of genes and information – have been bloody enough already. I believe that there will be no racial or sexual peace, no livable nature, until we learn to produce humanity through something more and less than kinship. I think I am on the side of the vampires, or least some of them. But, then, since when does one get to choose which vampire will trouble one's dreams? (Haraway 1997: 265)

In the English imaginary of the late nineteenth century, the historical forces of imperialism threw up a host of terrifying creatures that would come to haunt the proprietary sanctities of so-called Western Civilization. From Frankenstein's monster to Dr Jekyll's Mr Hyde, from Count Dracula to the Homosexual, the ignoble Aboriginal, the savage, threatened to undo the hegemony of civilization, its material powers of commodity wealth, its economies of spectatorship and display, and its governing strategies of infantilization and the marginalization of indigenous female leadership. Thus, Aboriginal Man was entirely necessary to bourgeois governance and its dissimulations of who was purportedly savage and who was civilized.

The figure of the Aboriginal, produced and reproduced through various technologies of representation, served as an alibi for the legitimation of the imperialist civilizing mission. 'The family' was one of those technologies of social life through which the reason and utility of 'civilization' were secured. In Canada, government legislation in the mid to late nineteenth century, such as An Act for the Better Protection of the Lands and Property of the Indians in Lower Canada (1850), An Act to Encourage the Gradual Civilization of the Indian Tribes in the Province, and to Amend the Laws Respecting Indians (1857), and the Indian Act (1876), helped to establish the institution of the European bourgeois family, its heterosexual norms, racial management, and patriarchal governing strategies, in colonial space. And what better way to ensure its 'peace' and propriety than through the making of a great and uncontrollable monstrosity that must be domesticated or expelled; hence, the legitimation of colonial violence in the face of an imaginary Other, the savage of imperial fantasy and invention.

Colonial violence was instrumental in the destruction of indigenous kinship relations. Specifically, colonial domicide was achieved by the implementation of residential schooling in the 1920s through the Indian Act, which forcibly took children from their homes to boarding schools. This act also excluded status Indian women from political governance and controlled band affiliation through the regulation of their marital and sexual relationships. In addition, at issue in the sexual regulation of female aboriginal bodies was control over white racial purity; thus racialized sexual citizenship in Canada was founded upon legislating the female aboriginal body to ensure that the fearful consequences of racial mixing proclaimed by nineteenth- and twentieth-century discourses of degeneration and eugenics would not *infect* the white heterosexual bourgeois family. Another key aspect of colonial domicide included the foster parenting of indigenous children into non-indigenous families. Alanis Obomsawin's film *Richard Cardinal: Cry from a Diary of a Métis Child* documents the tragic case of a fourteen-year-old Métis boy who, in the 1970s, committed suicide and left behind a diary detailing the abuse, loneliness, and isolation he suffered in a series of non-indigenous foster homes. The current focus by First Nations,

Métis, and Inuit women's social and political organizations on domestic and sexual violence within First Nations families points to what is currently recognized as one of the most significant areas in the work of combatting colonial domicide – the problem of intimate violence.

In its concentrated efforts to combat spousal violence and sexual assault in Inuit families and communities, Pauktuutit, the Inuit Women's Association of Canada, has produced several reports and publications, notably *Inuit Women: The Housing Crisis and Violence* (1994), prepared for the Canada Mortgage and Housing Corporation. The report states that 'Inuit are currently facing the worst housing crisis in Canada. While the initial causes of this crisis can be traced back over 40 years, the situation has become critical, as the Inuit population is rapidly increasing and housing stocks are eroding. Unlike other aboriginal peoples in Canada, Inuit do not have specific funding arrangements with the federal government for housing. This has resulted in severe overcrowding, and inadequate and unsafe housing conditions for many Inuit families. Overcrowding is widely considered among Inuit to be the most serious problem we face' (Pauktuutit 1994: 1). The impact of the housing crisis on Inuit women is enormous. As the report goes on to say: 'Increased rates of substance abuse, family violence and child sexual abuse have been linked by some to dehumanizing housing conditions. Inuit youth commit suicide at a rate ten times the national average. The housing needs of particularly vulnerable members of Inuit society, such as elders, persons with physical disabilities and single parents are simply not being met. The Arctic is one of the most difficult environments in the world for persons with disabilities' (Pauktuutit 1994: 1).[1]

Chandra Talpade Mohanty and M. Jacqui Alexander contend that the idea of a 'global sisterhood' is unworkable because the hegemony of global economic, social, and political relations is such that any attempt to create such a political constituency would define all women's knowledge within the narrow terms of white, western, middle-class women's experiences. Rather, they propose that a transnational feminism would take a situated approach to 'thinking about women in similar contexts across the world, in *different* geographical spaces, rather than as all women across the world' (Alexander and Mohanty 1997: xix). In creating a transnational 'domestic politics,' affiliative political kinships are even more important in light of some of the more dangerous and virulent revivals of 'the family' in various fundamentalist contexts, including, of course, Canada and the United States. But how do decolonizing,

> Sometimes I feel like a bridge. It's good that I have the responsibility of being a producer and director with the National Film Board of Canada. It's good to be in a position of power. It's important. The decisions of what goes into the film come from us. It doesn't come from the outside. It comes from the people who are involved and we can decide together. I'm really a bridge between two worlds. It comes through in my songs, my stories and my film work. I'm a fighter, a free spirit, but to be a free spirit at this time is very painful. You're choked by everything around you. You go outside and you're choked by the pollution. You're choked by the cars. You're choked by the traffic lights. You're choked by the law that tells you what you should be, what you have to be. How can you be free if you have to think of all those things they tell you to be? It puts to sleep what you are.
> – Alanis Obomsawin (Abenaki) in Petrone, ed., *First People, First Voices*

materialist feminists build such affiliations across the daunting powers of transnational capitalism and its global divisions of labour, the rise of fundamentalist nationalisms, and a centralized 'First World' military force? Not, I would argue, by accepting or condoning so-called traditional or culturally specific familial practices that perpetuate violence toward indigenous women, children, and youth.

One of the key sites of intervention by religious fundamentalisms is the everyday domain of the family. There are manifold reasons why the family has become such an economical site with which to establish a religio-political hegemony, some of which are historical, as in the destruction of indigenous kinship networks by British and French imperialist and colonialist forces during the nineteenth and early twentieth centuries. From the early Christian missionaries to late twentieth-century religious fundamentalism, religious institutions have invested heavily in familial relations as a key site for implementing and maintaining imperial rule. In Canada, the church-run residential schools throughout the twentieth century were mandated by the Indian Act to sever aboriginal children from their kinship filiations and affiliations and turn them into proper 'colonial subjects.' Several religious denominations participated in destroying the basis of aboriginal societies, but they did so not only by severing and obliterating kinship relations but also, along with government legislation and representational technologies, by holding up the Christian bourgeois family as an unobtainable ideal and model of domestic governance. A key import to colonial Canada for the regulation and management of so-called reproductive 'racial purity' through heterosexual relations, 'the family' emerged as a material force in the destruction of kinship societies and their subordination, socially and economically, to colonial and imperial nations. Other, more contemporary reasons under global capitalism for the use of the family as the site for establishing religious hegemony are the economic pressures either to do away with or to block the creation of social welfare programs, thus leaving a gap in the social fabric that is being quickly exploited by religious organizations which offer the impoverished the pseudo-social powers of moral superiority in the form of 'spiritual benefits' as compensation for the lack of material wealth and the real social power that accrues from it in late capitalist culture and society. Thus, religious fundamentalisms have made it their business to mediate between the political arenas of public culture and private familial life, that is, the allegedly private spheres of sexuality, intimacy, and reproduction, the familial relations between parents and children, husbands, wives, and siblings, common-law partners, and same-sex partners and spouses.

In his essay 'Nietzsche, Genealogy, History,' Michel Foucault characterized the importance of the genealogical method in terms of its capacity to '[oppose] itself to the search for "origins"' (Foucault 1977b: 140). Naming this oppositional strategy a genealogy is, of course, somewhat ironic, especially when considered in relation to the filiative legacies drawn up in such religious histories of 'mankind' as the Judeo-Christian Bible. The patrilineal accounts of father/son inheritances are seemingly endless and, in their exclusion of mothers, daughters, and sisters, function as a standard bearer of the autochthonous 'search for origins' beyond the female reproductive body. Thus, to overturn the search for origins is to insist upon its sites of construction and, in so doing, to denaturalize whatever dominant (i.e., racist and patriarchal) origin stories currently exist, be they religious or secular (i.e., Oedipal). It is also to put into question the reduction of the female body to a reproductive categorical imperative. For to erect a patrilineal genealogy of pure descent is to assume that what has been excluded – the female reproductive body – is its natural, as in taken for granted, correlative, and, therefore, *a priori* excluded from the domains of culture and society. Although the

implications I am drawing out of Foucault's understanding of a genealogical method may not have been included in his original vision of it –
and yet are in keeping with its oppositional strategy toward the search
for origins – I would like to suggest mobilizing institutional genealogies
that are responsive to the formation of sexual and racial differences in
nineteenth- and twentieth-century discourses and representational
technologies. In tracing such institutional and institutionalized genealogies, it becomes possible to write a different sort of history: one, for
example, that can take into account and critique the institutional link-
ages which maintain origin stories and their filiative bonds of inheritance at work in the formation of colonial and decolonial nationalisms.
This different genealogy, this genealogy with a difference, lies perhaps
somewhere in the future, somewhere in the journals, diaries, poems,
and notebooks of anti-racist feminists who already know how history
has failed to tell the 'other stories' at stake in colonial modernity. Nevertheless, I would like to imagine mobilizing genealogies of difference for
the particular purpose of discussing how religious fundamentalisms
have relied upon familial relations to perpetuate an ideological web of
fantasies about power, sexuality, and domination that is intimately
linked to the histories of aboriginality and colonization.

Aboriginality in (Post)colonial Desire

A sustained critique of the imperial history of sexuality almost always
has the uncanny effect of turning beloved assumptions on their head –
or, perhaps, setting them upright again. Take, for example, the progressive assumptions underlying gay, lesbian, bi-, and queer sexualities in
colonial and postcolonial studies today. In *Transgender Warriors: Making
History from Joan of Arc to Dennis Rodman*, Leslie Feinberg claims a place
for her book as 'a contribution to the demand for transgender liberation'
(Feinberg 1996: ix). In response to her fear that s/he 'would certainly be
killed before [s/he] could grow to adulthood' (6), Feinberg resolved to
find a community of transgendered people. Eventually, s/he writes, s/
he 'came full circle to one of my original questions as well: Have we
always existed?' (18). In her account of transgendered individuals
throughout history, she examines such figures of 'cultural diversity' as
the 'two-spirit,' a transgendered, predominantly male-to-female,
Native American. When coming across an archaeological figure in a
museum that raises her curiosity regarding the representation of male
and female indigenous bodies, s/he exclaims, 'I had found the first key

to a vault containing information I'd looked for all my life' (21). In her simultaneous historico-biographical narrative of transgendered identity, the two-spirit figures as an originary moment for Feinberg of the discovery of sexual diversity: 'What stunned me was that such ancient and diverse cultures allowed people to choose more sex/gender paths, and this diversity of human expression was honored as sacred' (23). Feinberg's personal history, perhaps best represented in her novel *Stone Butch Blues* (1993), is grounded in her working-class identity. The conflation of transgendered working-class oppression with the cultural figure of the two-spirit is a critical moment in Feinberg's narrative of the representational history of transgendered individuals. Unfortunately, it also marks a critical moment in the reproduction of representational imperialism when the Aboriginal is deployed – once again – as an original figure of 'discovery.' In Feinberg's text, the two-spirit is idealized as a representative subjugated figure of Western capitalist oppression and, in her novel especially, its redemption. If the politics of alliance-building between transgendered working-class oppression and First Nations colonization is at issue here, it lies, I would suggest, in a mutually invested critique of capitalist imperialism and globalization, its heterogeneous complicities and discontinuities, as well as in the interconnectedness and contingencies among multiple and discrete alterities. The narrative of discovery tends to position indigenous societies within a culturally relativist context, in this case, of sexual identities, and, furthermore, relegates indigenous people to a mythic past from which they have never advanced. While a plurality of sexual identities apparently valorizes 'inclusivity,' in the context of decolonization they more often than not signal a process of *assimilation*, the mimetic production of simulated figures of oppression and liberation that disavow the discontinuous realities of imperialism in the lives of indigenous people. Without acknowledging the specificities of imperialism and colonization and their effects on indigenous societies, the historical realities of resistance and change on the part of these societies also go unnoticed.

Michel Foucault's claim at the end of the first volume of *The History of Sexuality* that it is at best ironic and, at worse, a mistake to 'believe that our "liberation" is in the balance' when discourses of sexuality proliferate, would appear initially to stand in marked contrast, if not in defiance of, Feinberg's uncompromising defence of transgender liberation (Foucault 1978: 159). On the other hand, the contemporary and historical struggles of gays, lesbians, bisexuals, and transgendered individuals to be 'out' if they so choose, to live free of homophobic violence and its internalization, and to enjoy the benefits and annuities of their labours, loves, and citizenships, appear to contradict Foucault's claim. But the fact that sexuality is enlisted in the service of a politics of liberation or not, is not what is really at issue here. More to the point is how sexuality constitutes a specific mechanism that was deployed in nineteenth-century knowledge formations and institutions with, in some cases, the intention, or simply the unanticipated effect, of disrupting, producing, and/or maintaining forces of political domination and contestation.

In the contemporary moment, Lauren Berlant argues that the right-wing cultural agenda of the 'Reagan revolution' created a reactionary politics of public intimacy based in 'an affirmative rhetoric on a nationalist politics of intimacy, which it contrast[ed] to threatening practices of nonfamilial sexuality and, by implication other forms of racial and economic alterity' (Berlant 1997: 7). In competition with the counter-hegemonic politics of 'the personal is political,' agitated for by the radical feminisms of the 1960s and 1970s, the secular and religious fundamentalisms of present-day America dominate the legal and economic institutional organization and meaning of 'public intimacy.' In this example, the domain of heteronormative 'sexuality' or the public discourse on intimate relations is the arena of a nationalized political contestation working in tandem with, and perhaps even functioning as a site of mystification for, America's transnational economic dominance.

What Berlant understands critically and theoretically about the uses to which sexuality and intimate relations may be put in a network of contestatory political practices in the contemporary moment, can be broadened to include an historical perspective. For there is nothing new in the 'Reagan revolution' about the public use of sexuality in, for example, histories of colonization and imperialism, or occupation and globalization. As Foucault reminds us, the public use of sexuality cannot be so neatly divided between those for or against its liberation: 'it can never be inherent in the structure of things to guarantee the exercise of freedom' (Foucault 1984: 245). In Yvonne Johnson and Rudy Wiebe's collaborative text *Stolen Life: The Journey of a Cree Woman*, Johnson writes about same-sex intimacy between women in the former Women's Prison in Kingston, Ontario. In the following passage on the life of a woman's body in prison, Johnson observes the following:

> Two women near me are together, getting involved with each other. I can hear them tonight louder than usual. A place like this breeds a new kind of woman; they're driven to anything, maybe as a last-ditch try to hold onto

humanness. An act of sex may be the only free relationship you can have
in here, and I don't know, when will it be my turn? I don't want that. But
it's a reality behind bars, so it's acceptable; it's more or less expected. The
women here have to find a new way of thinking, to live; they fear to act
human, but who knows what that means in here, and so some keep trying.
The guards can hear and see them of course, but do nothing. If they listen,
it's just to tell each other ugly stories, and laugh. (Wiebe and Johnson 1998:
324)

Same-sex intimacy between women in prison is a consequence, not
necessarily of 'free choice,' but of the incarcerated circumstances that
incite desire and the need for love and intimacy. While sexual violence
in male prisons does not go unacknowledged in the public media, the
desire for sexual intimacy and love in male or female prisons is rarely
admitted. Thus, Foucault's critical challenge that sexuality is not necessarily 'progressive' is useful for understanding the social and historical
circumstances noted by Johnson in which same-sex intimacy between
women occurs under various circumstances, and in the case of prison
or compulsory heterosexuality, those circumstances are sometimes
ones of subjugation, although, of course, not all same-sex desire is necessarily or always overdetermined by such circumstances. The point is
that sexuality, as Foucault argued, is subject to the emergence of historical and political forces, deployed at certain times and in particular
institutional contexts and discourses as domains of power, where
power itself is recognized as pervasive and persistent even among
those marginalized or excluded from the dominant social formation of
the European middle-class patriarchal family of nineteenth-century
invention and in its present-day, mass-produced 'American' version.

Lauren Berlant's and Yvonne Johnson's discrete critical interventions
into the meanings of sexual politics illustrate that 'sexuality' is an effect
of certain relations of space and time, as much a tool of power over and
potential empowerment as a sign of the pervasiveness of power among
ruling political and economic elites, those who would desire to circulate within the orbit of that power, and those who would desire to do
otherwise.

Keeping in mind this matrix of corporealities – sexual, racial, aboriginal, and labouring – I want to consider how questions of the multiple
forms of physical, epistemic, and representational violence are being
used by religious fundamentalist forces to govern 'the body.'

The institutional limits of 'the family' are currently being negotiated by discourses of religious fundamentalism, on the one hand, and gay and lesbian marriage, on the other, especially in the domain of public media.[2] The larger question to which these concerns are directed is how this global competitive discourse on the family impacts on the significance of cultural practices, such as literature and film, their role in the academy (i.e., the classroom) and in contemporary society at large. While aboriginality in the representational technologies and techniques of colonial power was used to reproduce 'the family,' this historical reality also underlies how contemporary global religious fundamentalist movements are currently using the heteronormative domain of 'the family' to establish their hegemony in everyday life.

Religious fundamentalism, at least as it appears in Canadian media over the last decade or so, is largely represented as a phenomenon that happens 'elsewhere,' either in the United States and the broader Middle East, or in Canadian immigrant communities, where it is circumscribed by notions of cultural difference that function as racist codes for otherness and exclusion. Debate about religious difference in the public arena is directed toward questions of religious rights, freedoms, and equalities, and not those of power and religious oppression. The latter are often subsumed, for example, under the rhetoric of 'religious tolerance' (or intolerance) toward the existence, teachings, and practices of multiple, and in many cases monotheistic, religions, somewhat ironically, of course, since these particular religious practices are opposed to the very idea of plural godheads. In his critique of the cultural dimensions of religious fundamentalisms, Tariq Ali argues that the problem of religion and society today is how it is dominated by 'religious nationalism or its postmodern avatar, religious multiculturalism.' (Ali 2002: 6). One of the more problematic aspects of the multicultural alibi is how it silences and censors critical opposition to religious oppression. An additional problem emerges, however, when the ideology of nationalism dominates the discussion of religion, because of the tendency to ignore everyday life and thus to misrecognize the mediatory role played by religious fundamentalisms in creating as well as maintaining separate realms of private and public governance.

Although feminist critical debates of globalization have taken into account questions of identity formation and the impact of global political and economic forces in shaping the interrelated categories and experiences of gender, race, and sexuality, along with those of class and imperialism (Benhabib 2002 and Young 2002), the separation of public and private spheres has not been sufficiently recognized as an important site for interrogating how transnational hegemonies create and maintain themselves. As a result of this lacuna, critical globalization studies are reproducing at the level of epistemology (i.e., its particular relationship to power and knowledge) the separation of political powers within nation states, thus continuing to render micropolitical or domestic political governance as either supplemental to, secondary (as in 'ideological'), or entirely distinct from the macropolitical and economic interests of transnational capitalism. Both at the level of global political economy and knowledge production, the actual mechanisms that make the process of establishing global hegemonies possible remain hidden, thereby reinscribing the devaluation not only of particular arenas of study but the subjects whose lives are directly affected by the domestic politics of everyday life, including the poor, who are also predominantly women and children.

Questions of 'difference' have preoccupied intellectual and institutional horizons of academia for some time now. If a post–Second World War socialist consciousness challenged the elitism and ideological class biases of literary study, the 1980s and 1990s were dominated by feminist, lesbian and gay, and anti-racist critiques of the 'canon' and its humanist and not-so-humanist exclusions. Literary critics have learned and unlearned how different histories, bodies, and experiences constitute the writing, reception, and critical response to literature and the academic production of literary knowledge. While this history of difference(s) challenged colonial and neocolonial narratives of the nation and beyond, the emergence of new contradictions and conflicts among various social movements – between, for example, sexuality and decolonization – suggests that a genealogical approach to how such differences are imbricated in each other's political formations must be sought if the emerging tensions between domestic and public domains of power and governance currently being mediated by religious nationalisms are to be addressed and, I would add, transformed. Of particular importance here is why a cultural semiotics of 'the family' has become the most intense site of violent contestation for furthering the oppressive aims of religious nationalisms and familialisms. Moreover, we might consider how heteronormativity is implicated in the histories of imperialism and colonization as well as its connection to recent neo-liberal and neo-conservative global practices. To address these questions means going beyond the rhetoric of religious and cultural diversity toward destabilizing the very notion of 'religious fundamentalism,' and to do this by examining how religion is a site of both imaginary re-signification and political power. This cultural politics approach to the intersection of religion and literary studies is designed to focus on religious fundamentalists' own investments in cultural signification, thus making it possible both to comprehend and transform the violent opposition mounted by religious fundamentalist movements towards various literary and cultural works, such as Deepa Mehta's film *Fire* (Canada/India 1996), which was attacked in India in 1998 by Hindu fundamentalists for its depiction of a lesbian relationship in a Hindu family.[3] Cultural practices have become significant targets for religious fundamentalist violence precisely because, in many cases, they constitute an effective means for the dissemination of a critical resistance to and disclosure of the limits of democracy. Thus, I would argue, it is important to open up the discussion of 'religious fundamentalisms' to their imaginary as well as social and political interests. By doing so, Canadian literary scholars can participate meaningfully in important debates in educational institutions and elsewhere about the formation of the real and imagined communities of religious fundamentalisms as global and 'domestic' forces of power.

In pursuing these questions, I aim to move beyond the postmodern dilemma – what Jean-François Lyotard termed a postmodern incredulity toward metanarratives (Lyotard 1984) or, in Habermasian terms, the state of 'enlightened bewilderment' (as quoted in Torpey 2003, 1: see also Habermas 1998: 7) that currently exists toward grand projects of social change – by offering a different way of thinking about political affinities across the division between public and domestic or private spheres, especially as the latter are circumscribed by current notions of the 'familial.' While the critical attention currently directed toward public institutions is obviously important, the failure to understand how oppressive regimes of power operate through familial relations, parental and patriarchal authority, and heteronormative and racialized structures of knowing and being, means that the analysis of the public domain is complicit in perpetuating key mechanisms of power, such as sexual and domestic violence and the control and regulation of human reproduction and sexuality. It is these very mechanisms of corporeal power which provide the public domain with its authority and governance over everyday life and human subjectivity. To ignore these avenues of corporeal power will ensure that democracy will never reach women and the poor.

I would also argue that just how this so-called religious revolution is impacting on, as well as being challenged by, multiple institutions of public learning involves not only educational institutions such as the universities but also less obvious sites of knowledge acquisition and transmission, such as television programming, the Internet, and other aspects of public media. The next part of this chapter focuses specifically on the intersection of sexuality and aboriginality in the made-for-television movie *Where the Spirit Lives* and Tomson Highway's novel *The Kiss of the Fur Queen*.

Declassified Knowledge

In the fall of 1989, the made-for-television movie *Where the Spirit Lives* was first aired on Canadian television. *Where the Spirit Lives* is a narrative melodrama about the violent effects of residential schools on Native students during the 1930s. Specific amendments made to the Indian Act in the 1920s gave the state and its representative proxies the power to enforce compulsory attendance in residential schools for First Nations children:

> The Superintendent General may appoint any officer or person to be a truant officer to enforce the attendance of Indian children at school, and for such purpose a truant officer shall be vested with the powers of a peace officer, and shall have authority to enter any place where he has reason to believe there are Indian children between the ages of seven and fifteen years, and when requested by the Indian agent, a school teacher or the chief of a band shall examine into any case of truancy, shall warn the truants, their parents or guardians or the person with whom any Indian child resides, of the consequences of truancy, and notify the parent, guardian or such person in writing to cause the child to attend school. (Indian Act, Section 10 (3), c. 98. 1927 R.S.C.)

Two children, Komi, a girl of about twelve or thirteen years, and Pita, her younger brother, are removed from their northern band, the Kainah, and taken to an Anglican-run residential school located on the southern prairie. The heroine of the movie is a Miss Kathleen Willambury (played by Ann-Marie MacDonald), a young teacher who embodies the missionary spirit. She has left Cape Breton and the heartache of marital rejection to devote herself to educating the 'Indian children' of the Prairies.[4] Although the film is presented as fiction, the scriptwriter, Keith Ross Leckie, uses references and figures of authenticity to suggest that his dramatization transcodes elements of real events. The following appears, for example, on the screen at the conclusion of the movie: 'The last two Indian residential schools closed in 1988.' Leckie's film stands as the first and last word on the issue of First Nations compulsory education as an aid to assimilation. The schools have closed down their doors and presumably their repressive agenda. Lenore Keeshig-Tobias criticized the film, saying that 'the decisions are made by whites in that script, any kind of mental agony lies with the white people' ('Minorities Go Toe to Toe with Majority' 1989: C1). In the same newspaper article, Leckie responds that 'he was never trying to write the story from a native perspective. "Seven years ago I didn't know these schools existed. Now I do and I wanted white Canadian audiences to know too. I'm telling a white story here."' Leckie has afterall exposed the problem of colonial dominance and its subjugation of First Nations, by narrating the punishments meted out to indigenous children if they spoke in their mother tongues and engaged in spiritual practices. At the same time, however, the representation of victimized indigenous children is ultimately displaced by the sacrifice of another subject to the logic of power/victimization, a subject who becomes, within the film's subtext, a displaced figure of demonization. In other words, a well-meaning liberal subject-position exonerates itself, only to sacrifice another subject to the knowledge of its representational violence. In this case, that subject is the lesbian.

Cloaked in a liberal ethic to transform female homosocial relations in cinema, *Where the Spirit Lives* dramatizes the fraught relationship between an aboriginal woman (Komi) and a white woman (Miss Willambury). Although Willambury is complicit in the colonial oppression of Komi, she is forgiven. Within a heterosexual matrix, female relations that have been disrupted by 'the Father' may be bound by the suture of their common oppression due to his acknowledged power. Cross-cultural female homosocialities that do not depend upon this triangulation of mutual submission for their bonding, however, are a different matter.

> I move in-between
> Careful not to shame either side
> – Gregory Scofield, 'Between Sides,' in *Thunder through My Veins: Memories of a Métis Childhood*

The subtext of the film is a case of sexual abuse between Miss Appleby, a teacher, and a student named Rachael. The sexual abuse of

Rachael by Miss Appleby is never named as such, and, as a result, a dangerous ambiguity opens up in the narrative over what constitutes abuse and what constitutes the sexual expression of love between women. The teacher's sexual abuse of Rachael is represented in one scene by Miss Appleby leaving a sprig of purple flowers under Rachael's pillow. Rachael discovers the flowers and throws them on the floor in disgust as Appleby is seen to be watching from a distance. The scene confuses sexual abuse and female love, suggesting that it is lesbianism, the non-named sexual relations between women, rather than the violence of sexual abuse, that constitutes the sub-figure of monstrosity in this film. While Reverend Buckley is the acknowledged patriarchal enemy, it is lesbianism that comes to figure as an unnamed and unnameable figure of intrinsic evil. When Rachael's body is found dead, after she has escaped to catch up with her band, Taggart, a white man, who functions as the school's truant officer, asks the question: 'You tell me Reverend? What is it that makes a young girl run across the prairie for three days with no food and water, trying to get away from this place? It sure as hell isn't God's work.'

Where the Spirit Lives shifts the binary of colonializer/colonized to that of sexual difference thus maintaining the overall structure of power and domination but displacing the domination/subjugation opposition onto another figure who is equally powerless to resist the sacrifice of her body to the knowledge of imperial power.

This is what happens when the phallocratic economy of desire becomes the subject of its own critique. If the patriarch, Reverend Buckley, is made to figure as the enemy, then another essential form of intrinsic and immutable evil emerges in the lesbian, figured here as a sign of perversity. So long as aboriginal/non-aboriginal relations conform to the familiar and familial model of heterosexual colonial authority and governance, political homosociality may be incorporated into the hegemonic equilibrium of imperial power. Kinship affiliations that do not conform to this familial heterosexist matrix pose a genuine threat to the stability of colonial rule and end up being demonized into new imaginary vampires of perversity and abnormality.

Attempts to build political affinities across a gendered experiential horizon within seemingly progressive representations of postcoloniality often result in simple reversals and the somewhat insidious process of displacing one set of power dynamics by implicating another figure with which to redirect the spectator's gaze toward a savage Other.

But, of course, simple reversals don't always work. Richard Hill, in

> [T]hey live in a sort of frontier zone criss-crossed by ethnic, religious and other fault lines. But by virtue of this situation – peculiar rather than privileged – they have a special role to play in forging links, eliminating misunderstandings, making some parties more reasonable and others less belligerent, smoothing out difficulties, seeking compromise. Their role is to act as bridges, go-betweens, mediators between the various communities and cultures. And that is precisely why their dilemma is so significant: if they themselves cannot sustain their multiple allegiances, if they are continually being pressed to take sides or ordered to stay within their own tribe, then all of us have reason to be uneasy about the way the world is going.
>
> – Amin Maalouf, *In the Name of Identity:*
> *Violence and the Need to Belong*

his queering of decolonial mimicry, usefully observes that the result of such deconstructive manoeuvres 'may be paradoxical; it may turn out that some images contain contradictory meanings and pull in several directions at once as they strain under the descriptive inadequacy of the original binaries they undermine' (Hill 2001: 21). Inversions may retain the hierarchical logic of binary oppositions, displacing one antinomy for another by establishing new orders of normalization and domination, and often by pitting the subjectivities and experiences of 'race' and 'class' or 'sexuality' and 'gender' against one another. But 'reversals' can also set in motion multiple categories of embodiment, disclosing the partial and provisional tenuousness of the body and its inscriptions. Perhaps, for a brief moment, a reversal may crystallize relations of power and exploitation, and then, productively, release them. No longer burdened with the fixed immutability of god-forms and fetishes, this process of assemblage and dissassemblage, of solidification and melting, puts into play one sort of counter-hegemonic technique designed to challenge established codes of embodiment and inscription.

While the effects of reversals are neither always predictable nor guaranteed, history shows that they are nevertheless enormously productive, and not only to the extent that they shore up unconscious or unacknowledged binary hierarchies. Reversals also bring about new contradictions and problems. At their best, they challenge the logics and sequences of origin stories, the desire to fix and differentiate an original or authentic image from its seemingly impoverished copy.

The Phantom Child Always Arrives at His/Her Destination (?)

Perhaps one of the most important contemporary representations of colonial sexual violence, in part as a result of the Christian mission residential schooling, is to be found in Tomson Highway's novel *Kiss of the Fur Queen*.

Highway tells a story about two Cree brothers, who because of the colonial law are taken at the age of seven to a Christian mission school. There the boys, particularly the youngest, Dancer-turned-Gabriel, become the object of Father Lafleur's sexual abuse. The abuse is not always represented as violent and therefore easily viewed as an unusual and cruel act, but, rather, it is far more unsettling for its gentleness and persistence: Father Lafleur 'placed a hand on Champion's thigh and, like some large, furry animal, purred at him. "There, there. You'll be happy here with us." The scent of sacramental wine oozed off his tongue ...' (Highway 1999: 54–5). The boys survive their schooling on the strength of their artistic accomplishments, as a musician in Cham-pee-yun/Champion/Jeremiah's case and as a dancer in Dancer/Gabriel's. Jeremiah buries the pain and confusion of Father Lafleur's violence by throwing himself into an exclusively European artistic heritage, and yet he is always marked as a pre-eminent 'Indian Pianist' (191). Gabriel, on the other hand, doesn't bury the secret of his experience of violence but relives it in a parallel life to his dance career as a male prostitute on the streets. While the directions of Jeremiah's and Gabriel's lives seem very discontinuous – '"Haven't you feasted on enough human flesh?" Punching and punching, Gabriel all but broke Jeremiah's nose' (297) – due in part to Jeremiah's homophobia and misogyny, which replaced the emptiness left by the anger and violation of his childhood body, their mutual experience of colonial violence becomes the final place within which they reconnect and transform themselves through their artistic practices.

The novel incorporates two notable autobiographical aspects: Highway's brother, Rene, who died of AIDS and was trained in classical dance; and the murder of a school mate, Helen Betty Osborne, who in 1971 in The Pas, Manitoba, at the age of seventeen, was brutally gang-raped and murdered by four young men – 'her cunt was stabbed with a screwdriver fifty-six times' (Tompkins and Male 1994: 22). Highway's representation of sexual violence involves two characters: Evelyn Rose McCrae, the 'long-lost daughter of Mistik Lake ... is found in a ditch on the city's outskirts, a shattered beer bottle lying gently, like a rose, deep inside her crimson-soaked sex' (106–7); and Madeline Jeannette Lavoix, the 'erstwhile daughter of Mistik Lake ... found in a North Main alleyway behind a certain hotel of questionable repute, a red-handled screwdriver lying gently, like a rose, deep within the folds of her blood-soaked sex' (132). Another figure is the Madonna of North Main, Highway's appropriation and transformation of the Christian metaphor of emaculate conception. She is perpetually pregnant, standing in a door way on the street, surrounded by the fear and threat of violence towards her and her unborn child. Jeremiah imagines the child tumbling 'to a bed of broken beer bottles and screwdrivers filed sharp as nails' (144).

In response to this misogynist colonial violence, Highway says, 'What I want my work to do is (a) prevent that kind of thing happening to another native woman and (b) to educate our sons and our sons' sons that it's cruel to go around shoving screwdrivers up the cunts of women. That's the kind of event that changes the lives of people around it. It changed me, and I will write this sort of stuff until the world stops treating women so poorly' (Tompkins and Male 1994: 22). Diana Brydon argues that the novel both invites and deflects the autobiographical aspects of Highway's life. She insists that 'the novel must be read as a complex engagement with personal and social history, an engagement that locates the personal experience within a specific colonial context, and that seeks to carry the force of that personal anguish back into the public sphere to find appropriate forms of redress and progress' (Brydon 2001: 23). Highway's engagement with this personal dimension of colonial violence produces an 'embodied knowledge,' the knowledge that the body offers up through experience and memory, and the knowledge of how bodies are shaped, in Foucault's terms, by discourses and institutional powers. Such a corporeal mode of knowledge is essential to representations of sexuality, the body, and colonial violence. It is not only that coloniality and gender intersect in Highway's novel, but that such events of sexual colonial violence are themselves the site of the production of the Aboriginal body as the naturalized as well as heteronormalized site for such sexual violence.

Highway's novel, however, through its various forms of ironic designification and dissident reinscriptions, destabilizes the Aboriginal Body as the site of colonial violence. He does this primarily, I would argue, through the autochthonous birth of the phantom child, a figure of Aboriginality that does not necessarily reach its destination, as in its apparent destiny as the fulfilment of the subject of violence and savagery: the child tumbling toward 'a bed of broken beer bottles and screwdrivers filed sharp as nails' (144).

In *The Kiss of the Fur Queen*, a phantom child manifests in the body of a boy named 'Cham-pee-yun':

> The Fur Queen disappeared, leaving her cape and crown, and the ghost child drifting in the womb of space, the wisps of winter cloud its amniotic fluid, turning and turning, with a speed as imperceptable yet certain as the rhythm of the spheres. And slowly, ever so slowly, the ghost baby tumbled, head over heels over head, down, down to Earth. (12)

The phantom child enters the world of flesh, and it is this phantom-child-made-flesh – Champion – who will experience colonization as the inscription of what Beth Brant uncompromisingly calls 'our community rape.' Sexual abuse of indigenous children, male and female, in the Christian mission schools figures in the writings of Brant and Highway as a site of transformation from colonial violence to, in Brant's words, 'a new legacy of hope, truth and self-love' (Brant 1994: 73). Highway performs this transformation through an ironic de-signification of the Christian myth of origins. The autochthonous resurrection myth of Christ is replayed in the mythic birth of the phantom child, the Aboriginal. The Aboriginal belongs, in Jacques Derrida's words, to that 'irreducible species of the simulacrum or even of simulation, in the penumbral light of a virtuality that is neither being nor nothingness, nor even an order of the possible that an ontology or a mimetology could account for or subdue with reason. No more than myth, fable and phantasm are doubtless not truths or true statements as such, but neither are they errors or deceptions, false witnesses or perjuries' (Derrida 2002: 28). These apparitional significations play within the web of hegemonic forces, giving those forces a weight and strength they would otherwise not have. Like sacrificial lambs offered up to knowledge, indigenous children are molded, shaped, simulated, and slotted into the disciplines and institutions of regulation, representation, policing, and the law. Through the ironic play of de-signification, however, Highway contests the Christian myth of resurrection and its bloody symbolics, with an origin story of no origins that will not settle on its destination as 'the flesh' to be consumed by the ravenous and cannibalistic desires of 'Our Father.' To say the phantom child, the Aboriginal, reaches its destination in the flesh of a boy or a girl, as in the cases of Helen Betty Osborne, Pamela George, and Yvonne Johnson, is to say that this is his or her destiny, an immutable and inevitable fact. Such destinies and destinations are radically undone, however, through the transfigurations of Highway's phantasmatic bodies: the Fur Queen, the Madonna of North Main, the Two-spirit, the Apparitional Aboriginal.

People are not interchangeable, and often in the same family, whether it be Rwandan, Irish, Lebanese, Algerian or Bosnian, we find, between two brothers who have lived in the same environment, apparently small differences which make them act in diametrically opposite ways in matters related to politics, religion and everyday life. These differences may even turn one of the brothers into a killer, and the other into a man of dialogue and conciliation.

– Amin Maalouf, *In the Name of Identity*

In the case of Champion/'Jeremiah' and his brother Dancer/'Gabriel,' the act of renaming constitutes one mode of transfiguration through language and its identity subject-positions. Other modes of transfiguration occur through the corporealities of desire, sexuality, pain, pleasure, addiction, and love. Finally, it is storytelling itself that signifies the transfigurative possibilities for recoding the representational violence of colonization. *Thus, Anna May makes a real choice. She turns her car around and proceeds back home. She will begin the slow process of healing her mind. She will throw away the old messages, the old codes. She will make new ones, for herself, for her people* (Brant 1994: 70). But these old codes will not be discarded; they will be exposed first and then recycled into new narratives and new hybrid narrative forms that combine Cree stories and Christian myth, a new ecology of social life with new stories, new realities, and new histories.

Love in the Age of Decolonization

Church and state have long worked as consorts in the colonization of aboriginal peoples. With the guns came the Bible. With the Bible came the whiskey. With the whiskey came addiction and government over our affairs. With government came reserves, and loathing of all that was natural. With loathing came the unnatural; the internalization of all they told us about ourselves. And the beliefs hold fast in some. There are christian Indians and there are homophobic Indians ... The love that was natural in our world, has become unnatural as we become more consumed by the white world and the values therein. Our sexuality has been colonized, sterilized, whitewashed. (Brant 1994: 59–60)

The relationship between the family and the state must be the subject of rigorous historical research into how it was established not only through government legislation, although that is important, but also – and on a different register – through an examination of how everyday life and its corporeal knowledge, signified by such tropes as home and family, were essential to colonial and imperial governance beyond their merely metonymic value as a condensation of 'the nation' or 'the empire.' It is especially because of questions of violence, sexuality, and the subjugation of the body that it is time to theorize a de-familiar unconscious and perhaps to create an unfamiliar praxis, a network of political kinships strong enough to contest the use of intimate violence to maintain the hegemony of today's global military-communications-industrial complex.

One important challenge to the spectacle violence of neocolonization has been the emergence of the counter-figure of the cross-dresser, or transgendered representations in films such as Mohsen Makhmalbaf's *Kandahar: Journey into the Heart of Afghanistan* (Iran, 2001) and Shelley Niro's *Honey Moccasin* (Canada, 1998).

Kandahar is a fictional docudrama based on the story of Nelofer Pazira, who immigrated to Canada in 1989 to seek refuge from the tyranny of the Taliban in Afghanistan. One day, as Makhmalbaf's tells it, 'a young Afghan woman, who had taken refuge in Canada, came to see me. She had just received a desperate letter from her friend who wanted to commit suicide because of the harsh conditions in Kandahar. She wanted to go back and help her friend at all cost. She asked me to go with her and film her journey.' The story is based on Pazira's experience. In the film, Makhmalbaf created a central character named Nafas, whose name means respiration: 'it's an Afghan name. The *burka* (a gown worn by Afghan women which covers the entire body) prevents women from breathing and from being free.' The narrative of the film is a travelogue that documents Nafas's journey into Afghanistan. In one story on this journey, a group of women covered in their flowing and colourful *burkas* are walking across the Iranian desert to attend a wedding. At one point the group splits off, half going to the wedding and the other half going in the direction of the Afghanistan border. At the border, the women must lift their *burkas* only to reveal, in many cases, that the majority of the people are men, not women. In *Kandahar*, transgendering allegorizes the disappearing democratic citizen and how this disappearance is being furthered on the basis of familial corporeal power mediated by religious nationalisms.

Shelley Niro's film *Honey Moccasin* is an equally brilliant take on desire and the palimpsest of colonial power in everyday life. The film begins with a newscast on a slew of recent thefts in the reserve community. Someone is stealing powwow dress materials. Zachary John, the owner of the Inukshuk Café, is clearly the culprit. Honey Moccasin, owner of the Smokin Moccasin (MOCK-A-SIN as it appears on a stage backdrop in the bar), a bar once owned by 'Zack's' father, Johnny John, discovers not only that Zack is the perpetrator of the crimes but that he is using his stolen goods to cross-dress as a jingle dancer in his basement. Zack is gay, in love with 'Bow,' Honey's bouncer at the bar, and a cross-dresser. In addition to an avant-garde fashion show of powwow regalia, the film contains two other pieces of 'metropolitan' cultural representation, one a performance piece based on Peggy Lee's song 'Fever,' and the other a film, based on a poem by Daniel David Moses, titled 'Inukshuk,' both performed and filmed by Honey's talented daughter, Mabel, an art student. These artistic interventions in the film challenge the romantic myths of aboriginality, especially I would suggest, in the current critical context in which the figure of the berdache (indigenous male homosexuality) is being deployed as a site for the production of the distinction between modernity and 'savagery' or traditionalism. Rather, Niro's film critically engages with a prevalent social problem, homophobia, but its social critique is launched, not in order to insist upon the denial of continuing ways of life in favour of their so-called modernization, but as a strategy of decolonizing the multiple and complex forms of colonial violence and brutality. Creating strong and healthy individuals within communities means embracing their sexuality and gender, not unlike the narrative achievements in Witi Ihimaera's novel *The Whale Rider* and its filmic version, directed by Niki Caro, *Whale Rider*, in which a traditional Maori elder in New Zealand fails to see the leadership qualities in his grandchild simply because she is a girl – and not a boy (Ihimaera 1987, Caro 2002). Such works are unique in that the question of desire pulls in multiple directions, and the desire to be 'human' supercedes the sexualization of such desires. In the performance piece based on the Peggy Lee song, the lyrics are reclaimed and parodied, and its sexual connotations dissolve away as the trope of fever recalls the smallpox epidemic that wiped out a large proportion of the indigenous peoples in the seventeenth century. The lyrics include the following verse:

Captain Smith and Pocahontas
Had a very mad affair
When her daddy tried to kill him
She said daddy oh don't you dare.

The correlation of sexual desire and disease, of course, casts its ugly shadow over the meaning of homosexuality. And yet in the face of these horrific historical and material modes of violence, Zack emerges as a strong and healthy gay, cross-dressing man. Having paid his debt to society by suffering the humiliation of going on TV and giving back all of the stolen goods, the final scene has Zack in red lipstick being embraced by and embracing his father. The question of colonial and homophobic violence is intimately woven into this scene and recalls the words in Moses's poem, 'Inukshuk,' where he writes of 'hunters, who only hunt their brothers' – these hunters are discredited in the face of fathers who love their sons – and grandfathers who love their daughters – regardless of their gender.

Of course, transgendering is about gender and sexual identity, but it is also about crossing multiple zones of desirability and commodification: crossing borders between the spectacle and the commodity, between the technologically produced image and the materialities of economic and political power, between the public and private negotiations of identity, sexuality, love, and labour. In *Vested Interests: Cross-dressing and Cultural Anxiety*, Marjorie Garber traces the way the transvestite figure in a text 'that does not seem, thematically, to be primarily concerned with gender difference or blurred gender indicates a *category crisis elsewhere*, an irresolvable conflict or epistemological crux that destabilizes comfortable binarity, and displaces the resulting discomfort onto a figure that already inhabits, indeed incarnates, the margin' (Garber 1992b: 17). Garber's post-Foucauldian emphasis on the epistemic effects of transvestism tends, however, to relocate the power of social and political forces elsewhere, to the detriment, I think, of acknowledging the active dimension of such figures of transformation as deeply political engagements with changing political events of violence and oppression. In other words, such figures in the context of globalization and Third Worldism are not simply a response to binary difference, a way of trying to achieve an ideological resolution to a binary conflict. They do not only constitute a response to ideological forces of containment, but actively go beyond such forces by signalling the necessity for transformation and change. Contrary to Garber's theory of transgendering as a symptom of cultural anxiety, a 'categorical crisis,' films such as *Kandahar* and *Honey Moccasin* make use of the transformative codes of transgendering, with its emphasis on masquerade and binary cross-overs, to allegorize the transcultural powers of oppression that exist in today's neocolonial globalization, by signifying, first and foremost, a semiotic rupture with 'the Real' as a necessary critical response to the ideological mediations of religious nationalisms, familialisms, and other imperial fundamentalisms. Such necessary ruptures self-consciously mimic and overturn the weapons of mass deception delivered up by the likes of Ann Coulter and others in the U.S. religious fundamentalist mainstream.

The cultural work of Shelley Niro and Mohsen Makhmalbaf engage in various strategies of de-authorization that persistently critique as well as destabilize the making and remaking of religious fundamentalisms.

A cultural materialist approach to violence must include attention to representational violence and the making of such figures as the apparational Aboriginal. Keeping in mind the resignification of the figure of aboriginality, that the Aboriginal does not necessarily reach its destination, and that representations do not always have their intended liberatory or repressive effects, cultural criticism must nevertheless take note of the semi-autonomous aspects of representation and how technologies produce and reproduce such figures of aboriginality.

Too often, anti-racist feminist analyses of violence in representation reduce that violence to its symbolic dimension, as a sort of formalization of actual violent events. Any notion of epistemic or representational violence is subsumed as merely symbolic expressions of real social violence elsewhere. By acknowledging the discontinuous, though mutually related, aspects of representational, epistemic, social, economic, and political colonial violence, it is also possible to understand that cultural practices are as vital for their transformation as are legislative and economic acts. In the current climate of information-driven knowledge, the point cannot be made too clearly, that cultural politics and practices are necessary to decolonizing intimate violence in its representational and institutional forms. Furthermore, as we stare history in the face and observe the extraordinary legislative transformations in the creation of same-sex marriages and queer reproductive rights in Canada and the United States today, we would do well to remember that a persistent critique of those representational and institutional forms is essential because the global political economy has always worked in complicity with everyday life and such institutional technologies as 'the family,' in all its permutations and resignifications, to maintain the intimate violence that is essential to its hegemony.

'If it is true,' writes Franz Fanon, 'that consciousness is a process of transcendence, we have to see too that this transcendence is haunted by the problems of love and understanding' (Fanon 1967: 8). From the filiative symbolics of blood relations to the political affiliative kinships of 'women' and 'men,' 'lesbians' and 'gays,' 'First Nations' and 'non–First Nations,' emerges a tapestry of interwoven allegiances, truths, histories, and loves that cannot be easily pulled apart. To achieve these tough bonds, however, the silence must be broken, and the knowledge of sexual abuse and violence spoken out loud, heard, and responded to. The speech act must be reciprocated. Even in the most conservative of discourses, family practices, and religious traditions, de-significations emerge that, in a somewhat blasphemous way, make the world a safer place for the expression of love and for an ethics of engagement attuned to the social exchange of justice and healing.

Conclusion: De-signifying Kinship

The patriarchal, heterosexual, and imperial home in the late nineteenth and early twentieth centuries was constituted by a familial politics of power over the reproductive, sexual, and infantilized bodies of women and children. This corporeo-political formation of domestic relations transpired throughout the British Empire and its colonies, infiltrating the most intimate and intersubjective experiences of everyday life and the material economies of emotional and corporeal relations among the colonial bourgeoisie and colonized indigenous societies. It is in the home and in its corporealities that colonial violence can be gauged, and not only in its earlier inscriptions as in the legislative practices of the colonial state or in the representational and reproductive technologies of aboriginality, but also in those postcolonial discourses which perpetuate the Freudian legacy at the expense of systematically unravelling the history of sexual violence toward women and children as a material dimension of colonial power. The imperial text is multi-layered, a palimpsest of past significations and present resignifications.

The search for an original text on the part of a ruling imperial consciousness to justify and legitimate the violence of the state and its hierarchical division between domestic and public spheres of governance produced the figure of the Aboriginal. Nineteenth-century British patriarchy, with its privatization of the domestic sphere and women's labour, conjoined with economic imperialism to invent the figure of the Aboriginal precisely to eschew the contemporary realities of European imperialism and the political force of indigenous societies. This productive trope, the Aboriginal, was deployed in order to locate an originary violence elsewhere and outside the domain of 'civil society.' Civilization could not do without its Savage Other. The production of the Savage

Other is evident in the enormous cultural investments created throughout the twentieth century to reproduce "his" image in film, photography, advertising, and popular novels. Along with ethnographic and psychoanalytical discourses, representational technologies disseminated this imperial simulacrum of the Aboriginal, a hallucinatory figure of a European imperial imaginary.

Within this hugely productive zone of capital investments in aboriginality – the generative power of a representational autochthony – the Aboriginal Mother emerges as the key site of imperial conflict. Colonial power legislates her body, her sex, her children, and all her relations. She becomes an inscripted code in the writing of colonial power and its legislative practices to determine, for instance, Indian and non-Indian status through patrilineal descent. Hence, the Indian Act, put into place as the arbiter of aboriginal kinship relations, transcoded them into the classificatory system of bourgeois familial affiliations and its heteronormative codes of mother, father, son, and daughter, in all their Judeo-Christian and/or Oedipal formations.

While Freud's *Totem and Taboo* filled the contemporary moment of bourgeois power over the bodies of children, women, and domestic workers with a patriarchal narrative based on an imaginary history of patricide and the primal rule of the father, Engels, in *The Origin of the Family, Private Property and the State*, recalled the power of the primal mother via Bachofen's narrative of Mother Right and Morgan's 'communistic primitive household.' In Engels's case, this tiger's leap into the 'past' was a dialectical move because its invention of the aboriginal served to allegorize colonial power, whose goal was the destruction of indigenous women's political and economic power. In other words, Engels's representation of an historical transition from Mother Right to Father Right disclosed and anticipated the contemporary reality of colonial legislative powers and the installation, for example, of the Indian Act. Equally significant, and perhaps not surprising then, is that the struggle for decolonization emerged in the fold of the indigenous women's resistance movement. In the late 1970s, the Tobique women launched their national and international campaign against the gender discrimination of the Indian Act that resulted in Bill C-31 (1983) and the reinstatement of indigenous women's status. This struggle began over the dispossession of indigenous women and their children from the basic material necessities of housing, shelter, and the constitution of a home. The Aboriginal Mother was never a silent signifier of a conflict between tradition and modernity, but the very site of its production as an ideological displacement of the material antagonism over property rights and land ownership.

In Canada, the governing authority of the bourgeois family in colonial space was produced in the nineteenth and twentieth centuries by a multitude of visual and print cultural practices which constituted a mode of representational colonial violence. In the face of a pervasive semiotics of subjugation, indigenous artists and writers engage in various strategies of de-signification in order to challenge those textual and visual histories and their representations. A brilliant example of such work is Nadia Myre's *Indian Acts* (2000), also known as *Cont(r)acts* (2002). Myre, a renowned artist of Algonkin and French-Canadian heritage who was reinstated under Bill C-31, 'translates' the Canadian Indian Act (1876) into a beaded representation. By beading over its letters into fifty-six 'pages' of white lines on a red beaded background, Myre sets out to *write back* to the Indian Act – to engage in a *contrary* act against the *contractual* powers of colonial history.

Cont(r)acts is an interesting project for many reasons. It was a collaborative project in that Myre called upon some forty friends and relatives to do the meticulous beadwork. This collectivity of artisans eschewed the individual authority of the colonial signature. Furthermore, the material transformation of the Indian Act from its colonial grammatology into beads drew attention to the texturing of colonial legislative power. The material transformation that took place – and perhaps is still taking place – from indigenous oral storytelling to the print cultures of colonial ethnography is part of the palimpsest of imperialism that Myre's project both signifies and transforms through the combined labour of indigenous domestic craft and artistic practices. The white beaded lines on a red beaded background also put in motion a significant reversal in Canada's print and national cultures: it reverses, for example, the black on white regularity of printing as well as reversing the symbolic colours of Canada's national flag, which is red on white. These reversals signify the nation's symbolic inscription on the bodies and lands of indigenous peoples and simultaneously translates colonial state power into a contrary act of decolonization. Thus, this textual materialization of colonial state power transforms and subjects to erasure the previous documents of colonial representational violence. In another significant moment of reversal, Myre puts into motion the *palimpsest of decolonization* that is simultaneously working with political, juridical, and familial processes of historical change. Her work constitutes the ingredients of a counter-knowledge – one in which the truth claims of imperial violence are transformed into allegories of healing and a truly reparative textuality and testimonial consciousness.

Decolonization is the site of this complex interplay between savagery and civilization, between a primitivist archive of ethnographic, psychoanalytical, and representational investments, and its dialectical transformation via the careful, meticulous, and collective de-signifying practices of contemporary indigenous artists, film-makers, and writers.

Perhaps the greatest challenge indigenous people pose to imperialism and colonization is their vested interest in the materiality of everyday life and the continuing recognition of indigenous women in creating and maintaining that life. It is this material re-evaluation of indigenous women's political power and knowledge that I glimpse in the meticulous work of Nadia Myre's de-signified Indian Act – a reminder of an act of colonial legislation that was designed to aid in the destruction of indigenous societies by dispossessing indigenous women of their political role, by attempting to privatize the domestic sphere as a site of drudgery, slave labour, and unaccountable violence. But the palimpsest of decolonization reveals over and over the continuing struggle against the state and its imperial nationalisms, and that the formation of patriarchy and heteronormativity in the nineteenth century emerged as a political strategy to dispossess women, to privatize the equitable distribution of power and knowledge that was evident in contemporary indigenous societies. Nineteenth-century heteronormative patriarchy, therefore, underscores European imperialism, and it was directed not only toward European middle-class and working-class women but to their potential models and allies in the indigenous territories of North America and elsewhere. It is impossible, I would argue, to understand the one location of patriarchal imperialism and resistance to it without recalling and remembering this other one.

Notes

**Introduction: Of Soft and Savage Bodies in the
Colonial Domestic Archive**

1 In his essay 'The Noble Savage Theme as Fetish' Hayden White notes that metaphors, such as that of the Noble Savage, 'are crucially necessary when a culture or social group encounters phenomena that either elude or run afoul of normal expectations or quotidian experiences' (White 1978: 184). In his analysis, the significance of the Noble Savage to eighteenth-century Europe lay in its capacity to undermine the idea of nobility itself. The 'true referent' of the Noble Savage, argues Whites, was 'not the savages of the new or any other world ... the Noble Savage idea represents not so much an elevation of the idea of the native as a demotion of the idea of nobility' (191). Thus, White concludes 'the Noble Savage was a concept with which to belabour nobility, not to redeem the savage' (192). All that was considered evil or inassimilable to European bourgeois consciousness was projected, according to White, onto the 'natives,' specifically, 'a projection of repressed desires onto the lives of the native ... a desire tainted by horror and viewed with disgust' (187). This abject projection constituted, according to a particular aspect of White's definition of fetishism, 'a pathological displacement of libidinal interest and satisfaction to the fetish' (184). In other words, European bourgeois, patriarchal culture deployed the figure of the Noble Savage in order to secure knowledge about itself as civilized and enlightened.

2 At the heart of the salvage operation motif was Edward S. Curtis's photograph 'The Vanishing Race – the Navaho,' published in 1907 in volume 1 of his twenty-volume *The North American Indian* (1907–30). Concerning this image, Curtis writes that the photograph of the Navaho 'is meant to convey [...] that the Indians as a race, already shorn of their tribal strength and

stripped of their primitive dress, are passing into the darkness of an unknown future. Feeling that the picture expresses so much of the thought that inspired the entire work, the author has chosen it as the first of the series' (Curtis 1997: 36). Further to the question of salvage operations in ethnographic films and Canadian national cinema, see Gittings 2002 and Jessop 1999, 2002.

3 In her astute observation of a 1980s cover design of Bronislaw Malinowski's twentieth-century book *The Sexual Life of Savages in North-Western Melanesia: An Ethnographic Account of Courtship, Marriage, and Family Life among the Natives of the Trobriand Islands* (1929, rpt 1987), Marianna Torgovnick notes that 'the book's title and author's name occupy fully one-half of the cover ... The author's name penetrates the name of the book, a name which itself suggest penetration. If that explanation seems to go too far, the illustration at the bottom of the cover signals quite clearly themes of sexuality and gender. It merges the biological symbols of male and female, deploying half against the white field of title and author's name, half against an illustration below' (Torgovnick 1990: 5). The symbolic field of the book's cover rehearses the author's signature, and not simply as a collector of information but as both its author and authoritative producer.

4 Freud defines the uncanny as 'that class of the frightening which leads back to what is known of old and long familiar' (Freud 1995: 121). The uncanny belongs to the realm of the origin story, where defamiliarization brings the subject back to what is or was already known, but only by a certain reversal between 'fantasy' and 'reality,' between the representation and its non-existent referent.

5 Sander Gilman and Robert Young examine some of the pornographic fantasies that were pervasive in the imperial imagination (see Gilman 1985 and Young 1995). Both, however, evade the question of how such an imperial politics of desire created the figure of female aboriginality and its actual effects on indigenous women. For example, bell hooks notes Gilman's failure to attend to the specificity of Black female sexuality beyond the oppositional framework already at work in imperialist representations, which used Black female bodies to 'enforce the greater value of the white female icon' (hooks 1992: 64). Thus, Gilman and Young inadvertently reproduce representational violence by ignoring the material specificities and collusions of imperial and patriarchal representations on the lives of indigenous women.

6 Further to this point, see Barrett's and Eleanor Leacock's introductions to two separate editions of Engels's *The Origin of the Family, Private Property and the State*. Leacock has clearly found Engels's work useful to her analysis of egalitarian gender relations among the Montagnais-Naskapi Indians in

eastern Canada. Barrett is critical of Engels and Leacock's appropriation of his work (Barrett 1986 and Leacock 1972).

7 On 30 November 2000 a Speaker's Advisory Panel on Murals in the Parliament Buildings was struck by the Speaker of the British Columbia Legislative Assembly, Hon. Bill Hartley. A report, 'A Review of the Depiction of Aboriginal Artwork in the Parliament Buildings,' was issued 28 March 2001, with recommendations that the murals in question be removed. To date, they have not been removed.

8 Everyday domestic power relations were considered secondary and minor – if acknowledged at all – in comparison to relations of power largely constituted between and among men who embody national and imperial state powers. This imaginary boundary between domestic and state regimes of power has become more porous. Michèle Barrett observes, for example, that 'there is also now considerable awareness of the gendered character of the Hitler and Mussolini regimes which Woolf hated so much. Hence the extent to which the Nazis built a culture on the domestication of women, and the cultural politics of Mussolini's sexualization and domination of Italian women, are now seen as important issues' (Barrett 1989: xxxviii).

9 Anne Wheeler's film *Loyalties* was an early attempt during the 1980s to raise the question of sexual violence toward indigenous women as a neocolonial problem. See Emberley 1995 for a critical analysis of the film. Further to the specificity of rape and colonization, see also Layoun 1992 and Sharpe 1991, 1993.

1. An Origin Story of No Origins

1 Many of these problems were discussed in various publications during the 1980s by writers and critics such as Jeannette Armstrong (1989), Maria Campbell (1983), Marlene Castellano (1989), Beatrice Culleton (1984), Joyce Green (1985), Celia Haig-Brown (1988), and Kathleen Jamieson (1986). Collectively, this work drew attention to the specific effects of colonization on indigenous women and children.

2 Carol Summers, for example, examines how the British took control over midwifery to shape the Ugandan family by seizing control over reproduction: 'By promoting fertility, the administration sought to acquire taxpaying subjects and a labour force. By promoting new motherhood and attempting to reinforce social ties threatened through economic and political change, it endeavored to make itself self-perpetuating' (Summers 1991: 807).

3 Carol Smart notes that the government legislation regarding domestic violence (the Domestic Violence and Martrimonial Proceedings Act, 1976, and

the Domestic Proceedings and Magistrates' Courts Act, 1978) 'arose directly from the political lobbying of groups such as Women's Aid and the Women's Liberation Movement ... Yet its force lay in an argument which was based on establishing women's helplessness and vulnerability in the family and in marriage. It was not an argument based on the growth of women's independence in the public sphere, but an argument which relied on revealing women's powerlessness and their need for external intervention and help before they could help themselves' (Smart 1995: 156) Clearly, psychoanalysis or psychotherapy would play a significant role in 'helping' women who experienced domestic violence.

4 On British colonialism and white women, see Faymonville 1998 and Saxby 1982, and especially in the Canadian context, Valverde 1992, Henderson 2003, and Devereux 1999. Devereux, for example, notes that Anglo-Canadian women constituted a form of 'maternal feminism.' As part of the colonial importation of the New Woman, they were 'actively engaged in the expansion of the Empire and ... regarded themselves as struggling at the front lines of the imperial crusade' (Devereux 1999: 179).

5 Foucault defines 'oeconomy' as a pre-modernist mode of familial governance. He observes that 'upwards continuity in the sense that he who wishes to well govern the State must first learn how to govern himself, his goods and patrimony, after which he will be successful in governing the State. This upwards line characterizes the pedagogies of the Prince [i.e., Machiavelli's *Prince*] ... It is the pedagogical formation of the Prince, then, that will assure this upwards continuity. On the other hand, we also have a downwards continuity in the sense that, when a State is well-run then the head of the family will know how to look after his family, his goods and patrimony, which means that individuals will, in turn, behave as they should. This downwards line which transmits to individual behaviour and the running of the family the same principles as the good government of the State, is just at this time beginning to be called "police." The Prince's pedagogical formation ensures the upwards continuity of the forms of government, and police the downwards one. The central element of this continuity is the government of the family, termed "oeconomy."' (Foucault 1979b: 9–10). Importantly, and as in many conceptions of what constitutes modernity and what constitutes per-modernity, the notion of an oeconomy is historically situated in a pre-historical framework, which is to say, that it no longer exists. I would argue, however, that it does exist in a residual and thoroughly ideological way, to the extent that it exists simultaneously in its most naturalized and taken-for-granted mode with dominant public/private and public/domestic modes of nineteenth-century governance and with emergent

'public' modes of governance that have, for example, co-opted spheres of intimacy, privacy, and domesticity into the regulatory agencies of public institutions of health and education. Thus, I continue to deploy the notion of an *oeconomy* to signal its residual trace in global capitalisms today, as well as for its descriptive force in situating the emerging centrality of kinship relations to economic and political forms of power.

6 See Allen 1986 for an examination of the significance of the disentitlement of indigenous women in the United States.

7 See the following key texts: Delphy 1984; Kuhn and Wolpe 1978; O'Brien 1981; Sargent 1981.

8 Consider Foucault's observation that 'power in Western capitalism was denounced by Marxists as class domination; but the mechanics of power in themselves were never analyzed. This task could only begin after 1968, that is to say on the basis of daily struggles at grass roots level, among those whose fight was located in the fine meshes of the web of power ... So long as the posing of the question of power was kept subordinate to the economic instance and the system of interests which this served, there was a tendency to regard certain problems as of small importance' (Foucault 1980b: 116).

9 The notion of 'descent' already carries the trace of its eighteenth-century racial meaning. As Jean-Louis Flandrin explains, 'the word "famille" is usually understood to mean the entirety of several persons united by ties of blood or of affinity. Moreover, the dictionaries give as synonyms of the word "family" understood in this sense, "*race*," "house" (*maison*); "descent," "extraction" (*extraction, naissance*); "stock" (*souche, tige*); "branch," "parentage," "issue" (*lignage, parentage, parentelle*)' (Flandrin 1979: 6).

10 In the post–Bill C-31 period, some 40 per cent of the status Indian population adopted band membership codes. Most disturbing is that approximately 30 bands out of the 236 bands that had codes by 1992 opted for a type of membership rule based on blood quantum: 'A blood quantum rule sets a criterion for membership based on the number of Indian ancestors in an individual's family history. Blood quantum codes measure a person's quantum by adding the quantum of each parent and dividing by two. An individual with one parent of 100 per cent Indian blood and one parent of no Aboriginal blood is considered to be 50 per cent Indian. Similarly, if both parents are considered 50 per cent Indian, the child is considered 50 per cent Indian. A typical blood quantum criterion for band membership is 50 per cent, although there are codes where the quantum is set either above or below this level' (*Report* 1996).

11 For a summary of the political strategies deployed by the Tobique women that led to the implementation of Bill C-31, see Silman 1987.

12 See the following: Jones 1985, Kirby 1985, Kirkness 1987, and Emberley 1993: 87–91.
13 See also the more recent protest letter from the Inuit Women's Association, 'Letter to Premier Okalik of Nunavut' (Pauktuutit 2000a), which indicates to government officials that violence against women will not be tolerated.

2. The Spatial Politics of Homosocial Colonial Desire in Robert Flaherty's *Nanook of the North*

1 In his *Story of Comock the Eskimo*, Flaherty's fascination with the capacity of boats to contain mythical figures, in this case, hybrid 'half bird and half man' ones, is evident in the following account: 'We came to a ledge jutting off from the cliff face, landed upon it and, climbing up some fifty feet, sat down. I was looking through my glass at thousands of little specks, sea pigeons flying among the rocks of a nearby island. Suddenly on the water before the island I saw a small boat rowing toward us. It sprawled clumsily over the lumpy sea. It drew nearer. Its occupants were Eskimos. A man was steering at the stern, two others were at the oars. It drew nearer, close in. It was almost a third as broad as it was long, which was not more than fifteen feet, but within it we counted thirteen people, grown-ups and children, huddled together, and among them two dogs as well. Over the children and the dogs a woman held a stick to hit them if by moving suddenly they should threaten the balance of the cockleshell. Why the amazing craft did not capsize we could not understand, until I saw its waterline, a series of inflated seal bladders tied at intervals around it. They alone kept the craft afloat. The Eskimos, their dogs – as wild as wolves – cowering between their legs, stared at us out of their twinkling slant-eyes. They looked like something half bird and half man, for their costumes were not made of the usual deerskin or bearskin or hairy seal, but of the skins of the ivory duck, feathers and all, sewn together. They were not afraid' (Carpenter 1968: 13).
2 Sherene Razack outlines a strategy of 'unmapping' as a way of conjoining questions of identity, space, and race. She writes: 'In unmapping, there is an important relationship between identity and space. What is being imagined or projected onto specific spaces and bodies, and what is being enacted there? Who do white citizens know themselves to be and how much does an identity of dominance rely upon keeping racial Others firmly *in place*? How are people kept in their place? And, finally, how does place become race? We ask these questions here in the fervent belief that white settler societies can transcend their bloody beginnings and contemporary inequalities by remembering and confronting the racial hierarchies that structure our lives'

(Razack 2002: 5). While her questions are entirely relevant to this and other studies of 'race' and place, the notion of the 'unmappable' re-inscribes a naïve essentialism about nature and inscriptions of the earth, often attributed to indigenous peoples. Here the colonial paradigm of territorial conquest must be taken into account. Elsewhere I have argued that 'cartographies are technologies of space that can be altered or rewritten depending on the demands of the dominant mode of material relations. Cartographies "outside" the system of private property, outside, that is, cartographies of capital, are often conceived of as precartographic when they are in fact written maps that re-present a politics, a history, and an economy of writing in the graphic sense of the word. Cartographies can be different. They can bear the imprint of different agencies of land usage. How one *stores* the land in regulated shapes – and this is the image the map neatly draws – differs from "mapping" that, in *storying* the land, shows movement across space, delineations of mobility that are not quantifiable by measured or striated space' (Emberley 1997: 90).

3 On the generative principles of capital David Harvey writes: 'When Marx argues that "capital does" or "capital creates" he is *not* arguing that a thing called capital has causal power, but that the process of capital circulation, understood as a whole, is at the center of vital social transformations and for that reason has to be looked upon as *embodying a powerful generative principle affecting social life*' (Harvey 1996: 63; emphasis added).

4 Constitutive to demonstrating those contradictions can be added a remark by an earlier commentator on the film, Luc de Heusch, who went so far as to as to term the 'Alaskan Eskimo' a 'primitive Protestant' with the noble virtues of 'independence, perseverance, and patriarchy' (quoted in Rony 1996: 108).

5 Stoler's remarks here also cast light on Hayden White's essay 'The Noble Savage Theme as Fetish.' More than a repressive or exclusionary function, Stoler notes that the politics of desire often operated to contain and to rationalize the exorbitant and the excessive. Figures such as the Noble Savage were the repository of all manner of fears and anxieties about masculine sexuality. For Hayden White, the debate, for example, over whether Indians had souls, is 'much more illuminative of the confusion present in Europeans' minds over the nature of their own humanity than it is either of the nature of the natives (which goes without saying, of course) or of the attitudes toward and the beliefs about natives held by Europeans' (White 1978: 189). The problem, however, is not only the fact that ideas about Natives and the making of such figures as the Noble Savage worked as a critical trope within European Enlightenment debates, specifically Rousseau's *Dis-*

course on Inequality, over the problem of 'nobility'; it also worked to secure for an emerging European bourgeoisie its self-justification to rule over the colonies. Furthermore, White's concern for the European bourgeoisie's sense of its 'humanity' – what I would prefer to call its concern over its status as civilized and not savage – must be rethought in terms of the making of sexual and racial differences that underscored the very meaning of what it meant to European bourgeoisie male consciousness to be 'human': a fetish, if ever there was one, for containing the mystical powers of the ruling white, bourgeois, Christian father.

6 *Nanook of the North* has been the object of an interesting de-signification by Zacharias Kunuk's film *Atanarjuat: The Fast Runner.* Their interconnections are examined by Sophie McCall (2004). One of the most interesting intertextual moments concerns the ethno-pornographic representation of polygamy in *Nanook* and its de-signification in *Atanarjuat,* where the central character's two wives provide the narrative device that motivates the film's story of love, jealousy, murder, and revenge. Further to *Atanarjuat,* see the film script, interviews, and commentaries in *Atanarjuat: The Fast Runner* (Angilirq 2002).

3. Originary Violence and the Spectre of the Primordial Father

1 See especially chapter 2 of Leakey's *Origin of Humankind,* titled 'A Crowded Family,' in which he recounts the archaeological genealogy of 'homo sapien,' ironically with reference to his famous father's and mother's scholarship in the field.

2 In addition, writes David Macey, Foucault specifically meant that 'discourse was not an interplay of prior significations.' He goes on to quote Foucault: 'Discourse has to be seen as the violence we do to things, or in any case as a practice which we impose upon them; and it is within that practice that events in discourse find the principle of their regularity' (as quoted in Macey 1993: 244).

3 Foucault coins this term in his *Archaeology of Knowledge.* Dreyfus and Rabinow gloss this concept-metaphor in the following useful terms: 'The *dispositif* is, of course, a grid of intelligibility constructed by the historian. But it is also the practices themselves, acting as an apparatus, a tool, constituting subjects and organizing them' (Dreyfus and Rabinow 1982: 121). Michel de Certeau defines the microphysical dimensions of power as '"minuscule" technical procedures acting on and with details, redistributing a discursive space in order to make it the means of a generalized "discipline"' (Certeau 1984: xiv).

4 On de-disciplining the body, I mean to suggest how the notion of 'discipli-narity' signifies a new economy of violence since the late nineteenth century and the birth of regulatory practices in education, medicine, jurisprudence, and industrial capitalism. The bodies produced by these new regulatory practices are encoded by a semiotics of gender, race, class, and colonial identities. De-disciplining such bodily and embodied inscriptions undoes epistemic and representational violence.

5 Freud's anthropological sources include, for example, W. Robertson Smith's *Lectures on the Religion of the Semites* and *Kinship and Marriage in Early Arabia*.

6 Following this sentence, Freud writes: 'In my own judgment I am still some way from having achieved this end; and I may add that within the limits of the present paper I shall be able to bring forward only a part of such knowl-edge on the subject as I do possess.' Like an instance of infantile recurrence, Freud is repeatedly unable to consider the possibility of rejection in the face of sexual violence.

7 Passages indiscriminately quoted here can be found in Freud 1925.

8 Other notable films include *Tarzan Escapes* (1936), *Tarzan's Secret Treasure* (1941), and *Tarzan's New York Adventure* (1942).

9 McClintock summarizes Thomas Richards's analysis of the significance of this ad, which lies in 'its representation of the commodity as a magical medium capable of enforcing and enlarging British power in the colonial world, even without the rational understanding of the mesmerized Sudanese.' McClintock critiques Richards's imperiocentrism by adding: 'What the ad more properly reveals is the colonials' own fetishistic faith in the magic of brand names to work the causal power of empire' (see McClin-tock 1995: 225–6; and Richards 1990: 122–3).

10 The 'adulteration' of soap – 'objectionable substances used as substitutes for pure fat' – was a hotly debated issue in advertisements in the 1890s. Vinolia Soap advertisements in 1890 captured the readers attention by using a news-flash headline technique such as in 'Legislation against Impure Soaps' (see Mansell Collection, 'Commercial Advertisements: Soap,' Feb. 1891).

11 In *Black Skin, White Masks*, Fanon attends, very precisely, to the configura-tion of racism directed to and experienced by Black people. Constitutive to 'biological racism' against Black people, he argues, are metaphors and metonymies of physical and moral dirtiness, overdetermined by a Christian or religious ideology of sin and purity. He writes: '… the torturer is the black man, Satan is black, one talks of shadows, when one is dirty one is black – whether one is thinking of physical dirtiness or of moral dirtiness. It would be astonishing, if the trouble were taken to bring them all together, to see the vast number of expressions that make the black man the equivalent of sin.

In Europe, whether concretely or symbolically, the black man stands for the bad side of the character. As long as one cannot understand this fact, one is doomed to talk in circles about the "black problem." Blackness, darkness, shadow, shades, night, the labyrinths of the earth, abysmal depths, blacken someone's reputation; and, on the other side, the bright look of innocence, the white dove of peace, magical, heavenly light. A magnificent blond child – how much peace there is in that phrase, how much joy, and above all how much hope! There is no comparison with a magnificent black child: such a thing is unwanted!' (Fanon 1967: 189).

12 The new world scholar can purchase magazines, presumably those owned by Time Inc., or browse through them in libraries and bookstores. Once you've found your image(s), then you request copyright permission to reproduce and pay something in the order of US $100 to $250 US per image. Your publishing venue will have to have a significant distribution, preferably a trade publisher, to gain copyright permission to begin with. Covering the cost of reproduction can be negotiated with your publisher: either the publisher will pay, or the cost can be deducted from royalties; or possibly be covered by research grants.

13 For a reproduction of the Quaker State Oil advertisement, see McLuhan 1951: 116.

4. Post/Colonial Masculinities

1 See, for example, Sassoon's *Memoirs of George Sherston: Memoirs of a Fox-Hunting Man, Memoirs of an Infantry Offier, and Sherston's Progress* and *The War Poems of Siegfried Sassoon.*

2 See Rivers's well-known monograph *Kinship and Social Organization, Together with 'The Genealogical Method of Anthropological Enquiry.'*

3 As Showalter writes: 'For the officers, the male relationships of the army, as J.R. Ackerley observed in his autobiography, were "simply an extension of my public school" – chaste, intense, platonic, unacknowledged. J.B. Priestley agreed that the emotional training of all-male public schools prepared many officers to hail 'with relief ... a wholly masculine way of life uncomplicated by Woman." Witnessing the death of beloved male companions was a traumatic event that triggered much of the memorable poetry of the trenches, Richard Fein has said, "War poetry has the subversive tendency to be our age's love poetry"' (Showalter 1985: 171). On the subject of the rise of militarism, see M.C.C. Adams's *The Great Adventure: Male Desire and the Coming of World War I;* on the topic of militarism and Victorian public school experience, see G.F.A. Best's 'Militarism and the Victorian Public Schools.'

4 See also Laura A. Lewis, 'The Weight of Words: Domination through Mis-representation: The "Weakness" of Women and the Feminization of the Indian in Colonial Mexico.' For a summary of the history of the origins of the First World War, see Gordon Martel's useful account, *The Origins of the First World War.*

5 In Rey Chow's *The Protestant Ethnic and the Spirit of Capitalism*, the ends of 'Man' are figured in the following general terms: 'If Man is a historical invention, it is because he is a Western invention, which relies for its inventiveness – its originality, so to speak – on the debasement and exclusion of others' (Chow 2002: 2). Because the colonial context is constituted by subtle shifts in power across patriarchal, imperial, national, racist, and gendered lines, the 'ends' of Man tend to combine and recombine in ways that materially benefit some and dispossess others. It is important to work with the materialities of representational violence if the objective is to unfold the complex hegemonic formations of power that run along several intersecting and interlocking in/determinations including, among other things, the concept-metaphor of aboriginality.

6 For a fascinating reading of Barker's earlier novels and her interweaving of class and gender, see Peter Hitchcock's 'Radical Writing.'

5. The Family in the Age of Mechanical Reproduction

1 See the website of the International Council of Women of Canada at http:/www.ncwc.ca/aboutUs_history.html.

2 Further to this point, it is worth considering Duncan Campbell Scott's poem 'The Onondaga Madonna' published in *Labor and the Angel*:

The Onondaga Madonna

She stands full-throated and with careless pose,
This woman of a weird and waning race,
The tragic savage lurking in her face,
Where all her pagan passion burns and glows;
Her blood is mingled with her ancient foes,
And thrills with war and wildness in her veins;
Her rebel lips are dabbled with the stains
Of feuds and forays and her father's woes.
And closer in the shawl about her breast,
The latest promise of her nation's doom,
Paler than she her baby clings and lies,
The primal warrior gleaming from his eyes;

> He sulks, and burdened with his infant gloom,
> He draws his heavy brows and will not rest.

The title of Scott's volume of poetry gestures towards that nineteenth-century staple of feminine domesticity, the Angel in the House, juxtaposed with the figure of labouring aboriginal women in 'The Onondaga Madonna.' Such a gesture situates Scott's image of the Onandaga Madonna within the colonial gendering of First Nations women's bodies. Such bodies were made to represent a 'savage' nature, sexually and physically, as distinct from the proper body of civilization, the European female bourgeois body.

3 On domicide and its effects J. Douglas Porteous and Sandra E. Smith write that it 'may result in: the destruction of a place of attachment and refuge; loss of security and ownership; restrictions on freedom; partial loss of identity and a radical de-centring from place, family, and community. There may be a loss of historical connection; a weakening of roots; and partial erasure of the sources of memory, dreams, nostalgia, and ideals. If home has multiple, complex meanings that are interwoven, then so does domicide ... what is lost is not only the physical place, but the emotional essence of home - aspects of personal self-identity' (Porteous and Smith 2001: 63).

6. Inuit Mother Disappeared

1 All documents are from Library and Archives Canada, Record Group 86, vol. 920. All references to documents are contained in the text and indicated by date.

2 To maintain, for example, a rigid distinction between identifying a sex-undifferentiated body from a sexually undifferentiated body would be to deny an irreducible linguistic slide. It would also be to deny the libidinal investments of the colonial enterprise and the role of its ethno-pornographic gaze in circumscribing the rational discourses of the law.

3 These distinctions need some clarification. The difference between status and non-status Indians was determined by the Canadian state in the late nineteenth century through an ad-hoc process in which individuals were signed up, often given Christian names, and added to a registry. Métis constitute a cultural group of mixed Scottish/Cree or French/Cree descent. The Inuit are an independent cultural and linguistic group occupying what are now called the Northwest Territories, the Yukon, and the northern part of Labrador, in Canada. In 1993 the Canadian state recognized Nunavut, a third order of government constituted by the Inuit of the Eastern Arctic.

4 As we will see later, the suspicion on the part of this Ottawa bureaucrat

stems more from his ignorance of the realities of northern life than anything based on sustained knowledge of what would constitute suspicious behaviour and criminal activity within this environmentally 'alien' context.

5 According to Vic Satzewich and Terry Wotherspoon, it was not until the federal government census of 1951 that each Inuk was assigned 'a disc number' (Satzewich and Wotherspoon 1993: xv). The consistent usage of a name/number combination format (also referred to as 'E' numbers) in the RCMP reports suggests that some form of notation was in use before the census report systematized its usage. This systematic notation was purportedly initiated for the purposes of administering family allowance payments in the late 1940s.

6 During the course of the exhumation of Bertha's body and the exchange of reports between the various RCMP divisions on this topic, several other reports on the disappearance of Mrs A. were in circulation. During the period from Mrs A.'s disappearance (May 1948) to September of 1949, two dogs belonging to A.'s team as well as an abandoned toboggan were found, although it was concluded that the toboggan was not A.'s after all (7 November 1949, 29 November 1949, 10 May 1950).

7 It would appear, however, that A. had some of his own suspicions about what the RCMP were making of his story. In what is an ironic, or at least reflexive, moment in the text of these reports, the following comment is recorded, with quotation marks, from A.: '"it must look suspicious to you as a Policeman."' When asked what he meant by this comment, the following explanation is recorded: 'he said two of my children meeting their death by drowning and my wife and other child disappearing somewhere between my camp and Padlei and were never seen again, he then stated that he had been accused of murder, and he enlarged on this by stating that one dinner hour at the Army Camp, where he is employed, he was telling one of the other workmen about his troubles and how he lost four members of his family and this workman told him "[A.] YOU MURDERED THEM.' A. could not recall the name of this workman, however, during our conversation A. did inform the writer that his son John was buried on the top of the hill at the back of his cabin and that Bertha was buried on the side of the hill and that another baby boy that died at childbirth was buried across the lake from his cabin' (17 October 1949).

8 The contents of the statement leading up to this excerpt are as follows: 'Sometime in June, 1942, I was moving with my family, Bertha, John, Dianna and my wife from my tent which was approximately half a mile above my camp. On the way down with a canoe, a 16' Cruser Canoe, we hit fast water and it took the canoe towards a rock, where the canoe upset in the rolls

caused by the fast water and the rock. As the canoe started to upset I jumped into the water, the first one of my family, I saw was Bertha, I then looked for my wife, who was carrying Dianna on her back, I got hold of my wife and got her over to the canoe and told her to hold on to it, I then went to the other end of the canoe and started working it towards shore, when near shore the canoe hit another rock and righted itself, my son John was underneath the canoe, holding on to the thwart, John was about 3 1/2 years of age, I told him to hold on, we hit another rock and the canoe turned over and I managed to beach same, I could not see John when I righted the canoe, got my wife and child ashore and went out in the canoe to look for Bertha and John, I found Bertha, but could not find John ...'

9 This story was told to me by Frank Tester of the Faculty of Social Work, University of British Columbia, Vancouver, British Columbia, in the summer of 1991.

10 For a story about a shaman who wears a woman's dress and flies through the air, as told by the Tagish/Tlingit elder Angela Sidney, see Sidney 1990: 53–7.

11 Many acts of inscription take place, including a set of toboggan tracks and dogs' footprints in the snow outside Eskimo Point and a set of graves placed in the earth, dug, undug, and redug, as if to expose earth's 'mystery' and then to smother it. For a suggestive reading of narrative forms deriving from a process of deciphering animal tracks on the ground, see Ginzberg 1989: 102–3. While enamoured of 'man the hunter,' however, Ginzberg simply forgets about 'woman the gatherer' or 'woman the hunter,' for that matter. The essay is also problematic for its evolutionary and progressivist reading of footprints in the snow, read by Palaeolithic man, to written intellectual abstraction, read by postmodern (male) cultural historian.

12 Butler makes this move in *Gender Trouble*. Further to this point, Butler writes: 'Within feminist political practice, a radical rethinking of the ontological constructions of identity appears to be necessary in order to formulate a representational politics that might revive feminism on other grounds. On the other hand, it may be time to entertain a radical critique that seeks to free feminist theory from the necessity of having to construct a single or abiding ground which is invariably contested by those identity positions or anti-positions that it invariably excludes' (Butler 1990: 5).

7. The Possibility of Justice in the Child's Body

1 In 2001 Johnson was transferred to the Edmonton Institute for Women. In September 2005, at a hearing for early parole, the jury decided that she should be eligible to apply later that year.

2 In an effort to bring about 'restorative justice' in dealing with the high proportion of aboriginal people in Canada's correctional facilities, the Criminal
Code introduced in 1996 a directive to judges to 'always consider alternatives to jail in sentencing, particular for native people. Section 718.2 (e)
states: "all available sanctions other than imprisonment that are reasonable
in the circumstances should be considered for all offenders, with particular
attention to the circumstances of aboriginal offenders." In its interpretation
of this section, the high court directed sentencing judges to use a different
approach when sentencing first nations people so as to help ameliorate the
serious problem of overrepresentation of aboriginal people in prisons'
(Anand 2000: 412). See also Roach and Rudin 2000. Legal pluralism extends
the idea of restorative justice but differs from it in that it uses principles
based on aboriginal cultural practices such as the 'sentencing circle' as a
means of providing an alternative to incarceration.

3 In the following passage, Wiebe recalls his earlier work on Big Bear, and
although the interpretive emphasis may be the question of territorial dispossession, by his own account, Wiebe discloses that it is, in fact, 'daily life'
that is the governing issue for Big Bear:

> Facing Lieutenant-Governor Morris, Big Bear made the second of his pro-
> found, imagistic statements about Native-White relations:
> 'There is one thing that I dread: to feel the rope around my neck.'
> At first Morris understood this on a simple, literal level: it must refer to
> the White legal practice of hanging criminals, and since Big Bear was now
> definitely confirmed as 'troublesome,' no doubt he feared that fate if he
> signed. But Big Bear persisted, and at a certain point in the debate, which
> Morris himself recorded in his memoirs in 1880, the governor seemed to
> grasp the larger meaning of the statement: Big Bear was speaking for his
> people then alive and their children yet to be born in an all-inclusive
> image, and suddenly Morris made a radical concession in his interpreta-
> tion of what the treaty meant:
> 'I wish the Bear ... to understand fully, and tell the others [those people
> who are not here] ... The Government will not interfere with the Indian's
> daily life, they will not bind him.'
> Clearly, Morris understood what Big Bear was saying, and he
> responded with a transparent, official lie. Taking the Cree's immense
> land and forcing them to live in a reserve system was such an enormous
> 'interference' and 'binding' of their daily life – many Native people now
> speak of their reserves as 'prisons of grass'– that it seems the chiefs listen-
> ing to this debate in 1897 could not even imagine how enormous a lie it
> truly was. They all 'touched the pen,' and so signed. But Big Bear refused;

he and his people followed the buffalo south into Montana. (Wiebe and Johnson 1998: 10–11)

The meaning of 'daily life' might also be brought to bear on gender relations of power and economic exchange, so that the dynamics of colonial transformation in the history of indigenous peoples is made to include not only the dispossession of the land and its transformation into private property through individual settlement and labouring practices, but also the dispossession of the body through the transformation of kinship economies and their gender divisions of labour.

4 In her careful reading of *Stolen Life,* Deena Rymhs observes a significant shift in Wiebe's position from that of 'collaborator' to 'advocate': 'As Johnson's advocate, his job is to piece together a coherent picture of events from a mass of information' (Rymhs 2005: 96). The juridical bias toward determining just what constitutes evidence or information and just what sort of information needs to be presented coherently, once again, evades the question of justice.

5 For a detailed discussion of the palimpsest of imperialism and its inscriptions of *sati,* see Shetty and Bellamy 2000.

6 The federal prison for women in Kingston, Ontario, is a topic that will come up again in the text. In 1993 Johnson was chair of the Native Sisterhood, an internal organization formed by indigenous women. As Johnson notes, sometimes a quarter of the women in the prison are Native. The organization had built a sweat lodge. One of the issues Johnson recounts deals with the relocation of several Native women to the 'B Range,' an area of tighter security, which in Johnson's view, was an attempt on the part of prison authorities 'to keep them out of the Sisterhood because they were very solid together ... Staff said the B girls helped too many kill themselves' (34). In April 1990, *Creating Choices: The Report of the Task Force on Federally Sentenced Woman* was released. The suicide of twelve aboriginal women in P4W in 1994 prompted the Canadian government to follow up on its recommendation to close P4W. As a result of its closure and the report, the Okimaw Ohci Healing Lodge was established as, among other things, 'a safe place for Aboriginal women offenders' (http://www.csc-scc.gc.ca/text/facilit/institutprofiles/okima_e.shtn). Several Canadian academic journals have published articles and collections that examine the issues facing aboriginal women in correctional facilities. See, for example, Monture-Angus 1999, Sparling 1999, and Haq 1999. For an historical account of aboriginal women in prisons, see Sangster 1999.

7 Johnson reads the codes of white bourgeois femininity as a form of racial

and gendered violence, a necessary condition of feminine artifice under patriarchal colonial rule: 'My grandma Flora died with her palate as open as it was at birth ... Once she and Mom were drinking and I saw her wearing lipstick. It shocked me. She never wore any make-up that I saw, though Mom once said Grandma had one wish, to wear lipstick, but as a traditional woman she never did. But whoever put it on her this one time had not tried to reshape her mouth – when I put make-up on, I make my face appear normal – the lipstick just followed the deformity of her lip. Deep red; she sat there obviously drunk, and it made her look worse, so sad. Perhaps Mom was looking at her mother with pity, as she must look at me, but why put it on like that? I went to Grandma and asked, "Do you want this on?" but she didn't answer. So I rubbed it off, every bit' (31). When Wiebe remarks that Yvonne also wears lipstick sometimes, she responds: '"I know all about disguise," she says. "It's a wonder what I can do to myself with some Cover Girl, lip liner, and lipstick. But if you get close, you can see I'm wearing too much make-up. And it all bothers me still – when I saw Grandma like that, with lipstick and ... there are lots of reasons I don't want people close to me. My lip is only one"' (31). Femininity is a shield against the body gaze that is also a body search. It is a useful tool, but its uncharacteristic use by her grandmother only serves to reinforce the use of make-up to mimic a representation of white bourgeois femininity and, thus, self-loathing. Johnson astutely discloses the contradiction between colonial mimicry and strategic representation as a way of either reinforcing or disabling violence toward her and her grandmother's body. Johnson's father is of Norwegian ancestry. The racism of European notions of beauty unfolds in fights between Yvonne's mother, Celia, and her father, who threatens to leave Celia and find a 'nice blonde girl' (32). In narrating how her parents were 'pieced together,' individually and in relation to each other, Johnson observes the effects of the military masculinization of her father: 'Dad was pulled to pieces at seventeen and put together as a U.S. Marine to kill Japanese soldiers, and Mom was reassembled into something else in a Roman Catholic Indian residential school – when two people like that get together, what could they actually know about becoming and *being* a family? My dad did not recognize that he was the standard male chauvinist; for him, men do one thing and women another. His main way of doing things, as he always said, was work hard, pay the bills, put food on the table and clothing on our backs and a roof over our heads, but his place was not with the kids – that was women's work. The trouble was, there was often too little money because Dad drank so much, and so he and Mom always fought over who should have what responsibility for us. There were times when Mom felt we were burdens on her; often we'd hear her cry in her room at night' (33). The forces of patriarchal oppression led to her mother's own oppressive behaviour toward the children: 'strangely enough, Dad tells me now that Mom never beat us; that she was always after him to do it. Has he just forgotten, or did neither of them know what the other did with the kids, nor care?' (27–8). To divide is also to conquer; to separate so-called 'responsibilities' under capitalist patriarchy is to permit and sanction ignorance about who is doing what to whom. Under this regime of racist and sexist violence, Johnson learns to work with her body to protect herself: 'I learned very young to accept what I got; to hang my head, keep quiet, and hide behind my hair. I learned every fact about eye and body language, others as well as my own. Look, don't talk; move, don't speak' (34).

8 For example, Manina Jones challenges the collaborative moment in *Stolen Life*, noting that 'this work belongs in one reading to a long history of anthropological "as-told-to" accounts of Native lives edited by white writers ... if *Stolen Life* is literally and figuratively, an account of Johnson's reclaiming of her own powers of articulation, then why does she need a collaborator at all?' (Jones 2003: 207–8); and yet, in an optimistic tone, she affirms that 'the fact that Johnson and Wiebe are *co*-signatories may be read as an ambivalent renegotiating of the colonial representational contract, a gesture toward the postcolonial possibilities of collaboration' (Jones 2003: 210). Susanna Egan is more troubled by the claims of collaboration in *Stolen Life*, especially with respect to its testimonial possibilities, arguing that Wiebe's intervention does not create the conditions for Johnson's autonomy but rather situates her within 'a discursive assemblage through which Yvonne can be read and understood' (Egan 2000: 15). While I agree with Egan that the collaborative enterprise is unequal, it is not on the basis of discursive assemblages, which, as I argue in chapter 3, are, in fact, the conditions of possibility for the production of subjectivities – collaborative, testimonial, or otherwise. Rather, it is the *subject matter* – and not only *the* subject – that is determining in this text its collaborative subalternity. Both Jones and Egan emphasize too much the question of *the* subject without situating the question of the subject in relation to the *subject matter* of colonial, sexual, and racial violence, which is the material, historical, and discursive context of Yvonne's story.

9 The animal rights movements of the last twenty-five years or so escape Derrida's notice, especially in the United States, where the question of animal rights comes into conflict with the rights of the consumer. Since I have written about this at length elsewhere, I will only trouble to point out that Derr-

ida's claim for 'carnivorous sacrifice' cannot do without the category of 'the animal,' and, in fact, it underscores precisely the logic of animal rights activism. Derrida repeatedly claims that the category of the animal is confused, whereas he himself cannot overlook the problem: 'in the name of deconstruction, a set of questions on carno-phallogocentrism – we must reconsider in its totality the metaphysico-anthropocentric axiomatic that dominates, in the West, the thought of just and unjust' (Derrida 1992: 19). See Emberley 1997.

10 In addition to the focus on Big Bear and fraternal relations of governance is the feminine corollary to be found in the twin captivity narratives in *Two Months in the Camp of Big Bear: The Life and Adventures of Theresa Gowanlock and Theresa Delaney* (1885) (see Carter 1999, 1997). Another reading might situate this text and Wiebe's in relation to the continuing displacement in indigenous women's experience, in general, and Yvonne Johnson's, in particular, of a sexualized form of colonial violence. In other words, captivity narratives themselves displace the realities of sexualized colonial violence directed toward First Nations women and children.

8. Genealogies of Difference

1 Other publications on spousal abuse and sexual assault include, *Naalatsiarlutit: A Presentation of Artwork by Northern Artists on Spousal Abuse* (Pauktuutit 1992); *No More Secrets: Child Sexual Abuse in Inuit Communities* (Pauktuutit 1991); *Does Your Husband or Boyfriend Beat You?* (Pauktuutit 1990); *What to Do If You are Abused and/or Battered (Safety Plan)* (Pauktuutit 2000b).

2 Further to the rhetoric of globalization and its intersection with lesbian and gay bodies, see Mary K. Bloodsworth-Lugo and Carmen R. Lugo-Lugo, '"The War on Terror" and Same-Sex Marriage: Narratives of Containment and the Shaping of U.S. Public Opinion,' *Peace & Change* 30(4) (October 2005).

3 Movie theatres showing *Fire* in New Delhi, Bombay, and other cities were attacked for showing the film in December 1998. For a useful list of newspaper articles reporting the controversy during 1998–9, see http://www.saw-net.org/news/fire.html.

4 The film revolves around these two women, both of whom are represented in differing, and at times opposing, relations of dominance, victimization, and heroism. The crux of the story occurs when Komi and Pita's father comes to take them back to the North for the summer. Komi, who has been rechristened Amelia, and Kathleen have been led to believe by Reverend

Buckley and Taggart, an Indiana Jones–like truant officer, that Komi and Pita's parents died in a smallpox epidemic. It is on the basis of this information that Miss Willambury agrees to support Komi's adoption by the rich widow Barrington - an adoption which would result in a substantial donation to the school, enough to purchase a library. When Komi and Pita's father arrives, Reverend Buckley lies to him about their presence at the school, and Miss Willambury, standing by, remains silent. Miss Willambury doesn't tell Amelia the truth, but Amelia finds out anyway from her friend Ester, who overhears a conversation between Reverend Buckley and Miss Willambury. In the final scene, Miss Willambury rides out to meet Komi and her brother, who have decided to escape. Miss Willambury asks for Komi's forgiveness and gives her a Bible and prayer book. Amelia reciprocates with a gift, her bundle. Amelia turns and goes off with her brother into the prairie horizon. The second to last shot is a close-up of Miss Willambury's somewhat sad and disenchanted face. The final shot is of empty prairie landscape.

Bibliography

Adams, M.C.C. 1990. *The great adventure: Male desire and the coming of World War I*. Bloomington: Indiana UP.

Alexander, M. Jacqui, and Chandra Talpade Mohanty. 1997. *Feminist geneaologies, colonial legacies, democratic futures*. New York: Routledge.

Ali, Tariq. 2002. *The clash of fundamentalisms: Crusades, jihads and modernity*. London: Verso.

Allen, Paula Gunn. 1986. *The sacred hoop: Recovering the feminine in American Indian traditions*. Boston: Beacon Press.

Anand, Sanjeev. 2000. The sentencing of aboriginal offenders, continued confusion and persisting problems: A comment on the decision of *R. v. Gladue*. *Canadian Journal of Criminology* 42(3): 405–18.

Anderson, Kim. 2000. *A recognition of being: Reconstructing native womanhood*. Toronto: Second Story Press.

Armstrong, Jeannette. 1989. Cultural robbery, imperialism: Voices of native women. *Trivia: A Journal of Ideas* 14: 21–3.

Ashcroft, Bill, Gareth Griffiths, and Helen Tiffin. 2000. *Post-colonial studies: The key concepts*. London: Routledge.

Attorney-General of Canada v. Lavell; Isaac et al. v. Bédard, [1974] S.C.R. 1349.

Babington, Anthony. 1997. *Shell-shock: A history in the changing attitudes of war neuroses*. London: Leo Cooper.

Bachofen, J.J. 1967. *Myth, religion, and mother right: Selected writings of J.J. Bachofen*. Translated by Ralph Manheim. Princeton, NJ: Princeton University Press.

Bal, Mieke. 1996. Reading art? In *Generations and geographies in the visual arts*. Edited by Griselda Pollock. New York: Routledge.

Barker, Pat. 1982. *Union street* London: Virago Press.

– 1984. *Blow your house down*. Virago: London.

- 1991. *Regeneration*. Toronto: Penguin Books.
- 1993. *The eye in the door*. Toronto: Penguin Books.
- 1995. *The ghost road*. Toronto: Penguin Books.
- 1998. *Another world*. New York: Farrar, Straus and Giroux.

Barrett, Michèle. 1986. Introduction to *The origin of the family, private property and the state*, by Frederick Engels. Toronto: Penguin Books.
- 1989. *Women's oppression today*. 2nd ed. London: Verso.
- 1993. Introduction to *A room of one's own / Three guineas*, by Virginia Woolf. Toronto: Penguin Books.

Barrett, Michèle, and Mary McIntosh. 1982. *The anti-social family*. London: Verso.

Barrie, J.M. 1911. *Peter and Wendy*. London: Hodder and Stoughton.

Beeton, Isabella Mary. 1861. *The book of household management*. London.

Bell, Lynne, and Janice Williamson. 2001. High tech storyteller: A conversation with performance artist Lori Blondeau. *Fuse* 24(4): 27–34.

Benhabib, Seyla. 2002. *The claims of culture: Equality and diversity in the global era*. Princeton, NJ: Princeton University Press.

Benjamin, Walter. 1969. Theses on a philosophy of history. In *Illuminations*. Translated by Harry Zohn. Edited by Hannah Arendt. New York: Schocken.
- 1978. Critique of violence. In *Reflections: Essays, aphorisms, autobiographical writings*. Translated by Edmund Jephcott. Edited by Peter Demetz. New York: Harcourt Brace Jovanovich.

Berger, John. 1980. The suit and the photograph. In *About looking*. New York: Pantheon Books.

Berlant, Lauren. 1997. *The queen of America goes to Washington City: Essays on sex and citizenship*. Durham, NC: Duke University Press.

Best, G.F.A. 1975. Militarism and the Victorian public schools. In *The Victorian public school: Studies in the development of an educational institution*. Edited by Brian Simon and Ian Bradley. Dublin: Gill and Macmillan.

Bhabha, Homi. 1997. The world and the home. In *Dangerous liaisons: Gender, nation and postcolonial perspectives*. Edited by Anne McClintock, Aamir Mufti, and Ella Shohat. Minneapolis: University of Minnesota Press.

Blair, Jennifer, et al., eds. 2005. *Recalling early Canada*. Edmonton: University of Alberta Press.

Boal, Augusto. 1985. *Theatre of the oppressed*. Translated by Charles A. and Maria-Odilia Leal McBride. New York: Theater Communiations Group.

Bourke, Joanna. 1996. *Dismembering the male: Male bodies, Britain and the great war*. London: Reaktion Books.

Braidotti, Rosi. 1994. *Nomadic subjects: Embodiment and sexual difference in contemporary feminist theory*. New York: Columbia University Press.

Brant, Beth. 1994. *Writing as witness: Essay and talk*. Toronto: Women's Press.

Bridging the Cultural Divide: A report on Aboriginal people and criminal justice in Canada. 1996. Royal Commission on Aboriginal Peoples Special Report. Ottawa: The Commission. CD-ROM.

Brill, A.A., trans. 1918. Introduction to *Totem and taboo: Resemblances between the psychic lives of savages and neurotics*, by Sigmund Freud. New York: Vintage.

Brydon, Diana. 2001. Compromising postcolonialism: Tomson Highway's *Kiss of the fur queen* and contemporary postcolonial debates. In *Compr(om)ising post/colonialism(s): Challenging narratives and practices*. Edited by Greg Ratcliffe and Gerry Turcotte. Sydney: Dangaroo Press.

Buchbinder, David. 1994. *Masculinities and identities*. Melbourne: Melbourne University Press.

Burroughs, Edgar Rice. 1912. *Tarzan, the ape man*. New York: Grosset and Dunlap.

– 1915. *Jungle girl*. Gutchogue, NY: Buccaneer.

Burton, Antionette. 1995. Fearful bodies into disciplined subjects: Pleasure, romance, and the family drama of colonial reform in Mary Carpenter's six months in India. *Signs* 20(3): 545–74.

Butler, Judith. 1990. *Gender trouble: Feminism and the subversion of identity*. New York: Routledge.

Campbell, Maria. 1983. *Halfbreed*. Toronto: Goodread Biographies. Originally published by McClelland and Stewart, 1973.

Canadian Press. 1993a. 'Substance abuse rampant in Labrador village.' *Globe and Mail*. A4.

– 29 Jan.: 1993b. 'Care called lacking as more Innu children found sniffing glue.' *Globe and Mail*, 1 Feb.: A4.

Canadian Woman Studies / Les Cahiers de la femme. 1989. Special issue: 'Native women.' 10(2–3).

Carpenter, Edward, ed. 1968. *The story of Comock, the Eskimo*. New York: Simon and Schuster.

Caro, Niki, dir. 2002. *Whale Rider*. Video. New Zealand.

Carter, Sarah. 1997. *Capturing women: The manipulation of cultural imagery in Canada's West*. Montreal and Kingston: McGill-Queen's University Press.

– 1999. 'Captured women': A re-examination of the stories of Theresa Delaney and Theresa Gowanlock. In *Two months in the camp of Big Bear: The life and adventures of Theresa Gowanlock and Theresa Delaney*. Edited by Sarah Carter. Regina: Canadian Plains Research Center.

Castellano, Marlene, et al., eds. 1989. 'Native women.' Special issue of *Canadian Woman Studies / Les Cahiers de la femme*, 10(2–3).

Certeau, Michel de. 1984. *The practice of everyday life*. Translated by Steven Rendall. Berkeley: University of California Press.

Chaussonnet, Valérie. 1988. Needles and animals: Women's magic. In *Crossroads of continents: Cultures of Siberia and Alaska*. Edited by William W. Fitzhugh and Aron Crowell. Washington, DC: Smithsonian Institution Press.

Cheyfitz, Eric. 1991. *The poetics of imperialism: Translation and colonization from 'The Tempest' to 'Tarzan.'* Toronto: Oxford University Press.

Childers, Erskine B. 1962. *The road to Suez*. London: MacGibbon and Kee.

Chow, Rey. 2002. *The Protestant ethnic and the spirit of capitalism*. New York: Columbia University Press.

Chrisjohn, Roland D., Sherri L. Young, and Michael Maraun. 1997. *The circle game: Shadows and substance in the Indian residential school experience in Canada*. Penticton, BC: Theytus Books.

Clifford, James. 1988. *The predicament of culture: Twentieth-century ethnography, literature and art*. Cambridge, MA: Harvard University Press.

Cornell, Drucilla. 1991. Feminist legal reform, systems theory and the philosophy of the limit. In *Deconstruction and the possibility of justice*. New York: Routledge.

Culleton, Beatrice. 1984. *April Raintree*. Winnipeg: Pemmican.

Curtis, Edward S. 1997. *The North American Indian: The complete portfolios, 1907–1930*. New York: Taschen.

Darwin, Charles. 1871. *The descent of man and selection in relation to sex*. London: J. Murray.

Davidoff, Leonore, and Catherine Hall. 1987. *Family fortunes: Men and women of the English middle class, 1780–1850*. Chicago: University of Chicago Press.

Davin, Anna. 1997. Imperialism and motherhood. In *Tensions of empire: Colonial cultures in a bourgeois world*. Edited by Frederick Cooper and Ann Laura Stoler. Berkeley: University of California Press.

Delphy, Christine. 1984. Our friends and ourselves: The hidden foundations of various pseudo-feminist accounts. In *Close to home: A materialist analysis of women's oppression*. Edited and translated by Diana Leonard. Amherst: University of Massachusetts Press.

Department of Indian and Northern Affairs Canada. 1981. *Indian acts and amendments, 1868–1950*. 2nd ed. Ottawa.

Derrida, Jacques. 1977. Signature event context. Translated by Samuel Weber and Jeffrey Mehlman. *Glyph* 1: 172–97.

– 1992. Force of law: 'The mystical foundation of authority.' In *Deconstruction and the possibility of justice*. Edited by Drucilla Cornell, Michel Rosenfeld, and David Gray Carlson. Routledge: New York.

– 2002. *Without alibi*. Translated by Peggy Kamuf. Stanford, CA: Stanford University Press.

Devereux, Cecily. 1999. New woman, new world: Maternal feminism and the new imperialism in the white settler colonies. *Women's Studies International Forum* 22(2): 175–84.

Donzelot, Jacques. 1979. *The policing of families*. Foreword by Gilles Deleuze. Translated by Robert Hurley. New York: Pantheon.

Dreyfus, Hubert L., and Paul Rabinow. 1982. *Michel Foucault: Beyond structuralism and hermeneutics*. Chicago: University of Chicago Press.

D'Souza, Louwellyn John A. 1993. Engendering the spirit: Language, myth and two-spiritedness in the theatre of Tomson Highway, Bill Merasty and Drew Hayden Taylor. MA thesis, University of Western Ontario.

Dumont, Marilyn. 1996. *A really good brown girl*. London, ON: Brick Books.

Egan, Susanna. 2000. Telling trauma: Generic dissonance in the production of *Stolen Life*. *Canadian Literature* 67: 10–29.

Elias, Norbert. 1994. *The history of manners* (1939). Translated by Edmund Jephcott. In *The civilizing process*. London: Blackwell.

Ellison, Ralph. 1952. *Invisible man*. New York: Modern Library.

Emberley, Julia V. 1993. *Thresholds of difference: Feminist critique, Native women's writings, postcolonial theory*. Toronto: University of Toronto Press.

– 1995. History, gender, and imperialism: Anne Wheeler's *Loyalties*. In *Feminism, postmodernism, and development*. Edited by Marianne H. Marchand and Jane L. Parpart. International Studies of Women series. New York: Routledge.

– 1997. *The cultural politics of fur*. Ithaca, NY: Cornell University Press.

Engels, Friedrich. 1972. *The origin of the family, private property, and the state, in the light of the researches of Lewis H. Morgan*. New York: International Publisher.

Etienne, Mona, and Eleanor Leacock, eds. 1980. *Women and colonization: Anthropological perspectives*. New York: Praeger.

Eze, Emmanuel Chukwudi, ed. 1997. *Race and the enlightenment: A reader*. Oxford: Blackwell.

Fabian, Johannes. 1983. *Time and the other: How anthropology makes its other*. New York: Columbia University Press.

Fanon, Frantz. 1967. *Black skin, white masks*. Translated by Charles Lam Markmann. New York: Grove Press.

Faymonville, Carmen. 1998. 'Waste not, want not': Even redundant women have their uses. In *Imperial objects: Essays on Victorian women's emigration and the unauthorized imperial experience*. Edited by Rita Kranidis. New York: Twayne.

Feinberg, Leslie. 1993. *Stone butch blues*. Milford, CT.: Firebrand Books.

– 1996. *Transgender warriors: Making history from Joan of Arc to Dennis Rodman*. Boston: Beacon Press.

Findlay, L.M., ed. and trans. 2004. *The communist manifesto*, by Karl Marx and Friedrich Engels. Peterborough, ON: Broadview Press.

Fireweed. 1986. Special issue: Native Women. 22.

Fiske, Jo-Anne. 1994. The womb is to the nation as the heart is to the body: Ethnopolitical discourses of the Canadian indigenous women's movement. Paper presented at the 13th World Congress of Sociology, International Sociology Association, Beilefeld, Germany, 18–23 July.

Flaherty, Robert J., dir. 1976. *Nanook of the North* (1922). Home Vision Video.

Flaherty, Robert J., and Frances Hubbard Flaherty. 1924. *My Eskimos friends: 'Nanook of the North.'* New York: Doubleday.

Flandrin, Jean-Louis. 1979. *Families in former times: Kinship, household and sexuality*. Cambridge: Cambridge University Press.

Foucault, Michel. 1972. *The archaeology of knowledge*. Translated by Alan Sheridan. London: Tavistock. Originally published in French as *L'Archéologie du savoir*. Paris: Gallimard, 1969.

– 1973. *Madness and civilization: A history of insanity in the age of reason*. Translated by Richard Howard. New York: Vintage Books.

– 1975. *The birth of the clinic: An archaeology of medical perception*. Translated by A.M. Sheridan Smith. New York: Vintage Books.

– 1977a. Fantasia of the library. In *Language, counter-memory, practice: Selected essays and interviews*. Edited by Donald F. Bouchard. Translated by Donald F. Bouchard and Sherry Simon. Ithaca, NY: Cornell University Press.

– 1977b. Nietzsche, genealogy, history. In *Language, counter-memory, practice: Selected essays and interviews*. Edited by Donald F. Bouchard. Translated by Donald F. Bouchard and Sherry Simon. Ithaca, NY: Cornell University Press.

– 1978. *The history of sexuality*. Volume 1. *An introduction*. Translated by Robert Hurley. New York: Pantheon Books. First published as *La Volonté de savoir*. Paris: Editions Gallimard, 1976.

– 1979a. *Discipline and punish: The Birth of the prison*. Translated by Alan Sheridan. New York: Vintage Books. Originally published in French as *Surveiller et punir: Naissance de la prison*. Paris: Gallimard, 1975.

– 1979b. Governmentality. Translated by Rosi Braidotti. *Ideology and Consciousness* 6: 6–18.

– 1980a. The eye of power. In *Power/knowledge: Selected interviews and other writings, 1972–1977*. Edited by Colin Gordon. New York: Pantheon Books.

- 1980b. The politics of health in the eighteenth century. In *Power/knowledge: Selected interviews and other writings, 1972–1977*. Edited by Colin Gordon. New York: Pantheon Books.
- 1980c. Truth and power. In *Power/knowledge: Selected interviews and other writings, 1972–1977*. Edited by Colin Gordon. New York: Pantheon.
- 1984. On the genealogy of ethics: An overview of work in progress. In *The Foucault reader*. Edited by Paul Rabinow. New York: Pantheon.
- 1994. What is an author? In *Michel Foucault: Aesthetics, method and epistemology*. Edited by James D. Faubion. Essential works of Foucault, 1954–1984. Series editor, Paul Rabinow. New York: New Press.

Fournier, Suzanne, and Ernie Crey. 1997. *Stolen from our embrace: The abduction of First Nations children and the restoration of aboriginal communities*. Vancouver: Douglas and McIntyre.

Frazer, J.G. 1910. *Totemism and exogamy: A treatise on certain early forms of superstition and society*. 4 vols. London: Macmillan.

Freud, Sigmund. 1918. *Totem and taboo: Resemblances between the psychic lives of savages and neurotics*. Translated by A.A. Brill. New York: Vintage.
- 1925. *Case histories I: 'Dora' [1905/1901] and 'Little Hans' [1909]*. Translated by Alix and James Strachey. London: Penguin Books.
- 1995. The Uncanny. In *Psychological writings and letters*. Edited by Sander L. Gilman. New York: Continuum.

Fuss, Diana. 1989. *Essentially speaking: Feminism, nature and difference*. New York: Routledge.

Gage, Matilda Joslyn. 1893. *Women, church and state: A historical account of the status of women through the Christian ages*. New York: The Truth Seeker Company.

Garber, Marjorie. 1992a. The Occidental tourist: *M. Butterfly* and the scandal of transvestism. In *Nationalisms and sexualities*. Edited by Andrew Parker, Mary Russo, Doris Sommer, and Patricia Yaeger. New York: Routledge. A revised version of this essay appears in Garber 1992b.
- 1992b. *Vested interests: Cross-dressing and cultural anxiety*. New York: Routledge.

George, Jane. 1997. Anglican minister jailed eight months on sex charges. *Nunatsiaq News*, 3 Oct.: 3.

Gilbert, Sandra M. 1983. Soldier's heart: Literary men, literary women, and the great war. *Signs* 8: 418–32.

Gilman, Sander L. 1985. Black bodies, white bodies: Toward an iconography of female sexuality in late nineteenth-century art, medicine, and literature. In *Race, writing, and difference*. Edited by Henry Louis Gates, Jr. Chicago: University of Chicago Press.

Gimenez, Martha E. 1998. Marxist feminism / materialist feminism. http://
www.utc.edu/-kswitala/Feminism/Marxist.html.

Ginzberg, Carlo. 1989. Clues: Roots of an evidential paradigm. In *Clues, myths,
and historical method*. Translated by John and Anne C. Tedesch. Baltimore:
Johns Hopkins University Press.

Girard, René. 1977. *Violence and the sacred*. Translated by Patrick Gregory. Baltimore: Johns Hopkins University Press.

Gittings, Christopher E. 2002. *Canadian national cinema*. New York: Routledge.

Goldie, Terry. 2003. Eaten up: *Kiss of the fur queen*. In *Pink snow: Homotextual possibilities in Canadian fiction*. Peterborough, ON: Broadview Press.

Green, Joyce. 1985. Sexual equality and Indian government: An analysis of Bill
C-31 amendments of the Indian Act. *Native Studies Review* 1(2): 81–95.

Grewal, Inderpal. 1996. *Home and harem: Nation, gender, empire, and the cultures
of travel*. Durham, NC: Duke University Press.

Grinde, Donald A., Jr, and Bruce E. Johansen. 1991. *Exemplar of liberty: Native
America and the evolution of democracy*. Los Angeles: American Indian Studies
Center, University of California.

Habermas, Jürgen. 1998. Vorwort. In *Die postnationale konstellation: Politische
essays*. Frankfurt: Suhrkamp.

Haig-Brown, Celia. 1988. *Resistance and renewal: Surviving the Indian residential
school*. Vancouver: Tillacum Library.

Hall, Stuart. 1991. Reconstruction work: Images of post-war Black settlement.
In *Family snaps: The meaning of domestic images*. Edited by Jo Spence and Patricia Holland. London: Virago Press.

– 1996. On postmodernism and articulation: An interview with Stuart Hall. In
Stuart Hall: Critical dialogues in cultural studies. Edited by David Morley and
Kuan-Hsing Chen. New York: Routledge.

– 1997. The spectacle of the 'other.' In *Representations: Cultural representations
and signifying practices*. Edited by Stuart Hall. London: Sage in association
with the Open University.

Haq, Rana. 1999. Ontario's regressive approach to prisons: The negative
impact of superjails on women and their children. *Canadian Woman Studies /
Les Cahiers de la femme* 1(1–2): 133–5.

Haraway, Donna. 1991. A cyborg manifesto: Science, technology and socialist-
feminism in the late twentieth century. In *Simians, cyborgs, and women: The
reinvention of nature*. New York: Routledge.

– 1997. *Modest_witness@second millennium.FemaleMan©_meets_OncoMouse*™.
New York: Routledge.

Harris, Greg. 1998. Compulsory masculinity, Britain, and the Great War: The
literary-historical work of Pat Barker. *Critique: Studies in Contemporary Fiction*
39(4): 290–304.

Harvey, David. 1996. *Justice, nature and the geography of difference*. Cambridge, MA: Blackwell Publishers.

Henderson, Jennifer. 2003. *Settler feminism and race-making in Canada*. Toronto: University of Toronto Press.

Higginson, Kate. 2005. Feminine vulnerabiltiy, economics and the colonial rape scare: *Two Months in the Camp of Big Bear*. In *Recalling Early Canada*. Edited by Jennifer Blair et al. Edmonton: University of Alberta Press.

Highway, Tomson. 1998. *The kiss of the fur queen*. Toronto: Doubleday Canada.

Hill, Richard William. 2001. Drag racing: Dressing up & (messing up) white in contemporary First Nations arts. *Fuse Magazine* 23(4): 18–27.

Hirsch, Marianne. 1997. *Family frames: Photography, narrative and postmemory*. Cambridge, MA: Harvard University Press.

Hitchcock, Peter. 1991. Radical writing. In *Feminism, Bakhtin, and the dialogic*. Edited by Dale M. Bauer and Susan Jaret McKinstry. New York: State University of New York Press.

Hobsbawm, Eric. 1987. *The age of empire, 1875–1914*. New York: Vintage Books.

hooks, bell. 1992. Selling hot pussy. In *Black looks: Race and representation*. Toronto: Between the Lines.

Hourani, Albert. 1991. *A history of the Arab peoples*. Cambridge, MA: Harvard University Press.

Huhndorf, Shari. 2000. Nanook and his contemporaries: Imagining Eskimos in American culture, 1897–1922. *Critical Inquiry* 27(1): 122–48.

Ihimaera, Witi. 1987. *The whale rider*. Toronto: Harcourt.

The Imperial Colonialist. London: 1902–27.

International Council of Women of Canada. Online. http://www.ncwc.ca/aboutUs_history.html.

Jamieson, Kathleen. 1986. Sex discrimination and the Indian Act. In *Arduous journey: Canadian Indians and decolonization*. Edited by J. Rick Ponting. Toronto: McClelland and Stewart.

Janoff-Bulman, Ronnie. 1992. *Shattered assumptions: Towards a new psychology of trauma*. Toronto: Maxwell Macmillan Canada.

Jessop, Lynda. 1999. Tin cans and machinery: *Saving the Sagas* and other stuff. *Visual Anthropology* 12: 49–86.

– 2002. Moving pictures and costume songs at the 1927 'Exhibition of Canadian West Coast Art, Native and Modern.' *Canadian Journal of Film Studies* 11(1): 2–39.

Jones, Camille. 1985. Towards equal rights and amendment of section 12(1)(b) of the Indian Act: A post-script to *Lovelace v. Canada*. *Harvard Women's Law Journal* 8: 195–213.

Jones, Manina. 2003. Stolen life? Reading through two I's in postcolonial collaborative autobiography. In *Is Canada postcolonial? Unsettling Canadian lit-*

erature. Edited by Laura Moss. Waterloo, ON: Wilfrid Laurier University Press.

Kane, Marlyn (Osennontion), and Sylvia Maracle (Skonaganleh:ra). 1989. Our world. *Canadian Woman Studies / Les Cahiers de la femme* [special issue: 'Native women'] 10(2–3): 7–19.

Keller, Evelyn Fox. 1992. *Secrets of life / secrets of death: Essays on language, gender and science*. New York: Routledge.

Kincaid, Jamaica. 1988. *A small place*. Markham, ON: Penguin Books.

– 1992. Biography of a dress. *Grand Street* 11(3): 93–100.

Kirby, Peter. 1985. Marrying out and loss of status: The charter and the new Indian Act legislation. *Journal of Law and Social Policy* 1: 74–83.

Kirkness, Verna. 1987. Emerging native women. *Canadian Journal of Women and the Law* 2: 408–15.

Krafft-Ebing, Richard von. 1965. *Pyschopathia sexualis: A medico-forensic study*. Introduction by Ernest van den Haag. Translation by Harry E. Wedeck. New York: Putnam.

Kristeva, Julia. 1980. Motherhood according to Giovanni Bellini. In *Desire in language: A semiotic approach to literature and art*. Edited by Leon S. Roudiez. New York: Columbia University Press.

Kuhn, Annette, and Ann Marie Wolpe. 1978. *Feminism and materialism*. Boston: Routledge.

Landes, Joan B. 1988. *Women and the public sphere in the age of the French revolution*. Ithaca, NY: Cornell University Press.

– ed. 1998. *Feminism, the public, and the private*. New York: Oxford University Press.

Lawrence, Bonita. 2002. Rewriting histories of the land: Colonization and indigenous resistance in eastern Canada. In *Race, space, and the law: Unmapping a white settler society*. Edited by Sherene H. Razack. Toronto: Between the Lines.

Layoun, Mary. 1992. The female body and 'transnational' reproduction; or, rape by any other name? In *Nationalisms and sexualities*. Edited by Andrew Parker, Mary Russo, Doris Sommer, and Patricia Yaeger. New York: Routledge.

Leacock, Eleanor. 1972. Introduction to *The origin of the family, private property and the state*, by Frederick Engels. New York: International Publishers.

– 1980. Montagnais women and the Jesuit program for colonization. In *Women and civilization: Anthropological perspectives*. Edited by Mona Etienne and Eleanor Leacock. New York: Praeger.

Leakey, Richard. 1994. *The origin of humankind*. New York: Basic Books.

Lefebrve, Henri. 1991. *Critique of everyday life: Introduction*. Vol. 1. Translated by John Moore. London: Verso.

– 2002. *Critique of everyday life: Foundations for a sociology of the everyday.* Vol. 2. Translated by John Moore. London: Verso.

Leone, Hillary, and Jennifer Macdonald. 1992. Passio perpetuae. In *Incorporations.* Edited by Jonathan Crary and Sanford Kwinter. New York: Zone.

Lévi-Strauss, Claude. 1963a. Language and the analysis of social laws. In *Structural anthropology.* Translated by Claire Jacobson and Brooke Grundfest Schoepf. New York: Basic Books.

– 1963b. The structural study of myth. In *Structural anthropology.* Translated by Claire Jacobson and Brooke Grundfest Schoepf. New York: Basic Books.

– 1992. *Tristes tropiques.* Translated by Doreen Weightman and John Weightman. Toronto: Penguin Books.

Lewis, Laura A. 1996. The weight of words: Domination through misrepresentation: The 'weakness' of women and the feminization of the Indian in colonial Mexico. *Colonial Latin American Review* 5(1): 73–94.

Lippard, Lucy, ed. 1992. *Partial recall: Photographs of Native North Americans.* New York: The New Press.

Lyman, Christopher M. 1982. How the Indian was made. In *Vanishing race and other illusions: Photographs by Edward S. Curtis.* Introduction by Vine Deloria. New York: Pantheon Books in association with the Smithsonian Institution.

Lyotard, Jean-François. 1984. *The postmodern condition: A report on knowledge.* Translated by Geoff Bennington and Brian Massumi. Minneapolis: University of Minnesota Press.

Maalouf, Amin. 2003. *In the name of identity: Violence and the need to belong.* Markham, ON: Penguin Books.

Macey, David. 1993. *The lives of Michel Foucault.* London: Hutchinson.

Makhmalbaf, Mohsen, dir. 2001. *Kandahar: Journey into the heart of Afghanistan.* Iran.

Malinowski, Bronislaw. 1929. *The sexual life of savages in north-western Melanesia: An ethnographic account of courtship, marriage and family life among the natives of the Trobriand islands, British New Guinea.* Preface by Havelock Ellis. London G. Routledge and Sons, Ltd.

Martel, Gordon. 1996. *The origins of the First World War.* 2nd. ed. London: Longman.

Marx, Karl, and Friedrich Engels. 2004. *The communist manifesto* (1888). Edited and translated by L.M. Findlay. Peterborough, ON: Broadview Press.

Masson, Jeffrey M. 1984. *The assault on truth: Freud's suppression of the seduction theory.* New York: Farrar Straus Giroux.

McCall, Sophie. 2004. 'I can only sing this song to someone who understands it': Community filmmaking and the politics of partial translation in *Atanarjuat, the Fast Runner.* ECW 83: 19–46.

McClintock, Anne. 1995. *Imperial leather: Race, gender and sexuality in the colonial contest*. New York: Routledge.

McGillivray, Anne, and Brenda Comaskey. 1999. *Black eyes all of the time: Intimate violence, Aboriginal women, and the justice system*. Toronto: University of Toronto Press.

McLuhan, Herbert Marshall. 1951. *The mechanical bride: Folklore of industrial man*. New York: Vanguard Press, Inc.

McMaster Gerald. 1992. Colonial alchemy: Reading the boarding school experience. In *Partial recall: Photographs of Native North Americans*. Edited by Lucy Lippard. New York: New Press.

Mehta, Uday S. 1997. Liberal strategies of exclusion. In *Tensions of empire: Colonial cultures in a bourgeois world*. Edited by Frederick Cooper and Ann Laura Stoler. Berkeley: University of California Press.

Mendes, Sam. 1999, dir. *American beauty*. U.S.

Miller, D.A. *The novel and the police*. Berkeley: University of California Press, 1989.

Milloy, John. 1999. *A national crime: The Canadian government and the residential school system, 1879–1986*. Winnipeg: University of Manitoba Press.

Minorities go toe to toe with majority. 1989. *Globe and Mail*, 30 Sept.: C1.

Modleski, Tania. 1997. Cinema and the dark continent: Race and gender in popular film. In *Writing on the body: Female embodiment and feminist theory*. Edited by Katie Conboy, Nadia Medina, and Sarah Stanbury. New York: Columbia University Press.

Mohanty, Chandra Talpade. 1984. Under western eyes: Feminist scholarship and colonial discourse. *Boundary 2* 12: 333–58. Reprinted in Mohanty 2003.

– 2003. *Feminism without borders: Decolonizing theory, practicing solidarity*. Durham, NC: Duke University Press.

Monture-Angus, Patricia. 1995. *Thunder in my soul: A Mohawk woman speaks*. Foreword by Mary Ellen Turpel-Lafond. Halifax: Fernwood Publishing.

– 1999. Women and risk: Aboriginal women, colonialism, and correctional practice. *Canadian Woman Studies / Les Cahiers de la femme* 19(1–2): 24–9.

Morgan, Lewis Henry. 1877. *Ancient society; or, researches in the lines of human progress from savagery, through barbarism to civilization*. New York: H. Holt and Co.

Morris, Rosalind C. 1994. *New worlds from fragments: Film, ethnography, and the representation of northwest coast culture*. Boulder, CO: Westview Press.

Musser, C. 1996. Documentary. In *The Oxford history of world cinema*. Edited by Geoffrey Nowell-Smith. Oxford: Oxford University Press.

My secret. By a survivor. 1991. In *Ijirartuaqarunnirniq* (No more secrets). Ottawa: Pauktuutit (Inuit Women's Association).

Niro, Shelley, dir. 1998. *Honey moccasin*. Canada.

NWAC et al. v Her Majesty et al. Federal Court of Appeal, 20 August 1992.

Nunavut Implementation Commission. 1994. *Two-member constituencies and gender equality: A 'made in Nunavut' solution for a effective and representative legislature.* NWT.

Obomsawin, Alanis, dir. 1985. *Richard Cardinal: Cry from a diary of a Métis child.* Montreal: National Film Board of Canada.

O'Brien, Mary. 1981. *The politics of reproduction.* Boston: Routledge, 1981.

Ouellette, Grace Josephine Mildred Wuttunee. 2003. *The fourth world: An indigenous perspective on feminism and aboriginal women's activism.* Black Point, NS: Fernwood Books.

Pauktuutit Inuit Women's Association of Canada. n.d. *Inuit women and justice: Progress report number one.* Ottawa.

– 1990. *Does your husband or boyfriend beat you?* Ottawa.

– 1991. *No more secrets: Child sexual abuse in Inuit communities.* Ottawa.

– 1992. *Naalatsiarlutit: A presentation of artwork by northern artists on spousal abuse.* Ottawa.

– 1994. *Inuit women: The housing crisis and violence.* Ottawa.

– 2000a. Letter to Premier Okalik of Nunavut. *Canadian Woman Studies / Les Cahiers de la femme* [special issue: 'Women 2000: Eradicating poverty and violence in the 21st century'. 20(3): 191–3.

– 2000b. *What to do if you are abused and/or battered (safety plan).* Ottawa.

Payne, Carol. 1999. *A Canadian document / Un document canadien.* Ottawa: Canadian Museum of Contemporary Photography / Musée canadien de la photographie contemporaine.

Petrone, Penny, ed. 1983. *First peoples, first voices.* Toronto: University of Toronto Press.

Philip, Nourbese M. 2002. Dis place – The space between. In *A genealogy of resistance and other essays.* Toronto: Mercury Press.

Porteous, J. Douglas, and Sandra E. Smith. 2001. *Domicide: The global destruction of home.* Montreal and Kingston: McGill-Queen's University Press.

Poster, Mark. 1978. *A critical theory of the family.* New York: Seabury Press.

Proulx, Jocelyn, and Sharon Perrault, eds. 2000. *No place for violence: Canadian aboriginal alternatives,* Halifax: Fernwood Publishing.

Public Archives of Canada, Record Group 86, Vol. 920.

Razack, Sherene H. 2002. *Race, space and the law: Unmapping a white settler society.* Toronto: Between the Lines.

Report of the royal commission on aboriginal peoples. 1996. Ottawa, Canada. CD-ROM.

Richards, Thomas. 1990. *The commodity culture of Victorian Britain: Advertising and spectacle, 1851–1914.* London: Verso.

Rivers, W.H.R. 1968. *Kinship and social organization, together with 'The genealogi-*

cal method of anthropological enquiry.' London School of Economics Monographs on Social Anthropology, 34. London: Athlone Press.

Roach, Kent, and Joanthan Rudin. 2000. *Gladue*: The judicial and political reception of a promising decision. *Canadian Journal of Criminology* 42(3): 355–88.

Rony, Fatimah Tobing. 1996. Taxidermy and romantic ethnography: Robert Flaherty's *Nanook of the North*. In *The third eye: Race, cinema, and ethnographic spectacle*. Durham, NC: Duke University Press.

Roscoe, Will. 1998. *Changing ones: Third and fourth genders in Native North America*. New York: St Martin's Press.

Rose, Jacqueline. 2003. Response to Edward Said. In *Freud and the non-European*, by Edward Said. London: Verso.

Rowbotham, Sheila. 1986. *Friends of Alice Wheeldon*. London: Pluto Press.

Rutherford, Jonathon. 1997. *Forever England: Reflections on masculinity and empire*. London: Lawrence and Wishart.

Rymhs, Deena. 2005. Auto/biographical jurisdictions: Collaboration, self-representation, and the law in *Stolen Life: The Journey of a Cree Woman*. In *Auto/biography in Canada: Critical directions*. Edited by Julie Rak. Waterloo, ON: Wilfrid Laurier University Press.

Said, Edward. 1983. The world, the text, and the critic. In *The world, the text, and the critic*. Vintage: London.

– 1990. Figures, configurations, transfigurations. *Race and Class* 32(1): 1–16.

– 1993. *Culture and imperialism*. New York: Knopf.

– 2003. *Freud and the non-European*. Introduction by Christopher Bollas. London: Verso.

Sangster, Joan. 1999. Criminalizing the colonized: Ontario Native women confront the criminal justice system, 1920–60. *Canadian Historical Review* 80(1): 32–60.

Sargent, Lydia, ed. 1981. *Women and revolution: A discussion of the unhappy marriage of Marxism and feminism*. Montreal: Black Rose Books.

Sassoon, Siegfried. 1936. *Memoirs of George Sherston: Memoirs of a fox-hunting man, memoirs of an infantry officer, and Sherston's progress*. New York: Doubleday, Doran and Company.

– 1983. *The war poems of Siegfried Sassoon*. London: Faber and Faber.

Satzewich, Vic, and Terry Wotherspoon. 1993. *First Nations: Race, class, and gender relations*. Scarborough, ON: Nelson Canada.

Saxby, Jessie M. Women Wanted. 1982. In *A flannel shirt and liberty: British emigrant gentlewomen in the Canadian West, 1880–1914*. Vancouver: University of British Columbia Press.

Scarry, Elaine. 1985. *The body in pain: The making and unmaking of the world*. New York: Oxford University Press.

Schäffer, Mary T.S. 1911. *Old Indian trails: Incidents of camp and trail life, covering two years' exploration through the Rocky Mountains of Canada.* Toronto: William Briggs.

Scofield, Gregory. 1999. *Thunder through my veins: Memories of a Métis childhood.* Toronto: Harper Flamingo Canada.

Scott, Duncan Campbell. 1898. *Labor and the angel.* Boston: Copeland and Day.

Scott, Jamie. 2005. *Mixed messages: Materiality, textuality, missions.* New York: Palgrave/Macmillan.

Scott, Jamie, and Alvyn Austin, eds. 2005. *Canadian missionaries, indigenous peoples: Representing religion at home and abroad.* Toronto: University of Toronto Press.

Sedgwick, Eve Kosofsky. 1990. *Epistemology of the closet.* Berkeley: University of California Press.

Segal, Lynne. 1990. *Slow motion: Changing masculinities, changing men.* London: Virago Press.

Sharpe, Jenny. 1991. The unspeakable limits of rape: Colonial violence and counter insurgency. *Genders* 10: 25–46.

– 1993. *Allegories of empire: The figure of woman in the colonial text.* Minneapolis: University of Minnesota Press.

Shelley, Mary. 1977. *Frankenstein.* Introduction by Leonard Wolf. New York: C.N. Potter.

Shetty, Sandya, and Elizabeth Jane Bellamy. 2000. Postcolonialism's archive fever. *Diacritics* 30(1): 25–48.

Showalter, Elaine. 1985. *The female malady: Women, madness, and English culture, 1830–1930.* New York: Pantheon Books.

– 1997. *Hystories: Hysterical epidemics and modern culture.* London: Picador.

Sidney, Angela. 1990. *Life lived like a story: Stories of three Yukon elders.* Edited by Julie Cruikshank in collaboration with Angela Sidney, Kitty Smith, and Annie Ned. Lincoln: University of Nebraska Press.

Silman, Janet, ed. 1987. *Enough is enough: Aboriginal women speak out.* Toronto: University of Toronto Press.

Sinha, Mrinalini. 1995. *Colonial masculinity: The 'manly Englishman' and the 'Effeminate Bengali' in the late nineteenth century.* Manchester: Manchester University Press.

Smart, Carol. 1995. *Law, crime and sexuality: Essays in feminism.* London: Sage Publication.

Smith, Andrea. 2005. *Conquest: Sexual violence and American Indian genocide.* Boston: South End Press.

Smith, W. Robertson. 1894. *Lectures on the religion of the Semites.* 2nd. ed. London.

– 1903. *Kinship and marriage in early Arabia*. London.

Soja, Edward. 1996. *Thirdspace: Journeys to Los Angeles and other real-and-imagined-spaces*. Cambridge, MA: Blackwell.

Solanke, Adeola. 1991. Complex, not confused. In *Family snaps: The meanings of domestic photography*. Edited by Jo Spence and Patricia Holland. London: Virago.

Sparling, Lori. 1999. A suitable place: Positive change for federally sentenced aboriginal women in Canada. *Canadian Woman Studies / Les Cahiers de la femmes* 1(1–2): 116–21.

Spence, Jo, and Patricia Holland, eds. 1991. *Family snaps: The meaning of domestic photography*. London: Virago.

Spivak, Gayatri Chakravorty. 1986. Imperialism and sexual difference. *Oxford Literary Review* 8: 225–40.

– 1987. Feminism and critical theory. In *In other worlds: Essays in cultural politics*. New York: Methuen.

– 1988. Can the subaltern speak? In *Marxism and the interpretation of culture*. Edited by Cary Nelson and Lawrence Grossberg. Chicago: University of Illinois Press.

– 1992a. The politics of translation. In *Destabilizing theory: Contemporary feminist debates*. Edited by. Michèle Barrett and Anne Phillips. Stanford, CA: Stanford University Press.

– 1992b. Woman in difference: Mahasweta Devi's 'Douloti the bountiful.' In *Nationalisms and sexualities*. Edited by Andrew Parker, Mary Russo, Doris Sommer, and Patricia Yaeger. New York: Routledge.

– trans. 1995. Afterword to *Imaginary maps: Three stories by Mahasweta Devi*. New York: Routledge.

– 1999. *A critique of postcolonial reason: Toward a history of the vanishing present*. Cambridge, MA: Harvard University Press.

– 2000. Poststructuralism, marginality, postcoloniality and value. In *Postcolonialism: Critical concepts in literary and cultural studies*. Edited by Diana Brydon. Vol 1. London: Routledge.

– 2003. *Death of a discipline*. New York: Columbia University Press.

Stevenson, Robert Louis. 1929. *The strange case of Dr. Jekyll and Mr. Hyde*. New York: Random House.

Stevenson, Winona. 1999. Colonialism and First Nations women in Canada. In *Scratching the surface: Canadian anti-racist feminist thought*. Edited by Enakshi Dua and Angela Robertson. Toronto: Women's Press.

Stoler, Ann Laura. 1989. *Race and the education of desire: Foucault's 'History of sexuality' and the colonial order of things*. Durham, NC: Duke Unversity Press.

– 2003. *Carnal knowledge, imperial powers: Race and the intimate in colonial rule.* Berkeley: University of California Press.

Summers, Carol. 1991. Intimate colonialism: The imperial production of reproduction in Uganda, 1907–1925. *Signs: Journal of Women in Culture and Society* 16(4): 787–807.

Tarzan and his mate. 1934. Directed by Cedric Gibbon. Metro-Goldwyn-Mayer Pictures.

Tarzan escapes. 1936. Directed by James McKay. Metro-Goldwyn-Mayer Pictures.

Tarzan finds a son! 1939. Directed by Richard Thorpe. Metro-Goldwyn-Mayer Pictures.

Tarzan's New York adventure. 1942. Directed by Richard Thorpe. Metro-Goldwyn-Mayer Pictures.

Tarzan's secret treasure. 1941. Directed by Richard Thorpe. Metro-Goldwyn-Mayer Pictures.

Tarzan, the ape man. 1932. Directed by W.S. Van Dyke. Metro-Goldwyn-Mayer Pictures.

Taussig, Michael. 1987. *Shamanism, colonialism, and the wild man: A study in terror and healing.* Chicago: University of Chicago Press.

Tester, F.J. and P. Kulchyski. 1994. *Tammarniit (mistakes): Inuit relocation in the eastern Arctic, 1939–63.* Vancouver: University of British Columbia Press.

Tompkins, Joanne, and Lisa Male. 1994. 'Twenty-one Native women on motorcycles': An interview with Tomson Highway. *Australasian Drama Studies* 24: 13–28.

Torgovnick, Marianna. 1990. *Gone primitive: Savage intellects, modern lives.* Chicago: University of Chicago Press.

Torpey, John. 2003. 'Introduction.' In *Politics and the past: On repairing historic injustices.* Oxford: Rowman & Littlefield Publishers, Inc.

Trinh, T. Minh-ha. 1992. Why a fish pond? In *Framer framed.* New York: Routledge.

– 1998. *Cinema interval.* New York: Routledge.

– 1999. Jumping into the void. In *Cinema interval.* New York: Routledge.

Turpel-Lafond, Mary Ellen. 1987. Discrimination and the 1985 amendments to the Indian Act: Full of snares for women. In *Rights and Freedoms* 64: 6–8.

– 1993. Patriarchy and paternalism: The legacy of the Canadian state for First Nations women. *Canadian Journal of Women and the Law* 6: 174–92.

Valverde, Mariana. 1992. 'When the mother of the race is free': Race, reproduction, and sexuality in first-wave feminism. In *Gender conflicts: New essays in women's history.* Edited by Franca Iacovetta and Mariana Valverde. Toronto: Uniersity of Toronto Press.

Van Kirk, Sylvia. 1980. *'Many tender ties': Women in fur-trade society in western Canada, 1670–1870.* Winnipeg: Watson and Dwyyer.

West, Rebecca. 1979. *The return of the soldier.* London: Virago Press.

Westlund, Andrea C. 1999. Pre-modern and modern power: Foucault and the case of domestic violence. *Signs: Journal of Women in Culture and Society* 24(4): 1045–66.

Wexler, Laura. 2000. *Tender violence: Domestic visions in an age of U.S. imperialism.* Chapel Hill: University of North Carolina Press.

Where the spirit lives. 1989. Directed by Bruce Pittman. Amazing Spirit Productions Ltd. Distributer, Atlantis Releasing Inc.

White, Hayden. 1978. The noble savage theme as fetish. In *Tropics of discourse: Essays in cultural criticism.* Baltimore: Johns Hopkins University Press.

Wiebe, Ruby, and Yvonne Johnson. 1998. *Stolen life: The journey of a Cree woman.* Toronto: Vintage.

Williams, Raymond. 1976. *Keywords: A vocabulary of culture and society.* New York: Oxford University Press.

– 1977. *Marxism and literature.* Oxford: Oxford University Press.

– 1980. Problems of materialism. In *Problems in materialism and culture.* London: Verso.

Williams, Walter L. 1986. *The spirit and the flesh: Sexual diversity in American Indian culture.* Boston: Beacon Press.

Wilson, Elizabeth. 1985. *Adorned in dreams: Fashion and modernity.* London: Virago.

Wittig, Monique. 1992. The straight mind. In *The straight mind and other essays.* Boston: Women's Press.

Woolf, Virginia. 1929. *Mrs. Dalloway.* London: Hogarth Press.

– 1938. *Three Guineas.* London: Hogarth Press.

– 1981. *A room of one's own.* (1929). New York: Harcourt.

Yealland, Lewis R. 1981. *Hysterical disorders of warfare.* London: Macmillan

Young, Iris. 2002. *Inclusion and democracy.* Oxford: Oxford University Press.

Young, Robert. 1995. *Colonial desire: Hybridity in theory, culture and race.* New York: Routledge.

Illustration Credits

British Columbia Archives: figure I.2 (B-06675); figure I.3 (B-06670); figure I.4 (B-06669); figure I.5 (B-06668); figure 5.1 (E-07422); figure 5.2 (I-33192); figure 5.3 (C-08539); figure 5.4 (B-01072); figure 5.5 (G-03877); figure 5.6 (C-07918); figure 5.7 (B-06052); figure 5.8 (B-01278); figure 5.9 (F-04996); figure 5.10 (D-411); figure 7.1 (F-06877).

Collection of the author: figure 3.1.

Jane Ash Poitras: figure 5.15 (image courtesy of Spirit Wrestler Gallery).

Whyte Museum of the Canadian Rockies: figure I.1 (V.263 NA71-3123); figure 5.11 (Original Photograph V.527 PS-5); figure 5.12 (V.527 PS-51); figure 5.13 (V.527 PS-705); figure 5.14 (V.439 PS-352); figure 7.2 (V. 701/LC-369, 1929).

Index

of, 59; economy of, 82; femininization of, 84; and gender relations, 55;
and housing crisis, 237; men, 78–9,
81, 89; midwife, 191; and sentencing circles, 67–9; woman's body,
182; women, 42, 59, 67–9, 79, 237
Inuit mother, figure of, 185, 187, 198–
9, 203
Inuit Tapirisat of Canada, 184, 186
Inuit Women's Association. *See*
Pauktuutit
Iroquois confederacy, 55; and women
56–7

Johnson, Yvonne, 42, 214–33, 254; as
author, 224–7; childhood memories, 217–18; experience of sexual
abuse, 214–16; *Stolen Life: The Journey of a Cree Woman*, 42, 207, 214–
28, 233
Jones, Manina, 282n8
justice, 43, 207, 227; in decolonization, 227; and healing, 227, 232–3,
259; and indigenous women and
children, 210–13; and the law, 222–
31; and prison, 242–3

*Kandahar: Journey into the Heart of
Afghanistan*, 255–6, 258
Kane, Marlyn, 185–6
Kant, Immanuel, 55–6
Käsebier, Gertrude, 176–7
Keller, Evelyn Fox, 200
Kincaid, Jamaica, 153; 'Biography of
a Dress,' 153–5
kinship: and anthropology, 26; and
de-signification, 260–3; and dispossession of the land, 213; indigenous, 100, 213, 236–8; Inuit, 73;
political, 9, 43, 151, 235–7, 249; rela-

tions, 5, 11, 40, 53–4, 73, 132, 178,
236–8; as system, 70
Kiss of the Fur Queen (Tomson High-
way), 43, 251–5
Kunuk, Zacharias: *Atanarjuat: The
Fast Runner*, 272n6
Kuptana, Rosemarie, 186

Lavell, Jeannette Corbière, 63
law, 207, 210–13, 227; and the 'ends of
man,' 232; and heterogeneity, 227;
natural law, 231–2; positive law,
231–2
law of the father, 227–8, 231
law of narrative, 213, 224; colonial,
226–7; and letter of the law, 227–8
Lawrence, Bonita, 23–4
Leacock, Eleanor, 4, 266n6
Leakey, Richard, 92, 272n1
'legal pluralism,' 68, 227, 279n2
legislative acts, colonial, 61–6. *See also*
Indian Act; and names of specific
acts
lesbian politics, 241, 242–4; and
Deepa Mehta's film *Fire*; and globalization, 283n1; and same-sex
marriage, 259; and *Where the Spirit
Lives*, 248–9
Lévi-Strauss, Claude, 78–9, 92
liberalism, as ideology, 71–2
Lippard, Lucy, 176
love, 6; and eroticism, 6; and political
transformation, 254–9; in prison,
243; and sexual violence, 249

Maalouf, Amin, 248, 254
McCall, Sophie, 272n6
McClintock, Anne, 122, 273n9
McGillivray, Anne, 211
McMaster, Gerald, 180